Hindu Superiority

Hindu Superiority:

**AN ATTEMPT
TO DETERMINE THE POSITION OF THE
HINDU RACE IN THE SCALE OF NATIONS.**

BY

HAR BILAS SARDA, F.R.S.L.

GYAN

Published by

Gyan Publishing House
5, Ansari Road
Daryaganj, New Delhi-110002
Phone: 011-47034999, 9811692060
E-mail: books@gyanbooks.com

Distribution Network
gyanbooks.com
India, USA, Canada, UK, Australia

ISBN: 978-93-6208-204-6 (PB)
First Published, 1906

2nd Impression 2024

Printed at: Gyan Press, Delhi.

HINDU SUPERIORITY
Author: HAR BILAS SARDA

MAHARANA PRATAP.

Hindu Superiority.

HAR BILAS SARDA'S WORKS.

		Price.
1.	Hindu Superiority (illustrated)	Rs. 6 0 0
2.	Maharana Kumbha (illustrated)	„ 2 0 0
3.	Maharana Sanga (illustrated)	„ 2 8 0
4.	Ajmer: Historical and Descriptive (with 29 full-page illustrations)	„ 5 0 0
5.	Hammira of Ranthambhor	„ 1 8 0
6.	Prithviraj Vijaya	„ 0 8 0
7.	Hindu Sciences	„ 0 12 0
8.	Hindu Arts	„ 0 4 0
9.	Commerce and Wealth (Ancient India)	„ 0 4 0

(The last three are reprints of Chapters from "Hindu Superiority.")

To be had from—

Har Bilas Sarda, Civil Lines, Ajmer.

Hindu Superiority:

AN ATTEMPT
TO DETERMINE THE POSITION OF THE
HINDU RACE IN THE SCALE
OF NATIONS.

BY

HAR BILAS SARDA, F.R.S.L.,

Member of the Royal Asiatic Society of Great Britain and Ireland
Fellow of the Royal Statistical Society of London; and
Member of the Statistical Association of Boston,
United States, America; etc.

AND

AUTHOR OF

Maharana Sanga; Maharana Kumbha; Ajmer: Historical and Descriptive; Hammira of Ranthambhor.

THIRD EDITION.

MY MOTHERLAND

INDIA,

PARADISE ON EARTH,

Thou gavest Civilization and Religion to the world;

Eternal, Immortal, Everlasting,

To THEE, in reverence and Love,

I inscribe this volume.

HAR BILAS SARDA.

"If I were to look over the whole world to find out the country most richly endowed with all the wealth, power, and beauty that nature can bestow, in some parts *a very paradise on earth*—I should point to India. If I were asked under what sky the human mind has most fully developed some of its choicest gifts, has most deeply pondered on the greatest problems of life, and has found solutions of some of them which well deserve the attention even of those who have studied Plato and Kant—I should point to India. And if I were to ask myself from what literature we here in Europe—we who have been nurtured almost exclusively on the thoughts of the Greeks and the Romans, and of one Semitic race, the Jewish—may draw that corrective which is most wanted in order to make our inner life more perfect, more comprehensive, more universal, in fact more truly human, a life, not for this only, but a transfigured and eternal life, again I should point to India."—Professor Max Muller's *India: What can it teach us?* p. 8.

"India is the source from which not only the rest of Asia but the whole Western World derived their knowledge and their religion."—Professor Heeren's *Historical Researches*, Vol. II, p. 45.

LIST OF ILLUSTRATIONS.

Preface to the First Edition.

This book has grown out of a pamphlet written years ago and put aside at the time. The object of the book is, by presenting a bird's eye view of the achievements of the ancient Hindus, to invite the attention of thoughtful people to the leading features of the civilization which enabled the inhabitants of this country to contribute so much to the material and moral well-being of mankind. And if this attempt succeeds in any way in stimulating interest in the study of the leading institutions of Hinduism and a proper appreciation of their merits, I shall be amply repaid for my labour.

I must take this opportunity of expressing my gratitude to Mr. J. Inglis, Superintendent, Scottish Mission Industries, Ajmer, for his valuable assistance in seeing the book through the Press.

HAR BILAS SARDA.

Ajmer:
November 1906.

TABLE OF CONTENTS.

CONSTITUTION.

ANTIQUITY.

GOVERNMENT.

SOCIAL SYSTEM.

CHARACTER.

FOREIGN RELATIONS.

HINDU COLONIZATION OF THE WORLD.

PAGE.

PAGE.

CHINA AND JAPAN.

AMERICA.

LITERATURE.

SANSKRIT LANGUAGE.

PAGE.

ART OF WRITING.

VEDIC LITERATURE.

POETRY.

EPIC POETRY.

PAGE.

DRAMA.

•LYRIC POETRY.

ETHICO-DIDACTIC POETRY.

PHILOSOPHY.

MIMANSAS.

SCIENCE.

I.—MEDICINE.

II.—MATHEMATICS.

ARITHMETIC.

GEOMETRY. PAGE.

III.—ASTRONOMY.

IV.—MILITARY SCIENCE.

V.—MUSIC.

VI.—OTHER SCIENCES.

ARTS.

IV.—STEEL AND IRON MANUFACTURES.

V.—OTHER ARTS.

COMMERCE AND WEALTH.

I.—COMMERCE.

II.—WEALTH.

RELIGION.

INTRODUCTION.

IN the history of the world, India occupies the foremost place. From the dawn of history to the present day India has been connected in one way or another with almost every event of world importance By endowing India with the best and the choicest of gifts it had in store, Nature herself ordained that this magnificent country, with a climate varied and salubrious, a soil the most fertile in the world, animal and plant life the most abundant, useful and diversified to be found anywhere on the face of the earth, should play the leading part in the history of mankind.

Mr. Murray says: "It (India) has always appeared to the imagination of the Western World adorned with whatever is most splendid and gorgeous; glittering, as it were, with gold and gems, and redolent of fragrant and delicious odours. Though there be in these magnificent conceptions something romantic and illusory, still India forms unquestionably one of the most remarkable regions that exist on the surface of the globe. The varied grandeur of its scenery and the rich productions of its soil are scarcely equalled in any other country."[1]

The historian Abdullah Wassaf, writing in the 14th century A.D. says of India in his history, *Tazjiyat ul Amsar*:[2] "India, according to the concurrent opinion of all writers, is the most agreeable abode on the earth and the most pleasant quarter of

[1] Murray's History of India, p 1.

[2] Elliot's History of India, Vol. III, pp. 28 and 29.

the world. Its dust is purer than air and its air purer than purity itself: Its delightful plains resemble the garden of paradise.

> If it is asserted that Paradise is in India,
> Be not surprised, because Paradise itself is not comparable to it"

"India is an epitome of the whole world,"[1] and possesses all the leading features of other lands—the most bewitching scenery, the most fertile soil, the most dense forests, the highest mountains, some of the biggest rivers, and intensely cold seasons may be found along with arid, treeless deserts, sandy waterless plains, and the hottest days. To a student of humanity or of Nature, India even now is most picturesque, and is the most interesting country in the world. Count Bjornstjerna says: "But everything is peculiar, grand and romantic in India—from the steel-clad knight of Rajasthan to the devoted Brahman in the temples of Benares; from the fierce Mahratta on his fleet and active steed to the Nabob moving gently on his elephant; from the Amazon who chases the tiger in the jungle to the Bayadere who offers in *volupte* to her gods. Nature, too, in this glorious country is chequered with variety and clad in glowing colours: see the luxuriance of her tropical vegetation and the hurricane of her monsoon; see the majesty of her snow-covered Himalayas and the dryness of her desert; see the immense plains of Hindustan and the scenery of her lofty mountains; but, above all, see the immense age of her history and the poetry of her recollections."[2]

Professor Max Muller says: "In the study of the history of the human mind, in the study of ourselves, of our true selves, India occupies a place second to no other country. "Whatever sphere of the human mind you may select for your special study,

[1] Chambers' Encyclopædia. p. 337.

[2] Theogony of the Hindus, p. 126. "The scenery of the Himalayas," says Elphinstone, "is a sight which the soberest traveller has never described without kindling into enthusiasm, and which, if once seen, leaves an impression that can never be equalled or effaced."—*History of India*, p. 181.

whether it be language, or religion, or mythology, or philosophy, whether it be laws or customs, primitive art or primitive science, everywhere you have to go to India, whether you like it or not, because some of the most valuable and most instructive materials in the history of man are treasured up in India only."[1]

The *Calcutta Review* for December 1861, says: "Though now degraded and abased, yet we cannot doubt that there was a time when the Hindu race was splendid in arts and arms, happy in government, wise in legislation and eminent in knowledge."[2]

"The ancient state of India," says Mr. Thornton, "must have been one of extraordinary magnificence."[3]

Colonel Tod asks: "Where can we look for sages like those whose systems of philosophy were the prototypes of those of Greece: to whose works Plato, Thales and Pythagoras were disciples? Where shall we find astronomers whose knowledge of the planetary system yet excites wonder in Europe, as well as the architects and sculptors whose works claim our admiration, and the musicians 'who could make the mind oscillate from joy to sorrow, from tears to smiles, with the change of modes and varied intonation?'"[4]

[1] Max Muller's India: What can it teach us? p. 15.

[2] The same Review says: "That the Hindus were in former times a commercial people we have every reason to believe—the labours of the Indian loom have been universally celebrated, silk has been fabricated immemorially by the Hindus. We are also told by the Grecian writers that the Indians were the wisest of nations, and in metaphysical wisdom they were certainly eminent; in astronomy and mathematics they were equally well versed; this is the race, who Dionysius records:—

'First assayed the deep,
'And wafted merchandise to coasts unknown,
'Those who digested first the starry choir,
'Their motions marked, and called them by their names"

"Hindustan has from the earliest ages been celebrated as one of the most highly-favoured countries on the globe, and as abounding in the choicest productions both of Nature and Art."—*Encyclopædia Britannica*, p. 446.

[3] Chapters of the History of British India.

[4] Tod's Annals and Antiquities of Rajasthan, pp. 608 and 609.

Mons. Pierre Loti, the great Frenchman, writing to the President of the Comiti Franco Hindou, thus expresses his veneration for India: "And now I salute thee with awe, with veneration and wonder, ancient India of whom I am the adept, the India of the highest splendours of art and philosophy......May thy awakening astonish that Occident, decadent, mean, daily dwindling, slayer of nations, slayer of gods, slayer of souls, which yet bows down still, ancient India, before the prodigies of thy primordial conceptions."[1]

The *Edinburgh Review*, for October 1872, says: "The Hindu is the most ancient nation of which we have valuable remains, and has been *surpassed by none in refinement and civilization*: though the utmost pitch of refinement to which it ever arrived preceded in time the dawn of civilization in any other nation of which we have even the name in history. The further our literary inquiries are extended here, the more vast and stupendous is the scene which opens to us."

It may be urged that there is not much apparent use in harping on the greatness of the ancient Hindus, in talking of old days which can never return. Why not confine attention to the present, to the stern realities of the irrepressible present and let the dead past bury its dead? "The India of old," says an American writer, "is a figment of the imagination, a faded picture of the memory; the India of to-day is a stern reality that confronts and supplicates us."

Objections such as these betray ignorance not only of the inner life of the Hindus and of the principles on which the fabric of Hindu Society is based but of the principle of continuity of life itself—the basic principle of all life, whether of an individual or an institution. The past is ever present to a Hindu. His daily communion with the spirit of the past gives him strength to work in the present: for him, the springs of action lie in the

[1] The *Arya* (Pondicherry) for August 1914, p. 59.

past. It is the past that gives him hope for the future. His glorious past, when properly understood, lights the path he is to tread and will eventually lead him to a future equally splendid and happy. For, "how can the present yield fruit or the future have promise, except their roots be fixed in the past."[1]

Professor Sylvain Levi of Paris, writing to Mr. P. C. Roy, says, that if mental and moral improvement is possible in India, "it is only through a study of national antiquities, national literature and national ethics."

Mr. Samuel Smiles says: "Nations, like individuals, derive support and strength from the feeling that they belong to an illustrious race, that they are the heirs of their greatness, and ought to be the perpetuators of their glory. It is of momentous importance that a nation should have a great past to look back upon. It steadies the life of the present, elevates and upholds it and lightens and lifts it up, by the memory of the great deeds, the noble sufferings and the valorous achievements of the men of old."[2]

To the Hindus, therefore it is a matter of supreme importance to study the history of their nation, to study and assimilate the teachings of their forefathers—from whom, came the light which has illumined the whole of Asia and Europe.

A glimpse of those mighty men and their mighty achievements is all that is possible now, centuries of neglect followed by centuries of cruel repression having destroyed all but the vestiges of the splendid achievements bequeathed by them to posterity.

An attempt has been made in the following pages, with the help of the results of the laudable labours of scholars like Sir W. Jones, Prof. H H. Wilson, Prof. Max Muller, Schlegel, Sir Monier Williams, Mr. Colebrooke, Colonel Tod, E. B. Havell,

[1] Life of Dr. Arnold, ii, 387-88, (edition 1858).

[2] Smiles' Character, p. 27.

and other European scholars and writers to whom the country owes a great debt of gratitude, to get such a glimpse which, according to the writer quoted above, has not yet been surpassed. And what is the result? What do we learn about the ancient Hindus? We learn that they were the greatest nation that has yet flourished on this earth,—

> "In the world there is nothing great but man,
> In man there is nothing great but mind,"

was the favourite aphorism of the philosopher Sir William Hamilton.[1] And Mrs. Manning says: "The Hindus had the widest range of mind of which man is capable."[2]

We find that the ancient Hindus, in every feature of national life were in the first rank. Take whatever department of human activity you like, you find the ancient Hindus eminent in it, and as occupying a foremost place. This is more than what can be said of any other nation You may find a nation great in arms or commerce; you may find a people eminent in philosophy, in poetry, in science or in arts; you may find a race great politically but not equally so morally and intellectually. But you do not find a race which was or is pre-eminent in so many departments of human activity as the ancient Hindus.

According to European writers, the ancient Hindus were "a poetical people," they were essentially "a musical race," and they were "a commercial people." "They were a nation of philosophers;" "in science they were as acute and diligent as ever." "Art seems to have exhausted itself in India." "The Hindu is the parent of the literature and the theology of the world." His language is the best and the most beautiful in the world. The national character of the ancient Hindus as regards truthfulness, chivalry and honour was unrivalled; their colonies

[1] See Jevon's Logic, p. 9.

[2] Ancient and Mediæval India, Vol. II. p. 148.

filled the world, their kings "are still worshipped as the gods of the sea," "their civilization still pervades every corner of the civilized world and is around and about us every day of our lives."

It may be urged that in the picture of Hindu civilization painted in the book, only roseate hues have been used; that while lights are purposely made prominent, the shadows are conspicuous by their absence, and that most has been made of the best points of Hinduism. Such critics will do well to remember that the mountains are measured by their highest peaks and not by the low heights to which they here and there sink; that the first rank among the mountains is assigned to the Himalayas by Mounts Everest, Dhavalgiri and Kanchanjanga, and not by the lower heights of Mussoorie and Darjeeling, and that the patches of level ground here and there found enclosed within this gigantic range are justly ignored.

It may also be remarked here that the object of this book[1] being to enable men to appreciate the excellencies of Hindu civilization—by giving them an idea of the character and achievements of the ancient Hindus, who were the creatures of that civilization, which has admittedly seen its best days—any discussion of modern India for its own sake is without the scope of

[1] It is no part of the plan of this book to run down any creed or nationality. Consequently, whenever any other religion or race is mentioned, it is only for the elucidation of some point of Hindu civilization or to show the comparative excellence of some feature of it. Thus, whenever the oppressive nature of the rule of some of the Muhammadan rulers is mentioned, or the havoc caused by some of the invaders from the North-western frontier of India is described, it is not to emphasize that fact itself, but to illustrate, explain, or elucidate some feature of the character of the Hindus or their literature and society. It may also be remarked that the evils of the rule of the Afghans, Turks, and others were due not to the religion they professed but to their ignorance and backwardness in civilization. The Arabs, though professing the same religion as the Afghans and the Moghals, kept the lamp of knowledge and science lit in Europe and Western Asia during the middle ages. The work of Al-Beruni, Abul Fazal, Faizi and others in India pulls to pieces the theory that whatever evils there were in Muhammadan rule were due to the religion of the rulers.

this book. Wherever, therefore, any fact relating to the society, religion, literature or character of the Hindus of the present day, or their capacities and capabilities is mentioned, it has reference only to the elucidation of some feature of that civilization as illustrated in the life, work or character of the people of ancient India.

It is the inherent truth of Hinduism, the vitality and greatness of the Hindu civilization that have enabled the Hindus yet to preserve their existence as such, despite all the political cataclysms, social upheavals and racial eruptions the world has seen since the Mahabharata. These calamities overwhelmed the ancient Egyptians, the Assyrians and the Phœnicians and destroyed the empires of ancient Greece, Persia and Rome.

Compared to the sun of Hindu civilization giving a constant and steady stream of of beneficent light, which while lighting up the heavens above, penetrates the farthest nooks and corners of the world, carrying comfort and contentment to mankind, these civilizations were like brilliant meteors that appear in the skies lighting the while, with their short-lived lustre, the parts of the earth immediately below them.

> Then—let me dive into the depths of time,
> And bring from out the ages that have rolled,
> A few small fragments of those wrecks sublime,
> Which human eye may never more behold;
> And let the guerdon of my labour be
> My fallen country! one kind wish for thee.

CONSTITUTION

CONSTITUTION.

> Clime of the unforgotten brave!
> Where land from plain to mountain cave
> Was freedom's home or glory's grave;
> Shrine of the mighty! Can it be
> That this is all remains of thee?
>
> —BYRON: *Giaour.*

No one acquainted with the history of the ancient Indians can reasonably deny the great merits of their ancient Constitution, which combined happiness with activity, tranquility with progress—"one lesson which in every wind is blown"—and conservation with advancement. Their astonishing subjective capacities and their extraordinary powers of observation and generalization led them irresistibly to trace Nature in all her multifarious solemn workings. They followed her in every thing they did: hence the halo of reality and conservation which surrounds their work. It is this reality and conservation, the happy results of following Nature—"which is wisdom without reflection and above it"—that have imparted that polish to Hindu laws and institutions which makes them at once durable and brilliant.

There was, anciently, an adjustment of forces in India which enabled each institution to describe its peculiar orbit and work in its own sphere, without interfering with the others; but now, alas! owing to the long-continued and unabated pressure of hostile circumstances, that adjustment is broken, and forces are consequently being let loose which bring the different institutions together. Their foundations, however, are still intact, owing to their exceeding firmness.

The turning point in the history of Ancient India was the Mahabharata, the Great War between the Pandavas and the

Kauravas. This momentous event decided the future of Ancient India, as it closed the long chapter of Hindu growth and Hindu greatness. The sun of India's glory was at its meridian about the end of Dvapara, and, following the universal law of Nature, with the beginning of the Kaliyuga, it turned its course towards the horizon, where it set on the plains of Thaneshwar amidst the romantic splendour of Sanjogta's love and Pithora's chivalry. As the Mahabharata marked the zenith of Hindu greatness, so Shahabud-din's victory at Thaneshwar marked the sinking of the great luminary below the horizon. The great war which, as will be seen hereafter, influenced so powerfully the destiny of nations was, in reality, the beginning of the end of Hindu greatness, and it was after this period that the political and social Constitution of India began to yield to those innovations which by their very contrast to the fundamental principles of that Constitution, are so prominent now.

ANTIQUITY.

Time is the root of all created beings,
And uncreate; of pleasure and of pain.
Time doth create existence. Time destroys,
Time shatters all, and all again renews.
Time watches while all sleep. Unvanquished Time!

—MAHABHARATA : *Adiparva.*

THE antiquity of the Hindu civilization is wonderful; its vitality miraculous. The fabulous age of the Greeks and the times of the Egyptian Soufi, are but as yesterday in the history of Hindu civilization. The age of this earth is not to be counted by a few thousand years, but by millions and trillions. And Hindu civilization is the earliest civilization in this world.

Nations have risen and fallen, empires founded and destroyed, races appeared and disappeared, but the Hindu civilization that saw their rise and fall, their foundation and destruction, their appearance and disappearance, still remains.

After fully discussing the claims of the ancient nations of the world to high antiquity, Count Bjornstjerna says: "No nation on earth can vie with the Hindus in respect of the antiquity of their civilization and the antiquity of their religion."[1]

Dr. Stiles, President of Yale College in America, formed such an enthusiastic expectation from the amazing antiquity of the Hindu writings that he actually wrote to Sir W. Jones to request him to search among the Hindus for the Adamic books.[2]

Mr. Halhed exclaims with sacred reverence, after treating of the four *yugas* of the Hindus: "To such antiquity the Mosaic creation is but as yesterday; and to such ages, the life of Methuselah is no more than a span."

In concluding his remarks on the antiquity of Hindu astronomy, Count Bjornstjerna says: "But if it be true that the Hindus more than 3,000 years before Christ, according to Bailly's calculation, had attained so high a degree of *astronomical* and *geometrical* learning, how many centuries *earlier* must the commencement of their culture have been, since the human mind advances only step by step in the path of science!"[3]

Pliny states that from the days of Bacchus to Alexander of Macedon, 154 kings reigned over India, whose reigns extended over 6,451 years.

Abul-Fazal, in his translation of the *Raja Tarangini*, quotes the names of the kings who appear in these annals, and whose

[1] Theogony of the Hindus, p. 50.

[2] Ward's Mythology, Vol. I., p. 144.

[3] Theogony of the Hindus, p. 37.

successive reigns are said to have occupied 4,109 years 11 months and 9 days. Prof. Heeren says: "From Dionysius (an Indian king) to Sandracottus (Chandragupta) the space of 6,042 years is said to have elapsed. Megasthenes says 6,042 years passed between Spatembas and Sandracottus.[1]

Professor Max Duncker[2] says "that Spatembas," which is perhaps another name of Dionysius, "began his reign in 6,717 years B. C." "The era of Yudhisthira indeed" he again asserts, "is said to have preceded that of Vikramaditya by the space of 3,044 years, and to have commenced about 3,100 years B. C."[3]

Count Bjornstjerna says: "Megasthenes, the envoy of Alexander to Kandragupso (Chandragupta), king of the Gangarides, discovered chronological tables at Polybhottra (Patna), the residence of this king, which contain a series of no less than 153 kings, with all their names from Dionysius to Kandragupso, and specifying the duration of the reign of every one of those kings, together amounting to 6,451 years, which would place the regin of Dionysius nearly 7,000 years B. C., and consequently 1,000 years before the oldest king found on the Egyptian tables of *Manetho* (*viz.*, the head of the *Tinite Thebaine* dynasty), who reigned 5,867 years B.C., and 2,000 years before *Soufi*, the founder of the Gizeh Pyramid."[4]

According to the *Purāṇas*, the race of the Brihadrathas had ruled over Magadha before Pradyotas (who reigned about 2,100 A.C., acording to Sir W. Jones), from Somapi to Ripunjaya[5] for a thousand years. And before the first Brihadrathas, Sahadeva,

[1] Historical Researches, Vol., II., p. 218.
[2] History of Antiquity, Vol, IV., p. 74.
[3] History of Antiquity, Vol., IV., p. 219.
[4] Theogony of the Hindus, p. 45.
[5] Max Duncker's History of Antiquity, Vol. I., p. 76.

Jarasandha and Brihadratha are said to have reigned over Magadha."[1]

The fact that dynasties and not individuals were units of calculation, is in itself a proof of the great antiquity of the ancient Hindu Empire.

Count Bjornstjerna, after discussing the antiquity of Hindu astronomy says: "Besides the proofs adduced of the great antiquity of the civilization of the Hindus, there are others perhaps still stronger, namely, their gigantic temples hewn out of lofty rocks, with the most incredible labour, at Elephanta, at Ellora and several other places which, with regard to the vastness of the undertaking, may be compared with the pyramids, and in an architectural respect even surpass them."[2]

Captain Troyer says: "I cannot refuse credence to this fact, namely, that great States, highly advanced in civilization, existed at least three thousand years before our era. It is beyond that limit that I look for Rama, the hero of the Ramayana."[3]

According to the Mahabharata, Ayodhya prospered for 1,500 years, after which one of its kings, of the dynasty of Sagaras, founded Kanauj. The foundation of the city of Delhi (Indraprastha) is as old as the fabulous age (Pober, Vol. I. p. 263), at which time it was already celebrated for its splendour (Vol. I., p. 606). Rennell[4] states that Kanauj was founded more than a thousand years before Christ.

But apart from these views of European writers—who, as Professor Wilson says, "in order to avoid being thought credulous, run into the opposite vice of incredulity," and would never concede anything for which there is not a demonstrable proof,

[1] Max Duncker's History of Antiquity, Vol. IV. p. 77.

[2] Theogony of the Hindus, p. 38.

[3] Asiatic Journal, 1841. Professor Heeren says: "We do not perhaps assume too much when we venture to place the origin of Ayodhya from 1,500 to 2,000 B.C."—Hist. Researches, Vol. II., p. 227.

[4] Memoirs, p. 54 (2nd edition).

especially as the history of Ancient India is a history of ages so remote as to hopelessly put out of joint their early conceived and limited notions of chronology and antiquity—there is an important piece of evidence in favour of the great antiquity of Indian civilization. Says Count Bjornstjerna: "The Bactrian document, called Dabistan[1] (found in Kashmir and brought to Europe by Sir W. Jones), gives an entire register of kings, namely, of the Mahabadernes, whose first link reigned in Bactria, 5,600 years before Alexander's expedition to India, and consequently several hundred years *before* the time given by the Alexandrine text for the appearance *of the first man upon the earth.*"

That these Bactrian Kings were Hindus is now universally admitted.[2] Thus according to Dabistan, India enjoyed splendid civilization 6,000 B.C., or nearly 8,000 years before the Victorian age.

This alone is sufficient to prove that the ancient Indians were incontestably the earliest civilized nation on earth. Another conclusive proof of their unrivalled antiquity will be found in the fact that all the great nations of the old world derived their civilization from India; that India planted colonies in all parts of the world and that these colonies afterwards became known as Egypt, Greece, Persia, America, etc., and that Scandinavia, China and other countries derived their civilization and their religion from the Hindus. In short, as will be seen hereafter, it was India which supplied the rest of the world with learning, civilization and religion.

The most ancient coinage in the world is that of the Hindus (Aryas), and the modern discoveries of the coins of Ancient India are conclusive proofs of the vast antiquity of Hindu civilization.

[1] Theogony of the Hindus, p. 134.

[2] See Mill's History of India, Vol. II., pp. 237, 238.

[3] The coinage of the Hindus, whatever may be its value and character, is certainly of a very remote antiquity—Elphinstone's India, p. 176.

Mr. Princep says: "At or about 800 B.C., the Hindus were already in possession of such a scheme of exchange as recognised the use of fixed and determinate weight of metal, not only as general equivalents and measures of value, but further that the system had already advanced so far as to adopt small and convenient sections of metal into the category of current money."[1]

But in India everything is astounding to the European. Notwithstanding the destructive ravages of barbarous fanaticism, enough material remains from which we can infer the age of the present earth.

Swami Dayananda Saraswati has treated the subject elaborately in his "Introduction to the Vedas," and also discussed it with the Reverend Scott of Bareilly at Chandapur (vide *Arya Darpana* for March 1880, pp. 67, 68).

The *Sankalpa*, which every educated Hindu in India knows well, and which is recited at every ceremony, even at a dip in the sacred Ganges, is the key to unfold the whole mystery that enshrouds the view of the time at which the earth assumed its present form.

ओ३म् तत्सत् श्रीब्रह्मणो द्वितीयप्रहरार्द्धे वैवस्वतमन्वंतरेऽष्टाविंशतितमे कलियुगे कलिप्रथमचरणे आर्य्यावर्त्तान्तर्गतैकदेशे अमुकनगरे अमुकसंवत्सरायनर्त्तुमासपक्षदिननक्षत्रमुहूर्तेऽत्रेदं कार्य्यं कृतं क्रियते वा ।

To understand what follows, it must be remembered that, according to the Hindu theory of creation, this world is alternately created from and dissolved into its material cause (कारण) after a fixed period. The world exists in one form for a fixed period, and then, *for* that very period, it exists only in its *material* cause. The former is called *Brahma Dina*, and the latter *Brahma Ratri*.

As the Atharva Veda says, the *Brahma Dina* is equal to 4,320,000,000 years.

[1] Princep's Essays on Indian Antiquities, p. 223.

शतं तेऽयुतं हायनान्द्वे युगे त्रीणि चत्वारि कृण्मः । अथर्व० प्र० ८। अनु० २ । मं० २१ ॥

This *Brahma Dina* is made up of 1,000 *Chaturyugis* (4 yugas) or *Divyayugas*, as they are also called. Manu (Adhyaya I) says:—

दैविकानां युगानान्तु सहस्रं परिसंख्यया । ब्राह्ममेकमहर्ज्ञेयं तावतीं रात्रिमेव च ॥ मनु० अ० १ । श्लो० ७२ ॥

A *Chaturyugi* or *Divyayuga* means a period of four *yugas*, Satyayuga, Treta, Dvapara and Kaliyuga, and consists of 12,000 Divya years—Satyayuga consisting of 4,800, Treta of 3,600, Dvapara of 2,400, and Kaliyuga of 1,200 Divya years. Manu (Chapter I. Sl. 71) says:—

यदेतत् परिसंख्यातामादावेव चतुर्युगम् । एतद् द्वादशसाहस्रं देवानां युगमुच्यते ॥ ७१ ॥ And again,

चत्वार्याहुः सहस्राणि वर्षाणां तु कृतं युगम् । तस्य तावच्छती संध्या सन्ध्यांशश्च तथाविधः ॥ इतरेषु स सन्ध्येषु ससंध्यांशेषु च त्रिषु । एकापायेन वर्तन्ते सहस्राणि शतानि च ॥ (मनु० अ० १ । श्लो० ७०)

Now, a Divya year is equal to 360 ordinary years. Thus

Satyayuga	=4,800 × 360=1,728,000	years.
Treta	=3,600 × 360=1,296,000	,,
Dvapara	=2,400 × 360= 864,000	,,
Kaliyuga	=1,200 × 360= 432,000	,,
	A Chaturyugi =4,320,000	,,

Thus, the *Brahma Dina*=4,320,000,000 years. This is the period for which the world will remain in its present form.

Again, the *Brahma Dina* is divided into 14 *Manwantra* and a Manwantra into 71 Chaturyugis. Manu says:—

यत् प्राग् द्वादशसाहस्रमुदितं दैविकं युगम् । तदेकसप्ततिगुणं मन्वंतरमिहोच्यते ॥ मनु० अ० १ । श्लो० ७९ ॥

The Surya Siddhanta also says:—

युगानां सप्ततिः सैका मन्वन्तरमिहोच्यते । कृताब्दसङ्ख्या तस्यान्ते सन्धिः प्रोक्तो जलप्लवः । ससन्धयस्ते मनवः कल्पे ज्ञेयाश्चतुर्दश । कृतप्रमाणः कल्पादौ सन्धिः पञ्चदश स्मृतः ॥ इत्थं युगसहस्रेण भूतसंहारकारकः । कल्पो ब्राह्ममहः प्रोक्तः शर्वरी तस्य तावती ॥ सूर्यसि० अ० १ श्लो० । १८ । १९ । २० ॥

According to the *Sankalpa* quoted above, six Manwantaras[1] have passed since the creation of the present Earth, the seventh is passing, and the remaining seven have still to come. Each Chaturyugi=4,320,000, as shown before, and 4,320,000 ×71=306,720,000=one Manwantara. Now, six Manwantaras =1,840,320,000 have passed, and this present Kaliyuga is the Kaliyuga of the 28th Chaturyugi. Of this Chaturyugi, 5,016 years of the Kaliyuga (the present Samvat being 1973 Vikrama) have passed, and 432,000–5,016=426,984 years of the Kaliyuga have yet to pass. Thus, of the seventh Manwantara, 116,340,000 (27 Chaturyugis 4,320,000×27)+3,893,016 (the period of the 28th Chaturyugi already passed, 4,320,000–426,984), total 120,533,016 years, have passed. The period yet to pass before the Day of Dissolution comes is 2 14,704,000 (remaining 7 Manwantaras) +186,186,984 (of the present [seventh] Manwantara)=2,333,226,984 years.

The Europeans, "accustomed as they are," to use the words of Professor Sir M. Williams, "to a limited horizon," will find this vast antiquity bewildering. Billions surely are incredible to ears accustomed to a scale the highest note of which rises no higher than 6,000 years. But matters are improving, and even these souls will in time come out into a world in which centuries will be replaced by millenniums.

Mr. Baldwin says: "Doubtless the antiquity of the human race is much greater than is usually assumed by those whose

[1] The six Manwantaras already passed are Svayambhuva, Svarochisha, Auttami, Tamas, Raivat and Chākshus. The seventh, Vaivasvata, is passing. And the seven Manwantaras to come are named Savarni, Dakshasavarni, Brahmasavarni, Dharenasavarni, Rudrasavarni, Rauchyasavarni and Indrasavarni.

views of the past are still regulated by mediæval systems of chronology. Archæology and linguistic science, not to speak of geology, make it certain that the period between the beginning of the human race and the birth of Christ would be more accurately stated if the centuries counted in the longest estimate of the rabbinical chronologies should be changed to millenniums. And they present also another fact, namely, that the antiquity of civilization is very great, and suggest that in remote ages it may have existed, with important developments, in regions of the earth now described as barbarous . . . The representation of some speculators that the condition of the human race since its first appearance on earth has been a condition of universal and hopeless savagery down to a comparatively modern date, is an assumption merely, an unwarranted assumption used in support of an unproved and unprovable theory of man's origin."[1]

GOVERNMENT.

Whate'er is best administer'd, is best.

—*Pope, E. M.*

The saying of the greatest English exponent of Political Philosophy, Edmund Burke, that no country in which population flourishes can be under bad government, introduces us to the subject of the political constitution of Ancient India. Burke lays down two important standards to test the good or bad government of a nation: (i) Population, and (ii) Wealth.

All the ancient Greek writers and travellers are agreed that the ancient Aryas were the largest nation on the earth.

[1] Baldwin's Ancient America, p. 181.

Appollodorus[1] states that "there were between the Hydaspes and Hypanis (Hypasis) 1,500 cities, none of which was less than Cos."

Megasthenes says that "there are 120 nations in India." Arrian admits that the Indians were the most numerous people,[2] and that it was impossible to know and enumerate the cities in Aryavarta. Strabo says that Eukratides was the master of 1,000 cities between Hydaspes and Hyphasis (Panjab). Professor Max Duncker[3] says "the Indians were the largest of the nations."

Ctesias states "that they (Hindus) were as *numerous as all the other nations put together.*"[4]

But the most important proof of the over-abundant population of Ancient India is to be found in the successive waves of emigration from India to the different parts of the world, founding colonies and planting settlements in what are now called the Old and the New Worlds. *Vide* "Hindu Colonization."

As regards wealth, India has always been famous for its immense riches. "Golden India" is a hackneyed phrase.[5] Both in population and in wealth, India at one time was not only pre-eminent but was without a rival.

What higher authority for, what more positive proof of good government of Ancient India can be given than the fact that "Ancient India knew no thieves,"[6] nor knew why to shut the doors of its houses even at the time when, according to

[1] Elphinstone's India, p. 241. See Strabo, Lib. XV.

[2] See his History of Nations (Chapter on India), Chapter VII., pp. 6, 22 and 23.

[3] History of Antiquity, Vol. V., p. 18.

[4] Strabo states that "Polibhothra was eight miles long and had a rampart which had 570 towers and 64 gates." As late even as the 16th century, Kanauj was reported to have contained no less than 30,000 shops of betelsellers and "sixty thousand sets of musicians." See Historical Researches, Vol. II., p. 220.

[5] For further information on this subject, see chapter on "Wealth."

[6] See Strabo, Lib, XV., p. 488 (1587 edition).

Dr. Johnson, "the capital of the most civilized nation of modern times is the true Satan-at-home."

> "Prepare for death, if here at night you roam.
> And sign your will before you sup from home."[1]

The form of government depends upon the character of a people, the conditions of life obtaining among them, and the principles of their social system. With changes in respect of these matters, the form of government also undergoes a change. Broadly speaking, the best form of government is that which enables only men of high character, noble minds, wide sympathies, men of sterling qualities and talents to rise to the top, and prevents men of shallow minds, mean capacities, narrow sympathies, and unscrupulous character from coming into power, it being always understood that the proper functions of Government, as Herbert Spencer says, are only (i) national defence, and (ii) protection of one individual or of one class from another.

The form of government may vary, but the spirit depends on the ethical side of a people's character. It is well said—

> Political rights, however broadly framed,
> Will not elevate a people individually depraved.

If high moral principles guide the people in their daily conduct as a nation, the Government of that nation is free from those party strifes, that incessant warfare raged by one individual against another and by one class against another for power or for protection. It is this law that discovers to us the eternal principle, that spiritual elevation not only helps material prosperity but is essential to the *happiness* of a people, and that it is an index to the realization of the aim and object of all government.

[1] Johnson's London.

Mr. Herbert Spencer says: "There has grown up quite naturally, and indeed almost inevitably among civilized peoples, an identification of freedom with the political appliances, established to maintain freedom. The two are confused together in thought; or, to express the fact more correctly, they have not yet been separated in thought. In most countries during past times, and in many countries at the present time, experience has associated in men's minds the unchecked power of a ruler with extreme coercion of the ruled. Contrariwise in countries where the people have acquired some power, the restraints on the liberties of individuals have been relaxed; and with advance towards government by the majority, there has, on the average, been a progressing abolition of laws and removal of burdens which unduly interfered with such liberties. Hence, by contrast, popularly-governed nations have come to be regarded as free nations; and possession of political power by all is supposed to be the same thing as freedom. But the *assumed indentity of the two is a delusion*—delusion, which, like many other delusions, results from confounding means with ends. Freedom in its absolute form is the absence of all external checks to whatever actions the will prompts; and freedom in its socially-restricted form is the absence of any other external checks than those arising from the presence of other men who have like claims to do what their wills prompt. The mutual checks hence resulting are the only checks which freedom, in the true sense of the word, permits. The sphere within which each may act without trespassing on the like sphere of others, cannot be intruded upon by any agency, private or public, without an equivalent loss of freedom; and it matters not whether the public agency is autocratic or democratic: the intrusion is essentially the same."[1]

It is due to a thorough recognition of this truth that the Indian sages laid so much stress on the necessity of formation of

[1] Herbert Spencer's Autobiography, Vol. I., p. 439.

Hindu character on ethical and altruistic principles, to secure political as well as social prosperity. The higher the ethical development of character, the greater the freedom enjoyed by a people. It is in this sense true that the best-governed people is the least-governed people. Over-government is an evil that defeats it own ends. The real object of government is frustrated: its proper functions are neglected.

Mr. Herbert Spencer says: "Among mechanicians it is a recognized truth that the multiplication of levers, wheels, cranks, etc., in an apparatus, involves loss of power, and increases the chances of going wrong. Is it not so with Government machinery, as compared with the simpler machinery men frame in its absence? Moreover, men's desires when left to achieve their own satisfaction, follow the order of decreasing intensity and importance: the essential ones being satisfied first. But when, instead of aggregates of desires spontaneously working for their ends we get the judgments of Governments, there is no guarantee that the order of relative importance will be followed, and there is abundant proof that it is not followed. Adaptation to one function pre-supposes more or less unfitness for other functions; and pre-occupation with many functions is unfavourable to the complete discharge of anyone. Beyond the function of national defence, the essential function to be discharged by a Government is that of seeing that the citizens in seeking satisfaction for their own desires, individually or in groups, shall not injure one another; and its failure to perform this function is great in proportion as its other functions are numerous. The daily scandals of our judicial system, which often brings ruin instead of restitution, and frightens away multitudes who need protection, result in large measure from the pre-occupation of statesmen and politicians with non-essential things, while the all-essential thing passes almost unheeded."[1]

[1] Autobiography. Vol. I. p. 422.

In Ancient India, owing to the high ethical and spiritual development of the people, they were not over-governed. They enjoyed the greatest individual freedom compatible with national cohesion and national security. It is owing to this want of ethical and altruistic development of character that freedom, in its true sense, is not yet fully enjoyed in the world.

Mr. Herbert Spencer says: "Only along with the gradual moulding of men to the social state has it become possible, without social disruption, for those ideas and feelings which cause resistance to unlimited authority, to assert themselves and to restrict the authority. At present the need for the authority, and for the sentiment which causes submission to it, continues to be great. While the most advanced nations vie with one another it is manifest that their members are far too aggresive to permit much weakening of restraining agencies by which order is maintained among them. The unlimited right of the majority to rule is probably as advanced a conception of freedom as can safely be entertained at present, if indeed, even that can safely be entertained."[1]

After the Mahabharata, when the first crash came, the efforts of Hindu statesmen were directed towards preserving as much of the old Constitution as possible, while providing for the assimilation of new elements consequent on the slightly-changed conditions of life. Burke truly says that the true statesman is he who preserves what is acquired and leaves room for future improvement. Thus, though the comparative neglect of the ethical and spiritual culture of the Hindus after the beginning of the Kali-yuga affected their individual freedom, yet the ground-work of the Constitution being sound, it was able to adapt itself to changing circumstances, and, as the necessities of the situation plainly demanded, more heed was paid to the conservative

[1] Autobiography, Vol. I., p. 441.

principles than the progressive ones. But the spirit of the Constitution was never affected till its practical dissolution with the advent of foreigners into India.

"Arrian[1] mentions with admiration that every Indian is free," Lieutenant-Colonel Mark Wilks,[2] while discussing the political system in its provincial working says: "Each Hindu township is, and indeed always was, a particular community or petty republic by itself." "The whole of India," he says again, "is nothing more than one vast congeries of such republics."

These facts do not seem to support the theory that representative government does not suit the genius of the Hindus. Even Mr. James Mill is forced to admit that "in examining the spirit of these ancient Constitutions and laws, we discover evident traces of a germ of repulicanism."[3]

As regards the strength of the representative institutions, Sir Charles Metcalfe[4] says: "The village communities are little republics having nearly everything they can want within themselves and almost independent of any foreign

[1] See Indica, Ch. X. See also Diodorus, Lib. II, p. 214 (edition 1604). See also Elphinstone's India, p. 239.

[2] Historical Sketches of the South of India, Vol. I. p. 119.

[3] That the people took active interest in politics is exhibited by their instigating Sambas to fly from Alexander and Musicanus to break the peace made with Alexander.

As regards the executive system, Professor Max Duncker says: "The king placed officers over every village (called pati), and again over ten or twenty villages (grama), so that these places with their acreage formed together a district. Five or ten such districts formed a canton which contained a hunred communities, and over this, in turn, the king placed a higher magistrate; ten of those cantons form a region which thus comprised a thousand villages and this was administered by a Governor. The over-seers of districts were to have soldiers at their disposal to maintain order (police.) This is of itself evidence of an advanced stage of administration."—History of Antiquity, Vol. IV, p. 215.

The Police of India was excellent. Megasthenes says that in the camp of Sandrocottus, which he estimates to have contained 400,000 men, the sums stolen daily did not amount to more than Rs. 30.—Elphinstone's India, p. 241.

[4] Report of the Select Committee of the House of Commons, 1832, Vol. III. Appendices, p. 33.

nation. They seem to last where nothing else lasts. Dynasty after dynasty tumbles down, revolution succeeds revolution, and Pathan, Mughal, Mahratta, Sikh, British are all masters in turn, but the village communities remain the same. This union of village communities, each one forming a separate little State in itself, is in a high degree conducive to their (Hindu) happiness, and to the enjoyment of a great portion of freedom and independence."

Old inscriptions recently discovered furnish incontestable proof of the representative form of government prevailing in India in ancient times. The inscription dated S. 920 (A.D., 863) of the reign of Parantaka I (S. 907-948) found in the Vaikuntha Parumal Temple at Uttaramallur village, near Madurantakum station on South Indian Railway in 1898 A.D., shows that all villages and towns enjoyed representative government. And it must not be supposed that Parantaka I started the system of government by assemblies and committees. "Inscriptions prior to his reign bear ample testimony to their existence. The great men of the 'annual committee' are mentioned as the trustees of an endowment in an inscription [1] of the Ganga-Pallava King Kampavarman (9th century A.D.), and village assemblies are referred to in several inscriptions of the Pallava period. 'The committee of the assembly' is spoken of in an inscription of Varaguna Maharaja at Ambasumardram, who reigned probably at the beginning of the ninth century A.D., while the *Pancavari* and *Varagosthi* (committee assembly) are mentioned in an Eastern Calukya copper-plate grant [2] of the first half of the tenth century from the Kistna District. The system therefore seems to have been in operation almost throughout Southern India at the beginning of the tenth century A.D."

[1] See South Indian Inscriptions, Vol. III, p. 9.
[2] Epigraphia Indica, Vol. V., p. 138.

The inscription[1] given below may be divided into the following sections:—(1) Qualifications of committee members. (2) Disqualified persons: (*a*) Defaulting committee members and their relations however remote, (*b*) Incorrigible sinners and their relations, (*c*) Outcastes until they perform expiatory rites, (*d*) Those who are mentally or morally disqualified, (*e*) Those who are themselves disqualified but do not transmit their disqualification to their relatives. (3) Method of selection of members of committees. (4) No. of committees to be appointed annually. (5) Two others which are perhaps not annually appointed. (6) Appointment of accountants. It will thus be seen that the document was drawn up with a definite plan and follows a natural order in the arrangement of its various parts." ...."The tank committee was probably entrusted with the annual removal of silt, occasional repairs, investment of endowments made to tanks and similar questions. The gold committee probably regulated the Currency. Committee members were expected to take an active part in discussing questions brought before them. In fact, an inscription

[1] Arch. Survey Report of India 1904-05, pp. 135-136.

ABSTRACT OF INSCRIPTION.

"We (the members of) the assembly of Uttirameru-caturvedimangalam in its own sub-division of Kaliyurkottam—Karanjai Kondaya—Kramavittabhattan *alias* Somasiperuman of Srivanganagar in Purangarambai nadu of the Cola country sitting and convening the committee in accordance with the terms of the royal command, made a settlement as follows, according to (the terms of) the royal letter for choosing once every year from this year forward (members for) the annual committee, garden committee and tank committee:—

I There shall be thirty wards.

II. In these thirty wards those that live in each ward shall assemble and shall choose for pot-tickets anyone possessing the following qualifications:—

(*a*) He must own more than a quarter of tax-paying land.

(*b*) He must live in a house built on his own site.

(*c*) His age must be below 70 and above 35.

(*d*) He must know the Mantrabrahman, *i.e.* he must know (it) by being able to teach others.

from the Telugu country refers to eloquence at committee assemblies as a special merit. The age restriction, the educational and property qualifications laid down, and the principle of membership by rotation are items which may commend themselves even to *modern* administrators."

The Archæological Reporter in the same Report says: "The Tanjore inscriptions of the Cola king Rajaraja I. (A.D. 985 to 1013) mention not less than 150 villages which had assemblies and 40 others where the villagers, as a body, seem to have managed their affairs. The system must have been in operation in thousands of other villages whose names and whose exact number remain to be disclosed by future researches. Neither the period nor the circumstances under which village assemblies arose in Southern India are known. But as the Greek ambassador, Megasthenes, in his account of Indian administration as it obtained at his time, makes mention of six committees of five each, it may be supposed that the system was carried into Southern India by the Aryan immigrants and that slight alterations were probably made to suit the conditions of the South." "The number of committees of village assemblies does not appear to have been the same everywhere. Local conditions seem to have influ-

III. Even if one owns one-eight of land (he shall have) his name written on the pot-ticket to be put into the pot, in case he has learnt one Veda and one of the four *bhashyas* by being able to explain (it to others).

IV. Among those (possessing the foregoing qualifications).—

(*a*) Only such as are well conversant with business and are virtuous shall be taken, and

(*b*) One who possesses honest earnings, whose mind is pure and who has not been on (any of) the committees for the last three years shall be chosen. "One who has been on any of the committees but has not submitted his accounts, and all his relations specified below shall not have their names written on the pot-tickets and put (into the pot): (1) His son, (2) His father (3-12) father-in-law, etc.

. . . .

"Excluding all these, thus specified, names shall be written for 'pot-tickets in the thirty wards, and each of the wards in these twelve streets

enced the number very much. In the subjoined inscriptions provision is made for five committees: 'annual committee,' 'garden committee,' 'tank committee,' gold committee,' and 'pancavara committee' Reference is also made to a sixth

(of Uttaramallur shall prepare a separate covering ticket for (each of the) thirty wards bundled separately. (These packets)! shall be put into a pot. When the pot tickets have to be drawn, a full meeting of the great assembly, including the young and old (members) shall be convened. All the temple priests (nambimar) who happen to be in the village on the day, shall, without any exception whatever, be caused to be seated in the inner hall (where) the great assembly (meets). In the midst of the temple priests, one of them, who happens to be the eldest, shall stand up and lift that pot, looking upwards so as to be seen by all people. One ward (i.e., the packet representing it) shall be taken out by any young boy standing close, who does not know what is inside, and shall be transferred to another (empty) pot and shaken. From this pot one ticket shall be drawn (by the young boy?) and made over to the arbitrator (madhyastha). While taking charge of the ticket thus given (to him), the arbitrator shall receive it on the palm of his hand with the five fingers open. He shall read out (the name on) the ticket thus received. The ticket read (by him) shall (also) be read out by all the priests present in the inner hall. The name thus read out shall be put down (and accepted). Similarly one man shall be chosen for (each of) the thirty wards. Of the thirty men thus chosen those who had (previously) been on the 'garden committee,' and on the tank committee, those who are advanced in age and those who are advanced in learning shall be chosen for the 'annual committee.' Of the rest, twelve shall be taken for the 'garden committee' and the remaining six shall form the 'tank committee.' These (last) two committees shall be chosen by showing the Karai. The great men of these three committees thus (chosen) for them shall hold office for full three hundred and sixty days and (then) retire. When one who is on the committees is found guilty of (any) offence, he shall be removed (at once). For appointing the committees after these have retired, the members of the committee for supervision of justice in the twelve streets (of Uttaramallur) shall convene an assembly (Kuri) with the help of the arbitrator. The committees shall be appointed by drawing pot-tickets according to this order of settlement. For the 'pancavara committee' and the 'gold committee,' names shall be written for pot-tickets in the thirty wards; thirty (packets with) covering tickets shall be deposited (in a pot) and thirty pot-tickets shall be drawn (as previously described). From (these) thirty (tickets) twelve men shall be selected. Six out of twelve (thus) chosen shall form the 'gold committee,' and the remaining, six the 'pancavara committee.' When drawing pot-tickets for these (two) committees next year, the wards which have been already represented (during the year in question) on these committees shall be excluded and the selection made from the remaining wards by drawing the Karai. One who has ridden on an ass and one who has committed forgery shall not have (his name) written on the pot-ticket to be put (into the pot). Any arbitrator who possesses honest earnings shall write the accounts (of the village). No accountant shall be

committee, *viz.*, 'justice committee.' But it is not said if it was a separate body or if it was identical with one of the above-mentioned five. Inscriptions found at Tiruparkadal, near Kāvēripāk in the North Arcot district, furnish the names of five more committees, *viz.*, 'the great men of the wards committee,' 'the great men of the fields committee,' 'the great men (numbering) two hundred,' 'the great men of the village committee,' and 'the great men of the *udāsina* committee' (Annual Report on Epigraphy for 1904-1905, part II, paragraph 7).

The benevolent nature of the Hindu civilization is proved by the fact that the Hindu Colonies and Dependencies enjoyed the same Constitution as the mother country. Sir Stamford Raffles[1] says about Bali, an island east of Java: "Here, together with the Brahmanical religion is still preserved the ancient form of Hindu municipal polity."

Hindu works on diplomacy, polity and government

appointed to that office again before he submits his accounts (for the period during which he was in office) to the great men of the big committee and (is declared) to have been honest. The accounts which one has been writing, he shall submit himself. Thus from this year onwards, as long as the moon and the sun (endure) committees shall always be appointed by 'pot-ticket' alone. To this effect was the royal letter received and shown (to us) graciously issued by the Lord of gods, the Emperor, one who is fond of learned men, the wrestler with elephants, the crest jewel of horses, whose acts (*i.e.*, gifts) (resembles those of) the celestial tree, the glorious Parakesarivarman. At the royal command Karanjai Kondaya-Kramavittabhattan, alias Soma'siperuman of Srivanaganagar in Puravgarambainadu (a district) of the Cola country sat with (us) and thus caused (this settlement) to be made. We the (members of the) assembly of Uttarameru caturvedimangalam, made this settlement for the prosperity of our village in order that wicked men may perish and the rest may prosper. At the order of the great men sitting in the assembly, I, the arbitrator Kadadippottan Sivakkuri—Rajamallamangalapriyan thus wrote the settlement"—Archæological Survey of India: Annual Report for 1904-1905 A.D., pp. 142-145.

[1] Description of Java, Vol. II, Appendix, p. 237.

After quoting some passages from Manu, Colonel Briggs says: "These extracts afford us sufficient proof of a well-organised system of local superintendence and administration."—Brigg's Land Tax of India, page 24.

(though few are now extant) show the high development that political thought reached in those days. Some of them have been translated into Persian and thence into European languages. Abu Sabhhad had the *Rajniti* translated into Persian in 1150 A.D., Buzarchameher, the renowned minister of Nausherwan the Just, received his political education and training in India.

Law is a test of good government. The great Hindu work on law is a marvel of simplicity and wisdom. Without being complex, it satisfied all the diverse wants of the people. Its provisions did not change every week, and yet they suited the varied circumstances of Hindu society. Sir W. Jones says:[1] "The laws of Manu very probably were considerably older than those of Solon or even of Lycurgus, although the promulgation of them, before they were reduced to writing, might have been coeval with the first monarchies established in Egypt and India."

The English derived their laws from the Romans, who, in their turn, derived them from Greece. During the Decemvirate, Greece seems to have been indebted to India for its laws. Sir W. Jones says:[2] "Although perhaps Manu was never in Crete,[3] yet, some of his institutions may well have been adopted in that island, whence Lycurgus a century or two after may have imported them into Sparta."

The *Bible in India* says that the Manu Smriti was the foundation upon which the Egyptian, the Persian, the Grecian and the Roman codes of law were built, and that the influence of Manu was still every day felt in Europe.

Professor Wilson[4] says the Hindu had "a code of laws adapted to a great variety of relations which could not have existed except in an advanced condition of social organization."

[1] Haughton's Institutes of Hindu Law, Preface, page x.
[2] Preface to Haughton's Institutes of Hindu Law, page xii.
[3] The oneness of Minas and Manu is highly probable.
[4] Mill's India, Vol. II, p. 282

Coleman[1] says: "The style of it (Manu) has a certain austere majesty that sounds like the language of legislation and extorts a respectful awe. The sentiments of independence on all beings but God, and the harsh administrations even to kings are truly noble."

Dr. Robertson says: "With respect to the number and variety of points the Hindu code considers it will bear a comparison with the celebrated Digest of Justinian, or with the systems of jurisprudence in nations most highly civilized. The articles of which the Hindu code is composed are arranged in natural and luminous order. They are numerous and comprehensive, and investigated with that minute attention and discernment which are natural to a people distinguished for acuteness and subtlety of understanding, who have been long accustomed to the accuracy of judicial proceedings, and acquainted with all the refinements of legal practice. The decisions concerning every point are founded upon the great and immutable principles of justice which the human mind acknowledges and respects in every age and in all parts of the earth. Whoever examines the whole work cannot entertain a doubt of its containing the jurisprudence of an enlightened and commercial people. Whoever looks into any particular title will be surprised with a minuteness of detail and nicety of distinction which, in many instances, seem to go *beyond the attention of European legislation*; and it is remarkable that some of the regulations with indicate the greatest degree of refinement were established in periods of the most remote antiquity."[2]

Mr. Mill says that "the division and arrangement of Hindu law is rude and shows the barbarism of the nation;"

[1] Coleman's Mythology of the Hindus, p. 8.

[2] Disquisition Concerning India, Appendix, p. 217.

upon which Professor Wilson, with his usual candour, remarks: "By this test, the attempt to classify would place the Hindus higher in civilization than the English."[1]

Mr. Mill's review of Hindu religion and laws is a peace of stupendous perversity, ignorance and stupidity. Professor Wilson, the editor of Mill's History of India, speaks of it in the following terms: "The whole of this review of the religion as well as of the laws of the Hindus is full of serious defects arising from inveterate prejudices and imperfect knowledge."[2]

He thus describes the object of that most mischievous book ever written on India: "Indignant at the exalted, and it may be granted, sometimes exaggerated descriptions of their (Hindus) advance in civilization, of their learning, their sciences, their talents, their virtues, which emanated from the amiable enthusiasm of Sir William Jones, Mr. Mill has entered the lists against him with equal enthusiasm, but a less commendable purpose, and has sought to reduce them as far below their level as their encomiasts may have formerly elevated them above it. With very imperfect knowledge, with materials exceedingly defective, with an implicit faith in all testimony hostile to Hindu pretensions, he has elaborated a portrait of Hindu *which has no resemblance whatever to the original and which almost outrages humanity.*"

Of Mill's History of British India, Prof. Max Muller says: "The book which I consider most mischievous, nay, which I hold responsible for some of the greatest misfortunes that have happened in India, is Mill's History of India, even with the antidote against its poison which is supplied by Professor

[1] Mill's India, Vol. II, pp. 224-25.

[2] Mill's India, Vol. II, p. 136 (Note).

Wilson's notes."[1] Professor H. H. Wilson says: "Its tendency is evil"

To say that the plant of the jury system is an exotic in India is to plead one's utter ignorance of Hindu law. The "Sacred books of the East" series, Vol. 25, translated by Dr. G. Buhler and edited by Prof. Max Muller, treats of the Laws of Manu. Chapter VII, deals with civil and ceremonial law. Section I of the chapter provides that "a king desirous of investigating law cases must enter his court of justice, together with Brahmans and with experienced councillors."

Sec. 10. provides "that man (in the absence of a king, a learned Brahman) shall enter that most excellent Court accompanied by (at least) three assessors.

Sec. 11. Where three Brahman assessors mentioned above versed in the Vedas and the learned judge appointed by the king sit down, they call that the Court of (four-faced) Brahman.

In Chapter XII—Manu deals with the constitution of a Court of Law to decide doubtful points in law. Section 110 of it provides: "Wherever an assembly consisting either of ten or of at least three persons, who follow their prescribed occupations declares to be law, the legal force of that one must not dispute."

While discussing Mill's views, Professor Wilson again says: "According to this theory (Mill's theory contained in his explanation of the causes of complex procedure in the English courts of law) the corruption of the judge is the best security for justice.

[1] India: What can it teach us? p. 42.

It would be dangerous to reduce this to practice."

An eminent authority, the late Chief Justice of Madras, Sir Thomas Strange, says of the Hindu Law of Evidence: "It will be read by every English lawyer with a mixture of admiration and delight, as it may be studied by him to advantage."

A writer in the Asiatic Journal (p. 14) says: "All the requisite shades of care and diligence, the corresponding shades of negligence and default are carefully observed in the Hindu law of bailment, and neither in the jurisprudence nor in the legal treatises of the most civilised States of Europe are they to be found more logically expressed or more accurately defined. In the spirit of Pyrrhus' observation on the Roman legions, one cannot refrain from exclaiming: "I see nothing barbarous in the jurisprudence of the Hindus."

[1] Mill's India, Vol. II., p. 512.—Mill says that because the Hindus lend money on pledges, therefore they are barbarous. On this, Professor Wilson says: "Lending on pledges can scarcely be regarded as proof of a state of barbarism, or the multitude of pawn-brokers in London would witness our being very low in the scale of civilization." Mill declares the Muhammadan Code to be superior to the Hindu Code." "In civil branch," replies Wilson, "the laws of Contract and Inheritance, it is not so exact or complete as the latter ('Hindu'). Its (Muhammadan) spirit of barbarous retaliation is unknown to the Hindu Code." Mill thinks that perjury is a virtue according to the Hindu Code. But Wilson clearly proves that this is a creation of Mill's diseased imagination.

It is further objected that the uncertainties of the Hindu law are very great. Prof. Wilson (Essays. Vol. III., page 5) remarks: If the uncertainties of the English law are less perplexing than those of the Hindu law, we doubt if its delays are not something more interminable. A long time elapses before a cause comes for decision, and abundant opportunity is therefore afforded for the traffic of underhand negotiations, intrigues and corruption. It is needless to cite instances to prove the consequence or to make any individual application: public events have rendered the fact notorious. It can scarcely be otherwise." But he returns to the charge and says: "They say that pandits don't agree in the discharge of Hindu law. But see in the case of Virapermah Pillay *versus* Narain Pillay, the opinion of the two English judges. The Chief Justice of Bengal declares that a decision pronounced and argued with great pains by the Chief Justice at Madras will mislead those by whom it may be followed, and that the doctrine which it inculcates is contrary to law." Professor Wilson again says: "The Chief Justice of Bengal says that "he would connive at immoral acts if he thought they led to useful results."

Of the Commentary of Calluca on Manu, Sir W. Jones says: "It is the shortest yet the most luminous; the least ostentatious yet the most learned; the deepest yet the *most agreeable commentary ever composed on any author ancient or modern, European or Asiatic.*"[1]

SOCIAL SYSTEM.

Hail, social, life! into thy pleasing bounds
Again I come to pay the common stock,
My share of service, and, in glad return
To taste the comforts, thy protected joys.

—THOMSON: *Agamemnon.*

THE Hindus perfected society. The social organization of the people was based on scientific principles, and was well calculated to encure progress without party strife. There was no accumulation of wealth in one portion of the community, leaving the other portion in destitute poverty; no social forces stimulating the increase of the wealth of the one and the poverty of the other, as is the tendency of the modern civilization. "Every society," says Carlyle, "has a spiritual principle, is the embodiment, more or less complete, of an idea." The keynote of the Hindu system, however, was *national service.* It afforded to every member of the social body, opportunities and means to develop fully his powers and capacities, and to use them for the advancement of the common weal. Everyone was to serve the nation in the sphere in which he was best fitted to act, which, being congenial to his individual genius, was conducive to the highest development of his faculties and powers.

There was thus a wise and statesmanlike classification which procured a general distribution of wealth, expelled misery and

[1] Preface to Houghton's Institutes of Hindu Law, p. 18.

want from the land, promoted mental and moral progress, ensured national efficiency and, above all, made tranquillity compatible with advancement; in one word, dropped *manna* all round and made life doubly sweet by securing external peace with national efficiency and social happiness—a condition of affairs nowhere else so fully realized.

This classification—this principle of social organization—was the *Varnashrama*. Mankind were divided into two classes, (1) the Aryas and (2) the Dasyus, or the civilized and the savage. The Aryas were subdivided into:—

(1) Brahmans, who devoted themselves to learning and acquiring wisdom and following the liberal arts and sciences.

(2) Kshatriyas, who devoted themselves to the theory and practice of war, and to whom the executive government of the people was entrusted.

(3) Vaishyas, who devoted themselves to trade and the professions.

(4) Sudras (men of law capacities), who served and helped the other three classes.[1]

This classification is a necessary one in all civilized countries in some form or other. It was the glory of ancient Aryavarta that this classification existed there in its perfect form and was based on scientific principles—on the principle of heredity (which has not yet been fully appreciated by European thinkers), the conservation of energy, economy of labour, facility of development, and specialization of faculties. Literary men, soldiers, doctors,

[1] Rev. F. D. Maurice says that "the Sudras are not in any sense slaves, and never can have been such. The Greeks were surprised to find all classes in India free citizens."—The Religions of the World, p. 43.

Mr. Elphinstone says: "It is remarkable that in the Hindu dramas there is not a trace of servility in the behaviour of other characters to the king."—History of India, p. 243.

lawyers, clergymen, traders, and servants are to be found in England, France, America, and in every other civilized country of modern times, as they were in Ancient India. The only difference is that in one case the division was perfect and the working of its marvellous mechanism regular, while in the other the classification is imperfect and its working irregular and haphazard.

The *Varnashrama* was not the same as the caste system of the present day—a travesty of its ancient original. No one was a Brahman by blood nor a Sudra by birth, but everyone was such as his merits fitted him to be. "The people," says Col. Olcott, "were not, as now, irrevocably walled in by castes, but they were free to rise to the highest social dignities or sink to the lowest positions, according to the inherent qualities they might possess."

The son of a Brahman sometimes became a Kshatriya, sometimes a Vaishya, and sometimes a Sudra. At the same time, a Sudra as certainly became a Brahman or a Kshatriya. *Shanker Dig Vijaya* says:—

जन्मना जायते शूद्रः संस्कारात्द्विज उच्यते ।
वेदपाठी भवेद्विप्रः ब्रह्म जानाति ब्राह्मण: ॥

"By birth all are Sudra, by actions men become *Dvija* (twice-born). By reading the Vedas one becomes *Vipra* and becomes *Brahman* by gaining a knowledge of God."

"The passage in the *Vanaparva* of the Mahabharata runs thus: "He in whom the qualities of truth, munificence, forgiveness, gentleness, abstinence from cruel deeds, contemplation, benevolence are observed, is called a Brahman in the Smriti. A man is not a Sudra by being a Sudra nor a Brahman by being a Brahman:"

The Mahabharata (Santiparva) says:—

न विशेषोऽस्ति वर्णानां सर्वं ब्राह्ममिदं जगत् ।
ब्रह्मणा पूर्वसृष्टं हि कर्मभिर्वर्णतां गतम् ॥

"There are no distinctions of caste. Thus, a world which, as created by Brahma, was at first entirely Brahmanic, has become divided into classes, in consequence of men's actions."

"We read in the Aitareya Brahmana (ii. 3. 19), for example, that Kavasha Ailusha, who was a Sudra and son of a low woman, was greatly respected for his literary attainments, and admitted into the class of Rishis. Perhaps the most remarkable feature of his life is that he, Sudra as he was distinguished himself as the Rishi of some of the hymns of the Rig-Veda (Rig., x. 30-34). It is distinctly stated in the Chhandogyuapanished that Jabala, who is otherwise called Satya-Kama, had no gotra, or family name whatever (Chhan. Upa, iv. 4); all that we know about his parentage is that he was the son of a woman named Jabala, and that he is called after his mother. Though born of unknown parents, Jabala is said to have been the founder of a school of the Yajur-Veda. Even in the Apastamba-Sutra (ii. 5-10) and the Manusmriti x. 65), we find that a Sudra can become a Brahman and a Brahman can become Sudra, according to his good or bad deeds. Panini mentions the name of a celebrated grammarian called Cakravarmana in the sixth chapter of his Ashtadhyayi (p. vi. 1. 130); now Cakravarmana was a Kshatriya by birth, since he has the prescribed Kshatriya termination at the end of his name, which is a patronymic of Cakravarmana."[1]

Who were Vishvamitra and Valmiki by birth but Sudras? Even so late as the time of the Greek invasion of India, the caste system had not become petrified into its present state. The Greeks describe four castes. Megesthenes says that a Hindu of any caste may become a Sophist (Brahman).[2]

[1] Paper on "Sanskrit as a Living Language in India," read before the International Congress of Orientalists at Berlin on 14th September 1881 A. D.

[2] Arrian counts seven classes: Sophists, agriculturists, herdsmen, handicrafts and artisans, warriors, inspectors and councillors (See Strabo, Lib. XV.).

Colonel Tod says:—"In the early ages of these Solar and Lunar dynasties, the priestly office was not hereditary in families; it was a profession, and the genealogies exhibit frequent instances of branches of these races terminating their martial career in the commencement of a religious sect or 'gotra' and of their descendants reassuming their warlike occupations."

There was no hereditary caste. The people enjoyed the advantages of hereditary genius without the serious drawbacks of a rigid system of caste based on birth.

As late as the 12th century A. D., King Bellala Sen of Bengal elevated one section of the Kaivartas, now called the Chasi Kaivartas, to the rank of a clean caste and degraded the Suvarna Vaniks. In Rajputana, Maharawal Amar Singh of Jaisalmer even in the seventeenth century readmitted amongst the Bhatti Rajputs all Bhattis who had become Muhammadans.

"The one great object which the promoters of the hereditary system seem to have had in view was to secure to each class a high degree of efficiency in its own sphere." "Hereditary genius" is now a subject of serious enquiry amongst the enlightened men of Europe and America, and the evolution theory as applied to sociology, when fully worked out will show the merits of the system.

Even the system in the present form has not been an unmitigated evil. It has been the great conservative principle of the constitution of Hindu society, though originally it was a conservative as well as a progressive one. It is this principle of the Hindu social constitution which has enabled the nation to sustain, without being shattered to pieces, the tremendous shocks given by the numerous political convulsions and religious upheavals that have occurred during the last thousand years. "The system of caste," says Sir Henry Cotton," far from being the source of all troubles which can be traced in Hindu society, has rendered most important service in the past, and still continues to sustain order and solidarity."

As regards its importance from a European point of view Mr. Sidney Low in his recent book, *A Vision of India*, says: "There is no doubt that it is the main cause of the fundamental stability and contentment by which Indian society has been braced for centuries against the shocks of politics and the cataclysms of nature. It provides every man with his place, his career, his occupation, his circle of friends. It makes him, at the outset, a member of a corporate body; it protects his through life from the canker of social jealousy and unfulfilled aspirations; it ensures him companionship and a sense of community with others in like case with himself. The caste organization is to the Hindu his club, his trade-union, his benefit society, his philanthropic society. There are no work-houses in India, and none are as yet needed. The obligation to provide for kinsfolk and friends in distress is universally acknowledged; nor can it by questioned that this is due to the recognition of the strength of family ties and of the bonds created by associations and common pursuits which is fostered by the caste principle. An India without caste, as things stand at present, it is not quite easy to imagine."

CHARACTER.

To those who know thee not, no words can paint,
And those who know thee, know all words are faint.

—HAN. MOORE: *Sensibility.*

THE happy results of government depend chiefly upon the character of the people. And what nation, ancient or modern, can show such high character as that of the Ancient Hindus? Their generosity, simplicity, honesty, truthfulness, courage, refinement and chivalry are proverbial. In fact, the elements were so mixed in them that nature might stand up and say to all the world, "These were men."

The first and highest virtue in man is truthfulness. As Chaucer says:—

Truth is the highest thing that man may keep.

From the earliest times, the Hindus have always been praised by men of all countries and creeds for their truthfulness.

Strabo says: "They are so honest as neither to require locks to their doors nor writings to bind their agreements."[1]

Arrian (in the second century), the pupil of Epictetus, says that "no Indian was ever known to tell an untruth."[2] This, making a due allowance for exaggeration, is no mean praise.

Hioven-thsang, the most famous of the Chinese travellers, says: "The Indians are distinguished by the straightforwardness and honesty of their character. With regard to riches, they never take anything unjustly; with regard to justice, they make even excessive concessions . . . . . straightforwardness is the leading feature of their administration."[3]

[1] Strabo, Lib. xv p. 488 (ed. 1587).
[2] Indica, Cap. xii, 6. See also McCrindle in "Indian Antiquary," 1876, p. 92.
[3] Vol. II. p. 83.

Khang-thai, the Chinese ambassador to Siam, says that Su-We, a relative of Fauchen, King of Siam, who came to India about 231 A.D., on his return reported to the king that "the Indians are straightforward and honest."[1]

"In the fourth century, Friar Jordanus tells us that the people of India are true in speech and eminent in justice."[2]

Fei-tu, the ambassador of the Chinese Emperor Yangti to India in 605 A.D., among other things points out as peculiar to the Hindus that "they believe in solemn oaths."[3]

Idrisi, in his Geography (written in the 11th century), says: "The Indians are naturally inclined to justice, and never depart from it in their actions. Their good faith, honesty and fidelity to their engagements are well known, and they are so famous for these qualities that people flock to their country from every side."[4]

In the thirteenth century, Shams-ud-din Abu Abdullah quotes the following judgment of Bedi-ezr Zeman: "The Indians are innumerable, like grains of sand, free from deceit and violence. *They fear neither death nor life.*"[5]

Marco Polo (thirteenth century) says: "You must know that these Brahmins are the best merchants in the world and the most truthful, for they would not tell a lie for anything on earth."[6]

Kamal-ud-din Ibd-errazak Samarkandi (1413-1482), who went as ambassador of the Khakan to the prince of Calicut and to the King of Vidyanagar (1440-1445), bears testimony to "the perfect security which merchants enjoy in that country."[7]

[1]Max Muller's India: What can it teach us? p. 55.
[2]Marco Polo, ed. H. Yule, Vol. II, p. 354.
[3]Max Muller's India: What can it teach us? p. 275.
[4]Elliot's History of India, Vol. I, p. 88.
[5]India: What can it teach us? p. 275.
[6]Marco Polo, ed. H. Yule, Vol. II, p. 350.
[7]Notices des Manuscrits, Tom. xiv, p. 436.

Abul Fazal says: "The Hindus are admirers of truth and of unbounded fidelity in all their dealings."[1]

"Two hundred years ago you did not need to give written receipts for money or written promise for a trust placed in your hands. Your immense banking business three centuries ago was carried on by word of mouth. So much so that Phillimore and later writers speaking of the Indians said that they were a peculiarly truthful people. Truth was specifically an Indian virtue"[2]

Sir John Malcolm says: "Their truth is as remarkable as their courage."[3]

Colonel Sleeman, who had better and more numerous opportunities of knowing the Hindu character than most Europeans, assures us "that falsehood or lying between members of the same village is almost unknown." He adds: "I have had before me hundreds of cases in which a man's property, liberty and life has depended upon his telling a lie and he has refused to tell it."

What is the pivot on which the whole story of Ramayana, the book which even now exercises the greatest influence in the formation of Hindu character throughout India, turns? To remain true, though life may depart, and all that is near and dear in this world may perish. What is the lesson taught by the life of the greatest character unfolded to view by the Mahabharata, Bheeshma Pitamah? To remain true and stedfast, come what may.

Professor Max Muller says: "It was love of truth that struck all the people who came in contact with India, as the prominent feature in the national character of its inhabitants. No one ever accused them of falsehood. There must surely be some ground for this, for it is not a remark that is frequently made by travellers in foreign countries even in our time, that their inhabitants invariably speak the truth. Read the accounts of English travellers in France, and you will find very little said about French honesty and veracity."[4]

[1]Tod's Rajasthan, Vol. I, p. 643.

[2]Lecture on "Education as the Basis of National Life" at Adyar.

[3]Mill's History of India, Vol. I, p. 523.

[4]Max Muller's India: What can it teach us? p. 57.

But it is not for truthfulness alone that the Hindus have been famous. Their generosity, tolerance, frankness, intelligence, courtesy, loyalty, gentleness, sobriety, love of knowledge, industry, valour and a strong feeling of honour are even now remarkable.

"Megasthenes[1] observed with admiration the absence of slavery[2] in India, the chastity of the women, and the courage of the men. In valour they excelled all other Asiatics, sober and industrious, good farmers and skilful artizans, they scarcely ever had recourse to a lawsuit, and lived peaceably under their native chiefs."

That acute observer, the historian Abul Fazal, says: "The Hindus are religious, affable, courteous to strangers, cheerful, enamoured of knowledge, lovers of justice, able in business, grateful, admirers of truth, and of unbounded fidelity in all their dealings."[3] Colonel Dixon dilates upon "their fidelity, truthfulness, honesty, their determined valour, their simple loyalty, and an extreme and almost touching devotion when put upon their honour."[4]

"The Indians," says Neibuhr, "are really the most tolerant nation in the world." He also says that "they are gentle, virtuous, laborious, and that, perhaps of all men, they are the ones who seek to injure their fellow-beings the least."

The high character, the noble self-sacrifice, the unbounded love of a Hindu for those who are near and dear to him are well illustrated by the refusal of Yudhisthira to accept salvation,

[1]Hunter's Gazeteer, "India," p. 266.

[2]Mr. Elphinstone says: "It is remarkable that in the Hindu dramas there is not a trace of servility in the behaviour of other characters to the king."—History of India, p. 243.

[3]Tod's Rajasthan, Vol. I., p. 643.

[4]Colonel Dixon was Commissioner of Ajmer-Merwara from 1845 to 1857 A.D.

while his wife and brothers were outside Heaven. The Mahabharata says:—

"Lo, suddenly, with a sound that ran through heaven and earth, Indra came riding on his chariot and cried to the king 'Ascend.' Then indeed did Yudhisthira look back to his fallen brothers and spoke thus unto Indra with a sorrowful heart: 'Let my brothers, who yonder lie fallen go with me. Not even into thy heaven, O Indra, would I enter, if they are not to be there; and yon fairfaced daughter of a king, Draupadi, the all-deserving, let her too enter with us!'"

Sir Monier Williams says:[1] "Natives never willingly destroy life. 'Live and let live' is their rule of conduct towards the inferior creation."

"The villagers," says Mr. Elphinstone,[2] "are inoffensive, amiable people, affectionate to their family, kind to their neighbours."

In 1813 A.D., when evidence was given before the British Parliament,[3] Mr. Mercer said: "They (Hindus) are mild in their disposition, polished in their general manners; in their domestic relations, kind and affectionate."

Mr. Chaplin, Commissioner of the Deccan, declared to the committee of the Commons on East India Affairs in 1831: "They will bear an advantageous comparison with the natives of any country in the world."[4]

Captain Sydenham said: "The general character of the Hindus is submissive, docile, sober, inoffensive, capable of great attachment and loyalty, quick in apprehension, intelligent, active; generally honest and performing the duties of charity, benevolence and filial affection with as much sincerity and regularity as any nation with which I am acquainted."

[1] Modern India and the Indians, p. 33.
[2] Elphinstone's History of India, p. 199.
[3] Mill's History of India, Vol. I., p. 523.
[4] Tod's Western India, p. lvii.

Abbe Dubois says: "The Hindus are not in want of improvement in the discharge of social duties amongst themselves."

Sir John Malcolm said: "The Hindu inhabitants are a race of men, generally speaking, not more distinguished by their lofty stature and robust frame, than they are for some of the finest qualities of the mind—they are brave, generous, humane, and their truth is as remarkable as their courage." At a subsequent examination, he said, with respect to the feeling of honour: "I have known innumerable instances of its being carried to a pitch that would be considered in England more fit for the page of a romance than a history. With regard to their fidelity, I think, as far as my knowledge extends, there is, generally speaking, *no race of men more to be trusted.*"

Sir Thomas Munro when asked if he thought the civilization of the Hindus would be promoted by trade with England being thrown open, replied: "I do not exactly understand what is meant by the 'civilization' of the Hindus. In the knowledge of the theory and practice of good government, and in an education which, by banishing prejudice and superstition, opens the mind to receive instruction of every kind, they are inferior to Europeans. But if a good system of agriculture, unrivalled manufacturing skill, a capacity to produce whatever can contribute to either luxury or convenience, schools[1] established in every village for teaching, reading, writing and arithmetic, the general practice of hospitality and charity amongst each other, and, above all, a treatment of the female sex, full of confidence, respect and delicacy, are among the signs which denote a civilized people, then the Hindus are not inferior to the nations of Europe.

[1] "In Bengal there existed 80,000 native schools, though doubtless for the most part of a poor quality. According to a Government Report of 1835 there was a village school for every 400 persons."—Missionary Intelligencer, IX, pp. 183-193.

Of the ancient Universities of Nalanda, Takshashila, Sridhanya, Kataka and others, Mr. Havell says: "The whole range of education in these great Universities was schemed and co-ordinated with a breadth and largeness undreamt of in Modern India."[1] Professor Max Muller[2] says: "During the last twenty years, however, I have had some excellent opportunities of watching a number of native scholars under circumstances where it is not difficult to detect a man's true character, I mean in literary work, and, more particularly, in literary controversy. I have watched them carrying on such controversies both among themselves and with certain European scholars, and I feel bound to say that, *with hardly one exception they have displayed a far greater respect for truth, and a far more manly and generous spirit than we are accustomed to even in Europe and America*. They have shown strength, but no rudeness; nay, I know that nothing has surprised them as much as the coarse invective to which certain Sanskrit scholars have condescended, rudeness of speech being, according to their view of human nature, a safe sign not only of bad breeding but of want of knowledge. When they were wrong they have readily admitted their mistake; when they were right they have never sneered at their European adversaries. There has been, with few exceptions, no quibbling, no special pleading, no untruthfulness on their part, and certainly none of that low cunning of the scholar who writes down and publishes what he knows perfectly well to be false, and snaps his fingers at those who still value truth and self-respect more highly than victory or applause at any price.

Sir Thomas Munro estimated the children educated at public schools in the Madras Presidency as less than one in three."—Elphinstone's History of India, p. 205.

[1]Havell's Indian Sculpture and Painting, p. 106.

[2]India: What can it teach us? p. 63.

Let me add that I have been repeatedly told by English merchants that commercial honour stands higher in India than in any other country, and that a dishonoured bill is hardly known there."

The first Governor-General of India, Warren Hastings, said: "The Hindus are gentle, benevolent, more susceptible of gratitude for kindness shown to them, than prompted to vengeance for wrongs inflicted, and as exempt from the worst propensities of human passion as any people upon the face of the earth. They are faithful, affectionate," etc. (Minutes of evidence before the Committee of both Houses of Parliament, March and April 1813).

Bishop Heber says: "To say that the Hindus are deficient in any essential feature of a civilized people is an assertion which I can scarcely suppose to be made by any who have lived with them."[1] Again, "they are decidedly by nature a mild, pleasing, intelligent race, sober and parsimonious, and, where an object is held out to them, most industrious and persevering[2] . . . They are men of high and gallant courage, courteous, intelligent, and most eager for knowledge and improvement, with a remarkable aptitude for the abstract sciences, geometry, astronomy, etc., and for imitative arts, painting and sculpture; dutiful towards their parents, affectionate to children, more easily affected by kindness and attention to their wants and feelings than almost any men I have met with."[3] Again, "I have found in India a race of gentle and temperate habits, with a natural talent and acuteness beyond the ordinary level of mankind."

Of the labourers and workmen in the Calcutta mint in India, Professor Wilson says: "There was considerable skill and ready

[1]Journal, II, p. 382. [2]Ibid, p. 329. [3]Ibid, p. 369.

docility. So far from there being any servility there was extreme frankness, and I should say that where there is confidence without fear, frankness is one of the most universal features in the Indian character. In men of learning I found similar merits of industry, intelligence, cheerfulness, frankness. A very common characteristic of Hindus especially was simplicity, truly childish, and a total unacquaintance with business and manners of life. Generally speaking, boys are much more quick in apprehension and earnest in application than those of our own schools. Men of property and respectability afforded me many opportunities of witnessing polished manners, clearness and comprehensiveness of understanding, liberality of feeling, and independence of principle that would have stamped them *gentlemen* in any country in the world. The capacity of lads of 12 and 13 is often surprising."[1]

Sir Thomas Munro, Mercer and others quoted above, says Professor Wilson, were "men, equally eminent in wisdom as in station, remarkable for the extent of their opportunities of observation and the ability and diligence with which they used them, distinguished for possessing, by their knowledge of the language and the literature of the country, and by their habits of intimacy with the natives, the best, the only means of judging of the native character, and unequalled for the soundness of their judgment and comprehensiveness of their views."[2]

Professor Monier Williams[3] says: "I have found no people in Europe more religious, none more patiently persevering in common duties."

Mr. Elphinstone says: "If we compare them (Hindus) with our own (English people) the absence of drunkeness and of

[1] Mill's History of India, Vol. I, pp. 530-532.

[2] Mill's History of India, Vol. I, p. 523.

[3] Modern India and the Indians, pp. 88 and 128.

immodesty in their other vices, will leave the superiority in purity of manners on the side least flattering to our self-esteem."[1] He adds, "No set of people among the Hindus are so depraved as the dregs of our own great towns."[2]

"The cleanliness of the Hindus," he says again, "is proverbial.[3] They are a cleanly people, and may be compared with decided advantage with the nations of the south of Europe, both as regards their habitations and their persons. There are many of their practices which might be introduced even into the North with benefit."

Mr. Elphinstone says: "The natives are often accused of wanting in gratitude. But it does not appear that those who make the charge have done much to inspire such a sentiment: when masters are really kind and considerate they find as warm a return from Indian servants as any in the world; and there are few who have tried them in sickness or in difficulties and dangers who do not bear witness to their sympathy and attachment. Their devotion to their own chief is proverbial and can arise from no other cause than gratitude, unless where caste supplies the place of clannish feelings. The fidelity of our sepoys to their

[1] History of India, p. 202.

[2] Elphinstone's History of India, pp. 375-381. The percentage of criminals in India is lower than in England. "By a series of reports laid before the House of Commons in 1832 (Minutes of Evidence No. 4., page 103) it appears that in an average of four years the number of capital sentences carried into effect annually in England and Wales is as 1 for 203,281 souls, and in the provinces under the Bengal Presidency 1 for 1,004,182; transportation for life, in England 1 for 67,173 and in Bengal, 1 for 402,010. The annual number of sentences to death in England was 1,232, in Bengal 59. The population of England is 13,000,000; the population of Bengal, 60,000,000." The great Darwin was struck with the Hindu convicts at Port Louis and he wondered that they were such noble-looking figures. He says: "These men are generally quiet and well-conducted; from their outward conduct, their cleanliness, and faithful observance of their strange religious rites, it is impossible to look at them with the same eyes as on our wretched convicts in New South Wales"—A Naturalist's Voyage Round the World, p. 484.

[3] Elphinstone's History of India, p. 202.

foreign masters has been shown in instances which it would be difficult *to match even among the national troops in any other country*." He again says: "It is common to see persons who have been patronised by men in power not only continuing their attachment to them when in disgrace, but even to their families when they have left them in a helpless condition."[1]

To the diet[2] and the sobriety of living is due the greater

[1] "A perfectly authentic instance might be mentioned of a gentleman in a high station in Bengal who was dismissed and afterwards reduced to great temporary difficulties in his own country: a native of rank, to whom he had been kind, supplied him, when in those circumstances, with upwards of Rs. 1,00,000, of which he would not accept repayment and for which he could expect no possible return. This generous friend was a Mahratta Brahman, a race of all others who have least sympathy with other castes, and who are most hardened and corrupted by power."—Elphinstone's Hist. of India, p. 201.

[2] Mr. J. H. Bourdillon, in his report on the Census of 1881, observes that the superior healthiness of middle-age among the Hindus is more strikingly shown, for out of each 100 living persons the number of those aged 40 years and over is among the—

Hindus	21·97
Christians	14·31
Muhammadans	19·81
Aboriginals	15·86

As regards the diet of the Hindus, Mr. Buckle tells us: "In India the great heat of the climate brings into play that law (of nature) already pointed out, by virtue of which the ordinary food is of an oxygenous rather than of a carbonaceous character. This, according to another law, obliges the people to derive their usual diet not from the animal but from the vegetable world, of which starch is the most important constituent. At the same time, the high temperature, incapacitating men for arduous labour, makes necessary a food of which the returns will be abundant, and which will contain much nutriment in a comparatively small space. Here, then, we have some characteristics which, if the preceding views are correct, ought to be found in the ordinary food of the Indian nations. So they all are. From the earliest period the most general food in India has been rice, which is the most nutritive of all cerealia, which contains an enormous proportion of starch, and which yields to the labourer an average return of at least sixty fold."—History of Civilization in England, Volume I, page 64.

Neibuhr says: "Perhaps the Indian lawgivers thought it was for the sake of health absolutely necessary to prohibit the eating of meat, because the multitude follows more easily the prejudice of religion than the advice of a physician. It is also very likely that the law of the Oriental insists so strongly on the purification of the body for hygienic reasons."

healthiness of the Hindus. There are three insanes in every 10,000 persons in parts of India peopled by the Hindus, as compared to 30 insanes in every 10,000 in England and Wales.[1]

Mr. Ward says: "In their forms of address and behaviour in company the Hindus must be ranked amongst the politest nations."

Speaking of the inhabitants of the Gangetic Hindustan, Mr. Elphinstone says: "It is there we are most likely to gain a clear conception of their high spirit and generous self-devotion so singularly combined with gentleness of manners and softness of heart, together with an almost infantine simplicity."

Even honest writers, who have had no opportunities of studying the Hindu character, sometimes hastily generalize from stray instances of untruthfulness and dishonesty they happen to come across in life. In respect of such, Professor Max Muller says: "We may, to follow an Indian proverb, judge of a whole field of rice by tasting one or two grains only, but if we apply this rule to human beings we are sure to fall into the same mistake as the English chaplain who had once on board an English vessel christened a French child, and who remained fully convinced for the rest of his life that all French babies had very long noses."

The physical structure of the Hindu is still as admirable as that of any other people on the globe.

Mr. Orme says: "There is not a handsomer race in the universe than the Banians of Gujrat."[2] We read in Chamber's Encyclopædia that "the body of the Hindu is admirably proportioned."[3]

A strong opponent of the Hindus admires their physical agility. Mr. Mill says: "The body of the Hindu is agile to an extraordinary degree. Not only in those surprising contortions and feats which constitute the art of the tumbler do they excel almost all the nations in the world, but even in running and marching they equal, if not surpass, people of the most robust constitutions."[4]

[1] See the comparative tabular statement on page 204 of the report on the Census of Bengal, Vol. I (1881).

[2] On the effeminacy of the inhabitants of Hindustan, pp. 461-465.

[3] Chamber's Encyclopædia, p. 539.

[4] Mill's India, Vol. I, p. 478.

The Hindus were renowned for wisdom in ancient times.

"Wisdom, my father, is the noblest gift
The gods bestow on man, and better far
Than all his treasures."

SOPHOCLES: *Antigone.*

"We are told by Grecian writers that the Indians were the wisest of nations."[1]

Mr. Coleman[2] says: "The sages and poets of India have inculcated moral precepts and displayed poetic beauties which no country in the world of either ancient or modern date need be ashamed to acknowledge."

The didactic poetry of the Hindus furnishes sufficient proof of their transcendent wisdom. Mr. Elphinstone[3] says: that "the Greeks had a great impression of their (Hindus) wisdom."

Mr. Burnouf says that the "Indians are a nation rich in spiritual gifts, and endowed with peculiar sagacity and penetration."

It is the wisdom of the Hindus that invented the best and the greatest of indoor games, the game of Chess, which is now universally acknowledged to be of Hindu origin, the Sanskrit *chāturanga* becoming *shaturanga* in Persian.

Sir W. Jones says:[4] "The Hindus are said to have boasted of three inventions, all of which indeed are admirable; the method of instructing by apologues, the decimal scale and the game of Chess, on which they have some curious treatises."

Professor Heeren[5] says: "Chess-board is mentioned in Ramayana, where an account of Ayodhia is given."

[1] See Introduction.

[2] Mythology of the Hindus, p. 7.

[3] History of India, p. 242.

[4] As quoted by Mill in his History of British India, Vol., II, p. 43.

[5] Historical Researches, Vol. II. p. 151,

Chess is thus proved to have been in use in India long before Moses and Hermes made their appearance in the world. Mr. J. Mill, however, with his characteristic prejudice against the Hindus, observes that "there is no evidence that Hindus invented the game, except their own pretentions." On this, Professor Wilson says: "This is not true; we have not the evidence of their pretentions. The evidence is that of Muhammadan writers; the king of India is said, by Firdausi in the *Shahnama*—and the story is therefore of the tenth century at latest—*to have sent a Chess-board and a teacher to Nausherawan.* Sir W. Jones refers to Firdausi as his authority, and this reference might have shown by whom the story was told. Various Muhammadan writers are quoted by Hyde, in his Historia Shahiludii, who all concur in attributing the invention to the Indians."[1]

Prof. Macdonell says: "Contemporaneously with the fable literature, the most intellectual game the world has known began its westward migration from India. Chess in Sanskrit is called "*Chater Anga* ...... The earliest direct mention of the game in Sanskrit literature is found in the works of Bana and the *kavyalamkana* of Rudradatta ...... Introduced into Persia in the sixth century Chess was brought by the Arabs into Europe, where it was generally known by 1000 A.D ...... Besides the fable literature of India, this Indian game served to while away the tedious life of myriads during the Middle Ages."[2]

Mr. Murray in his "History of Chess," after giving reasons for accepting the fact that Chess was originally a Hindu invention, says: "We must accordingly conclude that our European Chess is a direct descendant of an Indian game played in the 7th century with substantially the same arrangement and method as in Europe five centuries later, the game having been adopted

[1] Mill's India, Vol. II., p. 44, footnote.

[2] Macdonell's Sanskrit Literature, p. 121.

first by the Persians, then handed on by the Persians to the Moslem world and finally borrowed from Islam by Christian Europe."[1]

Mr. Murray adds: "Games of a similar nature exist to-day in other parts of Asia than India . . . . . . but there can be no doubt that all these games are equally descended from the same original Indian game."[2]

"The wisdom of Solomon" is proverbial. But the story most frequently quoted to show his wisdom, itself stamps that wisdom as inferior to that of the Hindus. Says, Professor Max Muller: "Now you remember the judgment of Solomon, which has always been admired as a proof of great legal wisdom among the Jews! I must confess that, not having a legal mind, I never could suppress a certain shudder when reading the decision of Solomon: 'Divide the living child in two, and give half to the one, and half to the other.'"[3] "Let me now tell you the same story as it is told by the Buddhists, whose sacred Canon is full of such legends and parables. In the Kanjur, which is the Tibetan translation of the Buddhist Tripitaka, we read of two women who claimed each to be the mother of the same child. The king, after listening to their quarrels for a long time, gave it up as hopeless to settle who was the real mother. Upon this, Visakha stepped forward and said: 'What is the use of examining and cross-examining these women? Let them take the boy and settle it among themselves.' Thereupon, both women fell on the child, and when the fight became violent, the child was hurt and began to cry. Then one of them let him go, because she could not bear to hear the child cry. That settled the question. The king gave the child to the true mother, and had the other beaten with a rod."

[1] History of Chess: Introductory, Chapter I, p. 27 (Ed. 1913).
[2] History of Chess: Introductory, Chapter I, p. 27.
[3] Kings iii. 25.

"This seems to me, if not the more primitive, yet the more natural form of the story, showing a deeper knowledge of human nature and more wisdom than even the wisdom of Solomon"[1]

Mr. Elphinstone speaks of the Hindu character in misfortune in glowing terms. "When fate," he says, "is inevitable, the lowest Hindu encounters it with a coolness that would excite admiration in Europe."[2]

The national character of a people necessarily suffers from unsympathetic domination of a less civilized people. Successful falsehood, says Bentham, is the best defence of a slave; and it is no wonder that the character of the Hindus deteriorated under the Moslem rule. The wonder is their character is still so high. Professor Max Muller says: "I can only say that after reading the accounts of the terrors and horrors of Muhammadan rule, my wonder is that so much of native virtue and truthfulness should have survived."[3] He also says:

"When you read of the atrocities committed by the Muhammadan conquerors of India after that time (1000 A.D.) to the time when England stepped in and, whatever may be said by her envious critics, made, at all events, the broad principles of our common humanity respected once more in India, the wonder, to my mind, is how any nation could have survived such an *Inferno*, without being turned into devils themselves."[4]

When, however, centuries of foreign (Moghul) domination have left the people as virtuous, truthful and refined as any

[1] India: What can it teach us? p. 11.

[2] Elphinstone's History of India, pages 198 and 199. Of the great grandfather of the present Maharaja of Jodhpur, Colonel Tod says: "The biography of Man Singh would afford a remarkable picture of human patience, fortitude and constancy never surpassed in any age or country."—Rajasthan, Vol. II, p. 711.

[3] Max Muller's India: What can it teach us! p. 72.

[4] Max Muller's India: What can it teach us? p. 54.

It must not be supposed from the condemnatory language used in more

free people to be found anywhere in the world, what further, evidence is necessary to prove the high character of the ancient Hindus, whose lives were regulated by ethical principles of the highest order!

than one place in this book with regard to the treatment of the Hindus and their literature by some of the Mussalman invaders and rulers of India, that the history of those reigns is one continuous record of cruelty and oppression, unredeemed by any humanitarian considerations or sympathetic treatment. As Sir Arthur Helps observes, no dark cloud is without its silver lining. There are instances on record which show a chivalrous and generous regard displayed by some of the Muhammadan kings for the Hindus. It is related that when, during the reign of Rana Bikramajit, son of Rana Sanga of Chitor, who was at the time in Haravati, Mewar was invaded by Bahadur, King of Gujrat, and Chitor was invested by the combined armies of Gujrat and Malwa, Maharani Karnavati, the mother of the infant son of Rana Sanga, who was in the fortress, appealed for help to Humayun, whom she had adopted as her *Rakhiband bhai* (bracelet-bound brother). Humayun, like a true cavalier, accepted the obligation laid on him by the laws of chivalry and honour, to come to her aid, and abandoning his conquests in Bengal, hastened to answer the call of her adoptive sister, the Dowager Maharani of Chitor. "He amply fulfilled the pledge, expelled the foe from Chitor, took Mandoo by assault and, as some revenge for her king's aiding the King of Gujrat, he sent for the Rana Bikramajit, whom following their own notions of investiture, he girt with a sword in the captured citadel of his foe."

Nor should it be forgotten that it was a Mussalman who preserved the King of Marwar at the most critical period of his life. Not satisfied with the blood of Jaswant and of his eldest son, Pirthi Singh, the unrelenting tyrant (Aurangzeb) carrying his vengeance towards the Maharaja of Marwar even beyond the grave, commanded that his infant son, Ajit, should be surrendered to his custody. "Aurang offered to divide Maroo (Marwar) amongst her nobles if they would surrender their prince, but they replied, "our country is with our sinews, and these can defend both it and our lord." With eyes red with rage they left the *Am-e-khas.* Their abode was surrounded by the host of the Shah." A fearful battle ensued. The first care of the Rajputs was to save the infant prince, and to avoid suspicion, the heir of Marwar, concealed, in a basket of sweetmeats, was entrusted to a Moslem, who rigorously executed his trust and conveyed him to the appointed spot, where he was joined by the gallant Durga Das and his Rajputs, who had cut their way through all opposition to Marwar.

CHIVALRY.

Let laurels, drench'd in pure Parnassian dews,
Reward the memory, dear to every muse,
Who with a courage of unshaken root,
In honour's field advancing his firm foot,
Plants it upon the line that justice draws,
And will prevail or perish in the cause.

—*Cowper.*

The innate chivalry of Hindu character is well known to those who have studied their history, or lived with them and studied their manners and customs. Their treatment of the female sex, their unwillingness to injure or take away life unnecessarily, their magnanimous treatment of their fallen foes, their unwillingness to take advantage of their own superiority to their adversaries, prove the chivalrous character of the Hindu race. The undaunted heroism and the unequalled valour of the Ancient Hindus, their magnificent self-confidence, their righteousness of conduct, and, above all, the sublime teachings of their Shastras, containing the loftiest spiritual ideals yet conceived by humanity, made them the most chivalrous and humane people on the face of the earth. So much is the warrior caste of the Hindus even now identified with chivalry that *Rajputi* and *Chivalry* have become convertible terms.[1] Rajputana is eminently the land of chivalry, and the Rajputs, the descendents of the ancient Kshatriyas, have preserved some of the latter's virtues, prominent among which is chivalry. Rama, Arjuna, Karna, Krishna, Bhima, Bali, Baldeo (Hercules), Sagara, and others were ideal characters; but coming down to modern times we find that Rana Pratap of Mewar, Durga Das of Marwar and Prithvi Raj of Ajmer were characters for whose equals in chivalry and patriotism we may search in vain the annals of other nations, European or Asiatic.

The annals of no nation record instances that outshine the romantic chivalry displayed by Sadoo, heir of the lord of Pugal, till

[1] Tod's Rajasthan, Vol. II, p. 601.

lately a fief of Jaisalmer, or the chivalrous conduct of his bride, Kurramdevi, daughter of the Mohil chief Manik Rao, who "was at once a virgin, a wife and a widow."[1]

Colonel Tod says: "Nor is there anything finer in the annals of the chivalry of the West than the dignified and the heroic conduct of the Raja of Duttea," who met with a glorious death in defence of the laws of sanctuary and honour, when on the death of Madhaji Scindhia, the females of his (Scindhia's) family, in apprehension of his successor, Daulat Rao, sought refuge and protection with the Raja.[2]

The author of the Annals and Antiquities of Rajasthan pays the highest tribute to the valour and chivalry of the Rajputs when he says: "Cœur de lion (King of England) would not have remained so long in the dungeons of Austria had his subjects been Rajputs."[3]

Professor H. H. Wilson says: "The Hindu laws of war are very chivalrous and humane, and prohibit the slaying of the unarmed, of women, of the old and of the conquered."

The innate chivalry of the Hindu character has given rise to a peculiar custom observed among all classes of people, irrespective of caste, nationality or age. It is the *Rakhi* (Rakshabandhan), by which Hindu ladies command loyal, disinterested, and whole-souled service of men, whom they deign to adopt as their brothers, though in most instances they never behold them. "There is a delicacy in this custom," says Colonel Tod, "with which the bond uniting the cavaliers of Europe to the service of the fair in the days of chivalry will not compare."[4]

[1] Tod's Rajasthan, Vol. II, p. 629.

[2] Tod's Rajasthan, Vol. I, p. 117.

[3] Tod's Rajasthan, Vol. I, p. 161.

[4] Tod's Rajasthan, Vol. I, p. 581. "It is one of the few (customs) when an intercourse of gallantry of the most delicate nature is established between the

The following incident will show the character of the Rajputs and the nature of their warfare. During the reign of Rana Rai Mal of Chitor, his first cousin, Suraj Mal, whom the prophetess of Charuni Devi at Nahra Mugra had promised a crown, made several attempts to gain one. With the help of Nasir-uddin Khilji, the sultan of Malwa, he took Sadri and Batarda and attempted even Chitor. Rai Mal met the attack on the river Gumbeeree. The second son of the Rana, Kanwar Pirthi Raj, "the Rolando of his age" as Colonel Tod calls him, selected his uncle, Suraj Mal, whom he soon covered with wounds. Many had fallen on both sides but neither party would yield: when worn out they retired from the field, bivouacked in sight of each other. Colonel Tod continues: It will show the manners and feelings so peculiar to the Rajput, to describe the meeting between the rival uncle and nephew—unique in the details of strife perhaps since the origin of man.'[1] It is taken from a manuscript of the Jhala Chief who succeeded Suraj Mal in Sadri. Pirthi Raj visited his uncle, whom he found in a small tent reclining on a pallet, having just had 'the barber' (*nae*) to sew up his wounds. He rose and met his nephew with the customary respect, as if nothing unusual had occurred; but the exertion caused some of the wounds to open afresh, when the following dialogue ensued:—

"PIRTHI RAJ—'Well, uncle, how are your wounds?'

"SURAJ MAL—'Quite healed, my child, since I have the pleasure of seeing you.'

"PIRTHI RAJ.—But, uncle (*kaka*), I have not yet seen the

fair sex and the cavaliers of Rajasthan......The Rajput dame bestows with the Rakhi (bracelet) the title of adopted brother; and while its acceptance secures to her all the protection of a *cavaliere servente*, scandal itself never suggests any other tie to his devotion."—p. 312.

[1] Tod's Rajasthan, Vol. I, pp. 296, 297.

The renowned Fort of Chitor.

Dewanji.[1] I first ran to see you, and I am very hungry; have you anything to eat?'

"Dinner was soon served, and the extraordinary pair sat down, and 'ate off the same platter;' nor did Pirthi Raj hesitate to eat the *pan* presented on his taking leave.

PRITHI RAJ.—'You and I will end our battle in the morning, uncle.'

"SURAJ MAL—'Very well, child; come early.

"They met, and the rebels were defeated and fled to Sadri. Pirthi Raj, however, gave them no rest, pursuing them from place to place. In the wilds of Baturro they formed a stockaded retreat of the *dho* tree, which abounds in the forest; and Sujah and his companion Sarungdeo, were communing on their desperate plight when their cogitations were checked by the rush and neigh of horses. Scarcely had the pretender exclaimed, 'this must be my nephew!' when Pirthi Raj dashed his steed through the barricade and, reaching his uncle, dealt him a blow which would have levelled him but for the support of Sarungdeo, who upbraided him, adding, 'a buffet now was more than a score of wounds in former days:' to which Suraj Mal added, 'only when dealt by my nephew's hand.' Suraj Mal demanded a parley; and calling on the prince to stop the combat, he continued: 'If I am killed, it matters not—my children are Rajputs, they will run the country to find support; but if you are slain what will become of Chitor? My face will be blackened and my name everlastingly reprobated.'

"The sword was sheathed, and as the uncle and nephew embraced, the latter asked the former, 'what were you about uncle, when I came? 'Only talking nonsense, child, after dinner.' 'But with me over your head, uncle, as a foe, how could you be so

[1] The Rana is called Divanji as he is the minister of the temple of Eklingji Mahadeva.

negligent?' 'What could I do? You had left me no resource, and I must have some place to rest my head.'"[1]

An episode from the annals of Jaisalmer will illustrate the chivalrous nature of the Rajput and his desire to die fighting, as becomes a Rajput.

After a long course of victorious warfare, in which he subdued various tracts of country, even to the heart of the Panjab, disease seized on Rawul Chachick. In this state he determined to die as he had lived, with arms in his hand; but having no foe near with whom to cope he sent an embassy to the Langa prince of Multan, to beg as a last favour the *jood-dān*, or "gift of battle," that his soul may escape by the steel of his foeman, and not fall a sacrifice to slow disease. The prince, suspecting treachery, hesitated; but the Bhati messenger pledged his word that his master only wished an honourable death, and that he would bring only five hundred men to the combat. The challenge being accepted, the Rawul called his clansmen around him, and on recounting what he had done, seven hundred select Rajputs, who had shared in all his victories, volunteered to take the last field and make (*sankalp*) oblation of their lives with their leader.[2]

On reaching Dhooniapur, he heard that the prince of Multan was within two coss. His soul was rejoiced. He performed his ablutions, worshipped the gods, bestowed charity, and withdrew his thoughts from the world.

The battle lasted two hours, and the Yadu prince fell with all his kith and kin, after performing prodigies of valour. Two thousand Khans[3] fell beneath their swords and the Bhati gained the abode of Indra.

[1] Tod's Rajasthan, Vol. I. p. 298.

[2] Tod's Rajasthan, Vol. II, pp. 258, 259.

[3] These were Hindus [Solanki Rajputs] as was their prince The Rawul Chachick had married Sonaldevi, the grand-daughter of Hybat Khan, the Chief of the Sota tribe. or the Swatees. See Tod's Rajasthan, Vol. II, p. 233.

The chivalry of the Chief of Nimaj (a fief of Marwar in Rajputana), in the reign of Raja Maun Singh, excites the admiration of Colonel Tod, to which he gives expression in the following memorable words: "The brave Chief of Nimaj has sold his life but dearly. *In vain do we look in the annals of Europe for such devotion and generous despair as marked his end and that of his brave clan.*"[1]

"Have we anything in European chivalry," exclaims Mr. Edward Thomas, author of the *Chronical of Pathan Kings of Delhi,*" to compare with the act of the Suktawat chief, who is related to have voluntarily submitted himself for impalement on the spikes of the gate of a beleagured town, to enable his own elephant to force an entry?"[2]

Of Rana Raj Singh, the great opponent of Aurangzeb, Colonel Tod says: "As a skilful general and gallant soldier, in the defence of his country, he is above all praise. As a chivalrous Rajput, his braving all consequences when called upon to save the honour of a noble female of his race, he is without parallel."[3]

"The son of Rana Pertap, Umra, the foe of Jehangir," says Colonel Tod, "was a character of whom the proudest nation might be vain."[4]

[1] Tod's Rajasthan, Vol. I, p. 197. Mercenary bands, to the number of 8,000, with guns, attacked Surtan Singh in his haveli [dwelling] at Jodhpur, under the orders of Raja Maun Singh. With 180 of his clan he defended himself against great guns and small arms as long as the house was tenable, and than sallied forth, sword in hand, and with his brother and 80 of his kin fell nobly in the midst of his foes.

[2] Colonel Tod describes this event in detail. After the loss of Chitor during the reign of Jahangir, the Rana was in his mountain fastnesses when an opportunity offered itself of conquering the fortress of Ontala, 80 miles from Udaipur, which had only one gate to give admission to the castle. The rival clans Suktawats and Chondawats claimed the honour of leading the vanguard (herole) when the Rana said, "Herole to the clan which first entered Outala."—Annals and Antiquities of Rajasthan, Vol. I, p. 150.

[3] Annals and Antiquities of Rajasthan, Vol. I, p. 389.

[4] Tod's Rajasthan, Vol. I, p. 133.

Even of the Indians of the present day, Mr. Elphinstone says:[1] "They often display bravery unsurpassed by the most warlike nations, and will always throw away their lives for any consideration of religion or honour."

Mr. Bailie Fraser, author of the military memoirs of Lt.-Col. James Skinner says: "But if we seek for a picture of chivalrous gallantry, unswerving fidelity, and fearless self-devotion, we have only to turn to the chivalry of the Rajput States; and particlularly to that of the Rathors. We shall there find acts of resolute heroism that have not been surpassed by the troops of any age or country."[2]

The chivalrous character of the Hindu has handicapped him in his fight against his unscrupulous foes. To the advantage derived by the opponents of the Hindus from the latter's mutual jealousies and disunion was added also that of their (Hindu) unwillingness to do anything against the dictates of humanity or the demands of chivalry. Unlike other nations they do not believe in the maxim, "everything is fair in love and war." "To spare a prostrate foe," says Colonel Tod, "is the creed of the Hindu cavalier, and he carried all such maxims to excess."[3]

If the chivalrous nature of the latter-day Hindu had only been tempered with political discretion, India would not have suffered as she has done. The cruel Hun invader in the sixth century, Mihirgula, who practiced great oppression in the Panjab, when defeated and taken prisoner about 528 A.D. was spared and sent home in the North with all honour by Baladitya, King of Magadha, only to treacherously murder the King of Kashmir, and seize the kingdom.[4]

[1] Elphinstone's History of India, p. 199.

[2] Military Memoirs of Colonel J. Skinner, Vol. I., pp. 89, 90.

[3] Tod's Rajasthan, Vol. I, p. 287.

[4] Early History of India, by V. Smith, p. 276.

Maharana Sanga.

Sultan Shah-bud-din Ghori, when captured by Prithi Raj on the field of Tilaori, was liberated and allowed to return to his country, only to come back with a fresh army, and with the assistance of the traitors of Kanauj and Patan and of the Haoli Rao Hamir, to overturn the Hindu throne.

Again, when Mahmud, the Ghilzi King of Malwa, was defeated and taken prisoner by Maharana Sanga of Chitor in 1520 A.D., not only was he set at liberty without ransom, but was loaded with gifts and sent back to Malwa and reinstated on his throne, with the result that soon after Sanga's death this ungrateful man, to quote Ferishta, "without any provocation, deputed Shirza Khan with a force from Mandu to attack Rana Ratan Singh," son of Rana Sanga.[1]

When during the invasion of Mewar by the Imperial forces of the Emperor Aurangzeb—when all the resources of the mighty Moghul Empire were placed at the disposal of the Mussalman generals, and the Emperor himself repaired to the scene of action to direct the operations in person—the heir-apparent of Delhi and his army, cut off from all asssistance, were at the absolute mercy of the heir of Mewar, the magnanimous Rajputs, in pursuance of mistaken notions of chivalry and humanity not only spared the whole army, but gave them guides to conduct them by the defile of Dilwara and escorted them to Chitor. Nay, we learn from the historian Orme, that Aurangzeb himself owed his life to the clemency of the Rajputs. He says: "The division which moved with Aurangzeb himself was unexpectedly stopped by insuperable defences and precipices in front; while the Rajputs in one night closed the streights in his rear, by felling the overhanging trees; and from their stations above prevented all endea-

[1] Rana Sanga dressed his wounds, attended him in person, and after his recovery sent him with an escort of 1,000 Rajputs, to Mandu and seated him on the throne.—Brigg's Ferishta, Vol. IV., pp. 263-266.

vours of the troops, either within or without, from removing the obstacle. Udeperri, the favourite and Circassian wife of Aurangzeb, accompanied him in this arduous war, and with her retinue and escort was enclosed in another part of the mountains; her conductors, dreading to expose her person to danger or public view, surrendered. She was carried to the Rana, who received her with homage and every attention. Meanwhile, the Emperor himself might have perished by famine, of which the Rana let him see the risk, by a confinement of two days, when he ordered his Rajputs to withdraw from their stations, and suffer the way to be cleared. As soon as Aurangzeb was out of danger the Rana sent back his wife, accompanied by a chosen escort, who only requested in return that he would refrain from destroying the sacred animals of their religion which might still be left in the plains; but Aurangzeb, who believed in no virtue but self-interest, imputed the generosity and forbearance of the Rana to the fear of future vengeance, and continued the war. Soon after he was again well-nigh enclosed in the mountains. This second experience of difficulties beyond his age and constitution, and the arrival of his sons, Azim and Akbar, determined him not to expose himself any longer in the field, but to leave its operations to their conduct, superintended by his own instructions from Ajmer, to which city he retired with the households of his family, the officers of his court, and his bodyguard of four thousand men, dividing the army between his two sons, who each had brought a considerable number of troops from their respective Governments."[1]

Well may Colonel Tod exclaim: "But for repeated instances of an ill-judged humanity, the throne of the Moghals might have been completely overturned."[2]

[1] Tod's Rajasthan, Vol. I., p. 383.

[2] Tod's Rajasthan, Vol. I., p. 379.

Twice owing to political indiscretion on the part of the Ranas of Mewar, in the reigns of Akbar and Jehangir, did the Hindus lose their chance of supremacy. Were it not for the ill-fated interview between Rana Pratap and Man Singh of Jaipur on the Udaisagar lake, on the latter's return home from the conquest of Sholapur, Akbar would never have succeeded in consolidating his power and founding the Moghal Empire[1] in India, which, after a brilliant career of two centuries, was finally shattered to pieces by the Mahrattas.

PATRIOTISM.

Breathes there the man, with soul so dead,
Who never to himself hath said,
This is my own, my native land!

—SCOTT: *Lay of the Last Minstrel.*

LOVE of one's own country is inborn in all civilized men. *Matri Bhumi*—Motherland—was the constant refrain of the Hindus' song. The intensity of the feeling may be gauged from the fact that when during his fall, political foresight became a waning substance in the mental horizon of the Hindu, he ruled that no one should go out of the sacred limits of this holy land, that life here and death here alone shall be the necessary conditions of gaining Heaven hereafter. It is of course universally known

[1] "To him Akbar was indebted for half his triumphs, from the snowclad Caucasus to the shores of the 'golden Chersonese.' Let the eye embrace those extremes of his conquests, Kabul and the Paropamisan of Alexander, and Arracan (now well-known) on the Indian Ocean; the former reunited, the latter subjugated to the empire by a Rajput prince and a Rajput army," p. 336. "Prince Selim (afterwards Jehangir) led the war against Rana Pratap, guided by the councils of Raja Man and the distinguished apostate son of Sagurji, Mohabat Khan."—Vol. I, p. 337.

Again, when during Jehangir's reign, Mewar conceived the idea of putting up Prince Khurram against the Emperor Jehangir. and, in the Civil War, to wrest the supremacy for the Hindus, Bheem's indiscreet taunt to Raja Gaj Singh of Marwar at the critical moment alienated the Rathores, and the design was frustrated.

that the creed of the Rajput or the warrior caste of India even now is, that dying sword in hand in the cause of the country is the surest and the nearest way to the "mansions of the sun"—the highest paradise. Colonel Tod says: "The name of 'country' carried with it a magical power in the mind of the Rajput. The name of his wife or his mistress must never be mentioned at all, nor that of his country but with respect, or his sword is instantly unsheathed."[1]

Patriotism! In vain you ransack the annals of Greece and rome, of Modern or Mediæval Europe to find such noble patriots as Rana Pratap and Thakur Durga Das. Patriotism, chivalry and honour found their ideal embodiment in these two heroes. Pratap fought single-handed, with a handful of his Rajputs, against the mighty hosts of Akbar, "the greatest monarch that ever sat on an Asiatic throne," aided by the arms and counsels of his own countrymen, the Kuchhwahas, Rathores, Haras, Deoras of Abu and others, whose kingdoms lay round Mewar. He fought for a quarter of a century and died, leaving a name, unrivalled in the history of patriotism and chivalry. Colonel Tod says: "Pratap succeeded to the title and renown of an ancient house, but without a capital, without resources, his kindred and clans disspirited by reverses; yet possessed by the noble spirit of his race, he meditated the recovery of Chitor, the vindication of the honour of his house and the restoration of its power. The wily Moghal (Akbar) arrayed against Pratap, his kindred in faith as well as blood. The princes of Marwar, Amber, Bikaner and even Boondi, late his firm ally, took part with Akbar and upheld despotism. Nay, even his own brother, Sagarji, deserted him. But the magnitude of the peril confirmed the fortitude of Pratap, who vowed in the words of the bard, 'to make his mother's milk resplendent;' and he amply redeemed his pledge. Single-handed

[1] Tod's Rajasthan, Volume II, p. 429.

Akbar the Great.

for a quarter of a century did he withstand the combined efforts of the empire, at one time carrying destruction into the plains, at another flying from rock to rock, feeding his family from the fruits of his native hills, and rearing the nursling hero, Amra, amidst savage beasts and scarce less savage men, a fit heir to his prowess and revenge. The bare idea that 'the son of Bappa Rawal should bow the head to mortal man' was insupportable, and he spurned every overture, which had submission for its basis, or the degradation of uniting his family by marriage with the Tartar, though lord of countless multitudes."

Colonel Tod adds[1]: "It is worthy the attention of those who influence the distinies of States in more favoured climes to estimate the intensity of feeling which could arm the prince to oppose the resources of a small principality against the then most powerful empire in the world, whose armies were more numerous and far more efficient than any ever led by the Persians against the liberties of Greece. Had Mewar possessed her Thucydides or her Zenophon, neither her war of the Peleponnesus, nor the Retreat of the Ten Thousand would have yielded more diversified incidents for the historic muse than the deeds of this brilliant reign amid the many vicissitudes of Mewar. Undaunted heroism, inflexible fortitude, that which 'keeps honour bright,' perseverance with *fidelity such as no nation can boast* were the materials opposed to a soaring ambition, commanding talents, unlimited means and the fervour of religious zeal; all, however, insufficient to contend with one unconquerable mind. There is not a pass in the Alpine Aravali that is not sanctified by some deed of Pratap—some brilliant victory or often more glorious defeat. *Huldighat is the*[2] *Thermopylæ of Mewar, the field of Deweir her Marathon.*"

[1] Tod's Rajasthan, Vol. I., p. 349.

[2] "What says the Thermopylæ of India, Corygaum? Fine hundred firelocks against 20 thousand men! Do the annals of Napoleon record a more brilliant exploit?"—Rajasthan, Vol. I., p. 80.

"The last moments of Pratap," says Colonel Tod, "were an appropriate commentary on his life, which he terminated, like the Carthaginian, swearing his successor to eternal conflict against the foes of his country's independence. But the Rajput prince had not the same joyful assurance that inspired the Numidian Hamilcar; for his end was clouded with the presentiment that his son, Amra, would abandon his fame for inglorious repose A powerful sympathy is excited by the picture which is drawn of this final scene. The dying hero is represented in a lowly dwelling; his chiefs, the faithful companions of many a glorious day, awaiting round his pallent the dissolution of their prince, when a groan of mental anguish made Saloombra inquire 'what afficted his soul that it would not depart in peace?' He rallied: 'it lingered' he said, 'for some consolatory pledge that his country should not be abandoned to the Toorks,' and with the death pang upon him, he related and incident which had guided his estimate of his son's disposition, and now tortured him with the reflection, that for personal ease he would *forego the remembrance of his own and his country's wrongs.*"

"On the banks of the Peshola, Pratap and his chiefs had constructed a few huts (the site of the future palace of Udaipur) to protect them during the inclemency of the rains in the day of their distress. Prince Amra, forgetting the lowliness of the dwelling, a projecting bamboo of the roof caught the folds of his turban and dragged it off as he retired. A hasty emotion, which disclosed a varied feeling, was observed with pain by Pratap, who thence adopted the opinion that his son would never withstand the hardships necessary to be endured in such a cause: 'These sheds' said the dying prince, 'will give way to sumptuous dwellings, thus generating the love of ease, and luxury with its concomitants will ensue, to which the independence of Mewar, which we have bled to maintain, will be sacrificed; and you, my chiefs, will follow the pernicious example.' They pledged themselves, and became guarantees for the prince, 'by the throne of Bappa Rawal,' that they would not permit mansions to be raised till Mewar had recovered her independence. The soul of Pratap was satisfied, and with joy he expired". [1]

As regard Durga Das and the Rathores, the noble historian of Rajputana says: "Let us take a retrospective glance of the transactions of the Rathores from the year 1737, the period of Raja Jaswunt's death at Cabul, to the restoration of Ajit, presenting a continuous conflict of 30 years' duration. In vain might we search the annals of any other nation for such inflexible devotion as marked the Rathore character through this period of strife, during which, to use their own phrase, 'hardly a Chieftain died on his pallet.' Let those who deem the Hindu warrior void of patriotism read the rude chronicle of this thirty years' war; let them compare it with that of any other country, and do justice to the magnanimous Rajput. This narrative, the simplicity of which is the best voucher for its authenticity, presents an uninterrupted record of patriotism and disinterested loyalty. It was a period when the sacrifice of these principles was rewarded by the tyrant king with the highest honours of the State; nor are we without instances of the temptation being too strong to be withstood: but they are rare, and serve only to exhibit in more pleasing colours the virtues of the tribe which spurned the attempts at seduction. What a splendid example is the heroic Durga Das of all that constitutes the glory of the Rajput! Valour loyalty, integrity, combined with prudence in all the difficulties which surrounded him, are qualities which entitle him to the admiration which his memory continues to enjoy. The temptations held out to him were almost irresistible; not merely the gold, which he and thousands of his brethren would alike have spurned,

[1] Tod's Rajasthan, Vol. I, pp. 348, 349.

but the splendid offer of power in the proffered 'munsub of five thousand,' which would at once have lifted him from his vassal condition to an equality with the princes and chief nobles of the land. Durga had, indeed, but to name his reward; but, as the bard justly says, he was '*Amolac*' beyond all price, '*Unoko*' unique. Not even revenge, so dear to the Rajput, turned him aside from the dictates of true honour. The foul assassination of his brother, the brave Soning, effected through his enemies, made no alteration in his humanity whenever the chance of war placed his foe in his power; and in this his policy seconded his virtue. His chivalrous conduct in the extrication of Prince Akbar from inevitable destruction had he fallen into his father's hands, was only surpassed by his generous and delicate behaviour towards the prince's family which was left in his care, forming a marked contrast to that of the enemies of his faith on similar occasions. The virtue of the grand-daughter of Aurangzeb, in the sanctuary of Droonara, was in far better keeping than in the trebly-walled harem of Agra. Of his energetic mind and the control he exerted over those of his confiding brethren what a proof is given, in his preserving the secret of the abode of his prince throughout the first six years of his infancy! But, to conclude our eulogy in the words of their bard: he has reaped the immortality destined for good deeds; his memory is cherished, his actions are the theme of constant praise, and his picture on his white horse, old, yet in vigour, is familiar amongst the collections of the portraits of Rajputana." [1]

"In the history of mankind," adds Colonel Tod, "there is nothing to be found presenting a more brilliant picture of fidelity than that afforded by the Rathore clans in their devotion to their prince from his birth until he worked out his own and his country's deliverance." [2]

[1] Tod's Rajasthan, Vol. II, pp. 81, 82.
[2] Tod's Rajasthan, Vol. II. p. 94.

DURGA DAS, THE GREAT RATHOR LEADER.

Colonel Tod says, "Many anecdotes are extant recording the dread, Aurangzeb had of this leader of the Rathores, one of which is amusing. The tyrant had commanded pictures to be drawn of two of the most mortal foes to his repose, Sevaji and Durga: Sevaji was drawn seated on a couch; Durga in his ordinary position, on horseback, toasting *bhawties* or barley-cakes with the point of his lance, on a fire of maize-stalks. Aurangzeb at the first glance, exclaimed, 'I may entrap that fellow (meaning Sevaji), but this dog is born to be my bane." [1]

Patriotism, honour of his race, anxiety to maintain the good name of his country are inherent traits in the character of a true Hindu. A simple incident of no great political importance shows the living faith of the Rajput in his country and his race, for whose honour he is prepared at all times and in all circumstances to lay down his life unhesitatingly.

Humiliated by a night attack on his forces by a handful of men under Hamo, the Chief of Bundi, when his army was put to flight, in the course of a campaign against Haraoti, the Mahrana of Chitor re-formed his troops under the walls of his celebrated fortress, and swore that he would not eat anything until he was master of Bundi.

The rash vow went round; but Bundi was sixty miles distant, and defended by brave hearts. His chiefs expostulated with the Rana on the absolute impossibility of redeeming his vow; but the words of kings are sacred: Boondi must fall ere the King of the Gehlotes could dine. In this exigence a childish expedient was proposed to release him from hunger and his oath; 'to erect a mock Boondi, and take it by storm.' Instantly the mimic town arose under the walls of Chitor; and, that the deception might be complete, the local nomenclature was attended to, and each quarter had its appropriate appellation. A band of

[1] Tod's Rajasthan, Vol. II, p. 66.

Haras of the Pathar were in the service of Chitor, whose leader, Koombo Pairsi, was returning with his kin from hunting the deer, when their attention was attracted by this strange bustle. The story was soon told, that Boondi must fall ere the Rana could dine. Koombo assembled his brethren of the Pathar, declaring that even the mock Boondi must be defended. All felt the indignity to the clan, and each bosom burning with indignation, they prepared to protect the mud walls of the *pseudo* Boondi from iusult. It was reported to the Rana that Boondi was finished. He advanced to the storm; but what was his surprise when, instead of the blank cartridge, he heard a volley of balls whiz amongst them! A messenger was despatched and was received by Bairsi at the gate, who explained the cause of the unexpected salutation, desiring him to tell the Rana that 'not even the mock capital of a Hara should be dishonoured.' Spreading a sheet at the little gateway, Bairsi and the Kaawunts invited the assault, and at the threshold of *Gar-ca-Boondi* (the Boondi of clay) they gave up their lives for the honour of the race."[1]

Where can you find a more inspiring and ennobling example of a patriotic Hindu doing his duty than that of the eldest son of the Mehtri Chief during the Civil War between Bakht Singh and Ram Singh in Marwar? Colonel Tod says: "There is nothing more chivalrous in the days of Edward and Cressy than the death of the heir of Mehtri, who, with his father and brother sealed his fealty with his blood on this fatal field. He had long engaged the hand of a daughter of a chief of the Narookas, and was occupied with the marriage rites when tidings reached him of the approach of the rebels to Mairta. The knot had just been tied, their hands had been joined—but he was a Mairtea—he unlocked his hand from that of the fair Narooki, to court the

[1] Tod's Rajasthan Vol. II, pp. 463, 464.

Apsara in the field of battle. In the bridal vestments, with the nuptail coronet (Mor) encircling his forehead, he took his station with his clan in the second day's fight, and, 'obtained a bride in Indra's abode.' The bards of Maroo dwell with delight on the romantic glory of the youthful heir of Mehtri, as they repeat in their Doric verse.—

'Kan a moti bulbulla
Gulla soni a malla
Asi coss kurro ho aya
Kunwar Mehtri walla.'

The paraphernalia here enumerated are very foreign to the cavalier of the West: 'With pearls shining in his ears, and a golden chaplet round his neck, a space of eighty coss came the heir of Mehtri.'

"The virgin bride followed her lord from Jaipur, but instead of being met with the tabor and lute, and other signs of festivity, wail and lamentation awaited her within the lands of Mehtri, where tidings came of the calamity which at one deprived this branch of the Mairteas of all its supporters. Her part was soon taken, she commanded the pyre to be erected, and with the turban and toorah, which adorned her lord on this fatal day, she followed his shade to the mansions of the sun."[1]

Owing to certain reasons, Rai Singh, the their-apparent of Jaisalmer, during the reign of Mul Raj (who became king in A.D. 1762), was persuaded to put the minister to death. This was effected by the prince's own hands, in his father's presence; and as the Mehta, in falling, clung to Mul Raj (or protection, it was proposed to take off Mul Raj at the same time. The proposition, however, was rejected with horror by the prince, whose vengeance was satisfied. The Rawal was allowed to escape to the female apartments; but the chieftains, well knowing they

[1] Tod's Rajasthan, Vol. I, pp. 749, 750.

could not expect pardon from the Rawal, insisted on investing Rai Singh, and if he refused, on placing his brother on the *gadi*. The '*An*' of Rai Singh was proclaimed; but no entreaty or threat would induce him to listen to the proposal of occupying the throne; in lieu of which he used a pallet (khat). Three months and five days had passed since the deposal and bondage of Mul Raj, when a female resolved to emancipate him; this female was the wife of the chief conspirator, and confidential adviser of the regent prince. This noble dame, a Rathore Rajputni, of Mahecha clan, was the wife of Anop Singh of Jinjiniali, the premier noble of Jaisalmer, and who, wearied with the tyranny of the minister and the weakness of his prince, had proposed the death of the one and the deposal of the other. We are not made acquainted with any reason, save that of *swad'harma*, or 'fealty,' which prompted the Rahtorni to rescue her prince even at the risk of her husband's life; but her appeal to her son, Zorawar, to perform his duty, is preserved, and we give it *verbatim*: 'Should your father oppose you, sacrifice him to your duty, and I will mount the pyre with his corpse.' The son yielded obedience to the injunction of his magnanimous parent, who had sufficient influence to gain over Arjoon, the brother of her husband, as well as Megh Singh, Chief of Baroo. The three chieftains forced an entrance into the prison where there prince was confined, who refused to be released from his manacles, until he was told that the Mahechi had promoted the plot for his liberty. The sound of the grand *nakarra*, proclaiming Mul Raj's re-possession of the *gadi*, awoke his son from sleep; and on the herald depositing at the side of his pallet the sable *siropava*, and all the insignia of exile—the black steed and black vestments—the prince, obeying the command of the emancipated Rawal, clad himself therein, and, accompanied by his party, bade adieu to Jaisalmer, and took the road to Kottoroh. When he arrived at this town, on the southern frontier of the State, the chiefs proposed to "run the country"; but the replied that *the country was his mother and every Rajput his foe who injured it.*[1]

"This Rajputni," adds Colonel Tod, "with an elevation of mind equal to whatever is recorded of Greek and Roman heroines devoted herself and a husband whom she loved, to the one predominent sentiment of the Rajput—swadharma (duty).

The reply of the Deorah prince of Sirohi when instructed to perform that profound obeisance from which none were exempt at Delhi, where he had been carried by Mokundas, one of Jaswant Singh's generals after having been secretly captured whilst asleep in his palace, and his subsequent conduct, shows the high spirit and the independence of character of a true Rajput and his intense love for his country. He said that "his life was in the king's hands, his honour in his own; he had never bowed the head to mortal man, and never would." As Jaswant had pledged himself for his honourable treatement, the officers of the ceremonies endeavoured by stratagem to obtain a constrained obeisance, and instead of intorducing him as usual, they showed him a wicket, knee high, and very low overhead, by which to enter, but putting his feet foremost, his head was the last part to appear. This stubborn ingenuity, his noble bearing, and his long-protracted resistance, added to Jaswant's pledge, won the king's favour; and he not only proffered him pardon, but whatever lands he might desire. "Though the king did not name the return, Soortan was well aware of the terms, but he boldly and quickly replied, 'what can your Majesty bestow equal to Achilgurh? let me return to it is all I ask.' The king had the magnanimity to comply with his request; Soortan was allowed to retire to the castle of Abu, nor did he or any of the Deoras ever rank themselves amongst the vassals of the empire;

[1] Tod's Rajasthan, Vol. II, pp. 264, 265.

but they have continued to the present hour a life of almost savage independence."[1]

Colonel Tod says: "These *men of the soil*, as they emphatically designate themselves, cling to it and their ancient and well-defined privileges with an unconquerable pertinacity; in their endeavours to preserve them, whole generations have been swept away, yet has their strength increased in the very ratio of oppression. Where are now the oppressors? the dynasties of Ghazni, of Ghor, the Khiljis, the Lodis, the Pathans, the Timoors and the demoralising Mahratta? The native Rajput has flourished amidst these revolutions, and survived their fall; and but for the vices of their internal sway, chiefly contracted from such association, would have risen to power upon the ruin of their tyrants."[2]

How for this high character of the Rajputs will be influenced by the new condition of things remains to be seen. Colonel Tod says: "When so many nations are called upon, in a period of great calamity and danger, to make over to a foreigner, their opposite in everything, their superior in most, the control of their forces in time of war, the adjudication of their disputes in time of peace, and a share in the fruits of their renovating prosperity what must be the result, when each Rajput may hang up his lance in the hall, convert his sword to a ploughshare, and make a basket of his buckler? What but the prostration of every virtue? To be great, to be independent, its martial spirit must be cherished; happy if within the bounds of moderation."[3] It is to be hoped that education, travel and contact with enligtened Europeans will succeed in counteracting the baneful influences dreaded by the gallant Colonel.

[1] Tod's Rajasthan, Vol. II, pp. 56. 57,

[2] Tod's Rajasthan, Vol. II, p. 160.

[3] Tod's Rajasthan, Vol. I, p. 127.

"The Rajput, with all his turbulence, possesses in an eminent degree both loyalty and patriotism."[1]

What can be a more eloquent testimony to the patriotic fervour and the heroic valour of the Rajputs, than the following extract from the Annals and Antiquities of Rajasthan by Colonel Tod:—

"There is not a petty State in Rajputana that has not had its own Thermopylæ and scarcely a city that has not produced its Leonidas. But the mantle of ages has shrouded from view what the magic pen of the historian might have consecrated to endless admirations: Somnath might have rivalled Delphos; the spoils of Hind might have vied with the wealth of the Lybian King; and, compared with the army of the Pandavas, the army of Xerxes would have dwindled into insignificance."[2]

VALOUR.

No thought of flight,
None of retreat, no unbecoming deed
That argued fear; each on himself relied,
As only in his arm the moment lay
Of victory.

—MILTON: *Paradise Lost.*

THE Hindus were declared by the Greeks to be the bravest nation they ever came in contact with.[3] It was the Hindu King of Magadha that struck terror in the ever-victorious armies of Alexander the Great.

Abul Fazal, the minister of Akbar, after admiring their other noble virtues, speaks of the valour of the Hindus in these terms: "Their character shines brightest in adversity. Their soldiers (Rajputs) know not what it is to flee from the field of

[1] Tod's Rajasthan, Vol. I, p. 194.
[2] Tod's Rajasthan, Introduction, p. 16.
[3] Elphinstone's History of India, p. 197.

battle, but when the success of the combat becomes doubtful, they dismount from their horses and throw away their lives in payment of the debt of valour."

The traveller, Bernier, says that "the Rajputs embrace each other when on the battle-field as if resolved to die." The Spartans, as is well known, dressed their hair on such occasions. It is well known that when a Rajput becomes desperate, he puts on garments of saffron colour, which act, in technical language, is called *kesrian kasumal karna* (donning saffron robes).

After describing how, when Dara disappeared from the field of Dholpur, where the Imperial forces had made a last stand against the combined armies of Aurangzeb and Murad in their advance to Agra, and the Imperial forces took to flight, the Bundi chief, like Porus of old, continued fighting heroically till he was killed, saying, "Accursed be he who flees! Here, true to my salt, my feet are rooted to this field, nor will I quit it alive but with victory." And how Bharat Singh, his youngest son, maintained the contest nobly. Col. Tod says: "Thus in the two battles of Ujjain and Dholpur, no less than 12 princes of the blood, together with the heads of every Hara clan, maintained their fealty even to death. *Where* are we to look for such examples?"[1]

During a visit of the Bundi Chief, Rao Sooju to Chitor, Rana Ratna, at the instigation of an intriguing Poorbia, determined to slay the Rao in a hunt when the respective chiefs were attended only by a couple of servants. Finding a convenient opportunity, the Rana said to his companion, "now is the moment to slay the boar," and instantly an arrow from the bow of the Poorbia was sped at the Rao. With an eagle's eye he saw it coming, and turned it off with his bow. This might have been chance, but

[1]Tod's Rajasthan, Vol. II, p. 481. "The annals of no nation on earth can furnish such an example as an entire family, six royal brothers, stretched on the field and all but one in death."—Vol. II, p. 49.

another from the foster-brother of the Rana convinced him there was treachery. Scarcely had he warded off the second, when the Rana darted at him on horse-back, and cut him down with his *khanda*. The Rao fell, but recovering, took his shawl and lightly bound up the wound, and as his foe was making off, he called aloud, "Escape you may, but you have sunk Mewar." The Poorbia, who followed his prince, when he saw the Rao bind up his wound, said, "the work is but half done;" and like a coward, Ratna once more charged the wounded Rao. As his arm was raised to finish the deed of shame, like a wounded tiger the Hara made a dying effort, caught the assassin by the robe, and dragged him from his steed. Together they came to the ground, the Rana underneath. The Rao knelt upon his beast, while, with preternatural strength, with one hand he grasped his victim by the throat, with the other he searched for his dagger. What a moment for revenge! He plunged the weapon into his assassin's heart, and saw him expire at his feet. The Rao was satisfied; there was no more life left him than sufficed for revenge, and he dropped a corpse upon the dead body of his foeman.

The tidings flew to Bundi, to the mother of the Rao, that her son was slain in the *Aihura*. "Slain!" exclaimed this noble dame, "but did he fall alone? *Never could a son who has drunk at this breast depart unaccompanied;*" and as she spoke, "maternal feeling caused the milk to issue from the fount with such force that it rent the slab on which it fell." [1]

Colonel Tod thus relates an incident he witnessed in Haravati: "There was one specimen of devotion (to the prince of Kotah) which we dare not pass over, comparable with whatever is recorded of the fabled traits of heroism of Greece or Rome. The Regent's (Zalim Singh [2] of Kotah) battalions were advancing

[1] Tod's Rajasthan, Vol. II., pp. 468, 469.

[2] Col. Tod says: "Zalim Singh was a consummate politician, who can scarcely find a parallel in the varied pages of history. He was the *primum mobile* of the region he inhabited, a sphere far too confined for his genius, which required a wider field for its display, and might have controlled the destinies of nations.

in columns along the precipitous bank of a rivulet, when their attention was arrested by several shots fired from an isolated hillock rising out of the plain across the stream. Without any order, but as by a simultaneous impulse, the whole line halted to gaze at two audacious individuals, who appeared determined to make their mound a fortress. A minute or two passed in mute surprise, when the word was given to move on; but scarcely was it uttered ere several wounded from the head of the column were passing to the rear, and shots began to be exchanged very briskly, at least twenty in return for one. But the long matchlocks of the two heroes told every time in our lengthened line, while they seemed to have 'a charmed life,' and the shot fell like hail around them innocuous, one continuing to load behind the mound, while the other fired with deadly aim. At length two twelve-pounders were unlimbered; and as the shot whistled round their ears, both rose on the very pinnacle of the mound, and made a profound *salaam* for this compliment to their valour; which done, they continued to load and fire, whilst entire platoons blazed upon them. Although more men had suffered, an irresistible impulse was felt to save these gallant men; orders were given to cease firing, and the force was directed to move on, unless any two individuals chose to attack them manfully hand-to-hand. The words were scarcely uttered when two young Rohillas drew their swords, sprang down the bank, and soon cleared the space between them and the foemen. All was deep anxiety as they mounted to the assault; but whether their physical frame was less vigorous, or their energies were exhausted by wounds or by their peculiar situation, these

"When an English division in their pursuit of the Pindari leader, Karim Khan, insulted his town of Baran, he burst forth: 'If twenty years could be taken from his life, Delhi and Deccan should be one.'"—Tod's Rajasthan, Vol. II, pp. 517, 518.

EMPEROR JAHANGIR.

brave defenders fell on the mount whence they disputed the march of ten battalions of infantry and twenty pieces of cannon." [1]

Mukandas was the head of the Kunpanwat Rathores of Marwar. He incurred the displeasure of the Emperor Aurangzeb, by a reply which was disrespectful. The tyrent condemned him to enter a tiger's den, and contend for his life unarmed. Without a sign of fear he entered the arena where the savage beast was pacing, and thus contemptuously accosted him: "Oh tiger of the *Mian*, face the tiger of Jaswant," exhibiting to the king of the forest a pair of eyes, which anger and opium had rendered little less inflamed than his own. The animal, startled by so unaccustomed a salutation, for a moment looked at his visitor, put down his head, turned round and stalked from him. "You see" exclaimed the Rathore, "that he dare not face me, and it is contrary to the creed of a true Rajput to attack an enemy who dares not confront him."

Even the tyrant, who beheld the scene was surprised into admiration, presented him with gifts, and asked if he had any children to inherit his prowess. His reply, "how can we get children when you keep us from our wives beyond the Attock?' fully shows that the Rathore and fear were strangers to each other. From this singular encounter he bore the name of Naharkhan, "the tiger lord." [2]

"It was with the Sesodia Rajputs and the Shekhawats that Mohabat Khan performed the most daring exploit in Moghal history, making Jehangir prisoner in his own camp in the zenith of the power." [3]

[1] Tod's Rajasthan, Vol. II, pp. 579, 580.

[2] Tod's Rajasthan, Vol. II, pp. 55, 56.

[3] This Mohabat Khan was an apostate son of Sagarji, half-brother of Rana Pratap. "He was beyond doubt," says Tod, "the most daring Chief in Jehangir's reign."—Tod's Rajasthan, Vol. I, p. 356.

"The celebrated heroic charges of the Rathor horse at the battles of Tonga and Patun in 1791 A. D. against the disciplined armies of the French General De Boigne, carrying everything before them, show the unequalled dash and *élan* of the Rathor cavalry when inspired by patriotism.

About the part played by the Rathors at the battle of Malpura in 1799 A.D. Col. Skinner himself says: "The acts of these Rathors, and the cool intrepidity they showed in the square, surpasses all that I can say in their praise." [1]

There is no end to the recounting of the brave deeds performed by the Rajputs. Name a few heroes like Pratap, Durga Das, Jaswant, Hamir, Raj Singh, Maun, Prithvi Raj, Sivaji, and a volume is said. The rest

> 'Were long to tell; how many battles fought,
> How many kings destroyed and kingdoms won.'

But as the Rajputs were men of valour, so were they men of herculean build and strength. It was a Bhati Rajput—Soningdeo, a man of gigantic strength—who not only bent but broke the iron bow sent by the King of Khorasan to the Emperor of Delhi to string, when no one in Delhi could do so.[2]

"Homer's heroes," says Col. Tod, " were pigmies to the Kurus, whose bracelet we may doubt if Ajax could have lifted." [3]

Colonel Tod says: "Let us take the Rajput character from the royal historians themselves, from Akbar, Jehangir, Aurangzeb. The most brilliant conquests of these monarchs were by their Rajput allies; though the little regard the latter had for opinion alienated the sympathies of a race, who, when rightly managed, encountered at command the Afghan amidst the snows of Caucasus, or made the furthest Chersonese tributary to the

[1] Military Memoirs of Lt.-Col. James Skinner, by J. B. Fraser, Vol. I. p. 151.

[2] Tod's Rajasthan, Vol. II. p. 254.

[3] Tod's Rajasthan, Vol. II, p. 81.

EMPEROR AURANGZEB.

empire. Assam, where the British arms were recently engaged, and for the issue of which such anxiety was manifested in the metropolis of Britain, was conquered by a Rajput prince, whose descendant is now an ally of the British Government." [1]

"The Moghals were indebted for half their conquests to the *Lakh Tulvar Rathoran*" "(hundred thousand swords of the Rathores.) "But the Imperial princes knew not how to appreciate or to manage such men who, when united under one who could control them, were irressistible." [2]

Religious bigotry and Imperial vanity eventually disgusted the Rajputs, who were the bulwark of the Moghal throne, with the result that the empire came to an end sooner than was expected. "The spirit of devotion in this brave race by whose aid the Moghal power was made and maintained was irretrievably alienated," when Delhi was invaded by Nadir Shah. Even in the time of Emperor Aurangzeb, the Hindu princes of Rajputana, though disunited and jealous of each other, were some of them individually too strong to be openly defied by the Emperor. Jaswant Singh of Jodhpur was poisoned at Kabul,[4] and his heir, Prithvi Singh at Delhi, which freed the heart of Aurang from a terrible nightmare. It was only after these murders that the tyrant thought of imposing the hated Jazia. The great Jai Singh of Jaipur was also poisoned at his instigation by the Raja's son, Kirat Singh. Having recourse to poison, when unable to openly meet a strong opponent, was a favourite practice of the Moghal Emperors of India. Even the much-belauded Akbar, 'the arch-enemy of the Hindus' was not above it. Colonel Tod says:

[1] Tod's Rajasthan, Vol. I, p. 195.

[2] Tod's Rajasthan, Vol. II, p. 507.

[3] Tod's Rajasthan, Vol. I, p. 417.

[4] Tod's Rajasthan, Vol. I, p. 379, and Vol. II p. 52.

"A desire to be rid of the great Raja Maun of Amber to whom he was so much indebted, made the emperor to act the part of the assassin. He prepared a *majum* or confection, a part of which contained poison; but, caught in his own snare, he presented the innoxious portion to the Rajput and ate that drugged with death himself."[1] The cause appears to have been a design on the part of Raja Maun to alter the succession, and that Khusro, his nephew, should succeed instead of Selim.

The murder of Maharaja Ajit Singh of Marwar by his own son, Bakht Singh at the instigation of the Sayyads illustrates the policy of "covert guile," which became a stronger weapon than the sword in the hands of some of the Moghal rulers of India, who seem to have accepted the recommendation bestowed on this policy by Belial in the assembly of the Fallen Angels.

The inherent strength of the old Rajput character, his power of dogged resistence, his invincible attachment to his country, and, above all, the spiritual nature of the ideals that nurtured his soul, are fully recognised by Col. Tod, who says: "What nation on earth would have maintained the semblance of civilization, the spirit or the customs of their forefathers, during so many centuries of overwhelming depression, but one of such singular character as the Rajput? Though ardent and reckless he can, when required, subside into forbearance and apparent apathy and reserve himself for the opportunity of revenge. Rajasthan exhibits the sole example in the history of mankind, of a people withstanding every outrage barbarity can inflict, or human nature sustain, yet rising buoyant from the pressure and making calamity a whetstone to courage."[2]

As the Ancient Hindus were the bravest nation in the world, so did they give to the world its greatest hero. Hercules has

[1] Tods Rajasthan, Vol. I. pp. 351, 352.

[2] Tod's Rajasthan, Vol. I page 259.

Maharaja Ajit Singh.

been universally acknowledged to be the greatest warrior, the bravest and the most powerful man the world has produced. And Hercules was in reality a Hindu and not a Greek. Hercules was but Balram. This may sound paradoxical to those who have not studied comparative mythology, but to those who have done so there is nothing strange in this statement. The word Hercules is, according to Col. Tod derived from the Sanskirt word Heri-cul-es (हरिकुलेश).

Professor Heeren says: "We can hardly doubt that Bacchus and Hercules were both of them Hindu deities, since they are not only represented as objects of general worship but the particular countries and places are also specified where both the one and the other had temples erected to their services" (see Arrian, p. 174, and Strabo, Vol. XV, p. 489).

Diodorus says that Hercules was born amongst the Indians. "The combats to which Diodorus alludes are those in the legendary haunts of the Hercules during their twelve years' exile from the seat of their forefathers." [1]

Colonel Tod says: "Both Krishna and Baldeo (Balram) or Apollo and Hercules are *es* (lords) of the race (cul) of Heri (Heri-cul-es), of which the Greeks might have made the compound Hercules. Might not a colony after the Great War have migrated Westward? The period of the return of Heraclidæ, the descendants of Atreus (Atri the progenitor of the Hericula (हरिकुल) would answer: "It was about half a century after the Great War."

Colonel Tod cannot resist the inference that the Herculas of India and the Heraclidæ of Greece were connected. Arrian

[1] Tod's Rajasthan, Vol. I, p. 30. Arrian's story of Hercules is the same as that given in the Puranas.

notices the similarity of the Hindu and Theban Hercules, and cites as his authority the ambassador of Seleucus, Megasthenes, who says: "He used the same habit with the Theban, and is practically worshipped by the Sureseni, who have two great cities belonging to them, namely, Mathura and Clisoboros."

The points of resemblance between the Hindu and the Theban Hercules are most striking.

(1) The Heraclidæ claimed their origin from Atreus, the Hericulas from Atri.

(2) Euristhenes was the first great king of the Heraclidæ; Yudhistira has sufficient affinity in his name to the first Spartan king not to startle the etymologist—the *d* and *r* being always permutable in Sanskrit.

(3) The Greeks or Ionians are descended from Yavan or Javan, the seventh from Japhet. The Hericules are also Yavans claiming from Javan or Yavona, the thirteenth in descent from Yayat, the third son of the primeval patriarch.

(4) The ancient Heraclidæ of the Greeks asserted that they were as old as the sun, older than the moon. May not this boast conceal the fact that the Hericulidæ (or Suryavansa) of Greece had settled there anterior to the colony of the Indu (Lunar) race of Hericulas? Col. Tod says: "Amidst the snows of Caucasus, Hindu legends abandon the Hericulas, under their leaders Yudhistira and Baldeo: yet, if Alexander established his altars in Panchalica amongst the sons of Pooru and the Hericulas, what physical impossibility exists that a colony of them under Yudhistira and Baldeo, eight centuries anterior, should have penetrated to Greece? Comparatively far advanced in science and arms, the conquest would have been easy."

(5) When Alexander attacked the "free cities" of Panchalika, the Poorus and the Hericulas who opposed him evinced the recollections of their ancestor, in carrying the figure of Hercules as their standard.[1]

Comparison proves a common origin to Hindu and Greek mythology; and Plato says "the Greeks derived theirs from Egypt and the East. May not this colony of the Heraclidæ who penetrated into Peloponnesus (according to Volney) 1078 years before Christ, be sufficiently near our calculated period of the Great War?"[2]

"How refreshing," Colonel Tod concludes, "to the mind yet to discover amidst the ruins of the Yamuna, Hercules (Baldeo) retaining his club and lion's hide."

---

[1] "The martial Rajputs are not strangers to armorial bearings, now so indiscriminately used in Europe. The great banner of Mewar exhibits a golden sun on a crimson field, those of the chiefs bear a dagger. 'Amber displays the *Panchranga* or five-coloured flag. The lion rampant on an argent field is extinct with the State of Chanderi. In Europe, these customs were not introduced till the period of the Crusades, and were copied from the Saracens, while the use of them among the Rajput tribes can be traced to a period anterior to the war of Troy."—India in Greece, page 92.

[2] Tod's Rajasthan, Vol. I, page 51.

THE POSITION OF WOMEN.

Oh fairest of creasion! last and best
Of all God's works! Creature in whom excell'd
Whatever can to sight or thought be formed
Holy, divine, good, amiable, or sweet.

—MILTON: *Paradise Lost.*

MR. HERBERT SPENCER, the great apostle of individual freedom, says that the position of women supplies a good test of the civilization of a people.

Colonel Tod also says: "It is universally admitted that there is no better criterion of the refinement of a nation than the condition of the fair sex therein."[1]

The high position Hindu women have always occupied in India would argue a very advanced state of civilization in that country. Even of the modern Hindu society, Colonel Tod says: "If devotion to the fair sex be admitted as a criterion of civilization, the Rajput must rank very his. His susceptibility is extreme, and fires at the slightest offence to female delicacy, which he never forgives. A satirical impromptu, offending against female delicacy, dissolved the coalition of the Rathores and Cutchwahas, and laid each prostrate before the Mahrattas, whom when united they had crushed; and a jest, apparently trivial, compromised the right of primogeniture to the throne of Chitor, and proved more disastrous in its consequences than the arms either of Moghuls or Mahrattas."[2]

Professor H. H. Wilson says: "And it may be confidently asserted that in no nation of antiquity were women held in so much esteem as amongst the Hindus."[3]

[1]Tod's Rajasthan, Vol. I, page 603.
[2]Tod's Rajasthan, Vol. I, page 276.
[3]Mill's History of India, Vol. II, page 51.

In Ancient India, however, they not only possessed equality of opportunities with men, but enjoyed certain rights and privileges not claimed by the male sex. The chivalrous treatment of women by Hindus is well known to all who know anything of Hindu society.

"Strike not even with a blossom a wife guilty of a hundred faults," says a Hindu sage, "a sentiment so delicate," says Colonel Tod "that Rignald-de-Born, the prince of troubadours, never utterred any more refined."[1]

Manu (Chapter V, 130) says: "The mouth of a woman is constantly pure," and he ranks it with the running waters and the sunbeam"[2] He also says (Chapter II, 33): "Where the females are honoured, there the deities are pleased; but where dishonoured, there all religious rites become useless."

The Mahabharata says: "The wife is the half of man: the wife is the best of friends: the wife is the root of the three-fold worldly activity: the wife is the root of salvation."

The Hindus seem to have laid special stress on honouring the wife and treating her with *ever-increasing delicacy*. The nearest approach to these ideas are the views of Mr. Herbert Spencer, who, in a letter dated the 18th March 1845, to his friend Lott, says: "And on this ground I conceive that instead of there being, as is commonly the case, a greater familiarity and carelessness with regard to appearances between husband and wife, there ought to be a greater delicacy than between any other parties."[3]

A rather forcible illustration of this view is the reply of the Hariji, queen of the famous Raja Jai Singh of Jaipur. One day when the Raja was alone with the queen, he began playfully to contrast the sweeping *jupe* of Kotah with the more scanty robe

[1] Tod's Rajasthan, Vol. I, page 611.

[2] The women are recommended "to preserve a cheerful temper," and to remain always well-dressed "If the wife be not elegantly attired she will not exhilarate her husband. A wife gaily adorned, the whole house is embellished.

[3] Herbert Spencer's Autobiography, Vol. I, page 268.

of the belles of his capital; and taking up a pair of scissors, said he would reduce it to an equality with the latter. Offended at his levity, she seized his sword, and assuming a threatening attitude, said "that in the house to which she had the honour to belong, they were not habituated to jests of this nature; that mutual respect was the guardian not only of happiness but of virtue;" and she assured him that if he ever again so insulted her, he would find that the daughter of Kotah could use a sword more effectively than the prince of Amber the scissors.[1]

Manu commands that "whoever accosts a woman shall do so by the title of sister, and that way must be made for her even as for the aged, for a priest, a prince, or a bridegroom;" and, in the law of hospitality, he ordains that pregnant women, brides, and damsels shall have food before all the other guests." (Education, art. 129).

The legal status of a wife in Ancient India and her equal treatment with her husband is thus defined by Manu, the great law-giver of the Hindus:—

1. If a wife dies, her husband may marry another wife. (Manu, Chapter V. verse 168).

If a husband dies, a wife may marry another husband (Manu, quoted by Madhava and Vidyanatha Dikshita; Parasara; Narada; Yagnavalkya, quoted by Krishnacharya Smriti; Agni Purana; Smriti, quoted by Chetti Koneri Acharya and Janardana Bhatta).

2. If a wife becomes fallen by drunkenness or immorality, her husband may marry another (Manu, Chapter IX, verse 80; Yagnavalkya, page 416, verse 73).

If a husband becomes fallen, a wife may re-marry another husband (Manu, quoted by Madhava and several other authorities above mentioned).

3. If a wife be barren, her husband may marry another wife (Manu, Chapter IX, verse 81).

[1] Tod's Rajasthan, Vol I, page 626.

If a husband be impotent she may marry another husband (Manu, and several other authorities quoted above).

4. In particular circumstances, a wife may cease to cohabit with her husband (Manu, Chapter IX, verse 79).

5. If a husband deserts his wife, she may marry another (Manu, Chapter IX, verse 76, and several others).

6. If a wife treats her husband with aversion, he may cease to cohabit with her (Manu, Chapter IX, verse 77).

7. A husband must be revered (Manu, Chapter V, verse 154).

A wife must be honoured by the husband (Manu, Chapter III, verse 55).

8. A good wife irradiates the house and is a goddess of wealth (Manu, Chapter IX, verse 26).

A good husband makes his wife entitled to honour (Manu, Chapter XI, verse 23).

The high ethical teachings of the Hindu Shastras prepared the men to assign to women a peculiarly privileged position, keeping them safe from the rough and degrading work that now often falls to their lot in the West, in consequence of the severe struggle for existence raging there. While providing the freest possible scope for the exercise of their peculiar gifts, which enabled them to achieve, in the superlative degree, the high and noble work which it is the privilege of women to perform for the well-being and advancement of a people, the ancient Hindu constitution not only accorded to them the position which the mothers, the sisters, the wives, and the daughters of the highest and the lowest in the nation are justly entitled to, but which enabled their true feminine nature and character to receive full development, so as to fulfil their high destiny of giving to the world a race of men yet unequalled in intellect, character and energy.

In Europe, as well as in India, the woman is styled "the half of the man"—in Europe, as "the better half," in India, simple as *Ardhangini* (lit. half-self). In Europe, however, it is a meaningless phrase, rather pointing to the desirability of assigning woman a position which is hers by nature than signifying the position actually occupied by her—showing the desirable but yet unattained ideal rather than, as amongst the Hindus, an actual reality. True, in every grade of European society women are to be met with whose position, domestic as well as social, is not only perfectly happy and satisfactory, but, to all outward appearance, looks higher than that enjoyed by their Hindu sisters. In Europe, woman has a distinct and separate individuality of her own, which flourishes independently of man, though by his side and connected with him. Not so in India. Woman has no distinctive, independent individuality in Hindu social polity. From her birth to her death she is a part of man, and cannot be separated from him. With marriage, she merges her individuality into her husband's, and both together form a single entity in society. The one without the other is only a part and not a whole.

It must not, however, be supposed that the woman loses herself in the man, and is therefore inferior to him. The man, too, after his union with woman is, like her, only a part of the social entity. All important religious, social, and domestic concerns of life recognise the entity only when it is complete, *i.e.*, formed of a man and a woman.

In Europe, the power and position enjoyed by woman are not recognised by the authority which sanctions all social law, and on which the entire fabric of society is ultimately based. What position and privilege she enjoys she evidently cannot claim as of right—a right inherent in and inseparable from womanhood. In some of the most important concerns of life she is utterly ignored. Not so amongst the Hindus. In India she is in possession of her rights, which are ordained by religion and held inviolable by social law. The Hindu woman is not indebted for her position to a man's love or affectionate regard or to the exigencies of social life. It is her birth right, inalienable, and recognised by all; it lives with her and dies with her. Man is as much subject to it as the woman is to a man's. Take, for instance, the most important concern of life, the *marriage*. In Europe, the father gives away the daughter; in his absence, the brother, or the uncle or some near male relation, as the case may be. He by himself performs this sacred and most important function in life. Where comes in the *better half* of the father, the brother, the uncle or the other relation? She has no place in the rite, no *locus standi*, no indispensable, inalienable position in the function. She is not a necessary party. She may be happy in the event and join the festivities, but she is an utter outsider so far as the rite itself—the right of giving away—is concerned. But what do we find in India? Amongst the Hindus, in order that the ceremony of giving away (called Kayadan) may be complete, the *ardhangini*, or the wife of the father, the brother, the uncle or the other male relative must take part in it. The "giving away" is not complete till the husband and the wife both do it. Nay, there is something more to mark the unalterable position of the wife as the "other half" of the husband. If, owing to any cause—death, illness or unavoidable absence—the better half of the father, brother or the other relative cannot be present at the Sacrament, a piece of cloth or something else is placed by his side as a substitute for her, to show that he, by himself, is only an incomplete individual, and cannot perform the most important functions of life unless and until joined by his wife. And it is not so with marriage only. From the marriage down to a dip in the sacred Ganges; the worship of the sacred *bar tree* (the Ficus Indica) in the *Bar Tirat* (Vata Triratra) ceremony;[1] the worship of the household gods, and other simple, ordinary duties, ordained by religion or sanctioned

[1] When the wife keeps a fast for three days.

by social usage, no ceremony is complete unless the wife joins the husband in its performance. What a difference here between the respective positions of the European and the Hindu woman! How inferior is the position of a European woman to that of her Hindu sister! With all the love and devotion she receives and the freedom of action she enjoys, she in Europe is even now as far away from the position of the other half of a man as she was two thousand years ago. But society in Europe is still in its making. Important and far-reaching changes will yet have to be made before it arrives at a stage of evolution when it will come into line with its sister organization, the Hindu society, as it is found in the Shastras.

In the West, women's sphere is yet limited; women's position yet precarious, owing to the selfish and hypocritical conduct of man, the product of a material civilization divorced from spiritual ideals. Their principal interest in public affairs, however, is directed to secure for themselves rights which they regard as essential to assure their position in the cold, pitiless struggle for existence, which respects neither age nor sex. In Ancient India people never thought of usurping from women their rights and privileges. They were safe from the turmoil of life; they were secure against the attacks which all have to meet who are governed by the complicated machinery of a civilization based on the worship of Mammon, with its horizon bounded by the desires, aspirations and capabilities of the physical man.

Sri Madhavacharya says that Draupadi's part in the administration of the empire was to instruct the subjects as to the duties and rights of women, superintend the management of the palace and its treasuries, to assist in the management of the finances of the empire, and to supervise the religious institutions of the nation.

The character and ideals of Hindu women may be inferred from the conduct of Maitreyi, wife of Yagyavalkya, who declined to accept the estate offered to her by her husband on his entering the third Ashram (Vanaprastha.) She told him that she also would like to have that which he was going in search of, and that, if the estate had been worth having, he would not have given it away.

Damayanti and Savitri were women whose lives would have purified the national life of any people. The learning of Gargi, the intellect and character of Tara, the fidelity of Anusuya and the devotion and love of Sita would do honour to any nation.

The courage and valour displayed by Kaikeyi in the battle-field by the side of Dashratha are no less remarkable than the heroism displayed by Satyabhama, of whom Madhavacharya says that, when she saw her husband tired and his enemy exulting in strength, she fought with him and deprived him of his arms. These facts show that in ancient times the women of India were not unused to warfare, and that they accompanied their husbands everywhere. They did not lead secluded lives. *They were not kept in the zenana*. The *pardah* system, which marks the advent into India of foreigners of a much lower civilization, was unknown in Ancient India.

It has sometimes been urged by men unacquainted with the social life of the Hindus that the fact that daughters do not share in the paternal property in the same way as the sons, argues a low position of women in Hindu polity. In the first place, the law of inheritance in this respect is no proof of the high or the low refinement of a people; or the Arabs would be held to be more refined than the Hindus. In the second place, it is not a fact that women do not inherit or are incompetent to hold property.

Professor Wilson says: "Their right to property is fully recognised and fully secured."[1] He also says: "In the absence of direct male heirs, widows succeed to a life interest in real and absolute interest in personal property. Next, daughters inherit

[1] Mill's History of India, p. 446, footnote.

absolutely. Where there are sons, mothers and daughters are entitled to shares, and wives hold peculiar property from a variety of sources, besides those specified by the text, over which a husband has no power during their lives, and which descends to their own heirs, with a preference in some cases to females. It is far from correct, therefore, to say that women amongst the Hindus are excluded from the rights of property."

Commenting on Mr. James Mill's opinion that according to Manu (Chapter IV, 43) women among the Hindus are excluded from sharing in the paternal property, Professor Wilson says: "The reference is incorrect, so is the law; as the passage in the first volume adverted to might have shown had the writer remembered it. For, after stating in the text in the same unqualified manner, that daughters are altogether debarred from a share, it is mentioned in a note that those who are unmarried are to receive portions out of their brothers' allotments. It is mere quibbling, therefore, to say they have no shares. But the more important question, as affecting the position of women in society, is not merely the shares of daughters, although this is artfully put forward as if it was decisive of the rights of the whole sex, but what rights women have in regard to property; and as we have already shown, the laws do not very materially differ in this respect from those which are observed in the civilized countries of modern Europe." [1]

Foreigners imbibe unfavourable notions regarding the position of Hindu women from their ignorance of the working of Hindu society and of the principles on which it is based. The Hindu law of inheritance in this respect is somewhat different from that obtaining in Europe, but in no way behind the latter in safeguarding the position of women.

[1] Mill's History of India, Vol. I, p. 451.

When men in all grades of society recognise the rights and privileges of women, and the social system of the nation is so framed as to provide means to enforce those rights, the aid of legislation becomes unnecessary. Those who are acquainted with the working of the social system of the Hindus know that the rights of women are recognised in a far more substantial manner than by giving them a certain portion of the inheritence in final settlement of all their claims on the family.

Respect for feminine nature, considerations of honour and chivalry towards the sex, and the ingrained fealing of regard and esteem for womanhood, urged the Hindus to take measures to safeguard the position of women against all possible but avoidable contingencies. A woman accordingly has claims on her father and brothers and sons for a suitable maintenance under all circumstances. A father may leave nothing to his sons, yet they are bound to suitably maintain their mother so long as she is alive.

Sisters claim maintenance, their marriage expenses, and presents on all ceremonial occasions, no matter whether their brothers have inherited any paternal estate or not. And, not daughters and sisters alone enjoy such rights in Hindu society; their children too have certain well-defined claims, and Hindu society possesses means to see that those claims are satisfied. The ceremonial institutions of the Hindus controlled by the caste organization, recognize and fulfil these obligations. Those who are acquainted with the inner working of Hindu society know that the sisters and the daughter's not only enjoy certain rights in connection with every festival and every event of importance in their father's and brothers' families—at some of which functions they play the leading part—but that even after their marriages their connection with the families in which they were born is one of a perennial flow towards them of presents and gifts, to which they are entitled by social law, irrespective of the relations existing between them being cordial or strained.

Thus, while their rights are secured against contingencies, women altogether get from their fathers and brothers far more than generally received by them anywhere else in Asia or Europe. Moreover, the joint Hindu family system is highly conducive to the preservation of their influence—in some respects predominant—in the families in which they were born.

Even at the present day, though the women are not so prominent, their influence is supreme. It is not correct to say that Hindu women are prisoners in the *zenana*, that there condition is a pitiable one, that they claim the philanthropic efforts of men and women to alleviate their hard lot, and that they deserve all the sympathy that suffering humanity may receive. Colonel Tod says: "The superficial observer, who applies his own standard to the customs of all nations, laments, with an affected philanthropy, the degraded condition of the Hindu female, in which sentiment he would find her little disposed to join. He particularly laments her want of liberty and calls her seclusion imprisonment. From the knowledge I possess of the freedom, the respect, the happiness which Rajput women enjoy, I am by no means inclined to deplore their state as one of captivity." And, who does not know that amongst no people in India is *pardah* observed more strictly than by the Rajputs?

Every Sanskrit scholar knows in what respect and veneration ladies like Gargi, Draupadi, Sakuntala, Mandodari, and Rukmani,[1] were held. Who can listen without admiration and strong emotion, to the celebrated forest speech of Draupadi, after the banishment of the Pandavas?

[1] Within the last 100 years, the name of Maharani Ahilyabai Holkar was prominently before the world. She is known from the Himalayas to Cape Comorin, and her memory is actually worshipped in some places.

Prithviraja, The last Hindu Emperor of India.

"Hindu female devotion" is a hackneyed phrase. Colonel Tod says: "Nor will the annals of any nation afford more numerous or more sublime instances of female devotion than those of the Rajputs."[1] Even in mediaeval ages, India produced women that would make the darkest page of history resplendent. "The annals of no nation on earth," says Colonel Tod, "record a more ennobling or more magnanimous instance of female loyalty than exemplified by Dewalde, mother of the Binafur brothers."[2]

As the incident alluded to above throws a flood of light on the high character of the Rajput women, and fully illustrates the commanding influence they exercise in society, a short account of this inspiring episode that occurred when Hindu independence was about to be overthrown, may well be inserted.

While the last Hindu emperor of India, the chivalrous Prithviraj, was returning to Delhi from Sameta, some of the wounded, who covered his retreat, were assailed and put to death by Parmal, the Chundail prince of Mahoba. In order to avenge this insult, the emperor invaded the territory of the Chundail, whose troops were cut to pieces at Sirswah. The Chundail by the advice of his queen, Malundevi, demanded a truce of his adversary, on the plea of the absence of his chieftains, Ala and Udil. The envoy found the Chohan ready to cross the Pahouj. The chivalarous Prithviraj, unused to refusing such requests, granted the truce.

The two brothers, Ala and Udil, the Sardars of Mahoba, had been made to abandon their home because Ala had refused to part with one of his mares which Parmal desired to possess. They went away to Kanauj, where they were received with open arms by Jai Chand.

[1] Tod's Rajasthan, Vol. I, p. 613.

[2] Tod's Rajasthan, Vol. I, p 614.

The bard, Yagnuk, now repaired to Kanauj to beg the two heroes on behalf of Parmal to return to Mahoba, as their fatherland demanded their services. He said, "the Chohan is encamped on the plains of Mahoba, Nursing and Birsing have fallen, Sirswah is given to the flames, and the Kingdom of Parmal laid waste by the Chohan. For one month a truce has been obtained, while to you I am sent for aid in his griefs. Listen, Oh sons of Binafur, sad have been the days of Malundevi since you left Mahoba! Oft she looks towards Kanauj; and, while she recalls you to mind, tears gush from her eyes and she exclaims, "the fame of the Chundail is departing, but when gone, Oh, sons of Jasraj, great will be your self-accusing sorrow! yet; think of Mahoba."

"Destruction to Mahoba! Annihilation to the Chundail, who, without fault, expelled us our home, in whose service fell our father, by whom his kingdom was extended. Send the slanderous Purihara—let him lead your armies against the heroes of Delhi. Our heads were the pillars of Mahoba; by us were the Goands expelled, and their strong-holds, Deogarh and Chandbari, added to his sway. We maintained the field against the Jadoon, sacked Hindown, and planted his standard on the plains of Kuttair. It was I (continued Ala) who stopped the sword of the conquering Cutchwaha. The Amirs of the Sultan fled before us. At Gaya we were victorious, and added Rewah to his Kingdom. '*Anterved*' I gave to the flames and levelled to the ground the towns of Mewat. From ten princes did Jasraj bring spoil to Mahoba. This have we done; and the reward is exile from our home! Seven times have I received wounds in his service, and since my father's death gained forty battles; and from seven has Udil conveyed the record of victory to Parmal. Thrice my death seemed inevitable. The honour of his house I have upheld—yet exile is my reward."

The bard replies; "The father of Parmal left him when a child to the care of Jasraj. Your father was in lieu of his own; the son should not abandon him when misfortune makes him call on you. The Rajput who abandons his sovereign in distress will be plunged into hell. Then place on your head the loyalty of your father. Can you desire to remain at Kanuaj while he is in trouble who expended thousands in rejoicings for your birth? Malundevi (the queen), who loves you as her own, presses your return. She bids me demand of Dewalde, fulfilment of the oft-repeated vow that your life and Mahoba, when endangered, were inseparable. The breakers of vows, despised on earth, will be plunged into hell, there to remain while sun and moon endure."

Dewalde heard the message of the queen. "Let us fly to Mahoba," she exclaimed. Ala was silent, while Udil said aloud, "May evil spirits seize upon Mahoba. Can you forget the day when, in distress, he drove us forth? Return to Mahoba—let it stand or fall, it is the same to me; Kanauj is henceforth my home."

"Would that the gods had made me barren," said Dewalde, "that I had never borne sons who thus abandon the paths of the Rajput, and refuse to succour their prince in danger." Her heart bursting with grief, and her eyes raised to heaven, she continued: "Was it for this, O universal lord, thou mad'st me feel a mother's pangs for these destroyers of Binafur's fame? Unworthy offspring! the heart of the true Rajput dances with joy at the mere name of strife—but ye, degenerate, cannot be the sons of Jasraj—some carl must have stolen to my embrace, and from such ye must be sprung." This was irresistible. The young Chiefs arose, their faces withered in sadness. "When we perish in defence of Mahoba, and, covered with wounds, perform deeds that will leave a deathless name, when our heads roll in the fields, when we embrace the valiant in fight, and treading in the footsteps of the the brave, make resplendent the blood of both lines, even in the presence of the heroes of the Chohan, then will our mother rejoice."

The chieftains took leave of the King of Kanauj and returned to Mahoba. On their return a grand Council assembled at a final deliberation, at which the mother of the Binafurs and the queen Malundevi were present. The latter thus opens the debate: "Oh, mother of Ala, how may we succeed against the lord of the world? If defeated, lost is Mahoba; if we pay tribute, we are loaded with shame." Dewalde recommends hearing *seriatim* the opinions of the chieftains, when Ala thus speaks: "Listen, Oh mother, to your son! he alone is of pure lineage, who, placing loyalty on his head, abandons all thought of self, and lays down his life for his prince; my thoughts are only for Parmal. If she[1] lives, she will show herself a woman *or emanation of Parvati*. The warriors of Sambhur shall be cut in pieces. I will so illustrate the blood of my fathers that my fame shall last for ever. My son, Eendal, Oh prince! I bequeath to you, and the fame of Dewalde is in your keeping." The queen thus replies: "The warriors of the Chohan are fierce as they are numerous; pay tribute, and save Mahoba." The soul of Udil was inflamed, and turning to the queen said: "Why thought you not thus when you slew the defenceless? but then I was unheard. Whence now your wisdom? Thrice I beseeched you to pardon. Nevertheless Mahoba is safe while life remains in me, and in your cause, O Parmal! We shall espouse celestial brides."

"Well have you spoken, my son," said Dewalde, "nothing now remains but to make thy parent's milk resplendent by thy deeds. The calls of the peasant driven from his home meets the ear, and while we deliberate, our villages are given to the flames." But Parmal replied: "Saturn rules the day, to-morrow we shall meet the foe." With indignation, Ala turned to the king: "*He who can look tamely on while the smoke ascends from his ruined*

[1] Hindus do not call their wives now a days by their names.

towns, his fields laid waste, can be no Rajput: he who succumbs to fear *when his country is invaded*, his body will be plunged into the hell of hells, his soul a wanderer in the world of spirits for sixty thousand years; but the warrior who performs his duty will be received into the mansion of the sun, and his deeds will last for ever."

The heroes embraced their wives for the last time, and with the dawn, performed their religious rites. Then Ala, calling his son Eendel and Udil, his brother, he once more poured forth his vows to the universal mother, "that he would illustrate the name of Jasraj, and evince the pure blood derived from Dewalde, whenever he met the foe." "Nobly have you resolved," said Udil, "and shall not my *kirban*[1] also dazzle the eyes of Sambhur's lord? Shall he not retire from before me?" "Farewell, my children," said Dewalde, "be true to your salt, and should you lose your heads for your prince, doubt not you will obtain the celestial crown." Having ceased, the wives of both exclaimed, "What virtuous wife survives her lord?" For, thus says Goriji, "the woman who survives her husband who falls in the field of battle will never obtain bliss, but wander a discontented ghost in the region of unhallowed spirits."

The fidelity of a nurse is well exemplified by the conduct of Punna, the *dhai* of Udai Singh, son of Rana Sanga, who was a Kheechee Rajputni, when Bunbir, after killing the Rana, Bikarmajit, entered the Raola[2] to kill the heir-apparent, Udai Singh. Aware that one murder was the precursor of another, the faithful nurse put her charge into a fruit basket, and covering it with leaves, she delivered it to the *bari*, enjoining him to escape with it from the fort. Scarcely had she time to substitute her own infant in the room of the prince, when Bunbir, entering, enquired

[1] A scimitar.

[2] Queen's quarters in the palace.

for him. Her lips refused their office, she pointed to the cradle, and beheld the murderous steel buried in the heart of her babe.'[1]

The exploits of the heroic Tara Bai of Bednore and those of her gallant husband, Prithviraj, the brother of the celebrated Rana Sanga, who opposed Baber at Biana, would give a clear idea of the dominating influence which the Rajput fair exercise not only in the formation of Rajput character but on Rajput conduct throughout life.

Colonel Tod says: "Tara Bai was the daughter of Rao Surtan, the chieftain of Bednor. He was of the Solanki tribe, the lineal descendant of the famed Balhara kings of Anhulwara. Thence expelled by the arms of Alla in the thirteenth century, they migrated to Central India, and obtained possession of Tonk-Thoda and its lands on the Banas, which from remote times had been occupied (perhaps founded) by the Taks, and hence bore the name of Taksilla-nagar familiar, Takitpur and Thoda. Sham Singh had been deprived of Thoda by Lilla (Lalla Khan) the Afghan, and his son Soortan now occupied Bednore at the foot of the Aravalli, within the bounds of Mewar. Stimulated by the reverses of her family, and by the incentives of its ancient glory, Tara Bai, scorning the habiliments and occupations of her sex, learned to guide the war-horse, and to throw with unerring aim the arrow from his back, even while at speed. Armed with the bow and quiver, and mounted on a fiery Kathiawar, she joined the cavalcade in their unsuccessful attempts to wrest Thoda from the Afghan. Jaimul, the third son of Rana Raj Mul, in person made proposals for her hand. 'Redeem Thoda,' said the star of Bednore, 'and my hand is thine.' He assented to the terms; but evincing a rude determination to be possessed of the prize ere he had earned it, he was slain by the indignant father. Prithviraj, the brother of the deceased, was then an exile in

[1] Tod's Rajasthan, Vol. I, p. 315.

Marwar; he had just signalized his valour and ensured his father's forgiveness, by the redemption of Godwar, and the catastrophe at Bednore determined him to accept the gage thrown down to Jaimul. Fame and the bard had carried the renown of Prithviraj far beyond the bounds of Mewar; the name alone was attractive to the fair, and when thereto he who bore it added all the chivalrous ardour of his prototype, the Chohan, Tara Bai, with the sanction of her father, consented to be his, on the simple asseveration that 'he would restore to them Thoda or he was no true Rajput.' The anniversary of the martyrdom of the sons oj Alli was the season chosen for the exploit. Pirthviraj formed a select band of five hundred cavaliers and, accompanied by his bride, the fair Tara, who insisted on partaking of his glory and his danger, he reached Thoda at the moment the *tazzia*, or bier containing the martyr brothers, was placed in the centre of the chouk or 'square.' The prince, Tara Bai and the faithful 'Senger Chief, the insepar-able companion of Prithviraj, left their cavalcade and joined the procession as it passed under the balcony of the palace, in which the Afghan was putting on his dress preparatory to descending. Just as he had asked who were the strange horsemen that had joined the throng, the lance of Prithviraj and an arrow from the bow of his Amazonian bride stretched him on the floor. Before the crowd recovered from the panic, the three had reached the gate of the town, where their exit was obstructed by an elephant. Tara Bai with her scimitar divided his trunk, and the animal flying, they joined their cavalcade, which was close at hand.

"The Afghans were encountered, and could not stand the attack. Those who did not fly were cut to pieces; and the gallant Prithviraj conducted the father of his bride into his inheritance. A brother of the Afghans, in his attempt to recover it, lost his life. The Nawab, Mulloo Khan, then hold-ing Ajmer, determined to oppose the Sesodia prince in person, who, resolved upon being the assailant, advanced to Ajmer, encountered his foe in the camp at day-break, and after great slaughter entered Gurh Beetli, the citadel, with the fugitives, 'By these acts,' says the Chronicle, 'his fame increased in Rajwarra: one thousand Rajputs, animated by the same love of glory and devotion, gathered round the *nakarras* of Prithviraj. Their swords shone in the heavens, and were dreaded on the earth; but they aided the defenceless." [1]

The strong affection of a Hindu wife for her husband is typified in the conduct of Chandandas's wife, so beautifully described in the political drama of *Mudra Rakhshas*. [2]

The Rajput mother claims full share in the glory of her sons, who imbibes at the maternal fount his first rudiments of chivalry the importance of this parental instruction cannot be better illustrated than in the ever-recurring simile, "make thy mother's milk resplendent," the full force of which we have in the powerful though overstrained expression of the Bundi Queen's joy on the announcement of the heroic death of her son.

Nor has the Rajput mother failed to defend her son's rights with exemplary valour, and to teach her son how life should be sacrificed at the alter of the country and in defence of the country's independence. Look at the animated picture given by Ferishta of Durgavati, Queen of Gurrah, defending the rights of her infant son against Akbar's ambition. "Like another Boadcea, she headed her army and fought a desperate battle with Asafkhan, in which she was defeated and wounded. Scorning flight or to *survive the loss of independence*, she, like the antique Roman in such a predicament, slew herself on the field of battle." [3]

Durgavati was only following in the footsteps of the earlier queens, the exploits of some of whom are well known in

[1] Tod's Rajasthan, Vol. I, pp. 673, 674.
[2] See *Infra*, "Hindu Drama."
[3] Tod's Rajasthan, Vol. I, p. 642.

THE CITY OF AJMER.

Rajputana. For instance, after the death of the Rana of Chitor on the field of Thaneshwar, his heir, Kurna being a minor, Kurna's mother, Korum Devi, a princess of Patun, headed her Rajputs and gave battle in person to Kutbuddin Aibak, near Amber, when the Viceroy (Kutbuddin) was defeated and wounded."[1]

"In the second Saka of Chitor, when Bahadur, Sultan of Gujrat, invaded that far-famed fortrees, the queen-mother, Jawahir Bai, in order to set an example of courageous devotion to their country, appeared clad in armour and headed a sally, in which she was slain."[2]

During the famous assault on Chitor by Akbar, when the command of the fortrees fell on Fattah, who was only sixteen years of age at the death of the Chondawat leader, his mother displayed heroism unparalleled in history. Colonel Tod says: "When the Saloomra fell at the gate of the Sun, the command devolved on Putta (Fatta) of Kailwa. He was only sixteen: his father had fallen in the last shock, and his mother had survived but to rear this the sole heir of their house. Like the spartan mother of old, she commanded him to put on the 'saffron robe' and to die for Chitor: but surpassing the Greeian dame, she illustrated her precept by example; and lest any soft 'compunctious visitings' for one dearer than herself might dim the lustre of Kailwa, she armed the young bride with a lance, with her descended the rock, and the defenders of Chitor saw her fall, fighting by the side of her Amazonian mother. When their wives and daughters performed such deeds, the Rajputs became reckless of life."[3]

"Nor do I deem him worthy who prefers"
A friend, how dear so ever to his country.

—SOPHOCLES *Antigone.*

[1] Tod's Rajasthan, Vol I, p. 259.
[2] Tod's Rajasthan, Vol. I, p. 311.
[3] Tod's Rajasthan, Vol. I. p. 326.

An incident taken from the annals of Mewar will illustrate the strength, the courage and the general character of Rajput women. Ursi, the elder brother of the Rana Ajeysi, "being out on a hunting excursion in the forest of Ondwa, with same young chiefs of the court, in pursuit of the boar, entered a field of maize, when a woman offered to drive out the game. Pulling one of the stalks of maize, which grows to the height of ten or twelve feet, she pointed it, and mounting the platform made to watch the corn, impaled the hog, dragged him before the hunters, and departed. Though accustomed to feats of strength and heroism from the nervous arms of their countrywomen, the act surprised them. They descended to the stream at hand and prepared the repast, as is usual, on the spot. The feast was held, and comments were passing on the fair arm which had transfixed the boar, when a ball of clay from a sling fractured a limb of the prince's steed. Looking in the direction whence it came, they observed the same damsel, from her elevated stand, preserving her fields from ærial depredators; but seeing the mischief she had occasioned she descended to express regret, and then returned to her pursuit. As they were proceeding homewards after the sports of the day, they again encountered the damsel with a vessel of milk on her head, and leading in either hand a young buffalo. It was proposed, in frolic, to overturn her milk, and one of the companions of the prince dashed rudely by her; but without being disconcerted, she entangled one of her charges with the horse's limbs, and brought the rider to the ground. On inquiry the prince discovered that she was the daughter of a poor Rajput of the Chundano tribe. He returned the next day to the same quarter and sent for her father, who came and took his seat with perfect independence close to the prince, to the merriment of his companions, which was checked by Ursi asking his daughter to wife. They were yet more surprised by the demand being refused. The Rajput, on going home, told the more prudent mother, who scolded him heartily, made him recall the refusal and seek the prince. They were married, and Hamir was the son of the Chundano Rajputni.'[1]

"The romantic history of the Chohan Emperor of Delhi abounds in sketches of female character; and in the story of his carrying off Sanjogta, the princess of Kanauj, we have a faithful picture of the sex. We see her, from the moment when, rejecting the assembled princes, she threw the 'garland of marriage' round the neck of her hero, the Chohan, abandon herself to all the influences of passion, mix in a cambat of five days' continuance against her father's array, witness his overthrow and the carnage of both armies, and subsequently, by her seductive charms, lulling her lover into a neglect of every princely duty. Yet when the foes of his glory and power invade India, we see the enchantress at once start from her trance of pleasure, and exchanging the softer for the sterner passions, in accents not less strong because mingled with deep affection, she conjures him, while arming him for battle, to die for his fame, declaring that she will join him in the 'mansions of the sun."

What Hindu can read without emotion the reply of the brave and beautiful Sanjogta, then in the heyday of her honeymoon? On Prithvi's relating to her the dream, he saw the previous night, she said: "Victory and fame to my lord! Oh Sun of the Chohans, in glory or in pleasure, who has tasted so deeply as you? To die is the destiny not only of man but of the gods, all desire to throw off the old garment;

[1] Tod's Rajasthan, Vol. I, pp. 267, 268. It was this Rana Hamir who attacked, defeated and made prisoner the Khilji king, Mahmud, the sucessor of Allauddin. The king suffered a confinement of three months in Chitor. Nor was he liberated till he had surrendored Ajmer, Ranthambor, Nagaur and Soe Sopur, besides paying fifty lakhs of rupees and one hundred elephants. See Vol. I, p. 272.

but to die well is to live for ever. Think not of self, but of immortality; let your sword divide your foe, and I will be your *ardhanga* (the other half) hereafter."

The army having assembled and all being prepared to march against the Islamite, the fair Sanjogta armed her lord for the encounter. "In vain she sought the rings of his corslet; her eyes were fixed on the face of the Chohan, as those of the famished wretch who finds a piece of gold. The sound of the drum reached the ear of the Chohan; it was as a death-knell on that of Sanjogta: and as he left her to head Delhi's heroes, she vowed that henceforth water only should sustain her. I shall see him again in the region of Surya, but never more in Yoginipur."

A more recent instance of the high spirit, undaunted courage and a high sense of duty and honour displayed by a queen of Marwar, has been recorded by a Frenchman of note. In the Civil War for empire amongst the sons of Shah Jahan, when Aurangzeb opened his career by the deposal of his father and the murder of his brothers, the Rajputs, faithful to the Emperor, determined to oppose him. Under the intrepid Rahtore, Maharaja Jaswant Singh, thirty thousand Rajputs chiefly of that clan, with a Mussalman army, advanced to the Narbada, and with a magnanimity amounting to imprudence, they permitted the junction of Murad with Aurangzeb. During the night the Mussalman army treacherously passed over to Aurangzeb.

Next morning the action commenced, which continued throughout the day. The Rajputs behaved with their usual bravery, but were surrounded on all sides, and by sunset left ten thousand dead on the field. The Maharaja retreated to his own country, but his wife, "disdained (says Ferishta) to receive her lord, and shut the gates of the castle."

The French traveller, Bernier, who was present in India at the time, says: "I cannot forbear to relate the fierce reception

Emperor Shah Jahan.

which the daughter of the Rana gave to her husband, Jaswant Singh, after his defeat and flight. When she heard he was nigh, and had understood what had passed in the battle—that he had fought with all possible courage; that he had but four or five hundred men left; and at last, no longer able to resist the enemy, had been forced to retreat; instead of sending some one to condole him in his misfortunes, she commanded in a dry mood to shut the gates of the castle, and not to let this infamous man enter; that he was not her husband; that the son-in-law of the great Rana could not have so mean a soul; that he was to remember, that being grafted into so illustrious a house, he was to imitate its virtue; in a word, he was to vanquish, or to die. A moment after, she was of another humour. She commands a pile of wood to be laid, that she might burn herself; that they abused her; that her husband must needs be dead; that it could not be otherwise. And a little while after she was seen to change countenance, to fall into a passion, and break into a thousand reproaches against him. In short, she remained thus transported eight or nine days, without being able to resolve to see her husband, till at last her mother coming, brought her in time to herself, composed by assuring her that as soon as the Raja had but refreshed himself, he would raise another army to fight Aurangzeb, and repair his honour. By which story one may see a pattern of the courage of the women in that country."[1]

---

[1] Tod's Rajasthan, Vol. I. p. 622.

FOREIGN RELATIONS.

"In the theatre of the world
The people are actors all.
One doth the sovereign monarch play;
And him the rest obey."

—CALDERON.

WHEN such brilliant national character combines with such happy social organization of the people as to excite the admiration of all who study it, one can easily conceive what noble achievements of peace and war the Ancient Hindus must have accomplished. It is true, "peace hath her victories no less renowned than war"; still a peculiar halo of glory attaches to military achievements. The achievements of the Hindus in philosophy, poetry, sciences and arts prove their peaceful victories. But their military achievements were equally great, as will appear from their mastery of the science of war.

Their civilizing missions covered the globe, and Hindu civilization still flows like an under-current in the countless social institutions of the world.

In the Aiteriya Brahmana, Emperor *Sudas* is stated to have completely conquered the whole world, with its different countries.

That the Hindus were quite capable of accomplishing this feat, is clear from the remarkable article that appeared in the *Contemporary Review* from the pen of Mr. Townsend. He says: "If the Prussain conscription were applied in India, we should, without counting reserves or land'wehr or any force not summoned in time of peace, have two-and-a-half millions of soldiers actually in barracks, with 800,000 recruits coming up every year—a force with which not only Asia but the world might be subdued." [1]

[1] Contemporary Review for June 1888.

General Sir Ian Hamilton, in his Scrap Book on the first part of the Russo-Japanese War, says: "Why, there is material in the North of India and in Nepaul sufficient and fit, under good leadership, to shake the artificial society of Europe to its foundations."

The empire of India in ancient and even in mediæval times, was greater than it has ever been during the last thousand years. Pururawa is said to have possessed 13 islands of the ocean. See Mahabharata Adiparva, 3143, "*Trisdasa Samudra Ya dwipa Asnan Pururawah*, etc."

The Mahabharata (Sabha Parva, Ch. 51) describes the Romans coming to the Emperor Yudhisthira with precious presents on the occasion of the Rajasuya Yagya at Delhi.

That the Hindus were a great naval power in ancient times is clear from the fact that one of the ancestors of Rama was "Sagara, emphatically called the Sea-king, whose sixty thousand sons were so many mariners."[1]

Pliny, indeed, states that "some consider the four Satrapies of Gedrosia, Atachosia, Aria and Paropamisus to belong to India." "This would include," says Mr. Elphinstone, "about two-thirds of Persia."[2]

Chandragupta received from Seleucus, the successor of Alexander in Asia "the Satrapies of the Paropanisadai, Aria and Arachosia, the capitals of which were respectively the cities now known as Kabul, Herat and Kandahar. The Satrapy of Gedrosia, or at least the eastern portion of it, seems also to have been included in the cession."[3]

Strabo mentions a large part of Persia to have been abandoned to the Hindus by the Macedonians.[4]

[1] Tod's Rajasthan, Vol. I, p. 603.
History of India, p. 232.
[3] Vincent Smith's Early History of India, p. 112.
[4] See Strabo. Lib. XV, p. 474.

Colonel Tod says: "The annals of the Yadus of Jaisalmer state that long anterior to Vicrama, they held dominion from Ghazni to Samarkand, that they established themselves in those regions after the Mahabharata, and were again impelled on the rise of Islamism within the Indus." He adds: "A multiplicity of scattered facts and geographical distinctions fully warrants our assent to the general truth of these records, which prove that the Yadu race had dominion in Central Asia."[1] He also says: "One thing is now proved that princes of the Hindu faith ruled over all these regions in the first ages of Islamism, and made frequent attempts for centuries after to reconquer them. Of these, Baber gives us a most striking instance in his description of Gazni, or, as he writes, Ghazni when he relates how when the Rai of Hind besieged Subakhtagin in Ghazni, Subakhtagin ordered flesh of kine to be thrown into the fountain, which made the Hindus retire."[2] The celebrated Balabhi is said to have been reduced by the same stratagem.

"Bappa, the ancestor of the Ranas of Mewar, abandoned Central India after establishing his line in Chitor, and retired to Khorasan. All this proves that Hinduism prevailed in those distant regions, and that the intercourse was unrestricted between Central Asia and India."[3]

"The Bhatti Chronicle calls the Langas[4] in one page Pathan and in another Rajput, which are perfectly reconcilable, and by no means indicative that the Pathan or Afghan of that early period or even in the time of Rai Sehra was Mohammadan. The title of Rai is a sufficient proof that they were even then Hindus." Colonel Tod adds: "Khan is by no means indicative of the Mohammadan faith."[5]

[1] Tod's Rajasthan, Vol. II, p. 230.
[2] Tod's Rajasthan, Vol. II, p. 222.
[3] Tod's Rajasthan, Vol. II, p. 231.
[4] They were Solanki Rajputs.
[5] Tod's Rajasthan, Vol. II, p. 258.

Eminent Greek writers—eye-witnesses of the splendour of India—bear testimony to the prosperity of the country, which even in her decline, was sufficiently great to dazzle their imagination. The Indian Court was the happy seat to which Greek politicians repaired as ambassadors, and they all speak of it in glowing terms.

Mr. Weber says: "Thus Megasthenes was sent by Seleucus to Chandragupta,[1] Deimachus again by Antiochus and Dionysius,[2] and most probably Basilis by Ptolemy II to Amritaghata, son of Chandragupta."

Mr. Vincent Smith says: "Ptolemy Philadelphos, who ruled in Egypt from 285 to 247 B.C., also despatched an envoy named Dionysius to the Indian Court."[3]

Discussing the municipal regulations of Chandragupta, Mr. Vincent Smith says: "The existence of these elaborate regulations is conclusive proof that the Maurya Empire in the third century B.C., was in constant intercourse with foreign States and that large numbers of strangers visited the capital on business.[4]

Antiochus the Great concluded an alliance[5] with Sobhagsen about 210 B.C., but was eventually defeated and slain by him. Colonel Tod says: "The obscure legends of the encounters of the Yadus with the allied Syrian and Bactrian kings would have seemed altogether illusory did not evidence exist that Antiochus the Great was slain in these very regions by the Hindu king Sobhagsen."[6]

[1] Weber's Indian Literature, page 251, footnote.

[2] Max Duncker's History of Antiquity, Vol. IV, page 453.

[3] Early History of India, page 130.

[4] Early History of India, page 125.

[5] Wilson's Vishnu Purana, Vol. II, page 181.

[6] Tod's Rajasthan, Vol. II, page 230.

The Greek king Seleucus, even gave Chandragupta his daughter to wife.[1] Professor Weber says: "In the retinue of this Greek princess there of course came to Patliputra, Greek damsels as her waiting-maids, and these have found particular favour in the eyes of the Indians, especially of their princes. For not only are..............mentioned as articles of traffic for India, but in Indian inscriptions also we find Yavan girls specified as tribute; while in Indian literature, and especially in Kalidasa, we are informed that indian princes were waited upon by Yavanis (Greek damsels): Lassen, I. A. K. ii, 551, 957, and Preface to Malavika, page xlvii "[2]

Prof. MacDonell says: "Indian inscriptions mention Yavana or Greek girls sent to India as tribute, and Sanskrit scholars, specially Kalidasa describes Indian princes as waited on by them."[3]

Mr. Vincent Smith says that "European soldiers described as powerful Yavans and dumb Mlechhas (barbarians) clad in complete armour, acted as body-guards to Tamil Kings."[4]

Mr. Pillay says: "Roman soldiers were enlisted in the service of a Pandyan and other Tamil Kings," and further, "Raman soldiers were employed to guard the gates of the fort of Madura."[5]

Even the Ramayana says that in Ayodhia, ambassadors from different countries resided.[6] Augustus received at Samos an embassy from India The ambassadors brought elephants, pearls and precious stones.

[1] Lassen, I. A. K. ii, 208: T. Wheeler's History of India (1874), page 177.

[2] Weber's Indian Literature, pp. 251, 252, footnote.

[3] MacDonell's Sanskrit Literature, p. 415.

[4] Early History of India, pp. 400, 401.

[5] The Tamils Eighteen Hundred Years Ago, Chapter III.

[6] Mrs. Manning's Ancient and Mediæval India, Vol. II, page 27.

Strabo[1] mentions an ambassador from King Pandion to Augustus, who met him in Syria. It appears from Periplus and Ptolemy that Pandion was the hereditary title of the descendants of 'Pandya, who founded the kingdom in the fifth century B.C.[2]

The embassies to Augustus are alluded to by Dion Cassius,[3] by Florus[4] and Orosius.[5] There was an embassy from India sent to Emperor Claudius, of which Pliny gives an account. He received from the ambassadors, who were four in number, the information about Ceylon which he has embodied in his Natural History. Two other embassies from Hindu princes to Rome were sent before the third century A.C., one toTrajan (107 A.C.) and another to Antonius Pius. Dion Cassius (A.D. 180) speaks of Trajan receiving many embassies from Indians.[6] Ammianus Marcellinus speaks of embassies sent by Indians to Emperor Julian in 361 A.D.[7] These relations continued to exist as late as the time of Justinian (530 A.C.)

Mr. Vincent Smith says of the Buddhist propaganda of Asoka: "Before the year 256 B.C. when the Rock edicts were Published collectively, the royal missionaries had been despatched to all the protected States and tribes on the frontiers of the empire, to Ceylon and to the Hellenistic monarchies of Syria, Egypt, Cyrene, Macedonia, and Epirus, then governed respectively by Antrochostheos, Ptolemy Philadelphos, Magas, Antigonos

[1] Lib. XV, page, 663.

[2] Elphinstone's History of India, page 218. A Brahmin followed this ambassador to Athens, where he burnt himself alive,

[3] History of Rome IX, 73.

[4] Epitome of Roman History, IV. p, 12.

[5] History, VI, page 12.

[6] History of Rome, Vol. IX, page 58.

[7] History of Rome, Vol. XXII, VII, page 10.

Gonatas, and Alexander. The Missionary organization thus embraced three continents, Asia, Africa and Europe." [1]

Thus, when even in those days, India was so great as to exact the homage of all who saw her, though her grand political and social institutions had lost their pristine purity and vigour, and those mighty forces which worked for her welfare and greatness were disappearing, when even in her fall she was the idol of foreign nations, how mighty must she have been when she was at the height of her power, at the zenith of her glory! Her constitution still stands like some tall ancient oak in a forest shorn of foliage, but still defying the discordant elements that rage round it, still looking down, with a majesty and dignity all its own, upon the new-sprung, prosperous young trees growing round it in happy ignorance of the storms and gusts in store.

It is curious to learn that even in her decline, India was sufficiently strong to defy the great conquerors of the old world. It was threatened by the prosperous empire of Assyria, then at the meridian of her power, under the celebrated queen Semiramis. She used the entire resources of the empire in preparations to invade India, and collected a considerable army. "After three years spent in these extraordinary preparations, she sent forward her armies, which some writers discribe as amounting to several millions of cambatants, but the narrative of Ctesias estimates them at three hundred thousand foot, five hundred thousand horse, while two thousand boats and a great number of mock elephants were conveyed on the backs of camels" But what

[1] Early History of India, Vol. X, page 161. "In one of Asoka's inscriptions, five Greek princes appear: (1) Antiochus of Syria, (2) Ptolemy Philadelphos of Egypt, (3) Antigonos Gonatos of Macedon, (4) Magas of Cereno, (5) Alexander II of Epirus." "Great intercourse," says a writer, "formerly subsisted between the Hindus and the nations of the West." See Asiatic Researches, Vol. III, pp. 297-298.

was the result? "The army was utterly routed and Semiramis brought back scarcely a third of her host; some authors even maintain that she herself perished in the expedition"[1]

> Horrid suggestion! thinkest thou then the gods
> Take care of men who came to burn their altars,
> Profane their rites, and trample on their laws?
> Will they reward the bad? It cannot be.
>
> —SOPHOCLES: *Antigone*.

Alexander the Great with his fine army was able to gain only one victory over a small Hindu Kingdom and that with the aid of another Hindu chief, the King of Takshashila.[2] The advance of Maharaja Mahanand of Maghada struck terror in the army of Alexander and had he advanced further the Great Alexander would have shared the fate of the Assyrian Semiramis. The Macedonian general Kainos, foresaw the danger. Mr. Vincent Smith says: "Kainos and his fellow-remonstrants may be credited with having prevented the annihilation of the Macedonian army."[3]

In later times, the Yadu king, Gaj Singh, who founded Gajni (Ghazni), single-handed "defeated the combined armies of Shah Secunder Roomi and Shah Mamraiz."[4]

[1] Murray's History of India, page 30.

[2] Sir William Hunter says: "The Hindu King Mophis of Taxila joined Alexander with 5,000 men against Porus."—Imperial Gazetteer, "India," page 263. It may be remembered that it was with the help of the traitors Sasigupta (Sasikottos) and others that Alexander obtained a footing in the Swat valley and conquered the Usufzi country.

Professor Max Duncker says that when Alexander attacked Porus "his army was twice as strong and had been yet further increased by 5,000 Indians from Mophis and some smaller States."—History of Antiquity, Vol. IV, page 399.

[3] Early History of India, page 104.

[4] Tod's Rajasthan, Vol. II, page 222.

HINDU COLONIZATION OF THE WORLD.

All places, that the eye of heaven visits
Are to a wise man ports and happy heavens;
Teach thy necessity to reason thus:
There is no virtue like necessity.

—SHAKESPEARE: *Richard II.*

THE turning point in the history of India, nay, in the history of the world, was the Mahabharata—the death-stroke to Indian prosperity and glory. Before this catastrophe, Hindu civilization was in full vigour. It declined gradually after the Mahabharata, till it was attacked first by the semi-barbarism coming from the north-west, and then by the European civilization. Simplicity with refinement, honesty with happiness, self-denial with plenty, and glory with power and peace, were the splendid results of the Hindu civilization.

The Mahabharata was a war not only between man and man, but between the two aspects of the heart, the two phases of the mind.

There are two remarkable features of that period, differing in nature but coinciding in their effect on India. These were *destruction* and *emigration*. The good and the great men of India either emigrated or were killed: the effect upon India was the same—inimical to her prosperity. Whole tribes were killed: whole races emigrated. It is true that, in addition to many civilizing expeditions, there had been tribal emigrations before that momentous period too. These emigrations, like the settlements and colonies of Ancient Greece, differed in an important respect from the modern settlements of the Europeans. The Grecian settlements attracted the best men of Greece; and the

Indian emigrations helped powerfully to set in motion those disintegrating forces that have undermined our national superiority, destroyed our independence and ruined our society and religion.

But there is no evil that is an unmixed evil: to every cloud there is a silver lining. In the present case, India's loss was the world's gain. Though India's greatness began to decline, the entire Western world, from Persia to Britain, received in the colonists the seeds of their future greatness. The Mahabharata was thus fraught with world-wide consequences.

"But perhaps, in no similar instance have events occurred fraught with consequences of such magnitude, as those flowing from the great religious war which, for a long series of years, raged throughout the length and breadth of India. That contest ended by the expulsion of vast bodies of men, many of them skilled in the arts of early civilization, and still greater numbers warriors by profession. Driven beyond the Himalayan mountains in the north, and to Ceylon, their last stronghold in the south, swept across the valley of the Indus of the west, this persecuted people carried with them the germs of the European arts and sciences. The mighty human tide that passed the barrier of the Punjab, rolled onward towards its destined channel in Europe and in Asia, to fulfil its beneficent office in the moral fertilization of the world."[1]

It is, of course, true that emigration from India had been going on from time immemorial. Notwithstanding the marvellous fertility of the soil and the wonderful industries that flourished in the country, India had to plant colonies to provide for her superabundant population. Professor Heeren says: "How could such a thickly-peopled, and in some parts over-peopled country as India have disposed of her superabundant

[1] India in Greece, page 26.

population except by planting colonies; even though intestine broils (witness the expulsion of the Buddhists) had not obliged her to have recourse to such an expedient?"[1]

The earliest emigration appears to date sometime after Manu. One of the oldest colonies founded by the Hindus was in Egypt; America, with some other countries, was also colonised before the last great migration. The principal migration to Greece took place soon after the Great War. The word *Kapi*[2] for ape appears in the hieroglyphic writings of Greece of the 17th century B.C., which shows that the colonization of Greece must be dated long anterior to the era of Moses.

It would perhaps be interesting to know the exact time when the Mahabharata took place.

In determining dates our efforts are clogged by the dearth of historical records. But it is not in historical literature *alone* that we have to mourn this loss. Every branch of literature, every science and art has suffered from ravages of ignorant fanaticism. Some have disappeared completely; others have come down to us in a more or less mutilated form. The present scarcity of historical works, however, should not be regarded as a proof of the absence of the Art of History any more than the present poverty of the country be accepted as a proof of its indigence in ancient times.

For one thing, the enmity of Aurangzeb towards all historical writings is well known. But it is the Arab, the Afghan and the Tartar semi-barbarism that is responsible for the destruction of literature, whether in Egypt or in India, in Persia or in Greece. The destruction of the Alexandrian library was one of those notorious feats by which the progress of humanity was put back by a thousand years. But the loss to humanity

[1] Historical Researches, Vol II, page 310.

[2] Weber's Indian Literature, page 3.

by the wholesale destruction of the libraries of India is beyond calculation. That eminent antiquarian and explorer, Rai Bahadur Sarat Chander Das, says: "In the lofty nine-storied temple at Buddha Gaya, which was formerly called the Mahagandhola (Gandhalaya), the images of the past Buddhas were enshrined. The nine-storied temple called Ratandadhi of Dharamganja (university) of Nalanda was the repository of the sacred books of the Mahayana and Hinayana Buddhist schools. The temple of Odantapuri *Vihara*, which is said to have been loftier than either of the two (Buddha Gaya and Nalanda) contained a vast collection of Buddhist and Brahminical works, which, after the manner of the great Alexandrian Library, was burnt under the orders of Mohammad Ben Sam, General of Bakhtyar Khilji, in 1212, A.D."[1]

Sultan Alla-ud-din Khilji burnt the famous library at Anhalwara Pattan. The *Tarikh Firoz Shahi* says that Firoz Shah Tughlak burnt a large library of Sanskrit books at Kohana. Sayad Ghulam Husein, in his well-known book, *Sair-ul-Mutakhreen* (Vol. I, page 140), says: "Sultan Sikander (Aurangzeb) was the most bigoted of the Sultans, and burnt the books of the Hindus whenever and wherever he got them."

Instances of such savagery could be multiplied easily. These are all manifestations of that mental aberration to which humanity is evidently subject at intervals, the disease being the same; the occasion may be the outrages committed by the Goths and Vandals of earlier times or the Afghans and the Turks of the later day.[2]

[1] The Hindustan Review for March 1906, page 187 (Universities in Ancient India).

[2] The Turks who sacked Nishapur in Turkistan in Hijra era 549 burnt down all libraries at that place of learning.

Mr. Dow, in the Preface to his History of Hindustan observes: "We must not, with Ferishta, consider the Hindus as destitute of genuine domestic annals, or that those voluminous records they possess are mere legends framed by Brahmans." Mr. Wilson, with his usual fairness, remarks that "it is incorrect to say that the Hindus never compiled history. The literature of the south abounds with local histories of Hindu authors. Mr. Stirling found various chronicles in Orissa, and Colonel Tod has met with equally abundant material in Rajputana." [1]

Professor Heeren says: "Wilson's translation of *Raj Taranqini*, a history of Kashmir, has clearly demonstrated that regular historical composition was an art not unknown in Hindustan, and affords satisfactory grounds for concluding that these productions were once less rare, and that futher exertions may bring more relics to light." [2]

Professor Wilson's assertion that "genealogies [3] and chronicles are found in various parts of India recorded with some perseverance," will be supported by all who know Hindu society.

The critics who resolutely deny the existence of the art in Ancient India on the plea that very few of the productions of the art are to be found, will do well to consider the fact that even the Vedas would have been lost had the old regime continued a century or so longer without giving birth to a Dayanand. When such has been the lot of their most adored possession, what better fate could the poor Art of History have aspired to meet?

[1] Mill's India, Volume II, page 67, footnote.

[2] Heeren's Historical Researches, Vol. II, page 143.

[3] The genealogies are still kept and are to be found in almost every part of Hindustan proper. In Rajputana, where they are regularly kept, you may select any man, and after a little search you can generally find out the names and abodes of every member of his ancestral family for about twenty generations back. There is a clan named "*Jagas* who have made this their hereditary profession.

The illustrious Colonel Tod says: "If we consider the political changes and convulsions which have happened in Hindustan since Mahmud's invasion, and the intolerant bigotry of many of his successors, we shall be able to account for the paucity of its national works on history, without being driven to the improbable conclusion, that the Hindus were ignorant of an art which was cultivated in other countries from almost the earliest ages. Is it to be imagined that a nation so highly civilized as the Hindus, amongst whom the exact sciences flourished in perfection, by whom the fine arts, architecture, sculpture, poetry and music were not only cultivated, but taught and defined by the nicest and most elaborate rules, were totally unacquainted with the simple art of recording the event of their history, the characters of their princes, and the acts of their reigns?"[1]

He then asks, whence did Abdul Fazul obtain the materials for his Ancient History of India, if there were no historical records in existence at the time? This, he declares, sufficiently proves the existence of the art. Then, again, he says that in Chund's heroic account of Prithvi Raj, we find notices which authorise the inference that works similar to his own were then extant.[2]

It must not be supposed that the authors of these works were ignorant bards. We find that Chund's history contains chapters on laws for governing empires; lessons on diplomacy: home and foreign. See also the admirable remarks of the French Orientalist, Monsieur Abel Remsat, in his *Melanges Asiatiques*.

[1] Introduction to Tod's Rajasthan.

[2] In Rajputana many historcial works are to be found, such as (1) Vijaya Vilas, (2) Surya Prakash, (3) Kheat, (4) Jagat Vilas, (5) Raj Prakash, (6) Jai Vilas, (7) Khoman Rasa, (8) Maun Charitra. The last two are comparatively of recent date. See *Rasamala* or Hindu Annals of the Province of Gujrat, by the Honourable A. K. Forbes, 1890 (Bombay).

Since the time of Col. Tod, a number of historical works and books on political science have been discovered. Kautilya's *Artha Shastra* (4th century B.C.) has attained world-wide celebrity. Among the other historical works since found are: Harshacharita of Bana, Gaudavaho, Navasahasanka Charita, Vikramankadevacharita, Prithvirajavijaya, Ramacharita, Dvyashrayakavya, Ballalacharita, four Kumarapala Charitas, Kirtikaumudi Sukritasankirtana, Prabandhachintamani, Prabandhakosha, Vastupalacharita, Dammiramahakavya Mandalikakavya, etc.

But to return to the point. Swami Dayanand Saraswati, in his *Bhumika*, says that 5,007 years have passed since the beginning of the Kaliyuga era. The *Siddhanta Siromani*, one of the most popular of the Hindu works on Astronomy, says that the Kaliyug era, at the time of the establishment of the Salivahan era, was 3,179. It says: याताः षण्मनवो युगानि भमितान्यन्यद्युगाङ्घ्रित्रयं। नन्दाद्रीन्दुगुणास्तथा शकनृपस्यान्ते कलेर्वत्सराः॥

The Salivahan era at present (1916 A.D.) is 1838: so that the Kaliyuga era should now be 3179 + 1838 = 5017.

The *Varahi Sanhita* of Varahamihar says that the constellation *Saptarishi* was in *Magha Nakhshatra* in the reign of Yudhishtira, and that the date of his reign may be obtained by adding 2,526 to the Salivahan era. According to this, Yudhishtira reigned 2,526 + 1,838 = 4,364 years ago.

आसन् मघासु मुनयः शासति पृथ्वीं युधिष्ठिरे नृपतौ।
षड्द्विकपञ्चद्वि (२५२६) युतः शककालस्तस्य राज्ञश्च॥

वाराही संहिता। अ० १३॥

Kalhan Bhatta, in his famous work, *Raj Taringini*, says that Kauravas and Pandavas flourished when 653 years of the Kalyuga era had passed.

शतेषु षट्सु सार्द्धेषु त्र्यधिकेषु (६५३) च भूतले।
कलेर्गतेषु वर्षाणामभवन् कुरुपांडवाः॥

राजतरंगिणी, त० १, श्लोक ५१॥

This, too, shows that 4,364 + 653 = 5,017 years have passed since the commencement of the Kaliyuga era.

The astronomers, Parasar and Arya Bhatta respectively, hold that the Mahabharata took place $666\frac{2}{30}$ years and $662\frac{2}{5}$ years after the commencement of the Kaliyuga.[1]

Vrahadgarga Muni, on the contrary, holds that the *saptarishi* were in the *Magha Nakhshatra* at the junction of the Dwapar and the Kaliyuga. He says:—

कलिद्वापरसंधौ तु स्थितास्ते पितृदैवतम् (मघा) ।
मुनयोः धर्मनिरताः प्रजानां पालने रताः ॥

According to him, therefore, Yudhishtira flourished at the beginning of the Kaliyuga.

An inscription in a Jain temple on a hill near Ahole, Kaladagi district, Deccan, says that the temple, built by King Pulkeshi II, of the Chalukya family, was erected 3,735 years after the Mahabharata, and when 556 years of the *Saka* era had passed, thus proving that the Great War took place 3,735—556=3,179 years before the Saka era; in other words, 3173+1838 (Saka era)=5017 years ago. The inscription runs as follows:—

त्रिंशत्सु त्रिसहस्रेषु भारतादाहवादितः ।
सप्ताब्दशतयुक्तेषु श (ग) तेष्वब्देषु पञ्चसु (३७३५)
पंचाशत्सु कलौ काले षट्सु पंचशतासु च (५५६) ।
समासु समतीतासु शकानामपि भूभुजाम् ॥

Following evidently the view held by Vrahadgarga Muni, the author of the *Ayeen-i-Akbari* says that Vicramaditya ascended the throne in the 3,044th year of the Yudhishtira era. This also makes the Yudhishtira era begin 3044+1973 (Vicrama era) =5,017 years ago.

Thus, the authorities are all agreed that the Kaliyuga commenced 5,017 years ago: opinion, however, is divided as to when the Great war took place. Tradition seems to says that

[1] "Indian Eras," p. 8.

the Mahabharata took place at the commencement of the Kaliyuga, while the astronomers think that it took place about the middle of the 7th century of the Kaliyuga era. Whichever view is correct, we know, on a comparison of these times with the dates of Scriptural history, that the Kaliyuga era commenced before the birth of Noah, and that the Great War took place either before his time or soon after it.

The migrations from India, as stated before, took place Eastwards as well as westwards and northwards. The Eastern migrations were to the Transgangetic Peninsula, to China, to the islands of the Indian Archipelago, and to America. The Northern and the North-western to Turkistan, Siberia, Scandinavia, Germany and Britain, as well as to Persia, Greece, Rome and Etruria: the Western, to the eastern parts of Africa, and thence to Egypt. We find that Epypt, Persia, Assyria and Greece all derived the rudiments of their learning and civilization from India, and that the Egyptian, the Assyrian, the Grecian, the German, the Scandinavian and the Druidic mythologies were all derived from the Hindu mythology.

Sir Walter Raleigh strongly supports the Hindu hypothesis regarding the locality of the nursery for rearing mankind and that India was the first peopled country.[1]

The Central Asian theory of emigration is unable to meet the difficulty presented by the fact that "the Astronomy of the Hindus and of the Chinese appear to be the remains rather than the elements of a Science." The advocates of the theory are obliged to assume that in ancient times a nation existed more advanced than either, the remains of whose achievements in Science still survive in the literature of the Hindus and the Chinese.

[1] History of the World, p. 99. He would at once have found the origin of *Ararat* had he known that the Hindus call their country "Aryavarta."

"That the Hindus, the Persians, the Egyptians and the Chinese, from the earliest periods of their history, divided the time alike, namely, the year into 12 months and $365\frac{1}{4}$ days, and the day into 24 hours: that they divided the Zodiac alike into 12 signs: that they divided the week alike into seven days, which being an arbitrary division, could not be the result of accident, but proves that they obtained it from the common source of an ancient people who already possessed a high degree of civilization." But what nation flourished anterior to the Hindus, the Chinese and the Persians, no one has yet theorised; much less has it been proved that that primitive nation attained to a high degree of civilization. On the contrary, all competent authorities are unanimous in holding that "Hinduism (Hindu Literature, Science and Arts) developed itself on the shores of the Ganges and the Jumna," and that "the Hindu civilization originated and attained to its highest pitch only in India."

There is thus an abrupt break in the Central Asian theory of emigration. The theory sketched out in the following pages satisfactorily explains all such difficulties. Count Bjornstjerna[1] says: "It is there (Aryavarta) we must seek not only for the cradle of the Brahmin religion, but for the cradle of the high civilization of the Hindus, which gradually extended itself in the West to Ethiopia, to Egypt, to Phœnicia; in the East, to Siam, to China, and to Japan; in the South, Ceylon, to Java and to Sumatra; in the North, to Persia to Caldæa and to Colchis, whence it came to Greece and to Rome, and at length to the remote abode of the Hyperboreans."

Colonel Olcott says: "The modern school of comparative Philology traces the migration of Aryan civilization into Europe by a study of modern languages in comparison with the Sanskrit. And we have an equally, if not a still more striking means

[1] Theogony of the Hindus, p. 168.

of knowing the outflow of Aryan thought towards the West in the philosophies and religious of Babylonia, Egypt, Rome and Northern Europe. One has only to put side by side the teachings of Pythagoras, Socrates, Plato, Aristotle, Homer, Zeno, Hesiod, Cicero, Scœvola, Varro and Virgil with those of Veda-Vyasa, Kapila, Gautama, Patanjali, Kanada, Jaimini, Narada, Panini, Marichi, and many others we might mention, to be astonished at their identity of conceptions—an identity that upon any other theory than that of a derivation of the younger philosophical schools of the West from the older ones of the East would be simply miraculous. The human mind is certainly capable of evolving like ideas in different ages, just as humanity produces for itself in each generation the teachers, rulers, warriors and artisans it needs. But that the views of the Aryan sages should be so identical with those of the latter Greek and Roman philosophers as to seem as if the latter were to the former like the reflection of an object in a mirror to the object itself, without an actual physical transmission of teacher or books from the East to the West, is something opposed to common sense. And this again corroborates our convictions that the old Egyptians were emigrants from India; nearly all the famous ancient philosophers *had been to Egypt to learn her wisdom*, from the Jewish Moses to the Greek Plato."[1]

Sir William Jones says: "Of the cursory observations on the Hindus, which it would require volumes to expand and illustrate, this is the result, that they had an immemorial affinity with the old Persians, Ethiopians and Egyptians, the Phœnicians, Greeks and Tuscans, the Scythians, or Goths, and Celts, the Chinese, Japanese, and Peruvians."[2]

[1] See the Theosophist for March 1881, p. 124.

[2] Asiatic Researches, Vol. I, p. 426.

EGYPT AND ETHIOPIA.

In the afternoon they came unto a land,
In which it seemed always afternoon.

TENNYSON: *Lotus Eaters.*

EGYPT was originally a colony of the Hindus. It appears that about seven or eight thousand years ago a body of colonists from India settled in Egypt, where they established one of the mightiest empires of the old world. Colonel Olcott says: "We have a right to more than suspect that India, eight thousand years ago, sent a colony of emigrants who carried their arts and high civilization into what is now known to us as Egypt. This is what Brugsch Bey, the most modern as well as the most trusted Egyptologer and antiquarian, says on the origin of the old Egyptians. Regarding these a branch of the Caucasian family having a close affinity with the Indo-Germanic races, he insists that they 'migrated from India long before historic memory, and crossed that bridge of nations, the Isthmus of Suez, to find a new fatherland on the banks of the Nile. The Egyptains came, according to their own records, from a mysterious land (now shown to lie on the shore of the Indian ocean), the sacred Punt; the original home of their gods who followed thence after their people who had abandoned them to the valley of the Nile, led by Amon, Hor and Hathor. This region was the Egyptian "Land of the Gods." Pa-Nuter, in old Egyptian, or Holyland, and now proved beyond any doubt to have been quite a different place from the Holyland of Sinai. By the Pictorial hieroglyphic inscription found (and interpreted) on the walls of the temple of the Queen Haslitop at Der-el-babri, we see that this Punt can be no other than India. For many ages the Egyptians traded with their old homes, and the reference here made by them to the names of the Princes of Punt and its fauna and flora, especially the nomenclature of various precious woods to be found but in India, leave us scarcely room for the smallest doubt that the old civilization of Egypt is the direct outcome of that of the older India."[1]

The author of "India in Greece" says: "At the mouth of the Indus dwell a seafaring people, active, ingenious, and enterprising, as when, ages subsequent to this great movement, they themselves, with the warlike denizens of the Punjab, were driven from their native land to seek the far-distant climes of Greece. The commercial people dwelling along the coast that stretches from the mouth of the Indus to the Coree, are embarking on that emigration whose magnificent result to civilization, and whose gigantic monuments of art, fill the mind with mingled emotions of admiration and awe. These people coast along the shores of Mekran, traverse the mouth of the Persian Gulf, and again adhering to the sea-board of Oman, Hadramant and Yeman (the Eastern Arabia), they sail up the Red Sea; and again ascending the mighty stream that fertilises a land of wonders, found the kingdoms of Egypt, Nubia, and Abyssinia. These are the same stock that centuries subsequently to this colonization, spread the blessings of civilization over Hellas and her islands."[2]

Mr. Pococke thus summarises his researches: "I would now briefly recapitutate the leading evidences of the colonization of Africa from North-western India and the Himalaya province. *First* from the provinces or rivers deriving their names from the great rivers of India; *secondly*, from the towns and provinces of India or its northern frontiers; *thirdly*, from the Ruling Chiefs styled Ramas (Rameses), etc.; *fourthly*, similarity in the objects of sculpture; *fifthly*, architectural skill and its grand and gigantic

[1] See the Theosophist for March 1881, p. 123.
[2] India in Greece, p. 42.

character; and *sixthly*, the power of translating words, imagined to be Egyptian, through the medium of a modified Sanskrit."[1]

Apart from the historical evidence there are ethnological grounds to support the fact that the Ancient Egyptians were originally an Indian people. Professor Heeren is astonished at the "physical similarity in colour and in the conformation of the head" of the Ancient Egyptians and the Hindus. As regards the latter point, he adds: "As to the form of the head, I have now before me the skulls of a mummy and a native of Bengal from the collections of M. Blumenbach; and it is impossible to conceive anything more striking than the resemblance between the two, both as respects the general form and the structure of the firm portions. Indeed, the learned possessor himself considers them to be the most alike of any in his numerous collections."[2]

After showing the still more striking similarity between the manners and customs, in fact, between the social, religious and political institutions of the two peoples, Professor Heeren says: "It is perfectly agreeable to Hindu manners that colonies from India, *i.e.*, Banian families should have passed over into Africa, and carried with them their industry, and perhaps also their religious worship."[3] He adds: "It is hardly possible to maintain the opposite side of the question, *viz.*, that the Hindus were derived from the Egyptians, for it has been already ascertained that the country bordering on the Ganges was the cradle of Hindu civilization. Now the Egyptians could not have established themselves in that neighbourhood, their probable settlement would rather have taken place on the Coast of Malabar."

[1] India in Greece, p. 201.

[2] Heeren's Asiatic Nations, Vol. II, p. 303.

[3] Heeren's Historical Researches, Vol. II, p. 309.

The learned professor concludes: "Whatever weight may be attached *to Indian tradition and the express testimony of Eusebius* confirming the report of migrations from the banks of the Indus into Egypt, there is certainly nothing inprobable in the event itself, as a desire of gain would have formed a sufficient inducement." Decisive evidence of the fact, however, may be found in Philostratus and Nonnus. For further information on the subject, *vide* Religion.[1]

Ethiopia,[2] as is universally admitted now, was colonised by the Hindus. Sir W. Jones says: "Ethiopia and Hindustan were possessed or colonised by the same extraordinary race."[3]

Philostratus introduces the Brahman Iarchus by stating to his auditor that the Ethopians were originally an *Indian race* compelled to leave India for the impurity contracted by slaying a certain monarch to whom they owed allegiance.[4]

Eusebius states that Ethiopians emigrating from the river Indus settled in the vicinity of Egypt.[5]

In Philostratus, an Egyptian is made to remark that he had heard from his father that the Indians were the wisest of men, and that the Ethiopians, a colony of the Indians, preserved the wisdom and usage of their forefathers and acknowledged their ancient origin. We find the same assertion made at a later period,

[1] Mr. Pococke, who made the subject his life-long study, says: "The early civilization, the early arts, the indubitably early literature of India are equally the civilization, the arts and literature of Egypt and of Greece—for geographical evidences, conjoined to historical fact and religious practices, now prove beyond all dispute that the two latter countries are the colonies of the former."—India in Greece, p. 74.

[2] "The ancient geographers called by the name of Ethiopia all that part of Africa which now constitutes Nubia, Abyssinia, Sanaor, Darfur, and Dongola."—Theogony of the Hindus, p. 44.

[3] Asiatic Researches, Vol. I, p. 426.

[4] V. A. III, 6, See "India in Greece," p. 200.

[5] Lemp. Barker's edition; "Meroe."

in the third century, by Julius Africanus, from whom it has been preserved by Eusebius and Syncellus.[1]

Cuvier, quoting Syncellus, even assigns the reign of Amenophis as the epoch of the colonization of Ethiopia from India.[2]

The Ancient Abyssinians (Abusinians), as already remarked were originally migrators to Africa from the banks of Abuisin, a classical name for the Indus,[3]

As will appear from the accounts of the commercial position of India in the ancient world, commerce on an extensive scale existed between Ancient India and Abyssinia, and we find Hindus in large numbers settled in the latter country, "whence also," says Colonel Tod, "the Hindu names of towns at the estuaries of the Gambia and Senegal rivers, the Tamba Cunda and another Cundas." He continues: "A writer in the *Asiatic Journal* (Vol. IV, p. 325) gives a curious list of the names of places in the interior of Africa, mentioned in Park's Second Journey, which are shown to be all Sanskrit, and most of them actually current in India at the present day."[4]

PERSIA.

Not vainly did the early Persian make
His altar the high places, and the peak
Of earth—o'ergazing mountains, and thus take
A fit and unwalled temple, there to seek
The spirit, in whose honour shrines are weak,
Upreared of human hands.

BYRON: *Childe Harold.*

Professor Max Muller thus speaks of the colonization of Persia by the Hindus. Discussing the word 'Arya,' he says: "But it was more faithfully preserved by the Zoroastrians, who mig-

[1] See "India in Greece," p. 205.
[2] P. 18 of his "Discourse," etc.
[3] Heeren's Historical Researches, Vol. II, p. 310.
[4] See Tod's Rajasthan, Vol. II. p. 309, footnote.

rated from India to the North-west and whose religion has been preserved to us in the Zind Avesta, though in fragments only."[1] He again says: "The Zoroastrians were a colony from Northern India."[2]

Professor Heeren says: "In point of fact the Zind is derived from the Sanskrit, and a passage in Manu (Chapter X, Slokas 43-45) makes the Persians to have descended from the Hindus of the second or Warrior caste."[3]

शनकैस्तु क्रियालोपादिमाः क्षत्रियजातयः ।
वृषलत्वं गता लोके ब्राह्मणादर्शनेन च ॥
पौण्ड्रकाश्चौड्रद्रविडाः काम्बोजाः यवनाः शकाः ।
पारदाः पल्हवाश्चीनाः किराताः दरदाः खशाः ॥

Sir W. Jones says: "I was not a little surprised to find that out of ten words in Du Perron's Zind Dictionary, six or seven were pure Sanskrit."[4]

Mr. Haug, in an interesting essay on the origin of Zoroastrian religion, compares it with Brahminism, and points out the originally-close connection between the Brahminical and the Zoroastrian religions, customs and observances. After comparing names of divine beings, names and legends of heroes, sacrificial rites, religious observances, domestic rites, and cosmographical opinions that occur both in the Vedic and Avesta writings, he says: "In the Vedas as well as in the older portions of the Zind-Avesta (see the Gathas), their are sufficient traces to be discovered that the Zoroastrian religion arose out of a vital struggle against a form which the Brahminical religion had assumed at a certain early period."[5]

After contrasting the names of the Hindu gods and the Zoroastrian deities, Professor Haug says: "These facts throw

[1] Science of Language, p. 242.
[2] Science of Language, p. 253.
[3] Historical Researches, Vol. II, p. 220.
[4] Sir W. Jones' Works, Vol. I, pp. 82 and 83.
[5] Haug's Essays on the Parsees, p. 287.

some light upon the age in which that great religious struggle took place, the consequence of which was *the entire separation of the Ancient Iranians from the Brahmans* and the foundation of the Zoroastrian religion. It must have occurred at the time when Indra was the chief god of the Brahmans."[1]

It is not an easy matter to ascertain the exact period at which the Hindu colonization of Persia took place. It is certain, however, that it took place long before the Mahabharata. Col. Tod says: "Ujameda, by his wife, Nila, had five sons, who spread their branches on both sides of the Indus. Regarding three the Puranas are silent, which implies their migration to distant regions. Is it possible they might be the origin of the Medes? These Medes are descendants of *Yayat, third son of the patriarch, Menu:* and *Madai*, founder of the Medes, was of Japhet's line. *Aja Mede*, the patronymic of the branch of Bajaswa, is from Aja 'a goat.' The Assyrian Mede in Scripture is typified by the goat."[2]

Apart from the passage in Manu,[3] describing the origin of the Ancient Persians, there is another argument to support it. Zoroaster, the Prophet of the Ancient Persians, was born after the emigrants from India had settled in Persia long enough to have become a separate nation. Vyasa held a grand religious discussion with Zoroaster at Balkh in Turkistan, and was therefore his contemporary. Zanthus of Lydia (B.C. 470), the earliest Greek writer, who mentions Zoroaster, says that he lived about six hundred years before the Trojan War (which took place about 1800 B.C.). Aristotle and Eudoxus place his era as

[1] Haug's Essays on the Parsees, p. 288.

Of great importance for showing the originally-close relationship between the Brahminical and Parsi religions, is the fact that several of the Indian gods are actually mentioned by name in the Zind Avesta, some as demons, others as angels:—Haug's Essays, p. 272.

[2] Tod's Rajasthan, Vol. I, p. 41.

[3] Manusmriti is admittedly much older than the Mahabharata.

much as six thousand years before Plato, others five thousand years before the Trojan War (see Pliny: Historia Naturalis, XXX, 1-3). Berosus, the Babylonian historian, makes him a king of the Babylonians and the founder of a dynasty which reigned over Babylon between B.C. 2200 and B.C. 2000. It is, however, clear that the Hindu Colonization of Persia took place anterior to the Great War.

In the first chapter (Fargard) of the part which bears the name Vendidad of their sacred book (which is also their most ancient book), Hurmuzd or God tells Zapetman (Zoroaster): "I have given to man an excellent and *fertile* country. Nobody is able to give such a one. This land lies to the east (of Persia) where the stars rise every evening." "When Jamshed (the leader of the emigrating nation), came from *the highland in the east* to the plain, there were neither domestic animals nor wild, nor men." Count Bjornstjerna says: "The country alluded to above from which the Persians are said to have come can be no other than the north-west part of Ancient India—Afghanistan and Kashmir—being to the east of Persia, as well as highland compared to the Persian plains."[1]

[1] Theogony of the Hindus.

The Chaldeans were originally migrators from India. Count Bjornstjerna says: "The Chaldeans, the Babylonians and the inhabitants of Colchis derived their civilization from India."—Theogony of the Hindus, p. 168.

The Assyrians, too, were of Hindu origin. There first king was Bali, Boal or Bel. This Boal or Bali was a great king of India in ancient times. He ruled from Cambodia to Greece. Professor Maurice says: "Bali . . . was the puissant sovereign of a mighty empire extending over the vast continent of India."

The Hindu emigrations to Greece have already been mentioned. After describing the Grecian society during the Homeric times, Mr. Pococke says: "The whole of this state of society, civil and military, must strike everyone as being eminently Asiatic, much of it specifically Indian. Such it undoubtedly is. And I shall demonstrate that these evidences were but the attendant tokens of an Indian colonization with its corresponding religion and language. I shall exhibit dynasties disappearing from Western India appear again in Greece: clans, whose martial fame is still recorded in the faithful chronicles of North-western India, as the gallant bands who fought upon the plains of Troy."—India in Greece, p. 12.

TURKISTAN AND NORTHERN ASIA.

"At length then to the wide earth's extreme bounds,
To Scythia are we come, those pathless wilds
Where human footstep never mark the ground."

—ÆSCHYLUS: *Prometheus.*

THE Turanians extending over the whole of Turkistan and Central Asia were originally an Indian people. Colonel Tod says: "Abdul Gazi makes Tamak, the son of Turc, the Turishka of the Puranas His descendants gave their name to Tocharisten or Turkistan."[1] Professor Max Muller says: "Turvas and his descendants who represent Turanians[2] are described in the later epic poems of India as cursed and deprived of their inheritance," and hence their migration.

Colonel Tod says: "The Jaisalmer annals assert that the Yadu and the Balica branches of the Indu race ruled Korassan after the Great War, the Indo-Scythic races of Grecian authors." Besides the Balicas and the numerous branches of the Indo-Medes, many of the sons of Cooru dispersed over these regions: amongst whom we may place Ootooru Cooru (Northern Coorus) of the Puranas, the Ottorocuræ of the Greek authors. Both the Indu and the Surya races were eternally sending their superfluous population to those distant regions."[3]

A Mohammadan historian[4] says that the country of Khatha was first inhabited by a body of emigrants from India.

"But, if the evidences of Saxon colonization in this island (Great Britain)—I speak independently of Anglo-Saxon history—are strong both from language and political institutions, the evidences are still more decisive in the parallel case of an Indian colonization of Greece—not only her language, but her philosophy, her religion, her rivers, her mountains and her tribes; her subtle turn of intellect, her political institutes and above all the mysteries of that noble land irresistibly prove her colonisation from India." The primitive history of Greece " adds the author. "is the primitive history of India."—India in Greece, p. 10.

[1] Tod's Rajasthan, Vol. I, p. 103.
[2] Science of Language, p. 242.
[3] Tod's Rajasthan, Vol. I, p. 43.
[4] History of China, Vol. II, p. 10.

A band of Hindu settlers left India for Siberia, where they founded a kingdom, with Bajrapur as its capital. It is related that on the death of the king of that country in a battle, Parda man, Gad and Sambha, three sons of Sri Krishna Chandra, with a large number of Brahmans and Kshatriyas went there, and the eldest brother succeeded to the throne of the deceased Raja. On the death of Sri Krishna Chandra they paid a condolence visit to Dwarka.[1] "The sons of Krishna eventually left Indus behind and passed into Zabulisthan, and peopled those countries, even to Samarkand.[2]

Colonel Tod says: "The annals of the Yadus of Jaisalmer state that long enterior to Vikrama, they held dominion from Ghazni to Samarkand: that they established themselves in those regions after Mahabharata or the Great War, and were again impelled on the rise of Islamism within the Indus."[3] He further says: "The Yadus of Jaisalmer ruled Zabulistan and founded Ghazni."[4] They claim Chaghtaes as of their own Indu stock, "a claim which," says Colonel Tod, "I now deem worthy of credit."

The Afghans are the descendants of the *Aphghana*, the serpent tribe of the Apivansa of Ancient India. "According to Abu Haukal, the city of Herat is also called Heri. This adjoins Maru or Murve."[5] The country called Seestan, which events in the near future may yet bring more prominently before the public, was a settlement of the Hindus. Colonel Tod says: "Seestan (the region of cold, *see-sthan*) and both sides ef the valley were occupied in the earliest periods by another branch of the Yadus."[6] Colonel Tod again says: "To the Indu race of Aswa (the des-

[1] Hari Vansha, Vishnu Parva, Adhyaya, 97.
[2] Tod's Rajasthan, Vol I, p. 85.
[3] Tod's Rajasthan, Vol. I, p. 520.
[4] Tod's Rajasthan, Vol. I, p. 61.
[5] Tod's Rajasthan, Vol. II, p. 231.
[6] Tod's Rajasthan, Vol. II, p. 230.

cendants of Deomida and Bajaswa), spread over the countries on both sides of the Indus, do we owe the distinctive appellations of Asia."[1]

That the people of Bactria were an Indian people has already been shown. And that the migrations extended to Siberia and the northernmost part of Asia is evident from the fact that the descendants of the Aryan migrators are still found there. "The Samoyedes and Tchoudes of Siberia and Finland are really Samayadus and Joudes of India. The languages of the two former races are said to have a strong affinity and are classed as Hindu-Germanic by Klaproth, the author of 'Asia Polyglotta'"[2] Mr. Remusat traces these tribes to Central Asia, where the Yadus long held sway. Sama, Syam is a title of Krishna. They were Sama Yadus.

SCANDINAVIA.

The Swedish sage admires in yonder bowers,
His winged insects and his rosy flowers.

—CAMPBELL: *Pleasures of Hope.*

THE Scandinavians are the descendents of the Hindu Kshatriyas. The term Scandinavian and the Hindu "Kshatriya" or the warrior caste, are identical, "the former being a Sanskrit equivalent for the latter:" "Scanda Nabhi" (Scanda Navi) signifies Scanda Chiefs (Warrior Chiefs).

Colonel Tod says: "The Aswas were chiefly of the Indu race, yet a branch of the Suryas also bore this designation." In the *Edda* we are informed that the Getes or Jits who entered Scandinavia were termed Asi, and their first settlement was Asigard (*Asi Garh* fortress of the Asi)."

[1] Tod's Rajasthan, Vol. I, p. 63. "Europe, derived from Sarupa, 'of the beautiful face,' the initial syllable *su* and *eu* having the same signification in both languages, *viz.*, *good*. *Rupa* is countenance."—p. 515.

[2] Tod's Rajasthan, Vol. I, p. 529. The race of Joude is described by Baber as occupying the mountainous range, the very spot mentioned in the annals of the Yadus as their place of halt on quitting India twelve centuries before Christ, and thence called Yadu-ki-dang, or hill of Yadu.

Pinkerton concludes Odin to have come to Scandinavia in the time of Darius Hystaspes, 500 years before Christ, and that his successor was Gotama. This is the period of the last Buddha or Mahavira, whose era is 477 before Vicrama, or 533 before Chirst." [1]

"In the martial mythology and warlike poetry of the Scandinavians a wide field exists for assimilation." [2]

"We can scarcely question," says Count Bjornstjerna, "the derivation of the *Edda* (the religious book of Ancient Scandinavia) from the Vedas." [3]

The principle on which the seven days of the week are named in India is the same on which it has been done in Scandinavia:—

(1) *Sunday* is called by the Hindus *Adityawaram*, after *Addit*, the sun, after which also the Scandinavians call the day *Sondag*.

(2) *Monday* is called by the Hindus *Somawaram*, from *Soma*, the moon. Among the Scandinavians it is called *Mondag*.

(3) *Tuesday* is called *Mangalwaram* in India, after the Hindu hero, Mangala. It bears the name *Tisdag* amongst the Scandinavians, after their hero, *This*.

(4) *Wednesday* is termed *Budhawaram* by the Hindus, after *Budha*; by the Scandinavians it is denominated after Oden (Woden, Bodham, Budha), *Onsdag*.

(5) *Thursday* is called *Brahaspatiwaram* by the Hindus, after *Brahaspati*, or Brahma, their principal god; it bearsthe name *Thorsdag* amongst the Scandinavians, after their principal god, *Thor*.

[1] Tod's Rajasthan, Vol. I, p. 64.

[2] Tod's Rajasthan, Vol. I, p. 68.

[3] Theogony of the Hindus, p. 108.

(6) *Friday* is called by the Hindus *Sucrawaram*, after *Sucra*, the god of beauty; it is named by the Scandinavians after Freja, the goddess of beauty, *Frejdag*.

(7) *Saturday* is called *Saniwaram* by the Hindus, after *Sanischar*, the god who cleanses spiritually; it is named *Lordag* by the Scandinavians from *loger*, bathing.

"We have here," says, Count Bjornstjerna, himself a Scandinavian gentleman, "another proof that the myths of the Scandinavians are derived from those of the Hindus."[1]

[1] Theogony of the Hindus, p. 169.

The Ancient Germans appear to have migrated from India. Mr. Muir says: "It has been remarked by various authors (as Kuhn and Zeitschrift, IV. 94 ff) that in analogy with Manu or Manus as the father of mankind, or of the Aryas, German mythology recognises Manus as the ancestor of Teutons." The English 'man' and the German 'mann' appear also to be akin to the word 'manu,' and the German 'mensch' presents a close resemblance to 'manush' of Sanskrit"—Manning's Ancient and Mediæval India, Vol. I, p. 118.

The first habit of the Germans, says Tacitus, on rising was ablution, which Colonel Tod thinks must have been of Eastern origin and not of the cold climate of Germany, as also "the loose flowing robe, the long and braided hair tied in a knot at the top of the head so emblematic of the Brahmins."—Tod's Rajasthan, Vol. I, pp. 63 and 80.

The Germans may be the Brahmans or Sharmas of India. Sharma became Jarma and Jarma became Jerman. For, in Sanskrit *sh* and *j* and *a* are convertible into one another, as Arya, Arjya, and Arshya (see Max Muller's Rig Veda). Csoma-De-Coras in the Preface to his Tibetan Dictionary, says: "The Hungarians will find a fund of information from the study of Sanskrit respecting their origin, manners, customs and language."

Colonel Tod says: "I have often been struck with a characteristic analogy in the sculptures of the most ancient Saxon cathedrals in England, and on the continent to Kanaya and the Gopis. Both may be intended to represent divine harmony. Did the *Asi and Jits of Scandinavia*, the ancestors of the Saxons, bring them from Asia?"—Tod's Rajasthan, Vol. I (People's Edition). p. 570.

The Druids in Ancient Britain appear to have been Buddhistic Brahmans; they adopted the metempsychosis, the pre-existence of the soul, and its return to the realms of universal space They had a divine triad, consisting of a Creator, Preserver, and Destroyer, as with the Hindus. The Druids constituted a Sacerdotal Order which reserved to itself alone the interpretation of the mysteries of religion.

"The ban of the Druids was equally terrible with that of the Brahmans; even the king against whom it was fulminated 'fell,' to use the expression of the Druids, "like grass before the scythe"—Theogony of the Hindus, p. 104.

Mr. Pococke says: "It is in no spirit of etymological trifling that I assure the reader that the far-famed 'hurrah' of his native country (England)

EASTERN ASIA.

But, Oh! what pencil of a living star
Could paint that gorgeous car,
In which as in an ark supremely bright,
The Lord of boundless light
Ascending calm o'er the Empyreum sails,
And with ten thousand beams his beauty veils,

—HYMN TO SURYA: *Translated by S. W. Jones.*

THE eastward wave of Hindu emigration covered the whole of Eastern Asia, comprising the Transgangetic Peninsula, China, Japan, the isles of the Indian Archipelago, and Australia, and finally broke upon the shores of America.

The manners and institutions of the inhabitants of the Transgangetic Peninsula bear so strong an affinity to those of the Hindus that one cannot resist the idea of their having been a Hindu race at some distant period. The fundamental principles

is the war-cry of his forefather, the Rajput of Britain, for he was long the denizen of this island. His shout was 'haro! haro! (hurrah! hurrah!) Hark to the spirit-stirring strains of Wordsworth, so descriptive of this Oriental warrior. It is the Druid who speaks:—

Then seize the spear, and mount the *scythed wheel,*
Lash the proud steed, and whirl the flaming steel,
Sweep through the thickest host and scorn to fly,
Arise! arise! for this it is to die.
Thus, 'neath his *vaulted cave* the Druid sire
Lit the rapt soul, and fed the martial fire.

The learned Pictet says: "I here terminate this parallel of the Celtic idioms with the Sanskrit. I do not believe that after this marked series of analogies, a series which embraces the entire organization of their tongues, that their radical affinity can be contested"—Colebrooke's Miscellaneous Essays, Vol. II, p. 179, Translation of Jatimala.

"The Celtic race established in Europe from the most ancient times must have been the first to arrive there. The decisive analogies which these languages still present to the Sanskrit carry us back to the most ancient period to which we can attain by Comparative Philology. . . " Lettre a M. Humboldt, Journal Asiatique (1836). p. 455.

For further information regading the Hindu colonization of Great Britain see Godfrey Higgins' "Cetlic Druids," wherein it has been proved that the Druids were the priests of the Hindu colonists who emigrated from India and settled in Britain.

which underlie their polity, manners, morality and religion are the same as those of the Hindus. It may in fact be taken for granted that the Transgangetic Peninsula was but a part and parcel of India so far as society, religion and polity were concerned. There was no general change in India but was also wrought there. The propagation of Buddhism was not confined to India; the people of the Transgangetic Peninsula took their share in it.

China accepted the religion of the great Buddha. Thenceforward it became a rival power with India in the eyes of the inhabitants of the Peninsula. The Aryas of India soon reverted to their ancient faith, or rather to a modified form of the ancient faith but on the people of the Peninsula the grasp of the reformed faith was too firm to be so easily shaken off, and thus the silver cord of friendship that tied the two together was snapped. The inhabitants of the Transgangetic Peninsula thenceforward began to look up to the Celestials rather than to the Hindus for enlightenment and instruction. But as their political and social institutions had a Hindu cast, a total overthrow of Hinduism in consequence of this cleavage was impossible. Their civilization therefore retained its Hindu basis.

Lower Burma or Pegu was conquered by emigrants from the Telegu kingdoms.[1] One of Asoka's missions was to Suvarna-bhumi or Burma, and one of the most famous of Hindu settlements, the remains of which exist, was Thorakhetra near Prome.[2]

Mr. R. F. St. Andrew St. John says: "Somewhere about 300 A.D., people from the west-coast of the Bay of Bengal founded colonies on the coast of the Gulf of Martaban of which the principal appears to have been Thaton, or Saddhammanagar.[3]

[1] Sir A. P. Phayre's History of Burma, p. 28.

[2] *Ibid.*

[3] Sir A. Phayre's History of the Burman Race, J. A. S. B., 1864 and 1868 A. D.

"The Burmans, we are told by Symes, call their Code generally, Dharmasath or Sastra; it is one among the many commentaries on Manu. Mr. Syme speaks in glowing terms of the Code"[1]

Mr. Wilson says: "The civilization of the Burmese and the Tibetans is derived from India."

The name Burma itself is of Hindu derivation and proves the Hindu origin of the Burmans. The name Camboja is frequently mentioned in Sanskrit works, and who that has read accounts of it will deny its identity with Combodia?[2] In 1882 a Hindu temple was excavated in that country by a Frenchman,[3] whose writings prove that in ancient times, if not a part of the Indian empire, it was most closely connected with it.

As regards the colonization of Cambodia, Mr. Havell says: "About fourth century A.D. a band of adventurers from the country round Takshasila, called then Camboja, seems to have set off from the west coast of India, as the colonists of Java did a few centuries later, and eventually founded a Kingdom in the south-eastern corner of Asia which they named after their native country."[4]

Mr. Fergusson says:— "The splendid remains at Amravati show that from the mouths of the Krishna and Godavari the Buddhists of North and North-west India colonized Pegu, Cambodia and eventually the island of Java."[5]

Colonists from Chamba, near Bhagalpur, founded as settlement in Cochin China and named it after their famous town.[6]

[1] Syme's Embassy to Ava, p. 326. Also Journal of the R. A. S. for 1898.

[2] Compare Cambistholi of Arrian, Camba-sthala (Sthala-place or district). The world denotes the dwellers in the Kamba or Kambis country. So Kamboja may be explained as those born in Kamba or Kambos.—Wilson's Vishnu Purana, Vol. II, p. 182.

[3] The *Indian Mirror* of the 2nd September 1882.

[4] Havell's Indian Sculpture ana Painting, p. 136.

[5] Indian Architecture, p. 103.

[6] Rhys David's Buddhist India, p. 35.

According to the Siamese tradition, the Hindus settled in Siam before the birth of Buddha. The following extracts from the Chinese history, Ma-Tuan-lin, gives the route adopted by the Hindus when migrating to the trans-gangetic Peninsula, and the way in which they gained supremacy there: "Kaundinya, a Brahman from India, having been notified by an oracle that he was called to reign upon Fu-nan (Kamboja), proceeded south (from Eastern India) until he reached the country of Pan-Pan, whither a deputation from the people of Fu-nan came to meet him, and proclaimed him king. This occurred in about A.D. 420-450." (Pan-Pan was situated in the northern part of the Malay Peninsula. King Riddhi reigned in this kingdom between A.D. 502-507). "At his court may be seen many Brahmans who have come from India in order to profit by his munificence: they are all in great favour with him." What a deep root Hinduism had laid in Cambodia may be seen from a Sanskrit inscription of about A.D. 600. "It states that copies of the Mahabharata, Ramayana and of an unnamed Purana were presented to the temple of Veal Kantel, and that the donor made arrangements in order to insure their daily recitation in perpetuity."

The Hindu colonists of Siam built what is indisputably the most stupendous Hindu temple now standing. Speaking of the Angkor Wat of Siam, an English writer says: "The comparatively few European travellers who have visited this temple all unite in declaring it the most colossally stupendous as well as one of the most architecturally beautiful structures they have ever beheld, so that while it rivals or eclipses the Egyptian Pyramids in one respect, it hardly falls short of the highest Hellenic standard as regards artistic detail in the other. The huge building, which is between two and three miles in circumference, contains a multitude of courts, colonnades, and chambers...............The walls and portals are covered with sculptures, the exterior of the temple being ornamented with bas-reliefs of scenes from Ramayana, the great Sanskrit epic poem.........Angkor Wat was certainly commenced as a Brahmanic temple, but before its completion Buddhism had become the religion of the land, and so it is we find here, as in the temple of Borobaddav in Java, artistic representations of the deities of both the religions."

The wave of Indian migration before breaking on the shores of America submerged the islands of the Indian Archipelago. Col. Tod says: "The isles of the Archipelago were colonized by the Suryas (Surya-Vansa Kshtriyas), whose mythological and heroic history is sculptured in their edifices and maintained in their writings."[1]

Mr. Elphinstone says: "The histories of Java give a distinct account of a numerous body of Hindus from Kalinga who landed on their island, civilized the inhabitants and established on era still subsisting, the first year of which fell in the seventy-fifth year before Chirst."[2]

"The colonization of the eastern coast of Java" by Brahmans is "a fact well established by Sir Stamford Raffles."[3]

Later immigrants from India were evidently Buddhists. Mr. Sewell says: "Native tradition in Java relates that about the beginning of the seventh century (603 A. D. according to Fergusson), a prince of Gujrat arrived in the island with 5,000 followers and settled at Mataram. A little later, 2,000 more immigrants arrived to support him. He and his followers were Buddhists, and from his time Buddhism was firmly established as the religion of Java."[4]

[1] Tod's Rajasthan, Vol. II, p. 218, footnote.

[2] Elphinstone's History of India, p. 168.

[3] Heeren's Historical Researches, Vol. II, p. 303, footnote.

[4] Antiquarian Notes in Java, Journal R. A. S., p. 402 (1906). Also History of Java, by Sir Stamford Raffles, Vol. II, p. 82.

"The Chinese pilgrims who visited the island in the fourth century found it entirely peopled by the Hindus."[1] These pilgrims sailed from the Ganges to Ceylon, from Ceylon to Java and from Java to China in ships manned by crews professing the Brahminical religion.[2] Respecting the inhabitants of Java, Mr. Buckle says: "Of all the Asiatic islanders this race is the most attractive to the imagination. They still adhere to the Hindu faith and worship."[3]

Dr. Cust says: "In the third group we come once more on traces of the great Aryan civilization of India; for, many centuries ago some adventurous Brahmans from the Telegu coast (or from Cambodia) conveyed to Java their religion, their sacred books and their civilization, and Java became the seat of a great and powerful Hindu dynasty.[4] The author of Tazjiyatul Amsar, the celebrated history or the Mongal dynasty, says:. "Among the early conquests during the time of the reign of Kublai Khan was that of the island of Java, one of the countries of Hind in the year 691 H. (1294 A. D.). He then describes how Sri Ram, the King of Java, made peace with the Mongol army.[5]

As regards Borneo, the largest island of the Archipelago, another traveller[6] observes that "in the very inmost recesses of the mountains as well as over the face of the country, the remains of temples and pagodas are to be seen similar to those found on the continent of India bearing all the traits of Hindu mythology; and that in the country of Wahoo, at least 400 miles from the coast, there are several of very superior workmanship with all the emblematic figures so common in Hindu places of worship."

[1] See R. A. S. Journal, Vol. IX, pp. 136-138, on the History of Java.
[2] Elphinstone's India, p. 185.
[3] Beauties, Sublimities and Harmonies of Nature, Vol. I.
[4] Linguistic and Oriental Essays.
[5] Elliot's History of India, Vol. III, p. 27.
[6] See Dalton's account of the Diaks of Borneo in the Journal of the Asiatic Society, Vol. VII, p. 153.

Sir Stampford Raffles while describing the small island of Bali, situated towards the east of Java, says: "Here, together with the Brahminical religion, is still preserved the ancient form of Hindu municipal polity."[1]

The Bugis of the island of *Celebes* trace back their history to the Savira Geding, whom they represent to have proceeded in immediate descent from their heavenly mediator *Baitara Guru* (which is distinctly a Hindu name), and to have been the first chief of any celebrity in Celebes.

As regards Sumatra, the Bombay Gazeteer says: "The Hindu settlement of Sumatra was almost entirely from the east coast of India, and that Bengal, Orissa and Masulipatam had a large share in colonizing both Java and Cambodia cannot be doubted."[2] M. Coleman says: "Mr. Anderson in his account of his mission to the coast of that island (Sumatra) has, however, stated that he discovered at Jambi the remains of an ancient Hindu temple of considerable dimensions, and near the spot various mutilated figures, which would appear to clearly indicate the former existence of the worship of the Vedantic philosophy."[3] Even in A. D. 1510, Albuquerque found a strong Hindu element in Java and Malacca, and Sumatra ruled by a Hindu named Parameshwara.

The famous Chinese traveller, I-Tsing, mentions more than ten Indian colonies in farther India and the islands of the Indian Archipelago, where Indian manners, customs and religious practices prevailed, together with Sanskrit learning. Sri Bhoja in Sumatra, Kalinga in Java, Mabasin in Borneo, and the islands of Bali, Bhojapara and others all bearing Indian names were amongst such colonies.[4] Mr. Kakasu Okakura says: "Down to

[1] Description of Java, Vol. II, p. 236.
[2] Journal of the Bombay Branch of the R. A. S., Vol. XVII.
[3] Coleman's Hindu Mythology, p. 361.
[4] I-Tsing, by Dr. Taka-Kusu.

the days of the Muhammadan conquest, went by the ancient highways of the sea, the intrepid mariners of the Bengal coast founding colonies in Ceylon, Java, Sumatra, and binding Cathay (China) and India fast in mutual intercourse."[1]

CHINA AND JAPAN.

CHINA, too, was colonized to some extent by the ancient Hindus. According to the Hindu theory of emigration, Kshatriyas from India went and established colonies in China. Col. Tod says: "The genealogists of China and Tartary declare themselves to be the descendants of "Awar," son of the Hindu King, "Pururawa.""[2]

"Sir W. Jones says the Chinese assert their Hindu origin."[3]

According to the traditions noted in the *Schuking*, the ancestors of the Chinese, conducted by Fohi, came to the plains of China 2,900 years before Christ, from the high mountain land which lies to the west of that country. This shows that the settlers into China were originally inhabitants of Kashmir, Ladakh, Little Thibet, and the Punjab, which were parts of Ancient India[4]

[1] Ideals of the East. p. 182.

That the wave of Hindu civilization and emigration did at one time break on the shores of Australia is evident from the fact that many extraordinary things are found there. Among other things, the native races have got a kind of arrow, which clearly betrays its Hindu origin. This arrow, called *bomerang* by the natives is exactly the same as that used by Arjuna and Karana in the Mahabharata. Its great merit is that it returns to the archer if it misses the aim. For further information on the point see "Military Science."

[2] Annals of Rajasthan, Vol. I, p. 35.

[3] Annals of Rajasthan, Vol. I, p. 57.

[4] It may be reiterated that in the days of the Mahabharata and for long after, Afghanistan was a part of Aryawarta (India) The Raja of Kandhar was a Hindu, and his daughter, Khandhari or Gandhari, was the mother of Duryodhana. Even at the time of Alexander the Great it was a part of India. Hindu kings ruled in Kabul till the sixth century A. D.

The religion and culture of China are undoubtedly of Hindu origin. Okakura, speaking of the missionary activity of Indian Buddhists in China, says that at one time in the single province of Lo-yang there were more than 3,000 Indian monks and 10,000 Indian families to impress their national religion and art on Chinese soil."[1] Court Bjornstjerna says: "What may be said with certainty is that the religion of China came from India."

That Ancient India had constant intercourse with China no one can deny. China and Chinese products are constantly mentioned in the sacred as well as the profane literature of the time. Chinese authors, too, according to Elphinstone, note Indian ambassadors to the court of China. Professor Heeren says that "the name China is of Hindu origin and came to us from India." See also Vincent, Vol. II, pp. 574, 575.[3] The word *Sinim* occurs in the Bible, Isaiah xlix, 12.

According to Professor Lacouperie (*Western origin of Chinese civilization*) the maritime intercourse of India with China dates from about 680 B.C., when the "sea traders of the Indian Ocean" whose "Chiefs were Hindus" founded a colony called Lang-ga, after the Indian name Lanka or Ceylon, about the present gulf of Kiaotchoa. These Indian colonists had, however, to retreat before the gradual advance of the Chinese till they became submerged in the kingdom of Cambodia, founded by the Hindus about the first century A.D. But throughout this period the monopoly of the seaborne trade of China was in their hands. "The Chinese," says Mr. G. Phillips, "did not

[1] Ideals of the East, p. 113.

[2] Ramayana mentions Chinese silks and other manufactures.

[3] M. de Guigues says that Magadha was known to the Chinese by the name *Mo-kiato*, and its capital was recognized by both its Hindu names, *Kusumpura*, for which the Chinese wrote *Kia-so-mo-pon-lo* and *Pataliputra*, out of which they made *Patoli-tse* by translating *putra*, which means son in Sanskrit, into their own corresponding word, *tse*.—Journal of the Royal Asiatic Society, Vol. V. Such translation of names has thrown a veil of obscurity over many a name of Hindu origin. Hindu geography has thus suffered a great loss.

arrive in the Malaya Archipelago before the 5th century, and they did not extend their voyages to India, Persia and Arabia till a century later." [1]

In the second century A.D., Indians from the Sindhu (Sindh) during the time of Rudradaman, the Khshatrapa Satrap of Kattiawad, took presents by sea to China.[2]

An Indian named Buddhabhadra, a descendant of the Sakya Prince Amitodana, arrived in China in 398 A.D. *via* North India and Cochin China. In 420, Sangh Varmi reached China, and in 424 A.D. Gunavarman, grandson of an ex-king of Kabul, after visiting Ceylon and Java, arrived at the Capital of the Sung dynasty. In 433, according to *Bhikshuni Nidana*, a ship called Nandi brought to China a second party of Sinhalese nuns, who established the Bhikshuni order in China. In 434, another party of Sinhalese nuns, under the leadership of one Tissara, arrived in China to further Gunavraman's work for the foundation of the monastic system in China. In 438, eight Bhikshus came from Ceylon. In 526, Bodhidharma, son of a king of Southern India, embarked in old age from India and "reached Canton by sea," and was invited to Nanking, the Capital of the Emperor of South China. The Chinese geographer, Chia Tau, records his coming in his Huang-hua-hsi-ta-chi.[3] The *kwai yuen* catalogue records that in 548 A.D. Paramati, a native of Ujjain (Malwa), was invited by the Emperor Wu, of the L'lan dynasty, and arrived at the Southern Coast of China, and that Vajrabodhi entered the Chinese Capital and became the founder of mystical Buddhism in China. For constant intercourse between China and India, read Col. Yule's *Cathay and the Way Thither*.

[1] Journal of the R. A. S. 1895, p. 525.

[2] *Vide, Milinda Panha* pp. 127-327.

J. R. A. S. for 1896 A. D.

The sea route from India to China through the port of Tamralipti was under the special protection of the Indian kings. When the Chinese pilgrim, Hiuen-Tsiang, wanted to return to China in A.D., 645, Bhashkarvarman the Brahman king of Kamrup (Assam) and a vassal of the Emperor Harsha, told him: "But I know not, if you prefer to go, by what route you propose to return; if you select the southern sea route, then I will send official attendants to accompany you." Itsing sailed from China for India in A.D. 671 and returned to China twenty-four years later by the sea route from Tamralipiti. In one of his works, Itsing gives an account of no less than sixty Chinese, Corean, and Indo-Chinese pilgrims who visited India in the latter half of the seventh century, and some of whom travelled by the sea route through Tamrailpti.

The influence of Indian thought and culture on Japan was very great. Professor Winternitz, while reviewing *Geschichte der Japanischen Literature*, says: "In view of so much Indian influence in Japanese literature, it is possible to assume that the 'Keuyogen' or double meaning of Japanese poetry may in any way be connected with that form of *Alankara* of the Indian *Kavya*, which is exactly in the same method. The distinguished Japanese scholar, Mr. J. Taka Kusu, says: "But I should like to emphasize the fact that the influence of India, *material and intellectual*, must have been much greater in an earlier period than we at present consider to have been the case. There were, for instance, several Indians, whom the Kuroshiwo current, washing almost the whole southern coast, brought to the Japanese shore."[1] He further says: "It cannot be denied that several Indians came to Japan, especially in view of so many Indians finding their way to China by sea." He then relates how a Brahmin Bodhisen Bharadvaja, known generally as the

[1] Journal of the Royal Astiatic Society for 1905, p. 871.

"Brahmin Bishop," came with another priest from India *via* Champa (Cochin China) to Osaka, then to Nara, where they met another Indian ascetic and taught Sanskrit to the Japanese. "His monastry and tombstone, with a written eulogy, still exist in Nara. Just at this time a Japanese alphabet or syllabary is said to have been invented. The fifty syllables, Gojuin, are arranged by a hand evidently with a practical knowledge of Sanskrit method."[1]

Japanese tradition records the names of several Indians who visited Japan to propagate Buddhism. One of them, Bodhidharma, of South India, came to Japan and interviewed Prince Shotoku (A.D. 573-621). Subhkakara, a native of Central India, visited Japan from China and left at the Kumedera Temple a part of Mahavairochanabhis ambodhi Sutra on Buddhistic Tantrism.[2]

It is noteworthy that some of the scriptures of the Japanese priests preserved in the Horiuzi Temple of Japan are written in Bengali characters of the eleventh century.[3]

The influence of India on Japan, as Dr. Taka Kusu says, was not intellectual only. The official records of Japan, *Nihon-ko-ki* and *Ruijukokushi*, describe how cotton was introduced in Japan by two Indians who reached Japan in July 799 and April 800 A.D. *Vide* also Dr. Taka Kusu's "What Japan owes to India," in the Journal of the Indo Japanese Association for January 1910.

---

[1] Journal of the R. A. S. for 1905, pp. 872, 873.

[2] Rev Daito Shimaji's "India and Japan in Ancient Times," in the Journal of the Indo Japanese Association for January 1910.

[3] Ancedota Oxoniensis, Vol. III.

AMERICA.

America! half brother of the world!
With something good and bad of every land.

BAILEY: *Festus.*

THE fact that a highly-civilized race inhabited America long before the modern civilization of Europe made its appearance there, is quite clear from the striking remains of ancient and high refinement existing in the country. Extensive remains of cities which must have been once in a most flourishing condition, of strong and well-built fortresses, as well as the ruins of very ancient and magnificent buildings, tanks, roads and canals that meet the eye over a very wide area of the southern continent of America, irresistibly force us to the conclusion that the country must have been inhabited at one time by a very highly-civilized nation. Whence did this high civilization spring?

The researches of European antiquarians trace it to India. Mr. Coleman says: "Baron Humboldt, the great German traveller and scientist, describes the existence of Hindu remains still found in America,"[1]

Speaking of the social usages of the inhabitants of Peru, Mr. Pococke says: "The Peruvians and their ancestors, the Indians, are in this point of view at once seen to be the same people."[2] The architecture of ancient America resembles the Hindu style of architecture. Mr. Hardy says: "The ancient edifices of *Chichen* in Central America bear a striking resemblance to the topes of India."[3] Mr. Squire also says: "The Buddhist temples of Southern India, and of the islands of the Indian

[1] Hindu Mythology p. 350.

[2] India in Greece, p. 174.

[3] Eastern Monachism.

Archipelago, as described to us by the learned members of the Asiatic Society and the numerous writers on the religion and antiquities of the Hindus, correspond with great exactness in all their essential and in many of their minor features with those of Central America."[1] Dr. Zerfu remarks: "We find the remarkable temples, fortresses, viaducts, acqueducts of the Aryan group."[2]

A still more significant fact proves the Hindu origin of the civilization of ancient America. The mythology of ancient America furnishes sufficient grounds for the inference that it was a child of Hindu mythology. The following facts will elucidate the matter:—

(1) Americans worshipped Mother Earth as a mythological deity, as the Hindus still do—*dharti mata* and *prithvi mata* are well-known and familiar phrases in Hindustan.

(2) Footprints of heroes and deities on rocks and hills were worshipped by the Americans as devoutly as they are done in India even at the present day. Mexicans are said to have worshipped the footprints of Quetzal Coatle, as the Indians worship the footprints of Buddha in Ceylon, and of Krishna in Gokal, near Muttra.[3]

(3) The Solar and Lunar eclipses were looked upon in ancient America in the same light as in modern India. The Hindus beat drums and make noises by beating tin pots and other things. The Americans too, raise a frightful howl and sound musical instruments. *The Carecles (Americans) think that the demon Maleoyo, the hater of light, swallows the moon and the sun in the same way as the Hindus think that the demons Rahu and Ketu devour the sun and the moon.*

[1] Serpent symbol.

[2] A Manual of Historical Development of, Art.

[3] The people of Ajmer worship the footprints of Ajaipal, the founder of Ajmer, on a rock near the city.

(4) The priests were represented in America with serpents round their heads; *Siva*, *Kali* and others are so represented by the Hindu.

(5) The Mexicans worshipped the figure made of the trunk of a man with the head of an elephant. The Hindus, as is well-known, still worship this deity under the name of *Ganesh*. Baron Humboldt thus remarks on the Mexican deity: "It presents some remarkable and apparently *not accidental* resemblance with the Hindu *Genesh*."

(6) The legend of the Deluge,[1] as believed in by the Hindus was also prevalent in America.

(7) The American believed that the sun, stood still at the word of one of their saints. In India, it is said that the cries of Arjuna at the death of Krishna caused the sun to stand still.

(8) The tortoise myth is common to India and America. Mr. Taylor says: "The striking analogy between the tortoise myth of North America and India is by no means a matter of new observation; it was indeed noticed by Father Lafitan nearly a century and a half ago. Three great features of the Asiatic stories are found among the North American Indians in their fullest and clearest development. The earth is supported on the back of a huge floating tortoise, the tortoise sinks under and causes a deluge, and the tortoise is conceived as being itself the earth floating upon the face of the deep."[2]

(9) The serpent-worship was common to both countries. In India, even to the present day, the serpent is the emblem of wisdom, power, duration, life, eternity and a symbolic representation of the sun. The fact that serpent-worship is common to the Hindu, the Egyptian, the Syrian, the Grecian, the Chinese,

[1] Brahma caused the deluge when only one pious man named Satyavrata, and his family and some animals were saved.—Asiatic Researches, Vol. 1.

[2] Early History of Mankind.

the Scandinavian and the American mythologies has been held to be another proof of the Hindu mythology being the parent of these systems of mythology. Their philosophy was also derived from India. Their belief in the doctrine of the transmigration of souls shows their philosophy to be of Hindu origin.

Apart from mythology, the manners, customs and habits of the ancient Americans bore a very close resemblance to those of the Hindus. Their dress, costume, and sandals prove them to be of Indian origin. The dress of American women was the same as the national dress of Hindu women.

All that can be safely asserted as to the date of the Hindu colonization of America is, that it took place after the time of Sri Ram Chandra. That America was frequently visited by the Hindus till long after the Mahabharata is amply proved by historical records as well as the fictitious literature of the Hindus.

Sri Ram Chandra and Sita are still worshipped in America, and remarkably enough, under their original names. In America, an annual fair takes place, which closely corresponds with the Dashera (Ram Chandrajee-ka-Mela) of the Hindus.[1] Sir W. Jones says: "Rama is represented as a descendant from the sun, as the husband of Sita, and the son of a princess named Causelya. It is very remarkable that Peruvians, whose Inces boasted of the same descent, styled their greatest festival Rama-Sitva; whence we may suppose that South America was peopled by the same race who imported into the farthest parts of Asia the rites and the fabulous history of Rama.[2]

Mythology, architecture, philosophy, traditions, manners and legends of ancient America all argue the Hindu origin of the Americans. This is supported by what we find in the Puranas, the Mahabharata and other historical writings. It

[1] For full particulars see the Theosophist for 1886.

[2] Asiatic Researches, Vol. I, p. 426.

is expressly stated in the Mahabharata that Arjuna conquered Pataldesa (America) and married Alupi, daughter of the king of that country, named Kuroo, and that the fruit of this union was *Arawan*,[1] who afterwards distinguished himself as a great warrior.

A word regarding the route to America used by the Hindus. They seem generally to have taken the sea route from Ceylon or from some place in the Bay of Bengal to Java, Bali, or Borneo and thence to America—to Mexico, Central America or Peru. But more adventurous spirits appear sometimes to have chosen the land passage to America through China, Mongolia, Siberia,-Behring Straits (which, as geology has proved, was not in existence until recent times), and North America.

It has been urged that the Hindus, being prohibited from crossing the sea or even the river Attock, could not have gone to foreign climes in considerable numbers, either as traders or as settlers. Such criticism, however, only betrays ignorance of Hindu literature and Hindu history. Colonel Tod says: "It is ridiculous with all the knowledge now in our possession, to suppose that the Hindus always confined themselves within their gigantic barriers, the limits of modern India."[2]

The most ancient as well as the most authoritative work in Indian literature, the Veda, enjoins mankind to go to foreign countries in steamers and airships. The Yajur Veda (Adhyaya 6, Mantra 21), says:—

समुद्रङ्गच्छ स्वाहा अन्तरिक्षङ्गच्छ स्वाहा देवं सवितारङ्गच्छ स्वाहा ॥

"Oh men, who are fit to do administrative work righteously,

[1] Mahabharata, Bheeshma Parva, Adhayaya 91.

[2] Tod's Rajasthan, Vol. II, p. 218.

go to the seas in big, fast-going steamers, and to the high heavens in airships built on scientific principles." Also:—

तच्चक्षुर्देवहितं पुरस्ताच्छुक्रमुच्चरत् । पश्येम शरदः शतं जीवेम शरदः शतं शृणुयाम शरदः शतं प्रब्रवाम शरदः शतमदीनाः स्याम शरदः शतं भूयश्च शरदः शतात् ॥ यजु० अ० ३६ । मं० २४ ॥

Manu says:—

एतद्देशप्रसूतस्य सकाशादग्रजन्मनः ।
स्वं स्वं चरित्रं शिक्षेरन् पृथिव्यां सर्वमानवाः ॥
(मनु० अध्याय २ । श्लोक २०)

"Let mankind from the different countries of the world acquire knowledge from learned men born in this country (India)."

With regard to the adjudication of disputes regarding the amount of fares, Manu says:—

समुद्रयानकुशला देशकालार्थदर्शिनः ।
स्थापयन्ति तु यां वृद्धिं सा तत्राधिगमं प्रति ॥

"The final decision as to what is the suitable fare will rest with traders, who are fully acquainted with sea-routes as well as land-routes."

Manu again says:—

दीर्घाध्वनि यथोदेशं यथाकालान्तरो भवेत् ।
नदीतीरेषु तद्विद्यात् समुद्रे नास्ति लक्षणम् ॥
(मनु० अध्याय ८ । श्लोक ४०६)

There are numerous instances on record of political and religious leaders of India having gone to Europe and America on political and religious missions. Mahrishi Vyasa with Sukhadeva went to America and lived there for some time. Sukhadeva eventually returned to India *via* Europe (Heero Desha), Persia and Turkistan. The journey took him three years and is succinctly described in the Mahabharata, Shanti Parva, *Sukh utpatti*, Adh. 326.

Just before the Great War the Pandavas started on a conquering expedition to foreign countries. This journey was twice undertaken. On the first occasion they went to Burma, Siam, China, Tibet, Mongolia, Tartary, Persia and returned to India *via* Hirat, Kabul, Kandahar and Baluchistan. At Kandahar (Gandhar) they were the guests of the father-in-law of Dhritarashtra. The second mission was towards the West. Starting from Ceylon (Sinhala-dwipa) they went to Arabia, thence to Egypt, to Zanzibar and other parts of Africa. See Mahabharata, Sabha Parva, Adhyayas, 26-28.

The Sabha Parva of the Mahabharata describes how Sahadeva the youngest of the five Pandawas, conquered a number of islands.

सागरद्वीपवासांश्च नृपतीन् म्लेच्छयोनिजान् ।
निषादान् पुरुषादांश्च कर्णप्रावरणानपि ॥
द्वीप ताम्राह्वयञ्चैव वशे कृत्वा महामतिः ।

The magnanimous Sahadeva conquered and brought under his subjection the Mlechha kings, hunters and cannibals inhabiting the several islands in the sea, including the island called Tamra, etc.

The Great Arjuna, in the course of a voyage visited the following islands: (1) Agastha Tirtha, (2) Poolum Tirtha; (3) Subhadra Tirth, (4) Karandham Tirth, (5) Bharadwaja Tirth. See Mahabharata, Adi Parva.

Emperor Sagar's extensive foreign conquests are also well-known. His conquest of the islands of the Indian Archipelago is mentioned in the ancient traditions of those islands, where he is still worshipped as the "God of the Sea." See also Ramayana, *Balakanda*, V. 2.

The succession of the sons of Sri Krishna to the throne of Bajrapura[1] in Southern Siberia (to the north of the Altai Mountains) has already been mentioned.

It is also well-known that the emperors and kings of India often married foreign princesses. In addition to Dhritarashtra's marriage with the daughter of the king of Afghanistan, and

[1] See Hari Vansha Purana, Vishnu Parva, Adhyaya, 97.

Arjuna's with that of the American King Kuru, we find that Aniruddha, grandson of Sri Krishna, married the princess Ookha, daughter of Ban, King of Shonit, which belonged to Egypt.[1] Maharaja Chandragupta married the daughter of Seleucus, King of Babylon.

The obnoxious prohibition to cross the Attock is of recent origin. The Hindu possession of the Afghan and Persain territories was a relic of their ancient conquest. So late even as the first few centuries of the Christian era, the Hindus lived in thousands in Turkistan, Persia and Russia. The Chinese traveller, Hiuen Tsiang (630 A.D.), noticed that in the chief cities of Persia, Hindus were settled enjoying the full practice of their religion.[2] For an account of the Hindu commercial colony at Astrakhan, see the account given by Professor Pallas. Mr. Elphinstone says: "Even at the present day, individuals of a Hindu tribe from Shikarpur settle as merchants and bankers in the towns of Persia, Turkistan and Russia."[3] The same may be said of a large number of the natives of Jaisalmer.

A few passages from ancient Sanskrit works of historical importance may be quoted to show that the original founders and forefathers of many of the different nations of the world before they migrated to their respective countries, were inhabitants of India. As quoted above, Manu (Chapter X, page 43) says:—

शनकैस्तु क्रियालोपादिमाः क्षत्रियजातयः ।
वृषलत्वं गता लोके ब्राह्मणादर्शनेन च ॥
पौण्ड्रकाश्चौड्रद्रविडाः काम्बोजाः यवनाः शकाः ।
पारदाः पल्हवाश्चीनाः किराताः दरदाः खशाः ॥
मुखबाहूरुपज्जानां या लोके जातयो बहिः ।
म्लेच्छवाचश्चार्यवाचः सर्वे ते दस्यवः स्मृताः ॥

[1] See Hari Vansa, Vishnu Parva, Adh. 116-127.

[2] Beal's Buddhist Records, Vol. II, p. 269.

[3] Elphinstone's History of India, p. 135.

"The following tribes of Kshatriyas have gradually sunk into the state of Vrishalas (outcastes) from the extinction of sacred rites, and from having no communication with the Brahmans, *viz.*, Paundrakas, Odras, Dravidas, Kambojas, Yavanas, Shakas, Paradas, Pahlavas, Chinas, Kiratas, Daradas and Khasas," etc.

Sir W. Jones, in his treatise on the Chinese,[1] understands "by Chinas, the Chinese, who, as the Brahmins report, are descended from the Hindus." The other names, which are apparently those of other nations, may be thus explained. The Shakas were the ancient Sacæ. The Pahlavs were Medes speaking *Pahlavi* or the ancient Persian. The Cambojas were the inhabitants of Camboja or Combodia;[2] the Yavans as is well-known, were the Greeks. The Daradas of Daradasthan in the Chinese territory.

The Mahabbarata (Anushasana Parva, verses 2,103 and 2,104) says:—

शका यवनकाम्बोजास्तास्ताः क्षत्रियजातयः।
वृषलत्वं परिगता ब्राह्मणानामदर्शनात् ॥ २१०३ ॥
द्राविडाश्च कलिन्दाश्च पुलिन्दाश्चाप्युशीनराः।
कोलिसर्पा माहिषकास्तास्ताः क्षत्रियजातयः ॥ २१०४ ॥
वृषलत्वं परिगता ब्राह्मणानामदर्शनात्।

These tribes of Kshatriyas, *viz.*, Shakas, Yavanas, Kambojas, Dravidas, Kalindas, Pulindas,[3] Ushinaras, Kolisarpas, and Mahi-

[1] Sir W. Jones' Works, Vol. I, p. 99.

[2] That Kambojas meant the inhabitants of Cambodia is supported by two verses from the Mahabharata, where they are said to be living towards the north-east:—

दरदान्सह काम्बोजैरजयत् पाकशासनिः।
प्रागुत्तरां दिशं ये च वसन्त्याश्रित्य दस्यवः ॥
महाभारत सभापर्व १०३१-३२ ॥

"The son of Indra conquered the Daradas with the Kambojas and the Dasyus who dwelt in the north-east region."—Mahabharata. Book II, 1031, 1032.

The Khases are mentioned in the Ramayana also.

[3] The Andhras, Pundhars, Sabaras, Pulindas, Mutibas, are also mentioned in the Aitareya Brahmana.

shakas, have become outcastes (and exiled) from having cut off their connection with the Brahmans.

This is repeated in verses 2,158,2,159, where the following additional tribes are named: Mekalas, Latas, Konvasiras, Samdikas, Dorvas, Chauras, Savaras, Barbaras, and Kiratas.[1]

मेकला द्राविडा लाटा पौण्ड्राः कोन्वशिरास्तथा ।
शौण्डिका दरदा दर्वाश्चौरा शवरबर्वराः ॥
किराता यवनाश्चैव तास्ताः क्षत्रियजातयः ।
वृषलत्वमनुप्राप्ता ब्राह्मणानाममर्षणात् ॥
महाभारत अनुशासनपर्व अध्याय ३४ ॥

The Kambojas, Shakas, Shabaras, Kiratas, and Varvaras are again mentioned in the Mahabharata, Drona Parva, verse 4,747:—

काम्बोजानां सहस्रैश्च शकानां च विशांपते ।
शवराणां किरातानां वर्वराणां तथैव च ॥
अगम्यरूपां पृथिवीं मांसशोणितकर्दमाम् ।
कृतवांस्तत्र शैनेयः क्षपयंस्तावकं बलम् ॥
दस्यूनां स शिरस्त्राणैः शिरोभिर्लूनमूर्द्धजैः ॥
दीर्घकूर्चैर्मही कीर्णा विबर्हैरण्डजैरिव ॥
महाभारत द्रोणपर्व अध्याय ११९ ॥

"Shaineya destroying the host, converted the beautiful earth into a mass of mud with the flesh and blood of thousands of Kambojas, Shakas, Sabaras, Kiratas and Varvaras. The ground was covered with the shorn and hairless but long-bearded heads[2] of Dasyus, and their helmets as if with birds bereft of their plumes."

As many as 16 different foreign tribes are said in Shanti Parva (Section 65, line 1,429 ff.) to have descended from the Hindus. King Mandhatri asks Indra:—

[1] Vishnu Purana names over two hundred different peoples known to the Hindus, including Chinas, Pahlvas, Yavanas, Barbaras, Bahlikas (people of Balkh) and Huns.—See Wilson's *Vishnu Purana*, Vol. II, p. 156.

[2] Compare the hairless but long-bearded heads of the Arabs.

यवनाः किराता गांधाराश्चीनाः शवरबर्व्वराः ।
शकास्तुषाराः कंकाश्च पल्हवाश्चान्ध्रमद्रकाः ।
पौण्ड्राः पुलिन्दा रमठाः काम्बोजाश्चैव सर्व्वशः ।
ब्रह्मक्षत्रप्रसूताश्च वैश्याः शूद्राश्च मानवाः ॥
कथं धर्मांश्चरिष्यन्ति सर्वे विषयवासिनः ॥
मद्विधैश्च कथं स्थाप्या सर्वे वै दस्युजीविनः ॥
एतदिच्छाम्यहं श्रोतुं भगवंस्तद् ब्रवीहि मे ।
त्वं बन्धुभूतो ह्यस्माकं क्षत्रियाणां सुरेश्वरः ॥
महाभारत शान्तिपर्व अध्याय ६४ ॥

"The Yavanas, Kiratas, Gandharas, Chinas, Savaras, Varvaras, Shakas, Tusharas, Kankas, Pahlavs, Andhras, Madras, Paundras, Pulindas, Ramathas, Kambojas *men sprung from Brahmans and from Kshatriyas, persons of the Vaisha and Shudra castes.* How shall all these people of *different couutries* practice duty, and what rules shall kings like me prescribe for those who are living as Dasyus? Instruct me on these points, for thou art the friend of our Kshatriya race."

Manu's account of the origin of the Yavanas, Shakas, etc., is supported by the Vishnu Purana. When Sagara learnt from his mother all that had befallen his father Bahu, being vexed at the loss of his paternal kingdom, he vowed to exterminate the Haihayas and other enemies who had conquered it.

"Accordingly he destroyed nearly all the Haihayas. When the Shakas, Yavanas, Kambojas, Paradas and Pahlavas were about to undergo a similar fate, they had recourse to Vasishtha, the king's family priest, who interposed on their behalf in these words addressed to Sagara, representing them as virtually dead: 'You have done enough, my son, in the way of pursuing these men, who are as good as dead. In order that your vow might be fulfilled, I have compelled them to abandon the duties of their caste, and all association with the twice-born.' Agreeing to his spiritual guide's proposal, Sagra compelled these tribes to alter their costume. He made the Yavanas shave their heads, the Shakas shave half their heads, the Paradas wear long hair; and the Pahlavas beards. These and other Kshatriyas he deprived of the study of the Vedas and the Vashatkara. In consequence of their abandonment of their proper duties and of their desertion by the Brahmans, they became Mlechhas."

The Harivansa Purana also says: "*Shakah Yavana Kambojas Paradah Pahlavas tatha! Kolisarpah Samahishah Darvas Cholah Sa-Keralah! Sarve te Kshatriyas tata tesham dharmo nirakritah! Vasistha-vachanad rajan Sagarena Mahatmana!* The Shakas, Yavanas, Kambojas, Paradas, Pahlavas, Kolisarpas, Mahishas, Darvas, Cholas and Keralas had been all Kshatriyas, but were deprived of their social and religious position by the great Sagara (Hindu king) in accordance with the advice of Vasishtha. Some other tribes are also mentioned in the next verse to have received similar tereatment.[1]

Priyavrata, Swayambhuva's son, divided the earth into seven dwipas:—

(1) Jambu Dwipa (Asia).
(2) Plaksha " (South America).
(3) Pushkara " (North America).
(4) Krauncha " (Africa).
(5) Shaka " (Europe).
(6) Shalmali " (Antarcta, Australia).
(7) Kusa " (Oceania).

Owing to the destruction of the greater part of Sanskrit

[1] Mr. Colebrooke (Transactions of the Royal Asiatic Society, Vol. I, p. 453) quotes an ancient Hindu writer, who states that the barbaric tongues are called the Parasica, the Yavana, the Romaka and the Barbara; "the first three of which," says he, "would be the Persian, the Greek and the Latin. But which is the fourth and how Latin became known in India, it is difficult to say." And yet it is a well-authenticated fact that in the time of Emperor Asoka there was constant intercourse between India and Rome.

literature, it is impossible now to interpret correctly these geographical facts, not only because these are only the fragmentary remains of the science of geography inextricably mixed up with Puranic mythology and theology, but to a great extent because many of these ancient dwipas and countries have been so materially altered in consequence of the Cataclysm called the Deluge, as to have become impossible of identification now. The father of the modern geological science, *Cuvier*, expresses the following opinion regarding this Deluge in this *Descours Sur les Revolutions de la Surface du Globe*, p. 283 (5th Edition): "I consider with Messrs. Deluc and Dolomieu that if there is anything established in geology, it is the fact that the surface of the earth has been the subject of a great and sudden revolution, the date of which cannot go much further back than five or six thousand years; that this revolution has sunk (*enforce*) or caused to disappear (*fait-disparaitre*) some of those lands which were formerly inhabited by men, together with those species of animals which are now the most common."

We thus find that the Hindu civilization overran the entire universe, and that its landmarks are still to be seen all over the globe. Nay, it still lives and breathes around us. Says Monsieur Delbos: "The influence of the civilization worked out *thousands of years ago* in India is around and about us every day of our lives. It pervades every corner of the civilized world. Go to America and you find there, as in Europe, the influence of that civilization which came originally from the banks of the Ganges."

LITERATURE.

Was it not wisdom's sovereign power
That beamed her brightest, purest flame,
T'illume her sages' soul the thought to frame.
And clothe with words his heaven-taught lore?

—ÆSCHYLUS: *Prometheus Chained.*

THERE is no surer test of the real greatness of a nation than its literature. Literature embodies not only the intellect of a nation but also its spirit. It is a record of the learning, the wisdom, the refinement, the achievements, the civilization of a nation—a record of all that a nation thinks, says and does. Literature thus holds a mirror to the state of a nation, and serves as an index to mark its position in the scale of civilization and greatness.

Mr. W. C. Taylor thus speaks of Sanskrit literature: "It was an astounding discovery that Hindustan possessed, in spite of the changes of realms and chances of time, a language of unrivalled richness and variety; a language, the parent of all those dialects the Europe has fondly called classical—the source alike of Greek flexibility and Roman strength. A philosophy, compared with which, in point of age, the lessons of Pythagoras are but of yesterday, and in point of daring speculation Plato's boldest efforts were tame and commonplace. A poetry more purely intellectual than any of those of which we had before any conception; and systems of science whose antiquity baffled all power of astronomical calculation. This literature, with all its colossal proportion, which can scarcely be described without the semblance of bombast and exaggeration claimed of course a place for itself—it stood alone, and it was able to stand alone.

"To acquire the mastery of this language is almost the labour of a life; its literature seems exhaustless. The utmost stretch of imagination can scarcely comprehend its boundless mythology. Its philosophy has touched upon every metaphysical difficulty; its legislation is as varied as the castes for which it was designed."[1]

Count Bjornstjerna says: "The literature of India makes us acquainted with a great nation of past ages, which grasped every branch of knowledge, and which will always occupy a distinguished place in the history of the civilization of mankind."[2]

Professor Max Muller says: Although there is hardly any department of learning which has not received new light and new life from the ancient literature of india, yet nowhere is the light that comes to us from India so important, novel, and so rich as in the study of religion and mythology."[3]

Professor Macdonell says: "The intellectual debt of Europe to Sanskrit literature has been undeniably great. It may perhaps become greater still in the years that are to come."[4]

Captain Cunningham says: "Mathematical science was so perfect and astronomical observations so complete that the paths of the sun and the moon were accurately measured. The philosophy of the learned few was perhaps for the first time, firmly allied with the theology of the believing many, and Brahmanism laid down as articles of faith the unity of God, the creation of the world, the immortality of the soul, and the responsibility of man. The remote dwellers upon the Ganges distinctly made known that future life about which Moses is silent or obscure, and that unity and Omnipotence of the Creator which were unknown to the polytheism of the Greek and Roman multitude, and to the dualism of Mithraic legislators, while Vyasa perhaps surpassed Plato in keeping the people

[1] Journal of the Royal Asiatic Society, Vol. II (1834). W. C. Taylor's paper on Sanskrit Literature.

[2] Theogony of the Hindus, p. 85.

[3] Max Muller's India: What can it teach us? p. 140.

[4] History of Sanskrit Literature, p. 42.

tremblingly alive to the punishment which awaited evil deeds."[1]

Professor Heeren says: "The literature of the Sanskrit language incontestably belongs to a highly-cultivated people, whom we may with great reason consider to have been the most informed of all the East. It is, at the same time, a scientific and a poetic literature."[2] He also says: Hindu literature is one of the richest in prose and poetry."

Sir W. Jones says that "human life would not be sufficient to make oneself acquainted with *any considerable part* of Hindu literature."[3] Professor Max Muller says: "The number of Sanskrit works of which *MSS*. are still in existence amounts to ten thousand. This is more I believe, than the whole classical literature of Greece and Rome put together."[4]

Prof. Macdonell says that the Sanskrit literature in quantity exceeds that of Greece and Rome put together.[5]

Rev. Ward says: "No reasonable person will deny to the Hindus of former times the praise of very extensive learning. The variety of subjects upon which they wrote prove that *almost every science* was cultivated among them. The manner also in which they treated these subjects proves that the Hindu learned men yielded the palm of learning to scarcely any other of the ancients. The more their philosophical works and lawbooks are studied, the more will the enquirer be convinced of the depth of wisdom possessed by the authors."

Mrs. Manning says: "The Hindu had the widest range of mind of which man is capable."[7]

The high intellectual and emotional powers of the ancient

[1] Cunningham's History of the Sikhs.
[2] Heeren's Historical Researches, Vol. II, p. 201.
[3] Asiatic Researches, Vol. I, p. 354.
[4] Max Muller's India: What can it teach us? p. 84.
[5] History of Sanskrit Literature, p. 5.
[6] Ward's Antiquity of Hinduism, Vol. IV, conclusion.
[7] Ancient and Mediæval India, Vol. II, p. 148.

Hindus were in any case destined to produce a literature, remarkable for its sublimity and extent; but when these great gifts had the most perfect, melodious, and the richest language in the world to work with, the result could not but be a literature not only the most fertile and fascinating in the world but wonderful in range and astonishing in depth.

Sanskrit Language.

Sir W. Jones, one of the most intellectual of the European critics of Sanskrit literature, pronounced the Sanskrit language to be "of a wonderful structure, more perfect than the Greek, more copious than the Latin, and more exquisitely refined than either."[1]

Professor Bopp[2] also says that "Sanskrit is more perfect and copious than the Greek and the Latin and more exquisite and eloquent than either." Professor Max Muller calls Sanskrit the "language of languages," and remarks that "it has been truly said that Sanskrit is to the Science of language what Mathematics is to Astronomy."[3]

Professor Wilson says: "The Hindu had a copious and a cultivated language." "The Sanskrit," says Professor Heeren, "we can safely assert to be one of the richest and most refined of any. It has, moreover, reached a high degree of cultivation, and the richness of its philosophy is no way inferior to its poetic beauties, as it presents us with an abundance of technical terms to express the most abstract ideas."[4]

The distinguished German critic, Schlegel, says: "Justly it

[1] Asiatic Researches, Vol. I, p. 422 "Sanskrit has the most prodigious compounds, some of them extending to 152 syllables."—*Asiatic Researches* Vol. I, p. 360.

[2] Edinburgh Review, Vol. XXXIII, p. 43.

[3] Science of Language, p. 203.

[4] Historical Researches, Vol. II, pp. 109, 110.

As an example of Mr. James Mill's inveterate prejudice against everything Hindu, the following may be cited: La Pere Paolin says that "Sanskrit is more copious than Latin. It has several words to express the

is called Sanskrit, *i.e.*, perfect, finished. In its structure and grammar it closely resembles the Greek, but is infinitely more regular and therefore more simple, though not less rich. It combines the artistic fulness indicative of Greek development, the brevity and nice accuracy of Latin; whilst having a near affinity to the Persian and German roots, it is distinguished by expression as enthusiastic and forcible as theirs."[1] He again says: "The Sanskrit combines these various qualities, possessed separately by other tongues: Grecian copiousness, deep-toned Roman force, the divine afflatus characterising the Hebrew tongue."[2] He also says: "Judged by an organic standard of the principal elements of language, the Sanskrit excels in grammatical structure, and is indeed, the most perfectly-developed of all idioms, not excepting Greek and Latin."[3]

The importance of the "language of languages" is clearly recognised when we consider with Sir W. W. Hunter the fact that "the modern philology dates from the study of Sanskrit by the Europeans."[4]

Sir W. Jones' assertion that "Deonagri (old Nagari, *i.e.*, Brahmi) is the original source whence the alphabets of Western Asia were derived,"[5] not only proves the great antiquity of the Sanskrit literature but points out the channel through which Sans-

same thing. The sun has more than 30 names, the moon more than 20; a house has 20, a stone 5, or 6, a leaf 5, an ape 10, and a crow 9." Mr. James Mill thereupon says that "the highest merit of language would consist in having one name for everything which required a name and no more than one." On this Prof. Wilson exclaims: What would become of poetry, of eloquence, of literature, of intellect, if language was thus shorn of all that gives it beauty, variety, grace and vigour?"—*Mill's India*, Vol. II. p. 91.

[1] Schlegel's History of Literature, p. 117.

[2] Ibid, p. 105.

[3] Ibid, p. 106.

[4] Imperial Gazetteer, "India," p. 264. The foundation of the science of comparative philology was laid by the publication of Bopp's Comparative Grammar in 1848 A. D.

[5] Asiatic Researches, Vol. I, p. 423. Professor Heeren (Hist. Researches, Vol. II, pp. 201 and 202) says that Sanskrit literature is not only very rich but also extremely ancient.

krit philosophy and learning flowed towards the West, and, working in the new and fresh materials available there, produced Homer, Hesiod, Pythagoras, Socrates, Plato, Aristotle, Zeno, Cicero, Scarvola, Varro, Virgil, and others to divide the laurels of literary reputation with Vyasa, Kapila, Gautama, Patanjali, Kanada. Jamuni, Narada, Panini, Marichi, and Valmiki. The study of comparative philology, in so far as it has advanced, tends to show that Sanskrit is the mother of all Indo-European languages. From the Sanskrit were derived the original roots and those essentially necessary words which form the basis of all these languages. In other words, the part that is common to all or most of the languages of this group is supplied to each language by the Sanskrit.

The learned Dr. Pritchard says: "The affinity between the Greek language, and the old Parsi and Sanskrit is certain and essential. The use of cognate idioms proves the nations who used them to have descended from one stock. That the religion of the Greeks emanated from an Eastern source no one will deny. We must therefore suppose the religion as well as the language of Greece to have been derived in great part immediately from the East."[1]

Mr. Pococke says: "The Greek language is a derivation from the Sanskrit."[2] Sir W. Jones says: "I was not a little surprised to find that out of ten words in Du Perron's Zind Dictionary six or seven were pure Sanskrit."[3] Professor Heeren says: "In point of fact, the Zind is derived from the Sanskrit."[4]

As the Deonagri is the source from which the alphabets of Western Asia are derived, so are the Sanskrit names of the figures 1 to 10 the source from which most languages have derived their names of the said figures.

[1] Dr. Pritchard's Physical History of Man, Vol. I, p. 502.
[2] India in Greece, p. 18.
[3] Sir W. Jones' Works, Vol. I, pp. 82, 83.
[4] Heeren's Historical Researches, Vol. II p. 220.

The following table shows the connection of Sanskrit with the Zind, Greek, Latin and other Languages:—

English.	Sanskrit.	Lithunian.	Zind.	Tentonic.	Old Slavonic.	Latin.	Gothic.	Irish.	Greek.
I am	Asmi	Esmi	Almi	...	Yesme	Sum	...	...	...
Thou art	Asi	Esai	Ahi	...	Yesi	Es	...	...	...
He is	' Asti	Esti	Asti	...	Yesto	Est	...	...	...
We are	'Smas	Esmi	Hualie	...	Yesmi	Sumas	...	...	...
You are	'Stha	Esti	Sta	...	Yesti	Est is	...	...	...
Father	Pitar	......	Patar	...	...	Pater	Father	...	...
Mother	Matar	......	Matar	...	Mati	Mater	...	Mathair	...
Brother	Bhratar	......	Bratar	...	Brat	Fraater	Brother	Brothehir	...
Daughter	Duhitar	......	Dughdhar	...	Dukte	...	Daubtor	...	...
Father-in-law	Svasura	......	......	...	Svekt	Socer	Svailira	...	...
Mother-in-law	Svasru	......	......	...	Svekraj	Socrus (Italian)	Svailiro	...	...
Cattle	Pasu	(Penes, pecku)	Pasu	Gr. failur	...	Pecu	...	...	...
Ox and Cow	Go	Gow	Gao	Chuo	...	Bos	...	...	Bova,
Ox	Ukshan	Govjado	Ukhshan	Auhsan	...	Vacca	...	...	...
Steer	Sthura	Taura-S	Staoru	Stuir	...	...	...	...	...
Horse	Asva or Asu	Aszus	Aspa	Loh (avi-str)	...	Equims	...	...	Ois.
Sheep	Avi	Avi-S	......	Euve	...	Ovis	...	...	...
Sow	Su	......	......	Su	...	Sus	...	...	Vs.
Mouse	Mush	......	......	Mus	...	Mus	...	...	Uvs.
Fly	Makshika	Muse	Makshki	Micco	...	Musca	...	...	...
Matron	Matram	......	......	...	...	...	...	...	Metron.
...	Varuna	......	......	...	...	Uranus	...	...	...

[1] The Sanskrit *Duhitar* has dwindled down in Bohemian to *dci.* pronounced (tee).

Numerals.

Sanskrit.	Zind.	Greek (Doric).	Latin.	Gothic.
Prat'hama.	Frat'hema.	Prota.	Prima.	Fruma.
Dwitiya.	Bitya.	Deutera.	Altera.	Ant'hara
Tritiya.	Thritya.	Trita.	Tertia.	Thridyo.
Chaturtha.	Turiya.	Tetarta.	Quarta.	Fidvordo.
Panchama.	Pugdha.	Pempta.	Quinta.	Fimito.
Shasta.	Catva.	Hakta.	Sexta.	Saishto.
Saptama.	Haptat'ha.	Hebdoma.	Septima.	Sibundo.
Ashtama.	Astema.	Ogdoa.	Octava.	Ahtudo.
Navam.	Nauma.	Ennota.	Nova.	Nainudo.
Dasama.	Dasema.	Dekata.	Decima.	Taihundo.

Sanskrit.	Latin.	Greek.	Lithunian.	Welsh.
Eka.	Un.	Hen.	Wein.	Un.
Dva.	Du.	Du.	Du.	Dau.
Tri.	Tri.	Tri.	Tri.	Tri.
Chatur.	Quartur.	Tessar.	Kettuar.	Pedwar.
Panch.	Quinque.	Pente.	Penki.	
Shash.	Sex.	Hex.	Szestzi.	
Sapta.	Septem.	Hepta.	Septyni.	Saith.
Ashta.	Octo.	Okto.	Asztuui.	
Nava.	Movem.	Ennea.	Dewyni.	Naw.
Dasa.	Decem.	Deka.	Deszimt.	Deg.

To these numerals we subjoin a brief conspectus of the

Analogy of Verbs.

Singular.

Sanskrit.	Zind.	Greek.	Latin.
Dad a-mi.	Dadha mi.	Dido-mi.	Do.
Dada si.	Dodha si.	Dido s.	Da-s.
Dad-te.	Dadha te.	Dido-ti.	Da-t.

Plural.

Sanskrit.	Zind.	Greek.	Latin.
Dad mas.	Dade mahi.	Dido-mes.	Da-mus.
Dat t'ha.	Dasta ?	Dido te.	Da-tis.
Dad-te.	Dade-nti.	Dido-nti.	Da-nt.

General View of the Persons of the Verb.

First Person.

Sanskrit.	Zind.	Greek.	Latin.
Tishtami	... Histami ...	... Histemi ...	... Sto.
Dadami	... Dadhami ...	... Didomi ...	... D-o.
Asmi ...	... Ahmi ...	... Emmi ...	... Sum.
Bahrami ...	... Barami ...	... Phero ...	... Fero.
Vahami ...	... Vazami ...	... Ekho ...	... Veho.

Second Person.

Asi ...	... Ahi ...	... Easi ...	... Es.
Tishtasi ...	... Hisht'hahi	... Histos ...	... Stas.
Dadasi ...	... Dhdhahi ...	... Didos ...	... Das.
Bharasi ...	... Barahi ...	... Phereis ...	... Fers.
Tisht'hes	... Histois ...	... Histaies ...	... Stes.
Dadhyas	... Daidhya ...	... Didoies ...	... Des.
Bhares	... Bharois ...	... Pherois ...	... Feras.

Second Person Plural.

Tish-hat'ha	... Histh'at'ha	... Histate ...	... Statis.
Bharat'ha	... Bara'ha ...	... Pherete ...	... Fertis.
Tisht'het'ha	... Histaeta ...	... Histaiete ...	... Stetis.
Dadyata ...	... Daidhyata	... Dideiete ...	... Detis.
Bhareta ...	... Baraeta ...	... Pheroite ...	... Feratis.

Third Person.

Asti ...	... Ashti ...	... Esti ...	... Est.
Tishtati...	... Hishtoti ...	... Histate ...	... Stat.
Dadati ...	... Dadhaite ...	... Didote ...	... Dat.
Barati ...	... Baraite ...	... Phere (t)i ...	... Fert.
Bharet ...	... Baroit ...	... Pheroi ...	... Ferat.
Dadyat ...	... Daidhyat ...	... Dedoie ...	... Det.

Third Person Plural.

Santi ...	... Hente ...	... (S) enti ...	... Sunt.
Tishtanti	... Histenti ...	... Histanti ...	... Stant.
Dadati ...	... Dadenti ...	... Didonti ...	... Dant.
Bharanti	... Barenti ...	... Pheronti ...	... Ferunt.
Vahanti	... Vazenti ...	... Ekhonti ...	... Wehunt.

View of "Didomi" in the Future Tense.

Singular.

Zind.		Greek.
Da-syami	...	... Do so.
Da-saysi	...	... Do seis.
Da syati	...	... Do sei.

Dual.

Da syat'has	...	... Do-seton.
Da syatas	...	... Do seton.

Plural.

Da syamas	...	... Do.somen.
Da-syat'ha	...	... Do sete.
Da syanti	...	... Do sonti.

Supines and Infinitives.

Sanskrit.		Latin.
St'ha-tum. to stand	...	... Statum
Da tum. to give	...	... Datum.
Jna-tum. to know	...	... No-tum.
Patum. to drink	...	... Potum.
E tum. to go	...	... Itum.
Stra tum. to strew	...	... Stratum.
Ank tum. to anoint	...	... Unctum.
Svani-tum. to sound	...	... Son-i-tum.
Sarp-tum. to go	...	... Serptum.
Vami tum. to vomit	...	... Vomitum.
Pesh-tum. to bruise	...	... Pistum.
Jani tum. to beget	...	... Gen-i-tum.

The scale of calculation is common to all nations, and owes its origin to the Hindus. Dr. Ballantyne is inclined to support the theory that Sanskrit is the mother of all Aryan (Indo-European) languages.

Mr. Bopp[1] says that at one time Sanskrit was the one language spoken all over the world.

Mons. Dubois[2] says that Sanskrit is the original source of all the European languages of the present day.

[1]Edinburgh Review Vol. XXXIII, p. 43.

[2]Bible in India.

Miss Carpenter[1] says that though the original home of Sanskrit is Aryawarta, yet it has now been proved to have been the language of most of the countries of modern Europe in ancient times.

A German critic says that "Sanskrit is the mother of Greek, Latin and German languages, and that it has no other relation to them: this is the reason why Max Muller calls it the ancient language of the Aryas."

The great antiquity of Indian civilization is unquestionably beyond comparison; and the antiquarians are unanimous as to the incomparable antiquity of the Sanskrit literature also. The oldest writings of the oldest nations except the Hindus are, according to some Orientalists, the records of various developments of Buddhism, which took its rise in India after the decline of the Vedic religion. Count Bjornstjerna[2] says: "The so-called Hermes Scriptures (the names of all the sacred writings of the Egyptians) contain metaphysical treatises in the form of dialogue between Hermes (spiritual wisdom) and *Todh*, Bodh, Buddh (earthly wisdom), which throughout exhibit the doctrines of Buddhism." Again, "the early Egyptian writing which in the translation is called *Pimander's Hermes Trismegistus*, and forms a dialogue between Pimander (the highest intelligence) and Thodt (Bodh, Buddha), which develops the metaphysics of the Buddhists touching the trinity."

Prof. Weber says: "And while the claims of the written records of Indian literature to a high antiquity are thus indisputably proved by external geographical testimony, the internal evidence in the same direction, which may be gathered from their contents, is no less conclusive." [3]

[1] Journal of the Indian Association.

[2] Theogony of the Hindus, p. 100.

[3] Weber's History of Indian Literature, p. 5.

Art of Writing.

This introduces us to the important literary question as regards the art of writing in Ancient India. Apart from Mr. Weber's acceptance of "the claims of the written records of Indian literature to a high antiquity," Professor Wilson says: "The Hindus have been in possession of that (writing) as long as of a literature."[1]

Professor Heeren says: "Everything concurs to establish the fact that alphabetical writing was known in India from the earliest times, and that its use was not confined to inscriptions but extended also to every purpose of common life."[2] Count Bjornstjerna says that the Hindus possessed "written books of religion" before 2,800 B.C., or 800 years before Abraham.[3]

Professors Goldstucker, Bohtingk, Whitney and Roth hold that the authors of the *Pratisakhyas* must have had *written texts* before them.[4]

Mr. Vincent Smith says: "Writing was certainly in *common* use long before the days of Chandragupta."[5]

Considering the backwardness of other nations in the invention of the art of writing, and unwilling to give the second place to the nation to whom they owe all their learning and wisdom, the advocates of the theory of "Greek Culture" hesitate to assign high antiquity to the Hindu art of writing.

Professor Max Muller for one allows no written work before 350 B.C. This strange and absurd supposition is wholly inexplicable. Apart from the internal and direct evidence, one fact alone is sufficient to refute the supposition. When

[1] Mill's India, Vol. II, p. 49, footnote.

[2] Heeren's Historical Researches, Vol. II, p. 202.

[3] Theogony of the Hindus, p. 26.

[4] Weber's Indian Literature, p. 22, footnote.

[5] Early History of India, p. 127.

geometry and astronomy flourished so highly and extensively in India more than 3,000 years before Christ, according to the calculation of the celebrated astronomer, Bailly, is it at all conceivable that writing should have been unknown before 350 B.C.? Professor Max Duncker says that according to Max Muller's theory, the *Brahmanas* must have been retained in memory till 350 B.C., but "it seems to me," he says, "quite impossible considering their form." He adds: "If the *Brahmanas* which cite the Vedas accurately in their present arrangement, and speak not only of syllables but of letters arose between 800 and 600 B.C., it appears to me an inevitable conclusion that the Vedas must have existed in writing about 800 B.C.[1]

The paper on "The use of Writing in Ancient India," read by Mr. S. K. Varma, Oriental Lecturer, Balliol College, Oxford, before the International Congress of Orientalists[2] at Leyden, in 1883, deals with the subject in a masterly way, and shows that writing has been in use in India since the Vedic times. The learned writer[3] says: "I feel no hesitation in saying that there are words and phrases occurring in the Sanhitas of the Vedas in the *Brahmanas* and in the Sutra works, which

[1] History of Antiquity, Vol. IV, pp. 156, 157.

[2] Acta Du Aixieun Congres International Des Orientalistes tenuen 1883 a Leide, p. 305.

[3] To the objection that the word *Sruti*, as a synonym of Veda, conveyed the idea of what was learned and taught by hearing, thus proving the absence of written books he neatly replies that the word *Smriti*, derived from "*Smri*," to remember (as Sruti comes from *Sru* to hear), would equally convey the same idea and prove the same thing, though it is admitted by all that the art of writing was known to the authors of the Smritis. After quoting a part of a hymn in the 10th Mandala of the Rig Veda, "some one seeing the speech does not see it, while another hearing does not hear it," and showing that one could not see the speech unless it assumed some tangible shape like that of a book or manuscript; also that one could not possibly count a million without an acquaintance with writing, not to speak of having technical names for a million, a hundred million, nay, for a hundred thousand million, as we find them given in the seventh chapter of the white Yajur Veda—for we find that in Greece before writing became known, the highest number of what could be technically expressed was only

leave no doubt as to the use of the written characters in ancient India. It may be confidently asserted that the systematic treatises in prose which abounded at and long before the time of Panini could never have been composed without the help of writing. We know for certain that with the exception of the hymns of the Rig Veda, most of the Vaidik works are in prose, and it is difficult to understand how they could possibly have been composed without having recourse to some artificial means."

Katyayana says: यत्रपवत्वमपत्रा जलकः सहसादिभिः "When the writer and the witnesses are dead." Yagyavalka mentions written documents; and Narada and others also bear testimony to their existence. Even Max Muller himself is compelled to admit that "writing was known to the authors of the Sutras."

The supposition that writing was unknown in India before 350 B. C. is only one of the many instances calculated to show the strange waywardness of human intellect. If anyone of lesser authority than Max Muller had advanced such a supposition he might have been pronounced a maniac. It was left to the learned professor to conceive the possibility of a language of the structure of Sanskrit being cultivated to the extent of producing compositions like the Vedas, the Brahmanas and the Upanishads, and of a people achieving wonderful progress in mathematics and

10,000 and in Rome only a thousand—he goes on to show that the words "Kanda and Patala" which occur in Vedic literature prove the existence of written books in ancient times. After pointing out that the *Adhikara*, or heading rule, in Panini's grammar was denoted by Svarita, which proved conclusively that he employed writing and that the sixth chapter of Ashtadhyayi says that people in Panini's time used to mark the figures eight and five on the ears of their cattle, he concludes: The fact that Panini makes allusion to coins, for instance निष्क and रूप्य with which latter perhaps the word "rupee" is connected, and that he actually mentions the two words लिपि and लिबि both meaning writing, affords palpable proof of his acquaintance with the art of writing, without which, as I have said, he could never have produced his great grammar."

astronomy without being able to write A, B, C, or one, two and three!!![1]

The extraordinary vocal powers of the Hindus, combined with their wonderful inventive genius produced a language which, when fully developed, was commensurate with their marvellous intellectual faculties, and which contributed materially towards the creation of a literature unparalleled for richness, sublimity and range. The peculiar beauties inherent in the offspring of such high intellectual powers were greatly enhanced by its scientific upbringing, and by constant and assiduous exercise it has developed into what is now such a model of perfection as to well deserve the name of *deobani*, or "the language of the gods." The very excellence of the language and the scientific character of its structure have led some good people to doubt if this polished and learned language could ever have been the vernacular of any people. Fully realizing the significance of the fact that, with all their boast of high civilization and culture, they posses a language highly defective and irregular when compared to the Sanskrit, these critics find it difficult to believe that the Hindus ever spoke that perfect language.

In a learned paper on the subject read before the International Congress of Orientalists at Berlin, on 14th September 1881, Mr. Shyamji Krishna Varma, delegate of the Government of India to the Congress demolishes all the arguments advanced against the Sanskrit language having ever been a spoken vernacular of India, and proves that not only was "Sanskrit, as we find settled

[1] Ancient Sanskrit Literature, p. 523. "The Greeks praise the beauty of the writing of the Indians. See Strabo, Lib. XV, p. 493.

Megasthenes says that "the Hindus used letters for inscriptions on milestones, indicating the resting places and distances." Curtius also says that "the Indians wrote on soft rind of trees." Nearchus mentions that "the Indians wrote letters on cotton that had been well beaten together." Father Paulino says that "cotton paper was used in India before the Christian era."—*Historical Researches*, Vol. II, p. 107.

in the Ashtadhyayi of Panini, the spoken vernacular at the time when that grammarian flourished," but that "it is at present extensively used as the medium of conversation and correspondence among learned men in all parts of India, from Kashmir to Cape Comorin."

Professor Max Muller says: "Yet such is the marvellous continuity between the past and the present in India, that in spite of repeated social convulsions, religious reforms and foreign invasions, Sanskrit may be said to be still the only language that is spoken over the whole extent of that vast country." He adds: "Even at the present moment, after a century of English rule and English teaching, I believe that Sanskrit is more widely understood in India than Latin was in Europe at the time of Dante."[1]

Who after this can say that Sanskrit was or is a dead langauge?

THE VEDIC LITERATURE.

Veil after veil will lift—but there must be
Veil upon veil behind.

—*Buddha's Sermon.*[2]

PROFESSOR Max Muller says: "The Vedic literature" opens to us a chapter in what has been called the education of the human race, to which we can find no parallel anywhere else."[3]

The Vedic literature consists of (1) The Vedas, (2) The Brahmanas, (3) The Sutras.

The Vedas are four in number and are called the Rig Veda, the Yajur Veda, the Atharva Veda, and the Sama Veda. The Rig Veda and the Yajur Veda are the most important of the

[1] India: What can it teach us? pp. 78, 79.
[2] Light of Asia, p. 21.
[3] India: What can it teach us? p. 89.

Vedas, as they respectively deal with the knowledge of things physical, mental and spiritual and the application of that knowledge.

The Vedas are universally admitted to be not only by far the most important work in the Sanskrit language but the greatest work in all literature.

It is nothing short of a miracle that while important works in almost all departments of human learning that were cultivated in ancient India have perished, the most important of them all, the Vedas, the fountain-head of all knowledge and the parent of all literature and science, have come down to us secure and intact. While most of the important Sanskrit works from Manu Smriti, the most ancient code of law in the world, to the Ramayana and the Mahabharata have been tampered with, the Vedas, by the very inimitable grandeur of their language, and the unequalled sublimity of their contents have defied all attempts at interpolation.

As, however, the study of the Vedas has long been neglected, and a through knowledge of the Sutras and Vedangas by which alone the Vedic mantras may be interpreted is very rare, the Vedas are rarely well understood even by the learned amongst the Hindus.

When the Yajur Veda was presented to Voltaire, he expressed his belief that it was the most precious gift for which the West had been ever indebted to the East.[1]

Guigault says: "The Rig Veda is the most sublime conception of the great highways of humanity."

Mons. Leon Delbos speaks enthusiastically of the grandeur and sublimity of the Vedas. "There is no monument of Greece or Rome," he asserts, more precious than the Rig Veda."[2]

[1] Wilson's Essays, Vol. III, p. 304.

[2] Mons. Leon Delbos' paper on the Vedas read before the International Literary Association at Paris, on 14th July 1884, the Venerable Victor Hugo being in the chair.

Professor Max Muller says: "In the history of the world, the Vedas fill a gap which no literary work in any other language could fill."[1] He also says: "I maintain that to everybody who cares for himself, for his ancestors, for his history, for his intellectual development, a study of Vedic literature is indispensable."[2] The Hindus hold the Vedas to be the Revelation, and its study accordingly is indispensable to every man.

The Vedas are admittedly the oldest books in the world. "The age of this venerable hymnal (Rig Veda)," says Sir W. W. Hunter, "is unknown." Professor Max Muller says: "They (the Vedas) are the oldest of books in the library of mankind." They are without doubt," says Professor Heeren, "the oldest works composed in the Sanskrit."[3] "Even the most ancient Sanskrit writings allow the Vedas as already existing."[4] No country except India and no language except the Sanskrit can boast of a possession so ancient or venerable. No nation except the Hindus can stand before the world with such a sacred heirloom in its possession, unapproachable in grandeur and infinitely above all in glory. The Vedas stand alone in their solitary splendour, serving as a beacon of divine light for the onward march of humanity.

The Hindus hold that the Vedas contain the germs of all knowledge, and that their teachings are in complete consonance with the principles of science.[5] The late lamented P. Guru Datta of Lahore attempted to interpret a few mantras of the

[1] Wilson's Essays, Vol. III, p. 339.

[2] Max Muller's India: What can it teach us? p. 121.

[3] Historical Researches, Vol. II, p. 146.

[4] Heeren's Historical Researches, Vol. II, p. 127.

[5] See P. Guru Datta's Vedic Texts, No. 2, printed at the Virjanand Press, Lahore. Those who read their own historical theories in the Vedas will do well to consider the words of Professor Barth. After pointing out some of the metaphysical theories contained in the Vedas he proceeds: "These alone are sufficient to prove, if necessary, how profoundly sacerdotal this poetry is, and they ought to have suggested reflections to

Rig Veda on the strength of Swami Dayanand Saraswati's commentary on the Vedas. The result was astonishing. Interpreting the 7th Mantra of the Second Sukta of Rig Veda,—

मित्रं हुवे पूतं दक्षं वरुणं च रिशादसम् । धियं घृताचिं साधन्ता ॥

ऋ० अ० १ । सू० २ । मन्त्र ७ ॥

P. Guru Datta says: "This mantra describes the (*dhiyam*) process, or steps whereby the well-known of liquids, water, can be formed by the combination of *two* other substances (*gritachim sadhanta*). The word *sadhanta* is in the dual number indicating that it is two elementary bodies which combine to form water. What those two elementary substances, according to this mantra, are is not a matter of the least importance to determine. The words used to indicate those two substance are *mitra* and *varuna*.

"The first literal meaning of *mitra*[1] is measurer. The name is given to a substance that stands, as it were, as a measure or as a standard substance. It is the measurer of density, or of value, otherwise known as quantivalence. The other meaning of *mitra* is 'associate.' Now in this mantra, *mitra* is described as an associate of *varuna*[2] It will be shown

those who have *affected* to see in it only the work of primitive shepherds celebrating the praises of their gods as they lead their flocks to the pasture."—Barth's Religions of India, p. 38.

Professor Theilve of Leyden, too, expresses the same opinion, only more strongly in *Theologiche Tijdochrift* for July 1880. As Professor Max Muller admits, the Europeans "are still on the mere surface of Vedic literature," and must not reject it as useless if they do not find in it corroboration of their preconceived theories of anthropology and sociology, See India: What can it teach us? p 113.

[1] The word *mitra* is formed by adding the unadi suffix *kra* to the root *mi*, according to the Sutra अमिचिमिशसिभ्यः क्त्रः ॥ उणा० ४ । १६४ ॥ The meaning is मिनोति मान्यं करोति मित्रः । or one that measures or stands as a standard of reference.

[2] *Varuna* is formed by adding unadi suffix *unan* to root *vri* to accept कृवृदारिभ्य उनन् ॥ ५३ ॥ Hence it means that which is acceptable to all or seeks all.

how *varuna* indicates oxygen gas.[1] Now it is well-known that hydrogen is not only the lightest element known, nor is it only monovalent, but that it has a strong affinity for oxygen; hence it is that it is described as an associate of *varuna*. Many other analogies in the properties of *mitra* and *hydrogen* go on to suggest that what is in Vedic terms styled as *mitra* is in fact identical with hydrogen. *Mitra*, for instance, occurs as synonymous with *udana* in many parts of the Vedas, and *udana* is well characterized by its lightness or by its power to lift up.

"The second element with which we were concerned is *varuna*. *Varuna* is the substance that is acceptable to all. It is the element that every living being needs to live. Its well-known property is *rishadah*, *i.e.*, it eats away or rusts all the base metals, it burns all the bones, etc., and physiologically purifies the blood by oxidizing it, and thereby keeping the frame alive. It is by these properties that *varuna* is in general distinguished; but it is especially characterized here as *rishadha*. No one can fail to perceive that the substance thus distinctly characterized is oxygen gas.

"Another word used in the mantra is *puta daksham*. *Puta* is pure, free from impurities. *Daksha* means energy. *Puta daksham* is a substance, pure, possessed of kinetic energy. Who that is acquainted with the kinetic theory of gases cannot see in *puta dakhsha* the properties of a gas highly heated?

"The meaning of the mantra taken as a whole is this: Let one who is desirous to form water by the combination of two substances, take pure hydrogen gas highly heated and oxygen gas possessed of the properties *rishadha*, and let him combine them to form water."

The *Brahmanas*, too, are sometimes held by the ignorant to be

[1] Again, we have in Nighantu, the Vedic Dictionary, Chapter V Section 4, मित्र इति पदनामसु पठितम् ॥ Hence *mitra* means that which approches or seeks, association with others.

part of the Vedas, but as Professor Weber says: "Strictly speaking, only the Sanghitas are Vedas." The *Brahmanas* are either commentaries on the Vedas or philosophical disquisitions based on them.

Of the period when these *Brahmanas* were composed, Professor Weber says: "We have here a copy of the period when Brahmans with lively emulation carry on their enquiries into the highest questions the human mind can propound; women with enthusiastic ardour plunge into mysteries of speculation, impressing and astonishing men by the depth and loftiness of their opinion, and who solve the questions proposed to them on sacred subjects."[1]

The *Brahmanas*, composed by some of the wisest sages of the ancient world, though not enjoying the authority of the Vedas, are of the highest value to the student of the Vedic literature.

Professor Macdonell says they are notable as representing the oldest prose writing of the Indo-European family.[2]

The *Sutras* are divided into—

(1) Sikhsha (phonetic directory.)
(2) Chhandas (metre).
(3) Vyakarana (grammar).
(4) Nirukta (explanation of words).
(5) Jyotish (astronomy).
(6) Kalpa (ceremonial).

This division will show that the study of language was cultivated by the Hindus from the earliest time on scientific principles.

Speaking of the Pratisakhya (a sub-division of Sikhsha) of the white Yajush, Professor H. H. Wilon says: "Such laborious minutiæ and elaborate subtleties relating to the enunciation of human speech are not to be met with in the literature of any other nation."[3]

[1] Weber's Indian Literature, p. 22.
[2] Macdonell's Sanskrit Literature, p. 32.
[3] Wilson's Essays on Sanskrit Literature, Vol. III, p. 317.

Professor Macdonell says: "They (Pratisakhya) contain a number of minute observations, such as have only been made over again by the phoneticians of the present day in Europe."[1]

Professor Wilson again says: "It is well-known how long it took before the Greeks arrived at a complete nomenclature for the parts of speech. Plato only knew of noun and verb as the two component parts of speech, and, for philosophical purposes, Aristotle too, did not go beyond that number. It is only in discussing the rules of rhetoric that he is led to the admission of two more parts of speech—conjunctions and articles. The pronoun does not come in before Zenodotus, and the proposition occurs first in Aristarchos. In the Pratisakhya, on the contrary, we meet at once with the following exhaustive classification of the parts of speech."[2]

Mr. Alexander Thomson, the late learned Principal of the Agra College, and one of the best philologists in India, used to say that the consonantal division of the alphabet of the Sanskrit language was a more wonderful feat of human genius than any the world has yet seen. Even now the Europeans are far behind the Hindus in this respect. Professor Macdonell says: "We Europeans, 2,500 years later, and in the scientific age, still employ an alphabet which is not only inadequate to represent all the sounds of our language, but even preserve the random order in which vowels and consonants are jumbled up as they were in the Greek adaptation of the primitive Semitic arrangement of 3,000 years ago."[3]

Rev. Ward says: "In Philology the Hindus have, perhaps, excelled both the ancients (Greeks and Romans) and the moderns."[4]

[1] Macdonell's Sanskrit Literature, p. 38.

[2] Wilson's Essays on Sanskrit Literature, Vol. III, p 321 (3rd edition). Professor Jacobi of Bonn thinks the Vedic period goes back to 4,000 B.C.—Macdonell's Sanskrit Literature, p. 12.

[3] Macdonell's History of Sanskrit Literature p. 17.

[4] Mythology of the Hindus.

Professor Max Muller says: "The idea of reducing a whole language to a small number of roots, which in Europe was not attempted before the sixteenth century by Henry Estienne, was perfectly familiar to the Brahmans *at least* 500 years before Christ."[1]

"The science of language, indeed," says Sir W. W. Hunter "had been reduced in India to fundamental principles at a time when the grammarians of the West still treated it as accidental resemblances."[2]

Another branch of the science of language, the grammatical treatment of it, was cultivated to a degree which not only defies comparison, but is unique in the annals of literature. The most eminent Indian grammarian, Panini Muni, has achieved the most perfect work of its kind of which the human mind is capable. Professor Weber speaks in rapturous terms of Panini's achievement. He says: "We pass at once into the magnificent edifice which bears the name of Panini as its architect, and which justly commands the wonder and admiration of everyone who enters, and which, by the very fact of its sufficing for all the phenomena which language presents. bespeaks at once the marvellous ingenuity of its inventor and his profound penetration of the entire material of the language."[3]

Sir W. W. Hunter says: "The grammar of Panini stands supreme among the grammars of the world, alike for its precision of statement and for its thorough analysis of the roots of the language and of the formative principles of words. By applying an algebraical terminology, it attains a sharp

[1] Max Muller's Lectures on the Science of Language, p. 80. For H. Estienne, see Sir John Stoddart, Glossology.

[2] Imperial Gazetteer, "India," p. 214.

[3] Weber's Indian Literature, p. 216. "Those rules (of grammar) are formed with the utmost conciseness, the consequence of very ingenious methods."—Colebrooke on Sanskrit and Prakrit languages, *Asiatic Researches*, Vol. VII.

succinctness unrivalled in brevity, but at times enigmatical. It arranges in logical harmony the whole phenomena which the Sanskrit language presents, and stands forth as one of *the most splendid achievements of human invention and industry.* So elaborate is the structure that doubts have arisen whether its innumberable rules of formation and phonetic change, its polysyllabic derivatives, its ten conjugations with its multiform aorists and long array of tenses could ever have been the spoken language of a people."[1]

Manning says: The celebrated Panini bequeathed to posterity one of the oldest and most renowned books ever written in any language."[2] The scientific completeness of Sanskrit grammar appeared to Sir W. Jones so unaccountable that he wrote about it with amazement and admiration."[3]

In Europe, generally speaking, grammatical science does not yet treat of those high principles which underlie the life and growth of language. It is not fair to Panini to compare with his *Vyakarana*, the grammars of modern Europe, where the grammatical science has not yet grasped those principles of the formation and development of language, which it is the unique honour of Sanskrit grammars to classify and explain.

Professor MacDonell says: "The results attained by the Indians in the systematic analysis of language, surpass those arrived at by any other nation."[4]

Mrs. Manning says: "Sanskrit grammar is evidently far superior to the *kind* of grammar which for the most part has *contented* grammarians in Europe."[5]

[1] Imperial Gazetteer of India, "India," p. 214.
[2] Ancient and Mediæval India, Vol. I, p. 384.
[3] Ancient and Mediæval India, Vol. I, p. 379, "The grammatical works of the Hindus are so remarkable that in their own department they are said to exceed in merit nearly all, if not all, grammatical productions of other nations," p. 583.
[4] Macdonell's Sanskrit Literature, p. 39.
[5] Ancient and Mediæval India, Vol. I, p. 381.

"Vyakarana," says the same authoress, "was not merely grammar in the lower acceptation of being an explanation of declension, conjugation and other grammatical forms, but was from its commencement a scientific grammar or grammatical science in the highest sense which can be attributed to this term."[1]

Mr. Elphinstone says: "His works (Panini's) and those of his successors have established a system of grammar, the most complete that ever was employed in arranging elements of human speech."[2]

Professor Max Muller says: "Their (Hindus) achievements in grammatical analysis are still unsurpassed in the grammatical literature of any nation."

"Panini, Katyayana, and Patanjali are the canonical triad of grammarians of India," and, to quote Mrs. Manning once more, "such (grammatical) works are originated as are unrivalled in the literary history of other nations."[3]

Rev. Ward says: Their grammars are very numerous, and reflect the highest credit on the ingenuity of their authors."[4]

Professor Sir Monier Williams remarks: "The grammar of Panini is one of the most remarkable literary works that the world has ever seen, and *no other country can produce any grammatical system at all comparable to it, either for originality of plan or analytical subtlety.*" The Professor again says: "His Sastras are a perfect miracle of condensation."[5]

A commentary on Panini's grammar was written by Katyayana, author of *Varttikas*. He was criticised by Patanjali, who wrote the *Mahabhashya*, which is, according to Professor Sir

[1] See Goldstucker's Panini, p. 196. Vyakarana = undoing or analysis.
[2] Elphinstone's History of India, p. 116.
[3] Ancient and Mediæval History of India, Vol. I, p. 381. "Hindu grammarians have been engaged in the solution of interesting problems from times immemorial," p. 381.
[4] Ward's Mythology of the Hindus.
[5] Indian Wisdom, p 172.

Monier Williams, "one of the most wonderful grammatical works that the genius of any country has ever produced."[1]

The following grammarians are said to have preceded Panini: Apisali, Kasyapa, Gargya, Galava, Sakravarmana, Bharadwaja, Sakatyana, Sakalya, Senaka, and Sphotsyana.

As regards lexicons, the Rev. Ward says: "Their dictionaries also do the highest credit to the Hindu learned men, and prove how highly the Sanskrit was cultivated in former periods."

POETRY.

Blessings be with them and eternal praise.
The poets who on earth have made us heirs
Of Truth and pure delight by heavenly lays.

—*Wordsworth.*

Count Bjornstjerna says: "Poetry rules over all in India; it has lent its forms, its coloring, and its charms even to the most abstract sciences, yea, even to religion."[2]

Professor Max Duncker says: "The treasures of poetry in India are inexhaustible."[3]

Among such a "poetical people" as the Hindus—as Professor Heeren[4] aptly terms them—peotry flourished in wonderful luxuriance, and its various branches were cultivated with marvellous success. Professor Heeren says: "The various branches of poetry, such as the narrative and the dramatic, the lyric as well

[1] Monier Williams' Indian Wisdom, pp. 176 and 177. Patanjali is said to have been born at Gonarda in the east of India and lived for some time in Kashmir. His mother's name (according to some) was Ganika. Panini was, however, a native of Slatura, to the north-west of Attock on the Indus His mother, Dakshi, was descended from Daksha. Professor Goldstucker thinks he has grounds to decide that Panini lived before Buddha.

[2] Theogony of the Hindus, p. 80.

[3] History of Antiquity, Vol. IV, p. 27.

[4] Hist, Researches, Vol. II, p. 186.

the didactic and the apologue, have all flourished in Sanskrit literature, and produced the most excellent results."[1]

Professor Macdonell says: "The proneness of the Indian mind to reflection not only produced important results in religion, philosophy and science; it also found a more abundant expression in poetry *than the literature of any other nation can boast.*"[2]

Mr. Elphinstone says: "All who have read the heroic poems in the original are enthusiastic in their praise, and their beauties have been most felt by those whose own productions entitle their judgment to most respect. Nor is this admiration confined to critics who have peculiarly devoted themselves to Oriental literature. Milman and Schlegel vie with Wilson and Jones in their applause; and from one or other of these writers we learn the simplicity and originality of the composition; the sublimity, grace and pathos of particular passages; the natural dignity of actors; the holy purity of manners, and the inexhaustible fertility of imagination in the authors."[3]

EPIC POETRY.

And here the singer for his art,
Not all in vain may plead,
The song that nerves a nation's heart,
Is in itself a deed.

Tennyson.

Professor Heeren says: "The literature of the Hindus is rich in epic poetry."[4]

The Ramayana and the Mahabharata, however, are the

[1] Hist. Researches, Vol. II, p. 147.

[2] History of Sanskrit Literature p. 377.

[3] Elphinstone's History of India, p. 155.

[4] Historical Researches, Vol. II, p. 147.

principal epics, the epics *par excellence* of India. Professor Monier Williams thus speaks of them: "Although the Hindus, like the Greeks, have only two great epic poems, namely, the Ramayana and the Mahabharata, yet to compare these with the Iliad or the Odyssey is to compare the Indus and the Ganges rising in the snows of the world's most colossal ranges, swollen by numerous tributaries spreading into vast shallows or branching into deep divergent channels, with the streams of Attica or the mountainous torrents of Thessally. There is, in fact, an immensity of bulk about this, as about every other department of Sanskrit literature, which, to a European accustomed to a more limited horizon, is absolutely bewildering."[1]

Of these remarkable poems, the Ramayana is the older, while the Mahabharata is the larger of the two. Apart from their high poetical merits, in which they defy rivalry and discard comparison, their enormous bulk is a standing puzzle to European critics.[2]

A comparison with the other great epics of the old world will give an idea of their enormous size.

Mahabharata has	...	2,20,000 lines.
Ramayana has	...	48,000 „
Homer's Iliad has	...	15,693 „
Virgil's Ænead has	...	9,868 „

The Iliad and Odyssey together contain 30,000 lines. Schlegel calls the Ramayana "the noblest of epics."

"Ramayana," says Professor Monier Williams, "is undoubtedly one of the greatest treasures in Sanskrit literature."

Sir W. Jones says: "The Ramayana is an epic poem on the story of Rama, which, in unity of action, magnificence of imagery

[1] Indian Epic Poetry, p. 1.

[2] The Mahabharata is about 8 times as large as the Iliad and Odyssey put together.—Macdonell's Sanskrit Lit., p. 282.

and elegance of style far surpasses the learned and elaborate work of Nonnus."[1]

After giving the argument of the Ramayana, Prof. Heeren, with his usual moderation, says: "Such, in few words, is the chief subject of Ramayana, while the development and method of handling this simple argument is so remarkably rich and copious as to suffer little from a comparison in this respect with the most admired productions of the epic muse."[2]

Professor Sir M. Monier Williams says: "There is not in the whole range of the Sanskrit literature a more charming poem than the Ramayana. The classical purity, clearness and simplicity of its style, the exquisite touches of true poetic feeling with which it abounds, its graphic descriptions of heroic incidents, nature's grandest scenes, the deep acquaintance it displays with the conflicting workings and most refined emotions of the human heart, all entitle it to rank among *the most beautiful compositions that have appeared at any period or in any country*. It is like a spacious and delightful garden, here and there allowed to run wild, but teeming with fruits and flowers, watered by perennial streams, and even its most tangled jungle intersected with delightful pathways. The character of Rama is nobly portrayed. It is only too consistently unselfish to be human.[3] We must in fact bear in mind that he is half a god, yet though occasionally dazzled by flashes from his superior nature, we are not often

[1] Asiatic Researches, p. 255. A writer in the *Westminster Review* for April 1868 offers the Mahabharata such a remote antiquity as to leave behind not only Manu but even the writings of Asvalyana, etc. Count Bjornstjerna date, it at 2,000 B. C. Dr. Mitra points out that "the Mahabharata, in the course of its thousands of verses, nowhere alludes to Buddhism and Buddha, and must therefore, and on other grounds not worth naming here, date from before the birth of Sakya."—The Indo Aryans, Vol. I, p. 38.

[2] Heeren's Historical Researches, Vol. II, p. 149.

[3] "When identified with the deity, he seems himself unconscious of his true character. It is even possible that the passages which make him an incarnation of Vishnu may be later interpolations."

blinded or bewildered by it. At least in the earlier portion of the poem he is not generally represented as more than a heroic, noble-minded, pious, virtuous man, whose bravery, unselfish generosity, filial obedience, tender attachment to his wife, love for his brothers and freedom from all resentful feelings, we can appreciate and admire. When he falls a victim to the spite of his father's second wife, he cherishes no sense of wrong. When his father decides on banishing him, not a murmur escapes his lips. In noble language he expresses his resolution to sacrifice himself rather than allow his parent to break his pledged word. As to Sita, she is a paragon of domestic virtues." [1]

Sita is the noblest ideal of a waman. Her noble and calm devotion to her lord, her unbounded love, her exalted conception of the eternal, nay, divine relation of a wife to her husband are ideals unparalleled for loftiness and sublimity in any language or literature. What can be more noble than her address to Rama when she pleads for permission to accompany him into banishment?

A wife must share her husband's fate. My duty is to follow thee.
Where'er thou goest. Apart from thee, I would not dwell in heaven itself.
Deserted by her lord, a wife is like a miserable corpse.
Close as thy shadow would I cleave to thee in this life and hereafter.
Thou art my king, may guide, my only refuge, my divinity.
It is my fixed resolve to follow thee. If thou must wander forth
Through thorny trackless forests, I will go before thee, treading down
The prickly brambles to make smooth thy path. Walking before thee
Shall feel no weariness: the forest-thorns will seem like silken robes;
The bed of leaves a couch of down. To me the shelter of thy presence
Is better far than stately palaces and paradise itself.
Protected by thy arm, gods, demons, men shall have no power to harm me.
With thee I'll live contentedly on roots and fruits. Sweet or not sweet,
If given by thy hand, they will to me be like the food of life.
Roaming with thee in desert wastes, a thousand years will be a day;
Dwelling with thee, e'en hell itself should be to me a heaven of bliss.

[1] Indian Epic Poetry, p. 12.

"Juliet," says Prof. Dowden, "is but a passionate girl before this perfect woman," meaning, Brutus' Portia, but what becomes of Portia herself before this heavenly woman, this ethereal being, this celestial Sita?

As for Rama, his character stands simply unrivalled in all literature, ancient or modern, Asiatic or European.

Principal Griffith says: "Well may the Ramayana challenge the literature of every age and country to produce a poem that can boast of such perfect characters as a Rama and a Sita." He adds: "Nowhere else are poetry and morality so charmingly united, each elevating the other as in this really holy poem."

Miss Mary Scott says: "The Ramayana is full of poetry, and Sita one of the sweetest types of womanhood that I have ever read."[1]

As for the Mahabharata, Professor Hereen says: "It will scarcely be possible to deny the Mahabharata to be one of the richest compositions in Epic poetry that was ever produced."[2]

Dr. F. A. Hassler of America thus waxes eloquent in praise of the Mahabharata: "In all my experience in life, I have not found a work that has interested me as much as that noble production of the wise, and I do not hesitate to say, inspired men of ancient India. In fact I have studied it more than any other work for a long time past, and have made at least 1,000 notes, which I have arranged in alphabetical order for the purpose of study. The Mahabharata has opened to me, as it were, a new world, and I have been surprised beyond measure at the wisdom, truth, knowledge, and love of the right which I have found displayed in its pages. Not only so, but I have found many of the truths which my own heart has taught me in regard to the

[1] Letter to P. C. Roy, dated London, the 8th December 1883.

[2] Historical Researches, Vol. II. p. 164.

Supreme Being and His creations set forth in beautiful, clear language."[1]

"This poem[2] is really a series of religious, moral, metaphysical, philosophic and political disquisitions strung upon a thread of narrative. This not only gives to the modern world a living picture of Indian life, manners, politics, religion and philosophy as they existed more than 2,000 years ago, but they transmit to us some of the most sublime poetry and some of the deepest and noblest thoughts that have ever been given to the world."

Sri Krishna, the greatest politician the world has produced, says:—

"The wise grieve not for the departed, nor for those who yet survive.
Ne'er was the time when I was not, nor thou, nor yonder Chiefs, and ne'er
Shall be the time when all of us shall be not; as the unbodied soul
In this corporeal frame moves swiftly on through boyhood, youth and age,
So will it pass through other forms hereafter—be not grieved thereat.
The man whom pain and pleasure, heat and cold affect not, he is fit
For immortality: that which is not cannot be—and that which is
Can never cease to be. Know this: the being that spread this universe
Is indestructible; who can destroy the Indestructible?
These bodies that enclose the everlasting soul, inscrutable,
Immortal, have an end—but he who thinks the soul can be destroyed,
And he who deems it a destroyer, alike mistaken: it
Kills not, and is not killed; it is not born nor doth it ever die;
It has no past nor future—unproduced, unchanging, infinite: he
Who knows it fixed, unborn, imperishable, indissoluble,
How can that man destroy another, or extinguish aught below?
As man abandon old and threadbare clothes to put on others new,
So casts the embodied soul its worn out frame to enter other forms.
No dart can pierce it; flame cannot consume it, water wet it not,
Nor scorching breezes dry it: indestructible, incapable
Of heat or moisture or aridity—eternal, all-pervading,
Steadfast, immovable; perpetual, yet imperceptible,
Incomprehensible, unfading, deathless, unimaginable."

Professor Sylvain Levi of Paris says: "The Mahabharata is not only the largest, but also the grandest of all epics, as

[1] Letter to P. C. Roy, dated 21st July 1888. See Roy's Mahabharata.
[2] The "Hamilton Daily Spectator" of May 31st, 1884.

it contains throughout a lively teaching of morals under a glorious garment of poetry."[1]

The American ethnologist, Jeremiah Curtin says: "I have *never obtained more pleasure from reading any book in my life.* The Mahabharata will open the eyes of the world to the true character and intellectual rank of the Aryans of India. The Mahabharata is a real mine of wealth not entirely known, I suppose, at present to any man outside your country, but which will be known in time and valued in all civilized lands for the reason that it contains information of the highest import to all men who seek to know in singleness of heart, the history of our race upon the earth, and the relations of man with the Infinite Power above us, around us and in us."[2]

Saint Hilaire Bartholemy thus speaks of the Mahabharata in the *Journal Des Savantes* of September 1886: "When a century ago (1785) Mr. Wilkins published in Calcutta an extract from the grand poem (Mahabharata), and made it known through the episode of the Bhagavadgita, the world was dazzled with its magnificence. Vyasa, the reputed author of the Mahabharata, appeared greater than even Homer, and it required a very little indeed to induce people to place India above Greece. . . . . . . It has not the less been admitted that this prodigious Hindu epic is one of the grandest monuments of its kind of human intelligence and genius."

Sir Edwin Arnold, in his "Indian Idylls," claims for parts of it "an origin anterior to writing anterior to Puranic theology, anterior to Homer, perhaps to Moses." He further says: "What truer conception of a wife than this, written more than three thousand years ago: "She is a true wife who is skilful in household

[1] Letter to P. C Roy, dated the 17th March 1888. "Mahabharata is an inexhaustible mine of proverbial philosophy."—Macdonell's Sanskrit Literature, p. 378.

[2] See Roy's Translation of Mahabharata, part XXX.

affairs: she is a true wife whose heart is devoted to her lord; she is a true wife who knoweth none but her lord. The wife is man's half; the wife is the first of friends: the wife is the root of salvation. They that have wives have the means of being cheerful: they that have wives can achieve good fortune. Sweet-speeched wives are as friends on occasions of joy: they are as mothers in hours of sickness and woe. A wife, therefore, is one's most valuable possession. No man even in anger should ever do anything that is disagreeable to his wife, seeing that happiness, joy and virtue, everything depended on the wife," and concludes by saying: "we may well accept this great poem as one of the priceless possessions of the East."

Mr. Titus Munson Coan,[1] says: "The Hindu epics have a nearer significance for us than anything in the Norse Mythology. The Mahabharata, one of the longest of these poems, has wider romantic element in it than King Frithiof's *Saga*; its action is cast upon a grander scale, and its heroes belittle all others in mythology. The Hindu poems, early though they are, contain ethical and human elements that are unknown to the Norseman. It is in this that their enduring, their growing interest remains for the mind of Europe and America."

Mon. A. Barth says: "Some portions of the Mahabharata may well compare with the purest and most beautiful productions of human genius.[2] The Ramayana is three times as large as Homer's Iliad, and the Mahabharata four times as large as the Ramayana. Homer's Iliad and Odyssey have thirty thousand lines, the Mahabbarata has two hundred and twenty thousand

[1] The *New York Times* of 4th March 1888. The *Watertown Post* (Tuesday, June 22, 1886), calls Mahabharata, "one of the most wonderful poems of which we have any record," and says: "The poem is the Mahabharata the oldest, the most voluminous, and, according to Wheeler, the historian of India, the most valuable epic in any language. It consists of some 220,000 lines, is fourteen times longer than the Iliad."

[2] *Revue De L' Historic Des Religions*, Paris, 1889, p. 38.

lines, and in addition, a supplement of sixteen thousand three hundred and seventy-four couplets. But it is not in size alone that the sacred epics of Valmiki and Vyasa excel. They enchant by the wondrous story they tell of ancient Aryan life, faith and valour. There is also a lively teaching of morals under a glorious garment of poetry." "Matchless vivacity, unsurpassably tender and touching episodes, and a perfect store-house of national antiquities, literature and ethics."[1]

Speaking of a certain part of the Mahabhrata, a critic says: "We know of no episode, even in Homeric poems, which can surpass its grandeur or raise a more solemn dirge over the desolation of the fallen heart of men."[2]

The characters of the five Pandavas, of Krishna, Duryodhana, Drona, Bhishma and Karana, are drawn with a true poetic feeling "and with much artistic delicacy of touch." Yudhishtira, Arjuna, Bhima, are portraits worthy of the highest poets, and can only be drawn by men of extraordinary imagination, by soaring intellects as Vyasa.

"The Ramayana and the Mahabharata," says Wilson, "abound with poetical beauties of the first order, and particularly in

[1] The *Montreal Herald* (Thursday, Nov. 12th, 1891). Trubner's American, European and Oriental Literary Record, new Series, Vol. VII, No. 3, speaks of the Mahabbharata as "the wonderful epic," and regrets "how little has up to the present been done to unravel the mysteries it contains, or even to smooth a path leading to its golden treasures!"

[2] The *Westminster Review* for October 1842. "Many of its (Mahabharata's episodes of themselves would make perfect poems of the first grade, and would stand comparison with any European poems. There is a touching episode, full of true poetic feeling, in Adiparva 6104, called Bakabadha, as there are a thousand others."—Monier Williams' *Epic Poetry of India*.

Perfection is a merit known only to the Hindus. "A European poet would have brought the story to an end" after the termination of the war in favour of the Pandavas, but "the Sanskrit poet has a far deeper insight into man's nature," and would not end there, to the dissatisfaction of the reader but would wind up the story and end with the translation of the Pandavas to Heaven.

delineations of picturesque manners and situations, and in the expression of natural and amiable feeling."[1]

"There are many graphical passages," says Professor Monier Williams, "in the Ramayana and Mahabharata, which for beauty of description cannot be surpassed by anything in Homer, . . . that the diction of Indian epics is more polished, regular and cultivated, and the language altogether in a more advanced stage of development than that of Homer." Then, as to the description of scenery,[2] in which Hindu poets are certainly *more* graphic and picturesque than either Greek or Latin . . . he adds: "Yet there are not wanting indications in the Indian epics of a higher degree of cultivation than that represented in the Homeric poems. The battlefields of the Ramayana and the Mahabharata are not made barbarous by wanton cruelties, and the description of Ayodhya and Lanka imply far greater luxury and refinement than those of Sparta and Troy." Ramayana and Mahabharata rise above the Homeric poems also in the fact "that a deep religious meaning appears to underlie all the narrative, and that the wildest allegory may be intended to conceal a sublime moral, symbolizing the conflict between good and evil, teaching the hopelessness of victory in so terrible a contest with purity of soul, self-abnegation and the subjugation of the passions."[3]

Mr. Herbert Spencer, the greatest of the modern European thinkers, condemns the Iliad among other things for the reason "that the subject matter appeals continually to brutal passions and the instincts of the savage."[4]

[1] Mill's India, Vol p. 52, footnote

[2] "In Homer, the description of scenery and natural objects are too short and general to be really picturesque. Twining says that the Greek poets did not look upon Nature with a painter's eye."—Monier Williams' *Indian Epic Poetry*.

[3] Indian Epic Poetry, p. 4.

Herbert Spencer's Autobiography. Vol. I, p. 262.

The eminent scientist, Dr. A. R. Wallace, the codiscoverer with Darwin of the principle of Natural Selection says: "I have now finished reading the Mahabharata, which is on the whole very fine, finer, I think, than the Iliad."[1]

Sir Monier Williams says: "And in exhibiting pictures of domestic life and manners the Sanskrit epics are even more valuable than the Greek and Roman. In the delineation of women, the Hindu poet throws aside all exaggerated colouring, and draws from Nature. Kaikeyi, Mandodari, Kausalya, and even Manthra, are all drawn to the very life. Sita, Draupadi, and Damayanti engage our affections far more than Helen or even than Penelope. Indeed, Hindu wives[2] are generally perfect patterns of conjugal fidelity; nor can it be doubted that in these delightful portraits of the *pativrata* or devoted wife, we have true representations of the purity and simplicity of Hindu domestic manners in early times."

"Nothing," says the Professor further on, "can be more beautiful and touching than the picture of domestic and social happiness in the Ramayana and the Mahabharata. It is indeed in depicting scenes of domestic affection, and expressing those universal feelings and emotions which belong to human nature in all time and in all places, that Sanskrit epic poetry is *unrivalled*."[3]

[1] Letters and Reminiscences of Dr. Alfred Russel Wallace, by J. Maschant.

[2] Count Bjornstjerna says: "Among other remarkable particulars in this poem is the pure light in which it sets the noble character and highminded devotion of the women of India."—*Theogony of the Hindus*, p. 82.

[3] Indian Epic Poetry, pp. 57 and 58. "Contrast with the respectful tone of Hindu children towards their parents the harsh manner in which Telemachus generally speaks to his mother. Filial respect and affection is quite as noteworthy a feature in the Hindu character now as in ancient times. I have been assured by Indian officers that it is common for unmarried soldiers to stint themselves almost to starvation point that they may send money to their aged parents. In this, the Hindus might teach us (Englishmen) a lesson."—*Sir Monier Williams.*

In addition to these two most celebrated epics, there are a large number of smaller epics which would well stand comparison with similar poems of any country. Mr. Colebrooke speaks of *Raghuvansa* in the highest terms, and says, "*Sisupalbadh* is another celebrated epic poem."[1] "*Kirat Arjuniya* is remarkable," according to Colebrooke "for the variety of measures and the alliteration,[2] while *Maha Karyas* appears to the European reader very remarkable for verbal ingenuity." "*Bhattikavya*, by Bharteri Hari, is a poem of considerable reputation."[3] "*Kumar Sambhava* is charming and fanciful," and, adds Mr. Griffith, "the author must have tried all the fertility of resource, the artistic skill, and the exquisite ear of the author of *Lala Rookh*."[4]

Nalodaya, which is attributed to Kalidasa, "is remarkable for showing the extraordinary powers of the Sanskrit language, and it is impossible not to wonder at the ingenuity of the workman."[5] Mr. Colebrooke speaks of it as an instance of a complete poem, every canto of which exhibits variety of metre. "This," says Mrs. Manning also, "is an extraordinary peom."

Prof. Macdonell says: "The composition is so arranged that by the use of ambiguous words and phrases the story of the Ramayana and the Mahabharata is told at one and the same time. The same words, according to the sense in which they are understood, narrate the events of each epic. A *tour dè force* of this kind is doubtless unique in the literature of the world."[6]

Of *Nala Damayanti*, Professor Hereen says: "Remarkable as this episode appears for inventive merit it is not at all inferior

[1] Ancient and Mediæval India, Vol. II, p. 134.
[2] Manning's Ancient and Mediæval India, Vol. II, p. 135.
[3] Ibid, p. 137. "Verbal ingenuity is its most remarkable quality."
[4] Preface Griffith's translation of the "Birth of the War God."
[5] Old Indian Poetry.
[6] Sanskrit Literature, p. 331.

in point of style, and some passages *would do credit even to Homer himself.*"[1]

The imagination of the ancient Hindus was remarkable for fertility as well as range; in fact, like the whole face of nature, like those stupendous mountains, majestic rivers, and boundless expanse of the country around them, the ancient Hindu standards of strength and splendour are bewildering to some critics, who are "accustomed to a more limited horizon." Their (Hindu) creations are, therefore, not only unrivalled but unapproachable in beauty, richness and grandeur.

To the European everything is grand, sublime and magnificent in India, whether you look at the outward expression of nature, or at the physical and mental resources of the country. Look at the creation of God or the creation of man, you are absolutely struck with amazement and awe! The snowy peaks of her sublime Himavat seem to raise their heads higher than the highest heaven, while before their Indra and Brahma the Greeks Apollo and Jupiter sink into insignificance.

"If we compare," says Professor Hereen, "the mythology of the Hindus with that of the Greeks, it will have nothing to apprehend on the score of intrinsic copiousness. In point of æsthetic value, it is sometimes superior, at others, inferior to the Greek: while in luxuriance and splendour it has the decided advantage. Olympus, with all its family of gods and goddesses, must yield in pomp and majesty to the palaces of Vishnu and Indra."[2] "The Hindu mythology," he says, "like the sublime compositions of Milton and Klopstock, extends its poetic flight far into the regions of unlimited space." He adds: "The Hindu Epos has a greater resemblance to the religious poetry of the Germans and the English than Greeks, with this difference, that

[1] Heeren's Hist. Researches, Vol. II, p. 167.

[2] Heeren's Historical Researches, Vol. II, p. 285.

the poet of India has a wider range afforded to his imagination than the latter."

Some critics hold that the Ramayana is the original of the Iliad,[1] that the latter is only an adaptation of the former to the local circumstances of Greece; that Homer's description of the Trojan war is merely a mythological account of the invasion of Lanka by Ram Chandra. The main plot, of course, is the same. Troy stands for Lanka (Tabrobane), Sparta for Ajodhia, Menelaus for Rama, Paris for Ravana, Hector for Indrajit and Vibhishan; Helen for Sita, Agamemnon for Sugriva, Patroclus for Laksmana, Nestor for Jamvant. Achilles is a mixture of Arjuna, Bhima and Lakshmana.

Indeed it is very improbable, if not impossible, that the Greeks should produce all at once poems which stand amongst the greatest feats of human genius, and occupy a place in literature inferior only to the Indian epics (in some respects). Anterior to Homer, Greek literature has no existence, even no name, and it is difficult to believe that, without any previous cultivation whatever, some of the highest and the noblestwork in the whole range of literature should come into existence. The English literature did not begin with Milton, nor the Roman with Virgil; nor does the Sanskrit with Valmiki or Vyasa, as the Greek does with Homer.

Apart from external circumstances, the subject-matter lends support to the theory in a remarkable manner. The plot, the characters and the incidents resemble those of the Hindu epic poetry so strongly that it is difficult to explain this phenomenon except by assuming that the one has drawn extensively, if not wholly, from the other. And if we consider the external circumstances, the state of civilization of the two nations, their

[1] "Even the action of the Hindu Epic is placed in an age, far anterior to historical computation."—Heeren's Historical Researches.

literature, wealth and constitution, the learning and character of their creators, little doubt remains as to who were the real creators and who the adapters. M. Hippolyte Fauche, in the Preface to his French translation of the Ramayana, says that "Ramayana was composed before the Homeric poems' and that Homer took his ideas from it."

Apart from the fact that the main story has been adopted. and that the underlying plot of the one (Mahabharata) have been taken and fused together into a national epic by the Greeks, it is clear that episodes and separate incidents from the Indian epics have been taken and versified in the Greek tongue. Colonel Wilford asserts that "the subject of the *Dionysus* of Nonnus was borrowed from the Mahabharata."[1] About Ravana's invasion of the kingdom of Indra, Count Bjornstjerna says: "This myth is probably the foundation of the ancient Greek tradition of the attempt of the Titans to storm Heaven."[2]

Professor Max Duncker says: "When Dion Chrysostom remarks that the Homeric poems are sung by the Indians in their own language—the sorrows of Priam, the lamentations of Hecuba and Andromache, the bravery of Achilles and Hector—Lassen is undoubtedly right in referring this statement to the Mahabharata and putting Dhritrashtra in the place of Priam, Gandhari and Draupadi in the places of Andromache and Hecuba, Arjuna and Karna in the places of Achilles and Hector."[3]

[1] Asiatic Researches, Vol. IX, p. 93.

[2] Theogony of the Hindus, p. 81.

[3] History of Atinquity, Vol. IV, p. 81.

DRAMA.

To wake the soul by tender strokes of art,
To raise the genius and to mend the heart,
To make mankind in conscious virtue bold,
Live o'er each scene, and be what they behold.

—POPE: *Pro. to Addison's Cato.*

THE dramatic writings of the Hindus are equally remarkable. External nature, as might be expected in a country which is "the epitome of the word,"[1] is the special *forte* of the Hindu poets, and, in no country, ancient or modern, has Nature (in contradistinction to man) been treated so poetically or so extensively introduced in poetry. Though outward nature must attract, by its magnificance and its beauty, the attention of a people gifted with such marvellous power of observation and sense for beauty yet the Hindus being a people given more than any other nation to analyzing thoughts and feelings and investigating mental phenomena, have made explorations in the realms of mind that exact the homage of mankind and defy emulation. To this reason, therefore, is due that the internal nature of man, the human mind with all its thoughts, feelings, volitions, all its desires and affections, its tendencies and susceptibilities, its virtues and failings and their developments are all drawn with a pencil at once poetic and natural. Creation in perfect harmony with nature is a feature of the Hindu drama. The characters are all creations, perfect in themselves and in their fidelity to nature. Extravagance, contradiction and unsuitability in the development—either of the plot or the characters—is not permitted. The dramas hold the mirror to Nature and, in this respect, the Shakespearean dramas alone can be compared to them: while, as regards the language, Sanskrit, must of course, always stand alone in beauty and sublimity.

[1] Murray's History of India, p. 1.

With regard to the extent to which the dramatic literature has been cultivated in India, Sir W. Jones says that the *Hindu theatre would fill as many volumes as that of any nation of modern Europe.*

The Muhammadan conquest of India resulted in the effectual repression of Hindu dramatic writings. Instead of receiving further development, the Hindu drama rapidly declined, and a considerable part of this fascinating literature was for ever lost.

Professor Wilson says: "It may also be observed that the dramatic pieces which have come down to us are those of the highest order, defended by their intrinsic purity from the corrosion of time." *Rupaka* is the Hindu term for "Play," and "*Dasa Rupaka,*" or description of the ten kinds of dramatic compositions, is one of the best treatises on dramatic literature and shows the extent to which dramatic literature was cultivated by the Hindus.

Professor Macdonell says: "The drama has had a rich and varied development in India."[1] Professor Heeren says: "We might also conveniently transfer to them (Hindu dramas) the definitions of the European stage, and class them under the head of Tragedy, Comedy, Opera, Ballet Burletta, Melodrama and Farce." He adds: "There are specimens of Hindu comedy still extant no way inferior to the ancient Greek."[2]

Hindu drama, however, is in many respects superior to the Greek drama.

(1) Among the Hindus there are nine *rasa* or effects to be produced on the spectator. They are love, mirth, tenderness, fury, heroism, terror, disgust, wonder and tranquillity. "The serious part of this list is much more comprehensive than the Greek tragic *rasa* of terror and pity."

[1] Macdonell's Sanskrit, Literature, p. 348.

[2] Historical Researches, Vol. II, p. 191.

(2) "The love of Hindus is less sensual than that of the Greek and Latin comedy."—Wilson.

(3) Valour, whenever displayed in the Hindu drama, is calm, collected and dispassionate. The calm intrepidity of the hero of *Vir Charitra* presents a very favourable contrast to the fury of Tidides or the arrogance of a Rinaldo. The Hindu taste is much finer.

(4) "Women were represented in general by women." "Boy Cleopetra was unknown to the Hindu stage."

(5) The precise division of the Hindu play into acts is a feature unknown to the Greeks. The division into acts proves higher development.[1]

(6) There was, moreover, no want of instruction for stage business, and have the "asides" and "aparts" as regularly indicated as in the modern theatre in Europe.[2]

Following nature closely, the Hindu drama usually blended "seriousness and sorrow with levity and laughter." In this respect, the Hindu drama may be classed with much of the Spanish and English drama to which, as Schlegel observes, "the terms tragedy and comedy are wholly inapplicable, in the sense in which they are employed by the ancients."

The higher purpose of the dramatic art was never lost sight of by the Hindus. This is a distinguishing feature of the Hindu drama. Professor Wilson says: "We may, however, observe to the honour of the Hindu drama, that *Parakiya*, or she who is the wife of another person, is never to be made the object of a

[1] "In respect of dress and decorations, the resources of the Hindu theatre are sufficiently ample."—Heeren's Historical Researches, Vol. II.

[2] On Mill's instituting a comparison between the Chinese and the Hindu drama, Professor Wilson says: "The action of the Chinese plays is unskilfully conducted and they are wanting in the high poetic tone which distinguish those of the Hindus: at the same time they are ingenious and often interesting. They represent manners and feelings with truth. They are the works of a civilized people."—Mill's India, Vol. II, p. 60.

dramatic intrigue: a prohibition that would have sadly cooled the imagination and curbed the wit of Dryden and Congreve."[1]

Sir W. Jones says: "The dramatic species of entertainment must have been carried to great perfection when Vicramaditya, who reigned in the first century before Christ, give encouragement to poets, philologers, and mathematicians." But what a course of preliminary mental improvement," says Professor Heeren, "must the nation have gone through ere they could possess a writer like Kalidasa! ere they could understand and appreciated his genius!"

Greater masters of drama, however, lived and died in India before Kalidasa; *Bhasa* was one of them. Twelve or thirteen of his dramas have only lately come to light.

Love or *sringar*, which after hunger is the most powerful emotion in the world, is a leading principle in the dramatic literature of the world, and Mrs. Manning says: "Nowhere is love expressed with greater force and pathos than in the poetry of India."[2]

The best known dramatists of the Hindus are Kalidasa and Bhavbhuti. Kalidasa, "one of the greatest dramatists the world has ever produced," flourished in the reign of Vicramaditya in the first century B.C.,[3] while Bhavbhuti lived many centuries later.

The masterpiece of Kalidasa is the play of Sakuntala. The

[1] "Indeed nothing considered indecorous, whether of a serious or comic character, is allowed to be enacted in the sight or the hearing of the spectators."—Macdonell's Sanskrit Literature, p 348.

[2] Ancient and Mediæval India, Vol. II, p. 148.

[3] Professor Wilson says: "There having been two Kalidasas in India, and the existence of a Kalidasa at the court of Bhoja, is no argument against Amar's being contemporary with another bard of the same name, or their both having flourished long anterior to the reign of the prince." Professor Wilson then proceeds to explain the cause of such wild criticism, which he says is twofold, (1) The disputants run into the opposite vice of incredulity in order to avoid being thought credulous. (2) "Their opposition to the many claims of Hinduism is not founded so much in greater learning or superior talents as in strong prejudices in favour of their own country and high conceit of their own abilities." See Mill's History of India, Vol. I, p. 174.

plot of this "astonishing literary performance," as the great Gœthe calls it, is taken from the Mahabharata. Professor Heeren speaks in rapturous terms of this "far-famed drama,"[1] which is incomparable for its beauty, charm, tenderness and fidelity to nature, and which, in fact, stands at the head of the dramatic literature of the world. He says: "And we must, in truth, allow Kalidasa to be one of those poets who have done honor not merely to their nation but to all civilized mankind."[2]

Augustus Schlegel, the foremost German Sanskritist, says of *Sakuntala*, that it presents "through its Oriental brilliancy of colouring, so striking a resemblance to our (English) romantic drama that it might be suspected that the love of Shakespeare has influenced the translator, were it not that other Orientalists bore testimony to his fidelity."[3]

Alexander Von Humboldt also notes the masterly mode in which Kalidasa describes "the influence of nature upon the minds of lovers, his tenderness in the expression of feelings, and above all the richness of his creative fancy."[4]

"Her (Sakuntala's) love and sorrow," says Dr. Sir W. Hunter, "have furnished a theme for the great European poet of our age." Gœthe sings:—

> Wouldst thou the young years blossom and the fruit of its decline;
> And all by which the soul is charmed, enraptured, feasted, fed.
> Wouldst thou the Earth and Heaven itself in one sole name combine,
> I name thee, O Sakuntala! and all at once is said.

Professor Macdonell says: " It is a fact worth noting that

[1] Manning's Ancient and Mediæval India, Vol. II. p. 171.
[2] Historical Researches, Vol. II, p. 194.
[3] Monier Williams' Sakuntala, Preface.
Schlegel (History of Literature, p. 115) says: "What we chiefly admire in their poetry is that tender fondness of solitude and the animated vegetable kingdom that so attract us in the drama of Sakuntala, the traits 2 of female grace and fidelity and the exquisite loveliness of childhood, of such prominent interest in the older epics of India. We are also struck with the touching-pathos accompanying deep moral feeling."
[4] Ancient and Mediæval India, Vol. II, p. 142.

the beginning of one of the most famous of modern European dramas has been modelled on that of a celebrated Sanskrit play. The prelude of Sakuntala suggested to Gœthe the plan of the prologue on the stage in Faust."[1]

As regards the diction of the Hindu drama, Professor Wilson says: "It is impossible to conceive language so beautifully musical or so magnificently grand as that of the verses of Bhavbhuti and Kalidasa.,"[2]

Professor Macdonell[3] says: "In comparison with the Greek and the modern drama, Nature occupies a much more important place in Sanskrit plays." Of Sakuntala, Dushyanta says:—

> Her lip is ruddy as an opening bud,
> Her graceful arms resemble tender shoots.
> Attractive as the bloom upon the tree,
> The glow of youth is spread on all her limbs.

Another celebrated play of Kalidasa is *Vicrama and Urvasi*. Comparing this play with Sakuntala, Professor Wilson says: "There is the same vivacity of description and tenderness of feeling in both, the like delicate beauty in the thoughts and extreme elegance in the style. It may be difficult to decide to which the palm belongs, but the story of the present play is perhaps more skilfully woven, and the incidents arise out of each other more naturally than in Sakuntala, while, on the other hand, their is perhaps no one personage in it so interesting as the heroine of that drama." He adds: "The chief charm of this piece, however, is its poetry. The story, the situation and the characters are all highly imaginative, and nothing, if partiality for his work does not mislead the translator, can surpass the beauty and justice of many of the thoughts."

[1] History of Sanskrit Literature, p. 416.

[2] Wilson's Theatre of the Hindus, Vol. I, p. 63. As an instance of the great diversity of composition, I may mention the fact that the first 35 stanzas of Sakuntala exhibit eleven kinds of metre.

[3] History of Sanskrit Literature, p. 354.

Prof. Macdonell says: "The richness of creative fancy which Kalidasa displays and his skill in the expression of tender feeling, assign him a high place among the dramatists of the world."[1]

The story is founded on a legend from the *Satpath Brahmana*. *Vicrama* (a king) loves *Urvasi* (a nymph of Heaven), and his love is not rejected; but he is warned that if he is ever seen by her naked or unveiled, she shall be banished. This is a myth, and the high dramatic treatment of this scientific myth does the highest credit to the wisdom, observation and learning of Kalidasa. Explanations of this myth are given by Max, Muller in his "Comparative Mythology," as well as by Dr. Kuhn wherein he alludes also to the ideas of Weber. Max Muller makes *Urvasi*=dawn. Another explanation is that Pururavas (or Vicrama) personifies the sun, whilst *Urvasi* is the morning mist (see Chamber's Encyclopædia, S. V. Pururavas). *Urvasi* is an *apsara* and we find in Goldstucker's dictionary that the *apsaras* "are personifications of the vapours which are attached by the sun and formed into mists or clouds." *Apsaras* is derived from *ap*= waters, and *saras*=who moves.[2] Professor Goldstucker holds therefore, that the legend represents the absorption by the sun of the vapour floating in the air. When *Pururavas* becomes distinctly visible, *Urvasi* vanishes, because when the sun shines forth the mist is absorbed. *Urvasi* afterwards becomes a swan in the *Satpath*, but Kalidasa changes the nymph into a climbing plant. "In Greece, Daphne becomes a laurel, because the country abounds in laurels, which are manifest so soon as the sun has absorbed the mist."

Bhavbhuti's popularity perhaps rivalled that of Kalidasa. Professor Wilson bears testimony to the extraordinary beauty

[1] Macdonell's Sanskrit Literature, p. 353.

[2] See Wilson's Theatre of the Hindus, Vol. I, page 193.

and power of his language, and attributes his peculiar talent for describing nature in her magnificence to his early familiarity with the eternal mountains and forests of Gondwana. His best-known plays are the *Uttara Ram Charita* and *Malati Madhava*. As regards the former, Professor Wilson says: "It has more pretensions to genuine pathos than perhaps any other specimen of Hindu theatre. The mutual sorrows of Rama and Sita in their state of separation are pleasingly and tenderly expressed, and the meeting of the father and sons may be compared *advantageously* with similar scenes with which the fictions of Europe, both poetical and dramatic, abound. Besides the felicitous expression of softer feelings, this play has some curious pictures of the *beau ideal* of heroic bearing and of the duties of a warrior and a prince. *A higher elevation can scarcely be selected for either*. The true spirit of chivalry pervades the encounter of the two young princes. Some brilliant thoughts occur, the justice and beauty of which are not surpassed in any literature."[1]

As regards *Malati Madhava*, Prof. Wilson says: "It offers nothing to offend the most fastidious delicacy, and may be compared in this respect advantageously with many of the dramas of Modern Europe, which treat of the passion that constitutes its subject. The manner in which love is here depicted is worthy of observation, as correcting a mistaken notion of the influence which the passion exercises over the minds of the natives of at least one portion of Asia. However intense the feeling—and it is represented as sufficiently powerful to endanger existence—it partakes in no respect of the impetuosity which it has pleased the writers of the West to attribute to the people of the East.

> The barbarous nations whose inhuman love,
> Is wild desire, fierce as the sun they feel.

The heroine of this drama is loved as a woman. She is no

[1] Wilson's Theatre of the Hindus, Vol. I, pp. 383, 384.

goddess in the estimation of her lover. The passion of Malati is equally intense with that of Juliet. The fervour of attachment which unites the different personages of the drama so indissolubly in life and death is creditable to the Hindu national character. Unless instances of such disinterested union had existed, the author could scarcely have conceived, much less pictured it."

Altogether, *Malati Madhava* is one of the most charming, powerful and refined representations of the emotion of love to be found in the literature of any nation.

The political life and manners of the Hindus are well depicted by Visakhadatta in his celebrated play, *Mudra Rakshasa*. It has the stir and action of city life, the endless ingenuity of political and court intrigue, and the "staunch fidelity which appears as the uniform characteristic of servants, emissaries and friends, a singular feature in the Hindu character," which, Professor Wilson remarks, "it has not wholly lost." Professor Wilson adds: "It is a political or historical drama, and unfolds the political policy of Chanakya, the Machiavel of India, in a most ingenious manner. The plot of the drama singularly conforms to one of the unities, and the occurrences are all subservient to one action—the conciliation of Rakhshasa. This is never lost sight of from first to last without being made unduly prominent. It may be difficult in *the whole range of dramatic literature to find a more successful illustration of the rule.*"[1]

The *Mrichchhkati*, or the Toy Cart, by Maharaja Sudraka, possesses considerable dramatic merit. The interest is rarely suspended, and in every case the apparent interruption is with great ingenuity made subservient to the common design. The connection of the two plots is much better maintained than in

[1] Wilson's Theatre of the Hindus, Vol. II, p. 254. "The author is the Massinger of the Hindus."—*Wilson.*

the play we usually refer to as a happy specimen of such a combination, "The Spanish Frair." The deposition of Palaka is interwoven with the main story so intimately, that it could not be detached from it without injury, and yet it never becomes so prominent as to divert attention from that to which it is only an appendage." [1]

The hero of the play, however, is Samsthanaka, the Raja's brother-in-law. "A character so utterly contemptible has perhaps been scarcely ever delineated. It would be very interesting to compare this drama for its merit of unity with *The Merchant of Venice* or *The Two Noble Kinsmen*, two of the best English dramas, *in both of which the underplot is so loosely connected with the main plot.*"

One more play [2] and I have done. The celebrated drama, *Probadha Chandrodaya*, by Krishna Misra, is much admired by Professor Lassen,[3] who calls it peculiarly Indian, and "*unlike anything in the literature of other countries*. The alligorical personifications are not only well sustained but are wonderful, and the whole plot constructed with so much ability as to excite the admiration of all readers."

"Much of that of the Hindus," says Professor Wilson, "may compete successfully with the great number of dramatic productions of modern Europe, and offers no affinity to the monstrous and crude abortions which preceded the introduction of the legitimate drama in the West."

[1] Wilson's Theatre of the Hindus, Vol. I, p. 181.

[2] There are many other dramas of considerable merit and high repute. *Mahavir Charitra*, by Bhav Bhuti, *Ratnavali*, by Sri Harish Deva, Maharaja of Kashmir, and *Veni Samhara* are among those which can be advantageously compared with similar dramas in the literature of other nations.

[3] *Indische Allerthunskunde*, Vol. III, p. 790.

LYRIC POETRY.

> And fill this song of Jai Deva with thee,
> And make it wise to teach, strong to redeem,
> And sweet to living souls. Thou, mystery;
> Thou, Light of Life! Thou, Dawn beyond the dream!
>
> —*Hymn to Vishnu.*

THE Lyric poetry of the Hindus is the finest of its kind in the world, for the reason that the language in which it is written is the most melodious and musical on earth. As Professor Wilson remarks, the poetry of the Hindus can never be properly appreciated by those who are ignorant of Sanskrit. Moreover, owing to the peculiarities of life and character of the Hindus, Europeans can hardly be expected to fully appreciate and enjoy their poetry, as they neither fully understand their character, nor fully enter into their feelings and sympathise with them. To the Hindus, Bharata's conduct in following Rama into the jungle and entreating him to return to Ayodhia is as natural as anything in the world, while to Mr. Talboys Wheeler, the historian of India, it appears "contrary to human nature!!" As Mr. Wheeler regards the venerable Dasratha as shamming when he gives vent to sorrow after having sentenced Rama to exile to keep a vow, what would he have thought of the Hindu ladies of the present day had he known that they would die or suffer anything rather than open their lips even to those who are dearer to them than life itself, when they think modesty forbids their doing so, even when life itself is in danger? Hindu ideas of duty obedience and modesty are much more complex and advanced than those of other nations. Still, when Hindu Lyric Poetry has been properly judged, the praise has been liberal, and approbation emphatically expressed.

Professor Macdonell says: "It is impossible even for the Sanskrit scholar who has not lived in India, to appreciate fully the merits of this later poetry, much more so for those who can only become acquainted with it in translation. For, in the first place the metres, artificial and elaborate though they are, have a beauty of their own which cannot be reproduced in another language. Again, to understand it thoroughly the reader must have seen the tropical plains and forests of Hindustan steeped in intensive sunshine or bathed in brilliant moonlight; he must have viewed the silent ascetic seated at the foot of the sacred fig-tree, he must have experienced the feelings inspired by the approach of the monsoon, he must have watched beast and bird disporting himself in tank and river. He must know the varying aspects of Nature in the different seasons; in short, he must be acquainted with all the sights and sounds of an Indian landscape, the mere allusion to one of which may call up some familiar scene or touch chord of sentiment. Otherwise, for instance, the mango-tree, the red asoka, the orange kadamba, the various creepers, the different kinds of lotus, the mention of each of which should convey a vivid picture, are but empty names; without a knowledge, moreover, of the habits, modes of thought and traditions of the people, much must remain meaningless. But those who are properly equipped can see many beauties in classical Sanskrit poetry which are entirely lost to others. Thus a distinguished scholar known to the present writer has entered so fully into the spirit of that poetry that *he is unable to derive pleasure from any other*."[1]

Gita Govinda is the finest extant specimen of Hindu Lyric Poetry, and it is difficult to find in any language lyrics that can vie with it in melody and grace. Mr. Griffith says: "The exquisite melody of the verse can only be appreciated by those who can enjoy the original."[2]

[1] Macdonell's Sanskrit Literature, p. 279.

[2] Ancient and Mediæval India, Vol II, p. 269.

Professor Macdonell says: "The great perfection of form, Jayadeva has here attained, by combining grace of diction with ease in handling the most difficult metre, has not failed to win the admiration of all who are capable of reading the original Sanskrit. Making abundant use of alliteration and the most complex rhymes occurring as in the *Nalodaya*, not only at the end, but in the middle of metrical lines, the poet has adapted the most varied and melodious measures to the expression of exuberant erotic emotions, with a skill which could not be surpassed. It seems impossible to reproduce Jayadeva's verse adequately in English garb." [1]

Schlegel says: "Tender delicacy of feeling and elegaic love cast a halo over Indian poetry," and "the whole is recast in the mould of harmonious softness, and is redolent of elegaic sweetness." [2]

Gita Govinda has been analysed by Lassen in his Latin translation, beautifully translated in German by Ruckert, and has been dwelt upon with admiration by Sir W. Jones in his essay on the Mystical Poetry of the Hindus.

Professor Heeren says: "The Hindu lyric surpassed that of the Greek in admitting both the rhyme and blank verse." [3] He further says: "How much of the beauty of a lyric must inevitably be lost in a prose translation it would be superfluous to remark; and yet it is impossible to read the *Gita Govinda* without being charmed . . . . . . It is impossible, however, not to notice the extreme richness of the poet's fancy, the strength and vivacity of his sentiment particularly observable in his delicate

[1] Sanskrit Literature, p. 345. "It is not possible to imitate in English the almost infinite resources of the complicated and almost entirely quantitative classical Sanskrit measures." p. 349.

[2] Schlegel's History of Literature, p. 117.

[3] Historical Researches, Vol. II, p. 187.

taste for the beauties in general, and which not even the ardour of passion was able to extinguish."[1]

"*Gita Govinda* exhibits," says Mr. Elphinstone, "in perfection the luxuriant imagery and the voluptuous softness of the Hindu school."[2]

Another Hindu lyric is the *Ritu Sangrah*, something like "Thompson's Seasons" in the English language. Mrs. Manning says about it: "*Ritu Sangrah*, a lyric poem by Kalidasa, is much admired not only by the natives of India, but by almost all students of Sanskrit literature."[3]

Mr. Griffith, in his translation of *Ritu Sangrah* says: "Sir W. Jones speaks in rapturous terms of the beautiful and natural sketches with which it abounds," and after expressing his own admiration, adds, "it is much to be regretted that it is impossible to translate the whole."[4]

Professor Macdonell says: "Perhaps no other work (of Kalidasa) manifests so strikingly the poet's deep sympathy with nature, his keen power of observation and his skill in depicting an Indian landscape in vivid colours."[5]

Lyric poetry was extensively cultivated in India. Sir W. Hunter says: "The Mediæval Brahmans displayed a marvellous activity in theological as well as lyric poetry."

Professor Macdonell says: "Bearing evidence of great wealth of observation and depth of feeling, the Hindu Lyrics are often drawn by a master hand. Many of them are in matter and form gems of perfect beauty."[6] He adds: "Some of its gems are

[1] Ancient and Mediæval India, pp. 189 and 190. Jaideva, its author was born, as he himself says, at Kenduli, situated either in Calinga or in Burdwan.
[2] History of India, p. 156.
[3] Historical Reseaches, Vol. II. Professor Von Bohlen translated it into German and Latin in 1840 A.D.
[4] Manning's Ancient and Mediæval India, Vol. II, p. 265.
[5] Macdonell's Sanskrit Literature, p. 337.
[6] Ibid, p. 339.

well worthy of having inspired the genius of Heine to produce such lyrics as *Die Lotosblume* and *Auf Flugeludes Gesanges.*"

The *Sringara Satak* of Bhartari Hari is a matchless gem of perfect beauty. Of the Amara Satak, Professor Macdonell says: "The author is a master in the art of painting lovers in all moods, bliss, dejection, anger, and devotion. He is especially skilful in depicting the various stages of estrangement and reconciliation. It is remarkable how, with a subject so limited in situations and emotions so similar, the poet succeeds in arresting the attention with surprising turns of thought and with subtle touches which are ever new."[1]

Special charm must attach to Hindu Lyric Poetry, for, as Mrs. Manning remarks: "Nowhere is love expressed with greater force or pathos than in the poetry of the Hindus."[2]

Megh Duta is an excellent example of purely descriptive poetry. Professor H. H. Wilson says: "The language (of Megh Duta) although remarkable for the richness of its compounds, is not disfigured by their extravagance, and the order of the sentences is in general the natural one. The metre combines melody and dignity in a very extraordinary manner, and will bear an *advantageous* comparison with the best specimens of uniform verse in the poetry of any language, living or dead."[3]

Principal Tawney says: "The *Megh Duta* is a perfect work of art."

Fauche says: "The *Megh Duta* is without a rival in the whole elegiac literature of Europe."

Prof. Monier Williams says: "It combines the majesty of Homer with the tenderness of Virgil, the luxuriance of Ovid and the depth of Shakespeare. And yet it is simple and contains

[1] Macdonell's Sanskrit Literature, p. 342.

[2] Manning's Ancient and Mediæval India, Vol. II, p. 148.

[3] Wilson's Essays, Vol. II, p. 312.

enough to suggest the old Athenian boast of beauty without extravagance."[1]

Dr. Bhau Daji says: "The *Megh Duta* is one of the best and sublimest productions of the human mind."

Mr. R. C. Dutt says: "Kalidasa's *Megh Duta* is a lyrical gem so musical, so pathetic and yet so sublime that there is nothing equal to it either in Sanskrit or any other literature." "It is woven into such grand and majestic poetry and a theme so beautiful and sublime that imagination can conceive nothing lovelier or loftier than that."

Mr. Elphinstone says: "It is impossible to conceive language so beautifully musical or so magnificently grand as that of many verses of Kalidasa's *Cloud Messenger*."

Professor Max Muller says: It is a grand production."

Professor Macdonell says: "The theme is a message which an exile sends by a cloud to his wife dwelling far away. The idea has been borrowed and applied by Schiller in his Maria Stuart, where the captive queen of Scots calls on the clouds as they fly southwards to greet the land of her youth."[2]

ETHICO-DIDACTIC POETRY.

Thy power the breast from every error frees
And weeds out all its vices by degrees.

—GIFFORD: *Juvenal.*

THE Hindu achievements in this branch of literature establish once for all their intellectual superiority. It is this part of their literature that has made its way to the remotest corners of Europe and America. Its sway over the mind of the civilized world is almost despotic and complete.

[1] Monier William's Indian Wisdom.

[2] Macdonell's History of Sanskrit Literature, p. 335.

Professor Wilson says: "Fable constitutes with them (Hindus) practical ethics—the science of *Niti* or Polity—the system of rules necessary for the good government of society in all matters not of a religious nature—the reciprocal duties of the members of an organized body either in their private or public relations. Hence it is specially intended for the education of princes, and proposes to instruct them in those obligations which are common to them and their subjects, and those which are appropriate to their princely office; not only in regard to those over whom they rule, but in respect to other princes, under the contingencies of peace and war. Each fable is designed to illustrate and exemplify some reflection on worldly vicissitudes or some precept for human conduct; and the illustration is as frequently drawn from the intercourse of human beings as from any imaginary adventure of animal existence, and this mixture is in some degree a peculiarity of the Hindu plan of fabling or story-telling."[1]

It is now admitted by the learned everywhere that the fabulous literature of the world, which is such an important, and, in some respects, so necessary a part of the education of young men all over the world, apart from it being one of the most amusing, interesting and instructive diversions from labour and severe study, owes its origin solely to the intelligence and wisdom of the ancient Hindus.

Panchtantra is far and away the best masterpiece in the whole fabulous literature of the world; nay, it is the source from which the entire literature of fables, Asiatic or European has directly or indirectly emanated. Mr. Elphinstone says: "In the composition of tales and fables *they* (*Hindus*) *appear*

[1] Wilson's Essays on Sanskrit Literature, Vol. II, p. 85.

to have been the instructors of the rest of mankind.[1] The most ancient-known fables (those of Bidpai) have been found almost unchanged in their Sanskrit dress; and to them almost all the fabulous relations of other countries have been clearly traced by Mr. Colebrooke, the Baron-de-sacy and Professor Wilson."

The famous historian Ferishta, says: Panchtantra "was sent by the King of India to Nausherwan, King of Persia, with a chess board, when it was rendered into Pahlavi tongue by Buzoorjmehr, his vizier." The Kalala Damna, translated into Pahlavi from Sanskrit was rendered into Arabic by Ibn ool Mukba in the reign of Haroon-ul-Rashid, and in the reign of Sultan Beiram Ghiznavy it was converted into Persian from the Arabic and subsequently in the reign of Sultan Husein Mirza Khwaruzmy, Mulla Hassan Waiz Kashfy rendered the old Persian work, full of Arabic words and of Arabic poetry, into plain and elegant Persian, to which he gave the name of Anwar Suheli.[2]

Professor Macdonell says: "The Arabic version is of great importance as the source of other versions which exercised very great influence in shaping the literature of the Middle Ages in Europe. These versions of it were the later Syriac (C 1000 A. D.), the Greek (1180), the Persian (C 1130), recast later (C 1494) under the title of Anwar-i-Suhaili or Lights of Canopas, the old Spanish (1251) and the Hebrew one made about 1250 A. D.

[1] History of India, pp. 156 and 157. For a guide to further enquiry as to the Hindu origin of European fables, see Transactions of the R A. S., Vol. I, p. 155. "H. H. Wilson's analytical account of the Panchtantra." "The complicated system of story-telling, tale within tale like the Arabian Nights, seems also to have been of their invention, as are the subjects of many well-known tales and romances, Oriental and European."—Elphinstone's History of India, p. 157.

[2] Brigg's Ferishta, Vol. I, pp. 149 and 150. (Ed. 1829.)

The fourth stratum of translation is represented by John of Capua's rendering of the Hebrew version into Latin (C 1270), entitled Directorum Humanae Vitae, which was printed about 1480.

From John of Capua's work was made, at the instance of Duke Eberhardt of Wurtemberg, the famous German version, "Das Buch Der Byspel der alten Wysen," or Book of Apologues of the ancient sages, first printed about 1481. The fact that four dated editions appeared at Ulm between 1483 and 1485 and thirteen more down to 1492 is a suffieiently eloquent proof of the importance of this work as a means of instruction and amusement during the fifteenth and sixteenth centuries. The Directorum was also the source of the Italian version printed at Venice in 1552, from which came the English translation of Sir Thomas North (1570). The latter was thus separated from the Indian original by five intervening translations and a thousand years of time. [1]

Dr. Sir W. W. Hunter says: "The fables of animals, familiar to the Western world, from the time of Æsop downwards, had their original home in India. The relation between the fox and the lion in the Greek versions has no reality in nature, but it was based upon the actual relation between the lion and his follower, the jackal, in the Sanskrit stories. *Panchtantra* was translated into the ancient Persian in the sixth century A. D., and from that rendering all the subsequent versions in Asia Minor and Europe have been derived. The *most ancient animal fables of India are at the present day the Nursery Stories of England and America*. The graceful Hindu imagination delighted also in fairy tales, and the Sanskrit compositions of this class are the original source of many of the fairy stories of Persia, Arabia

[1] Macdonell's Sanskrit Literature, p. 417.

and Chiristendom."[1]

La Fontaine[2] acknowledges his indebtendness for a large part of his work to the Indian sage Pilpay (Bidpai=Vidyapati).

Professor Max Muller says: "The King of Persia, Khusro Nausherawan (531-579 A.D.), sent his physician, Barzoi, to India in order to translate the fables of the *Panchtantra* from Sanskrit into Pahlavi"[3] The Syriac translation was made about 570 A. D. and called *Kalilag* and *Damnag*. An Arabic translation from Pahlavi, called Kalilah and Dimnah, was made in the 8th century by a Persian convert who died in 760 A. D[4] *Hitopdesa* (*hita*=good and *updesa*=advice), as Mr. Manning says, is the form in which the old Sanskrit fables became introduced into the literature of nearly every known language.

Hitopdesa, owing to its intrinsic merit, is one of the most popular works in Sanskrit literature. The following stanzas dealing with the transitoriness of human life near the end of Book IV have a peculiar pensive beauty of their own:—

"As on the mighty ocean's waves
Two floating logs together come,
And having met for ever part:
So briefly joined are living things."

These lines are the source of Mathew Arnold's beautiful lines in his poem *The Terrace Berne*:—

Like driftwood spars, which meet and pass
Upon the boundless ocean-plain,
So on the sea of life, alas!
Man meets man—meets and quits again.

Prof. Macdonell says: The two Chinese encyclopædias, the

[1] Imperial Gazettar, "India," p. 238.
[2] Macdonell's Sanskrit Literature, p. 418.
[3] India: What can it teach us? p. 93. "The *Panchtantra* was translated into Persian in the sixth century by order of Nausherawan, and thence into Arabic and Turkish and lastly into French."—Heeren's Historical Researches, Vol. II, p. 200.
[4] Macdonell's Sanskrit Literature, p. 417.

older of which was completed in 668 A.D., contain a large number of Indian fables translated into Chinese, and cite no fewer than 202 Budhist works as their sources."[1]

Fabel maintains the Indian origin of the fables common to India and Greece, which proves the antiquity of the Hindu fables.[2]

Professor Weber says: "Allied to the fables are the fairy tales and romances, in which the luxuriant fancy of the Hindus has, in the most wonderful degree, put forth all its peculiar grace and charm."[3]

Professor Wilson says: "The fables of the Hindus are a sort of machinery to which there is no parallel in the fabling literature of Greece and Rome."[4] He also says that the Hindu literature contained collections of domestic narrative to an extent *surpassing those of any other* people.

Mrs. Manning thus remarks on the Panchtantra: "Each fable will be found to illustrate and exemplify some reflection on worldly vicissitude or some precept for human conduct; and instead of being aggregated promiscuously or without method, the stories are all strung together upon a connected thread and arranged in a framework of continuous narrative, out of which they successively spring."[5]

A careful study of the subject will show that even the books which appear to have a distinctive Persian character and are generally regarded to be of Persian origin are in reality Hindu to the core. Count Bjornstjerna remarks: "The thousand

[1] Macdonell's Sanskrit Literature, p. 369.

[2] Weber's Indian Literature, p. 211. "The fable reported by Arrian of Hercules having searched the whole Indian ocean and found the pearl with which he used to adorn his daughter, is of Hindu origin."—Heeren's Historical Researches, Vol. II, p. 271.

[3] Weber's Indian Literature, p. 213.

[4] Wilson's Essays, Vol. II, p. 85.

[5] Ancient and Mediæval India, Vol. II, p. 271.

and one Nights, so universally known in Europe, is a Hindu original translated into Persian and thence into other languages. In Sanskrit the name is *Vrihat katha.*"[1] Professor Lassen of Paris asserts that "The Arabian Nights Entertainments are of Hindu origin."[2]

Apart from the authority of so many learned Orientalists in favour of the Hindu origin of this literature, and the express historical evidence as to the transmission of the Hindu fables to Arabic and Persia, there is overwhelming internal evidence in the fables themselves to support the assertion that the Hindus have been the teachers of the rest of mankind in this important branch of literature. Take, for instance, the case of a particular fable. In the Panchtantra there is a story of a female bird who wished to make her nest further inland, because on the day of full moon the sea would be sweeping over the place where she then was. But the male bird objects, believing that he was as strong as the sea and that it could not encroach upon his nest. (Benfey, Vol. II, pp. 87-89). Now this story is, as Professor Wilson remarks, one of the decisive proofs of the Indian origin of the fables. The name of the bird in Arabic is *Titawi*, a word which cannot be resolved to any satisfactory Arabic root. It is "only a transcript of the Sanskrit *Tittibha*, Bengali *Titib* and Hindu *Titihir.*"

Wilson remarks that in the translation of Panchtantra, *Kalalawa Damna*, the name of the ox in Sanskrit, was *Sanjiwaka*, whence the Arabic *Shanzebeh*, and those of the jackals, Karataka and Damnaka, whence the Arabic *Kalala* and *Damna*. The tale of Ahmed and Pari Banu betrays palpably its Indian origin. *Pari Bhanu* is decidedly a Hindu name. The eldest of the three princes, Prince Husein, in search of some extraordinary rarity

[1] Theogony of the Hindus, p. 85.
[2] See his Ind. Alt. IV. p. 902.

which may entitle him to the hand of the Princess *Nuran Nihar*, repairs to the Indian city, Bisnagar (decidedly an Indian name) a metropolis of extraordinary wealth and population.

Mr. Deslongchamps says: "The book of Sindebad is of Indian origin," and adds that "the under-mentioned three stories were in a special degree derived from the original. (1) The Arabic story of a king, his son, his favourites and seven Vazirs. (2) The Hebrew romance of the Parables of Sendebar, and (3) the Greek romance of Syntipas." From the Hebrew romance above described, Deslongchamps derives "the history of the seven sages of Rome," *Historia septem sapicutan Romæ*, a very popular work in Europe for three centuries.

Professor Macdonell says: "Nothing perhaps in the history of the migration of Indian tales is more remarkable than the story of Barlaam and Josaphat. At the Court of Khalif Almansur (753-774), under whom Kalalah and Damnah was translated into Arabic, there lived a Christian known as John of Damascus who wrote in Greek the story of *Barlaam* and *Josaphat* as a manual of Christian theology......The hero of the story, Prince Josaphat, has an Indian origin, being in fact no other than Buddha. The name has been shown to be a corruption of Bodhisatwa, a well-known designation of the Indian reformer. Josaphat rose to the rank of a saint both in Greek and Roman Churches...... That the founder of an Oriental religion should have developed into a Christian saint is one of the most astounding facts in religious history."[1]

Professor Wilson says: "In a manuscript of the Parable of Sendebar, which existed in the British Museum, it is repeatedly asserted in anonymous Latin notes that the work was translated out of the Indian language into Persian and Arabic, and from

[1] Macdonell's Sanskrit Literature, p. 420.

one of them into Hebrew. Sendebar is also described as a chief of the Indian Brahmans, and Beibar, the king, as a king of India."—Ellis' *Metrical Romances*, Vol. III.

A decisive proof of Sindebad being an Indian is the direct evidence on the subject, of the eminent Arabic writer, Masudi. In his "Golden Meadows" (Miraj-ul-Zeheb), in a chapter on the ancient kings of India, he speaks of an Indian philosopher named Sindebad, who was contemporary with *Kurush*, and was the author of the work entitled, "The Story of Seven Vazirs, the tutor, the young man and the wife of the king." "This is the work," he adds, "which is called the book of Sindebad."

By his interesting analysis of the *Syntipas* and the *Parables of Sendebad*,[1] Professor Wilson clearly shows that the stories are one and all of Hindu origin.[2] He also shows that the "Seven Sages of Rome" is also of Hindu origin. Besides these fables and stories, says Professor Wilson, "various narratives of Indian origin forced their way individually and unconnectedly to Europe."[3]

Sir John Malcolm says: "Those who rank the highest among Eastern nations for genius have employed their talents in works of fiction, and have added to the moral lessons they desired to convey so much of grace and ornament that their volumes have found currency in every nation of the world."[4]

[1] Wilson's Sanskrit Essays, Vol. II, pp. 99 and 100.

[2] Ibid, p. 101.

[3] Wilson's Sanskrit Essays, Vol. II, p. 101.

[4] He fixed the Crusades as the time of the emigration to Europe of some of the well-known works of this kind, such as: (1) The Katha Saritasagar, (2) The Vital Panchvinsati, (3) The Siuhasana Dwatrinsati, and (4) The Sukasaptati. The first of these works was a translation of Brihat Katha in the Paisachi language and was translated for the amusement and instruction of Sri Harsh of Kashmir, by the order of his grandmother, Suryavati, who became *Sati* in 1093 A.D. But that the stories of which it is made up were of great antiquity is proved from the fact of one of them occurring in the Odyssey. In the fifth book of Katha Saritasagar there is a story of a man who being shipwrecked is caught

It is thus clear that the Hindus have produced a branch of literature the kind of which, in any considerable degree, has never been produced by any other nation in the world, Asiatic or European, ancient or modern. This wonderful phenomenon is thus explained by Professor Heeren. "The poetry of no other nation exhibits in such a striking manner the didactic character as that of the Hindus; for, no other people were so thoroughly imbued with the persuasion that to give and receive instruction was the sole and ultimate object of life."[1]

---

in a whirlpool, and escapes by jumping up and climbing the branch of a fig tree, apparently the banyan (*Ficus Indica*) celebrated for its pendulous roots. Professor Wilson here refers to Odyssey XII, pp. 101-104, where Ulysses escapes from a whirlpool by jumping up and clinging to the branches of a fig tree—probably the Indian fig tree or banyan, the pendulous branches of which would be more within reach than those of the Sicilian fig; and Homer, he thinks, may have borrowed the incident from some old Eastern fiction.

The tale of King Sibi, who offered up his life to save a pigeon from a hawk, "occurs in a Chinese as well as a Mohammedan form"—Macdonell's Sanskrit Literature, p. 377.

[1] Historical Researches, Vol. II, p. 197.

PHILOSOPHY.

How charming is divine philosophy,
Not harsh and crabbed, as dull fools suppose,
But musical as Apollo's lute,
And a perpetual feast of nectar'd sweets
Where no crude surfeit reigns.

—MILTON: *Comus.*

PHILOSOPHY is the real ruler of the globe: it lays down principles which guide the world. Philosophy shows how a transcendent genius exacts homage consciously or unconsciously from mankind. It is philosophy that blows the trumpet blast, and it is philosophy that blunts the edge of the sword. Philosophy reigns supreme, undisputed and absolute. It conquers the conqueror and subdues the subduer.

If it is true that a great nation alone can produce great philosophers or complete systems of philosophy, the ancient Indians may, without hesitation, be pronounced to have been the greatest nation, ancient or modern. "Philosophers," says Professor Max Muller, "arise after the security of a State has been established, after wealth has been acquired and accumulated in certain families, after schools and universities have been founded and taste created for those literary pursuits which even in the most advanced state of civilization must necessarily be confined to but a small portion of an ever-toiling community."[1]

To what high pinnacle of civilization, then, must the ancient Indians have reached, for, says Professor Max Muller further on, that "the Hindus were a nation of philosophers."[2]

[1] Ancient Sanskrit Literature, pp. 564, 565.

[2] Ancient Sanskrit Literature, p. 31.

The philosophy of the Hindus is another proof of their superiority in civilization and intellect to the moderns as well as the ancients. Manning says: "The Hindus had the widest range of mind of which man is capable."[1]

Schlegel speaks of the noble, clear and severely grand accents of Indian thought and says: "Even the loftiest philosophy of the Europeans, the idealism of reason, as is set forth by Greek philosophers, appears in comparison with the abundant light and vigour of Oriental idealism like a feeble promethean spark in the full flood of heavenly glory of the noonday sun—faltering and ever ready to be extinguished."[2]

Professor Weber, speaking of Hindu philosophy, says: "It is in this field and that of grammar that the Indian mind attained the highest pitch of its marvellous fertility."[3] "The Hindus," says Max Muller, "were a people remarkably gifted for philosophical abstraction."[4] Schlegel says: "India is pre-eminently distinguished for the many traits of original grandeur of thought and of the wonderful remains of immediate knowledge."[5]

Like all other things in India, the Hindu philosophy, too, is on a gigantic scale. Every shade of opinion, every mode of thought, every school of philosophy has found its expression in the philosophical writings of the Hindus and received its full development. Sir W. Hunter says: "The problem of thought and being, of mind and matter and soul apart from both, of the origin of evil, of the *sommum bonum* of life, of necessity and freewill, and of the relations of the creator to the creature, and the intellectual problems, such as the compatibility of evil with

[1] Ancient and Mediæval India, Vol. I, p. 114.

[2] History of Literature.

[3] Weber's Indian Literature, p. 27.

[4] Ancient Sanskrit Literature, p 566.

[5] History of Literature, p. 126.

the goodness of God and the unequal distribution of happiness and misery in this life, are endlessly discussed. *Brahmin philosophy exhausted the possible solutions of these difficulties* and of most of the other great problems which have since perplexed Greeks, Romans, Mediæval schoolmen and modern men of science."[1]

Speaking of the comprehensiveness of Hindu philosophy, Dr. Alexander Duff is reported to have said, in a speech delivered in Scotland, that "Hindu philosophy was so comprehensive that counterparts of all systems of European philosophy were to be found in it."

Professor Goldstucker[2] finds in the Upanishads "the germs of all the philosophies." Count Bjornstjerna says: "In a metaphysical point of view we find among the Hindus all the fundamental ideas of those vast systems which, regarded merely as the offspring of phantasy, nevertheless inspire admiration on account of the boldness of flight and of the faculty of the human mind to elevate itself to such remote ethereal regions. We find among them all the principles of Pantheism, Spinozism and Hegelianism, of God as being one with the universe; of the enternal spirit descended on earth in the whole spiritual life of mankind; of the return of the emanative sparks after death to their divine origin; of the uninterrupted alternation between life and death, which is nothing else but a transition between different modes of existence. All this we find again among the philosophers of the Hindus exhibited as clearly as by our modern philosophers more than three thousand years since."[3]

[1] Indian Gazetteer, pp 213, 214.

[2] Ancient and Mediæval India, Vol. I, p. 149.

[3] Theogony of the Hindus, pp. 29, 30. As an instance of Mr. James Mill's stupidity, one may cite his opinion that the Hindus were extremely barbarous, for they cultivated metaphysics so largely. Prof. Wilson takes exception to it,

Even with the limited knowledge of Hindu Philosophy and science that could be obtained at the time, Sir William Jones could say: "I can venture to affirm without meaning to pluck a leaf from the neverfading laurels of our immortal Newton, that the whole of his theology, and part of his philosophy, may be found in the Vedas, and even in the works of the Sufis. The *most subtle spirit* which he suspected to pervade natural bodies, and lying concealed in them, to cause attraction and repulsion, the emission, reflection and refraction of light, electricity, califaction sensation and muscular motion, is described by the Hindus as a *fifth element*, endued with those very powers."

Mrs. Besant says: "Indian psychology is a far more perfect science than European psychology."[1]

As Professor Max Muller has observed, "the Hindus talk philosophy in the street," and to this reason is due the thoroughly practical character of their philosophy. "In this respect," says says Bjornstjerna, "the Hindus were far in advance of the philosophers of Greece and Rome, who considered the immortality of the soul as problematical."[2] "Socrates and Plato with all their longings could only feel assured that the soul had more of immorality than aught else."[3] In India, however, the doctrine has not been accepted in theory only, it moulds the conduct of the whole nation. This is true philosophy. And it is due to

and says: "With regard to the writer's theory that the cultivation of metaphysics is a proof rather of barbarism than of civilization, it may be asked if Locke, Descartes, Leibnitz, Kant, Schelling were barbarous."—Mill's *History of India*, Vol. I, p. 74, footnote. Mr. James Mill is a conspicuous instance of a man whose mind becomes completely warped by prejudice. Mill's mind could conceive most absurd impossiblities. "Mr. Mill," says Wilson, "seems inclined to think that it was not impossible that the Pyramids had dropped from the clouds or sprung out of the soil." How this perverted intellect could educate one of the greatest English thinkers is a problem of some psycholgical interest.

[1] Lecture on National Universities in India (Calcutta), January, 1906.

[2] Theogony or the Hindus, p. 27.

[3] *Phædo*, Taylor's translation, Vol. IV, p. 324.

its practical character that Hindu philosophy has extended its sway over so wide an area of the globe. Hindus philosophy even now holds undisputed sway over the minds of nearly half the inhabitants of the world, whilst its partial influence is no doubt universal.

In ancient times people came to India from distant lands to acquire learning and gain wisdom, and Hindu Philosophy thus worked silently for centuries. That the Egyptians derived their religion, mythology and philosophy from the Hindus has been clearly established by Count Bjornstjerna; and that the Greek philosophy, too, was indebted almost wholly to the Hindu philosophy for its cardinal doctrines has also been shown by eminent Orientalists. The resemblance between the Hindu and the Greek philosophy is too close to be accidental. The Hindus, being far more advanced, must have been the teachers, and the Greeks the disciples. Mr. Colebrooke, the eminent antiquarian, decides in favour of Hindu originality and says: "The Hindus were, in this respect, the teachers and not the learners."[1]

A Frenchman observes that "the traces of Hindu philosophy which appear at each step in the doctrines professed by the illustrious men of Greece abundantly prove that it was from the East came their science, and that many of them no doubt drank deeply at the principal fountain.

The great Greek philosopher, Pythagoras, came to India to learn philosophy, and here imbibed the doctrine of the transmigration of souls propounded by the Hindu sages. Dr. Enfield says: "We find that it (India) was visited for the purpose of acquiring knowledge by Pythagoras, Anaxarches, Pyrrho, and others who afterwards became eminent philosophers in Greece."[2]

[1] Transactions of the R.A.S., Vol. I, p. 579.

[2] History of Philosophy, by Dr. Enfield, Vol. I, p. 65. "Some of the doctrines of the Greeks concerning nature are said to have been derived from the Indians," p. 70.

Discussing the question as to what constitutes human nature according to the Hindus, the Swedish Count says: "Pythagoras and Plato hold the same doctrine, that of Pythagoras, being probably derived from India, whither he travelled to complete his philosophical studies."[1]

Schlegel says: "The doctrine of the transmigration of souls was indigenous to India and was brought into Greece by Pythagoras."[2]

So long as philosophy was cultivated in Greece, India was often regarded as the ultimate and purest source of true wisdom, the knowledge of things divine. Even as late as Lucian's time, the middle of the 2nd century, the author concludes his evidently true history of Antiphilus and Demetrius by making the latter, a cynic philosopher by profession, resign all his property to his friend and depart for India, there to end his life among the Brahmans"[3]

Mr. Princep says: "The fact, however, that he (Pythagoras) derived his doctrines from an Indian source is very generally admitted. Under the name of Mythraic, the faith of Buddha had also a wide extention." Sir M. Monier Williams says that Pythagoras and Plato both believed in this doctrine, and that they were indebted for it to Hindu writers.[4]

Pyrrhon, according to Alexander Polyhister, went with Alexander the Great to India, and hence the scepticism of Pyrrhon is connected with the Buddhist philosophy of India.[5] Even Rev. Ward says: "The author is persuaded that he (the reader) will not consider the conjecture improbable that Pythagoras and

[1] Theogony of the Hindus, p. 77.
[2] History of Literature, p. 109.
[3] Toxaris, 34, quoted by C. W. King in his *Gnostics and their Remains*, p. 54.
[4] Indian Wisdom, p. 68.
[5] Max Muller's Science of Language, p. 86.

others did really visit India and that Gautama and Pythagoras were contemporaries."[1]

Professor Macdonell says: "According to Greek tradition, Thales, Empedocles, Anaxagoras, Democritus and others undertook journeys to Oriental countries in order to study philosophy."[2]

Professor H. H. Wilson says: "We know that there was an active communication between India and the Red Sea in the early ages of the Christian era, and that *doctrines* as well as articles of merchandise were brought to Alexandria from the former. Epipharius and Eusebius accuse Scythianus of having imported from India in the second century, books on magic and heretical notions leading to Manichæism; and it was at the same period that Ammonius Saccas instituted the sect of the New Platonists at Alexandria. The basis of the heresy was that true philosophy derived its origin from the Eastern nations."[3]

Mr. Davies says: "Scythianus was a contemporary of the Apostles, and was engaged as a merchant in the Indian trade. In the course of his traffic he often visited India and made himself acquainted with Hindu philosophy. According to Epiphanius and Cyril, he wrote a book in four parts, which they affirm to be the source from which the Manichæan doctrines were derived."[4]

Professor Macdonell says: "The influence of Indian philosophy on Christian Gnosticism in the second and third centuries seems at any rate undoubted. The Gnostic doctrine of the opposition between soul and matter, of the personal existence of intellect, will, and so forth, the identification of soul and light are derived from the Sankhya system. The division peculiar to several Gnostics of man into the three classes pnemnatikoi, psychikoi, and hylikoi, is also based on the Sankhya doctrine of

[1] Ward's Mythology of the Hindus, p. xxiii (Introduction).
[2] Macdonell's Sanskrit Literature, p. 422.
[3] Wilson's Vishnu Purana, Preface, p. xiv.
[4] Davies' Bhagwat Gita, p. 196.

the three gunas. Again Bardesanes, a Gnostic of the Syrian School, who obtained information about India from Indian philosophers, assumed the existence of a subtle ethereal body which is identical with the *linga sarira* of the Sankhya system. Finally the many heavens of the Gnostics are evidently derived from the fantastic cosmogony of later Buddhism."[1]

It is thus clear that the Hindu philosophy is the fountain-head of the Greek philosophy with regard to some of its cardinal points. True philosophy in fact originated with the Hindus. Man first distinguished the eternal from the perishable, and next he perceived within himself the germ of the eternal. "This discovery," says Professor Max Muller, "was an epoch in the history of the human mind, and the name of the discoverer has not been forgotten. It was Sandilya who declared that the self within the heart was Brahma."[2]

Excluding the extensive atheistic and agnostic systems of philosophy propounded by Charvakya and others, and those by the Jain and Buddhistic philosophers, the principal Hindu schools of philosophy are known as the *Darsanas*. But much of the philosophical literature of the Hindus is lost. Professor Goldstucker, too, thinks that "probably besides the Upanishads, there were philosophical works which were more original than those now preserved, and which served as the common source of the works which have come down to us as the six *Darsanas*."

The Darsanas are: Nyaya and Veisheshika; Sankhya and Yoga; and Purva and Uttara Mimansas.

NYAYA.

The Nyaya system was founded by Gautama, who says

[1] Macdonell's Sanskrit Literature, p. 423.

[2] Ancient Sanskrit Literature, p. 20.

that the way to salvation is the true knowledge of पदार्थ, substance or being, which he classifies as under:—

(1) Pramana.	(10) Bad.[1]
(2) Prameha.	(11) Jalp.[2]
(3) Sanshaya.	(12) Bitanda.[3]
(4) Prayojana.	(13) Haitwabhasya (parallelogism).
(5) Drishtant.	(14) Chhal.
(6) Siddhant (principle).	(15) Jati.
(7) Avayav (portion).	(16) Nigrahstan (when one is pushed to an utterly untenable position).
(8) Tarak (logic).	
(9) Nirnaya.	

The author then discusses (1) the nature of the argument and the proof, and their different kinds (प्रमेह या प्रमाण), (2) the nature of the soul as apart from senses, body and the mind. The relation of the soul with the body is through the medium of the mind or *man*. The soul and the body cannot affect each other directly but only through the medium of the mind. He then proceeds to prove the transmigration of souls, the omnipresence and omni science of God, and declares that He is separate from the souls, who are countless in number. The author believes the Vedas to be the Revelation, and advises all mankind to follow their teachings. The material cause of the universe, he declares, is Parmanu (atoms). The Parmanu are eternal. The author then proceeds to refute Atheism, and ends by giving reasons for a belief in God. An English critic says: "The great prominence given to the *method* by means of which *truth* might be ascertained has sometimes misled European writers into the belief that it is merely a system of logic. Far from being restricted to mere logic, the Nyaya was intended to be a complete system of

[1] *Bad*=a discussion with a sincere desire to get at the truth.

[2] *Jalp*=a discussion to refute the opponent.

[3] *Bitanda*=when one obstinately clings to his own doctrine and does not listen to the other side.

philosophical investigation, and dealt with some questions—such as the nature of the intellect, articulated sound, genus, variety and individuality—in a manner so masterly as well to deserve the notice of European philosophers."[1] Mrs. Manning after giving a brief outline of the *Naiyayic* syllogistic proof, says: "Even the bare outline here given shows Gautama's mental powers and practical mode of dealing with the deepest questions which affect the human mind."[2]

European logic employs phraseology founded upon classification, while the Nyaya system makes use of terms upon which a classification would be founded. The one infers that "kings are mortal because they belong to the class of mortal beings." The other arrives at the same conclusion, because mortality is inherent in humanity, and humanity is inherent in kings. The proposition given above would, as we have seen, be stated by a European logician as. "All men are mortal;" by a Hindu as, "Where there is humanity there is mortality." The reasoning is the same, but the Hindu method appears to be simpler.[3]

The German critic, Schlegel, says: "The Nyaya doctrine attibuted to Gautama, from all that we can learn, was an idealism constructed with a purity and logical consistency of which there are few other instances, and to which Greeks never attained."[4]

As regards the logical system of the Hindus, Max Duncker says: "The logical researches of the Hindus are scarcely behind

[1] Chamber's Encyclopædia, "Nyaya."

[2] Ancient and Mediæval India, Vol. I, p. 173. Mrs. Manning says: "His clearness of aim and his distinct perception of right means towards its attainment continue to be the invaluable guide of successive generations."

[3] The European is assisted by the abstract idea of *Class*; the Hindu makes use of what in Sanskrit is termed *Vyapti*. "It is difficult," remarks Dr. Roer, "to find an adequate word in English for this term." For further information see Translation of Bhashaparichheda, pp. 31 and 32, note.

[4] Schlegel's History of Literature, p. 126.

the similar works of modern times."[1] Mr. Elphinstone says: "An infinity of volumes have been produced by the Brahmins on the subject (Logic)"[2]

VEISHESHIK.

The Veisheshik is said to have been written not to oppose but to complete the Nyaya system: with slight modifications it is only a fuller development of the Nyaya. In Sanskrit these two schools of philosophy are comprised under one head, "Manan Shastra." Kanada, the founder of Veisheshik, reduces the contents of the universe under six categories only. They are:—

(1) Drabya (substance).
(2) Guna (quality).
(3) Karma (action or motion).
(4) Samanya (generality or class).
(5) Vishesha (atomic individuality or difference).
(6) Samvaya (intimate relation).
(7) Abhav (non-existence) was added afterwards.

Kanada's work is divided into ten books, of which the first book, after reducing the sixteen पदार्थ of the Nyaya to six only, as given above, discusses the nature of *Abhav* or non-existence. The second book discusses the nature of *Drabya*. In the third are discussed *Atma* and *Antahkaran* and their relation to each other. The *Atma* and *Antahkaran* correspond with the *Jeeva* and *Man* (मन) of the Nyaya. The fourth book discusses the nature of the human body and the external nature as affecting it, while the Vedic *dharma* is upheld in the sixth book. The seventh book discusses *Guna* and *Sambaya*, their natures, kinds and effects. The eighth book shows the way to what the Hindus

[1] History of Antiquity, Vol. IV, p. 310.

[2] Elphinstone's India, p. 122. Mrs. Manning says: "To the ability of the author may be attributed the yet continued popularity of the work (Nyaya)."

call *Gayàna*, or true knowledge of the mysteries of existence, non-existence and other metaphysical topics. The intellect and the *Vishesha* are discussed in the ninth book. The tenth book contains a detailed discussion on Atma and its *gunas*, etc.

The points of difference between the Nyaya and the Veisheshik are only two. (1) The Nyaya distributes the contents of the universe into sixteen categories, while the Veisheshik does so into seven only. (2) The Nyaya accepts four kinds of *Pramana* or arguments. The Veisheshik accept only two *Pratyakhsha* and *Anuman*—and rejects the remaining two, *Upman and Shabda*.

In the interesting introduction which Dr. Roer appends to the translation of Bhashaparichheda he compares Kanada's doctrine of atoms to that of Democritus, the Greek philosopher, and pronounces the former to be vastly superior.

"Veisheshik," says Mrs. Manning,[1] "leans towards physical science rather than metaphysical." The theory of sound propounded by the Hindus seems to be in accordance with the latest European advancement in science. After distinguishing between the articulate and the inarticulate sounds, Vishvanath, the author of Bhashaparichheda, says: "Some say its (sound) production takes place like a succession of waves; according to others, like the bud of *Kadamba* plant" (verses 165, 166). The *Tarak Sangrah*, another work of this school, says: "It is ether in which there resides the quality of sound. It is one, all-pervading and eternal."[2]

Sir P. C. Ray in his History of Hindu Chemistry says: "His theory of the propagation of sound cannot fail to excite our wonder and admiration even at this distant date. No less remarkable is his statement that light and heat are only different

[1] Ancient and Mediæval India, Vol. I, p. 181.

[2] Ancient and Mediæval India, Vol. I, p. 189.

forms of the same essential substance. But Kanada is anticipated in many material points by Kapila, the reputed originator of the Sankhya philosophy."[1]

According to the Veisheshik, as also according to Nyaya, there are five members of the syllogism instead of three as in the English syllogism.

They are: (1) Proposition, (2) Reason, (3) Example, (4) Application, (5) Conclusion.

For instance,—(1) The mountain is fiery.

(2) Because it smokes.

(3) Whatever smokes is fiery, as a culinary hearth.

(4) This does smoke.

(5) Therefore it is fiery as aforesaid.

A charge of deficiency, "inaccuracy of definition," has been brought against the five-membered syllogism. Dr. Ballantyne thus meets the accusation: "The five-membered expression, so far as the arrangement of its parts is concerned, is a summary of the *Naiyayik's* views in regard to rhetoric, 'an offshoot from logic' (see Whately's Rhetoric, p. 6), and one to which, after 'the ascertainment of the truth by investigation,' belongs the establishment of it to the satisfaction of another."[2] To this Mrs. Manning adds the following: "In fact, Gautama appears to have expressed bare logic in two-membered argument, and to have added two other members when he sought to convince rhetorically. After the declaration and the reason, he inserts an 'example' confirmatory and also suggestive, and an 'application,' that is, he shows in the fourth member of his syllogism that his example possesses the required character; and then he

[1] History of Hindu Chemistry, Vol. I, p. 1.

[2] Ballantyne on the Nyaya system.—*The Pandit*, Vol. I, p. 39.

winds up with the conclusion or Q. E. D., which is common to all syllogisms."

Principal B. Seal says: "The Hindu anuman (inference) it will be seen, anticipates J. S. Mill's analysis of the syllogism as a material inference, but is more comprehensive; for, the Hindu Udaharana, the third or general proposition with an example combines and harmonises Mill's view of the major premise as a brief memorandum of like instances already observed, fortified by a recommendation to extend its application to unobserved cases, with the Aristotelian view of it as a universal proposition which is the formal ground of inference."[1]

Dr. Seal discussing the Hindu logical methods of ascertaining causality says: "This Panchkarni, the joint method of Difference, has some advantages over J. S. Mill's method of Difference, or what is identical therewith, the earlier Buddhist Method; and the form of the canon bringing out in prominent relief the unconditionality and the immediateness of the antecedence is as superior from a theoritical point of view to J. S. Mill's canon and is as much more consonant than the latter to the practice of every experimenter, as the Hindu analysis of Anuman as a Formal Material Deductive Inductive Inference is more comprehensive and more scientific than Aristotle's or Mill's analysis of the syllogism (or Mediate Inference)."[2]

Evidently the difference between the Hindu and the Greek syllogism (for the Europeans have no syllogism of their own)[3] is due to the difference of aim of the reasoning of the two nations. The Greek wanted to prove his contention, but the Hindu, being more practical and thorough, wanted to convince his adversary.

[1] Roy's History of Hindu Chemistry, Vol. II, p. 234.

[2] History of Hindu Chemistry, Vol. II, pp. 242, 243.

[3] "There are only two nations in the whole history of the world who have conceived independently, and without any suggestion from others, the two

SANKHYA.

This remarkable system of philosophy was founded by Kapila, and is the oldest in the world. It teaches that there are twenty-four elements, and that the twenty-fifth, if it can be so-called, is *purusha* or *atma* (soul). The primary cause of the world is *Prakriti*, one of the twenty-four. Of itself, *Prakriti* is non-active, is, in fact, neither produced nor productive, but it becomes active by coming in contact with the *Purusha*.

The author holds that there are innumerable souls in the world, which fact constitutes one of its chief differences from the Vedanta. Sankhya says nothing of God, and on this account, some regard it as a system of scientific atheism: but that the system is theistic is proved by the fact that such a decided theist as Patanjali vindicates its character, and indeed supplements it by his own system, Yoga. Sankhya differs from Nyaya chiefly on the following two points: (1) According to Nyaya, *Purusha* is the agent, and is the legitimate party to enjoy the result of action (*Karma*). Sankhya, on the other hand, teaches that in its own nature, *Purusha* has neither happiness nor misery. It has nothing to do with *Karma* and its results, but by coming into contact with *Prakriti* it takes upon itself the good or the bad results of *Karma*. This is our ignorance. Knowledge would make us shun good or bad results. We will then be happy. The second point is this: Sankhya teaches that there cannot be anything which has not existed before. We cannot make a body round unless roundness already exists in it. It may not be seen,

sciences of Logic and Grammar, the Hindus and the Greeks."—Max Muller's *Ancient Sanskrit Literature*, p. 158. Considering that the Greek philosophers derived their philosophy from India, there may be a doubt regarding the Greek originality.

"It is interesting to note that the Indian mind independently arrived at an exposition of the syllogism as the form of deducting reasoning."—Macdonell's Sanskrit Literature, p. 404.

but still there it is. Nyaya holds the opposite theory.

"Sankhya doctrine," says Mrs. Manning, "is a very great effort at enravelling the deep mysteries of our existence. On the one side it exhibits the worthlessness of the perishable universe, including man with all his powers and qualities. On the other side it places the imperishable soul. The perishable portion of this division is fully and firmly dealt with, and has excited the admiration and interest of such men as Wilson, Ballantyne and others. But concerning the soul or the imperishable portion of his subject, one feels that the author is reserved, or that he has more thoughts than he chooses to express."[1]

The word Sankhya (*sam*=together and *khya*=reasoning) indicates that the system is based on synthetic reasoning.

Sir W. Hunter says: "The various theories of creation arrangement and development were each elaborated, and the views of the modern physiologists at the present day are a return with new light to the *evolution theory of Kapila*, whose Sankhya system is the oldest of the Darsanas."[2]

"Sankhya," says Prof. Macdonell, "for the first time in the history of the world, asserted the complete independence of the human mind and attempted to solve its problems by the aid of reason."[3]

Yoga.

Without a knowledge of *Yoga*[4] one cannot reach the real depths of human nature, and can never fathom the hidden

[1] Manning's Ancient and Mediæval India, Vol. I, p. 153.

[2] Indian Gazeteer, "India," p. 214.

[3] Macdonell's Sanskrit Literature, p. 386.

[4] "Al-Baruni translated Sankhya and Yoga into Arabic in the reign of Khalifa Al-Mamun."—Max Muller's *Science of Language*, p. 165.

mysteries and the realities of the heart, nor know the nature of the soul and of God. True metaphysics is impossible without *Yoga*, and so is mental philosophy. Pantanjali divides his work into four chapters. The first chapter, after discussing the nature of the soul and of *Yoga*, enumerates eight means or stages in the process by which *Yoga* can be accomplished. They are as under:—

YOGA.

1. Yama (forbearance). — Universal duty.
   (1) Not doing injury to living beings.
   (2) Veracity.
   (3) Avoidance of theft.
   (4) Chastity.
   (5) Non-acceptance of gifts.
2. Niyama (religious observance).
   (1) External and internal purity.
   (2) Cheerfulness or contentment.
   (3) Austerity.
   (4) Chanting Vedic hymns.
   (5) Devoted reliance on the Lord.
3. Asana (postures).
   There are 100 different postures of the body.
4. Pranayama (regulation of the breath).
   (1) Inhalation.
   (2) Exhalation.
   (3) Suspension (*Khumbhaka*).
5. Pratyahára (restraint of the senses).
6. Dhárana (steadying of the mind).
7. Dhyâna (contemplation).
8. Samâdhi (transportation of mind or unconsciousness).

After giving the above-mentioned sub-divisions the author describes the nature of *Samadhi* and its two divisions. The second chapter describes in detail the ways and means to perform *Samadhi*. The third chapter describes the powers developed in a Yogi when he has reached the last stage of *Yoga*. *Samadhi* on different objects imparts different powers to the yogi.

Samadhi on the Moon gives one particular power, on Jupiter another, and so on. The fourth chapter treats of *Mokhsha*. Patanjali declares that when a man becomes an adept at *Samadhi* he gains a knowledge of the past and the future, a knowledge of the sounds of animals, of the thoughts of others, of the time of his own death, etc.

It would be difficult to conceive all this but for the unimpeachable testimony of European scholars and officers. In an instance recorded by Pro. Wilson[1] a Brahman appeared to sit in the air wholly unsupported and to remain so sitting on one occasion for twelve minutes and on another for forty minutes.

Colonel Olcott records an account of a *yogi* described to him by Dr. Rajendralal Mitra: "It is not known when this *yogi* went into *Samadhi*, but his body was found about 45 years ago quite lifeless. All manner of tortures were used to bring him back to consciousness, but all to no purpose. He was then touched by the hand of a female and he instantly came back to his senses."[2]

Dr. McGregor says in his "History of the Sikhs": "A novel scene occurred at one of these garden houses in 1837. A *fakir* who arrived at Lahore engaged to bury himself for any length of time shut up in a box, without either food or drink? Ranjit disbelieved his assertions, and determined to put them to proof; for this purpose the man was shut up in a wooden box, which was placed in a small apartment below the level of the ground. There was a folding door to the box which was secured by a lock and key. Surrounding this apartment there was the garden house, the door of which was likewise locked; and outside of this a high wall having the door built up with bricks and mud.

[1] Essays on the Religion of the Hindus, Vol. I. p. 209. See description of the *Yogis* given by Onisicritus, a follower of Alexander. Also the account of Calanus.

[2] Col. Olcott's lecture on "Theosophy, the scientific basis of religion," p. 18.

Outside the whole there was placed a line of sentries, so that no one could approach the building. The strictest watch was kept for the space of forty days and forty nights, at the expiration of which period the Maharaja, attended by his grandson and several of his Sardars, as well as General Ventum, Captain Wade, and myself, proceeded to disinter the *fakir*." After describing the condition of the *fakir* after disinterment, in a few words, the author says: "When the fakir was able to converse, the completion of the feat was announced by the discharge of guns and other demonstrations of joy; while a rich chain of gold was placed round his neck by Ranjit himself."

"Another gentlemen of unimpeachable veracity describes the wonderful feat of a *lama* who became his guest in September 1887 at Darjeeling. After describing his postures, etc., the eye-witness proceeds: "Suddenly he, still retaining his sitting posture, rose perpendicularly into the air to the height of, I should say, two cubits (one yard), and then floated without a tremor or motion of a single muscle, like a cork in still water." The above are two out of numberless similar cases. In India not only these things but feats of a far more extraordinary nature are so common that they fail to evoke surprise at all."[1]

Fryer was quite astonished to see *yogis* who fixed their eyes towards the sun without lossing their sight.

The Yoga Philosophy is peculiar to the Hindus, and no trace of it is found in any other nation, ancient or modern. It was the fruit of the highest intellectual and spiritual development. The existence of this system is another proof of the intellectual superiority of the ancient Hindus over all other peoples.

[1] See also "The Court and Camp of Ranjit Singh."

MIMANSA.

Mimansa is the collective name of two of the six divisions of the Hindu Philosophy. They are the *Purva* and the *Uttara Mimansa*. The terms *Uttara* and *Purva*, meaning latter and former, do not apply to the relative ages of the Mimansas but to the sacred books which are indicated by them. Purva Mimansa treats of the Hindu ritual and *Karmakand* as promulgated in the *Brahmanas*, whilst the Uttara Mimansa treats of the nature of God and of the soul as taught in the Upanishads. And the two Mimansas are so-called because the Upanishads were composed later than the *Brahmanas*.

The Purva Mimansa gives in full detail the *Karma* we have to perform. The *Yagyas*, *Agnihotras*, gifts, etc., are all treated elaborately and minutely. The author, the venerable Jaimini, after discussing the nature of the *dharma* and *adhrma*, says that *dharma* consists in following the teachings of the Vedas. Dharma is essentially necessary to gain happiness.

The Uttara Mimansa is the work of the celebrated Vyasa, and is one of the most important of the six Darsanas. The school of philosophy of which the Uttara Mimansa is the best exposition is called Vedanta. The word Vedanta, means "the end or the ultimate aim of the Vedas," and the Vedanta system discusses the nature of the Brahma and the soul. The Uttara Mimansa is one of the grandest feats of the grand Hindu genius. The *Brahmasutra* of Vyasa begins with a refutation of atheism and a vindication of theism. It then lays down that the only way to salvation or *mukti* is *atmagyana*, or a true knowledge of the soul.

Professor Max Muller says: "Much that was most dear, that had seemed for a time their very self, had to be surrendered before they could find the self of selves, the old man, the looker-on, a subject independent of all personality, and existence independent of all life. When that point had been reached then the highest knowledge began to draw, the self within (the Pratyagatma) was drawn towards the highest self (the Paramatman), it found its true self in the highest self, and the oneness of the subjective with the objective self was recognized as underlying all reality, as the dim dream of religion—as the pure light of philosophy."

"This fundamental idea is worked out with systematic completeness in the Vedanta Philosophy, and no one who can appreciate the lessons contained in Berkeley's Philosophy will read the Upanishads and the Brahma Sutras without feeling a richer and a wiser man." [1]

There is a difference of opinion as regards the Vedantic view of the nature of the soul and of God. The great Shankeracharya believed that the Vedanta taught that there was only one Brahma and all else was *maya* or illusion.

Swami Dayanand Saraswati, however, holds the view originally held of Vedanta, and says that the Brahma Sutras or the real Vedanta Sutras do not teach the unity of God and soul. Popular belief, however, is swayed by the views of Shanker Swami, and the system is held to be an all-absorbing Pantheism. Anyway, it is the most sublime system of philosophy ever propounded by man.

Of Sankara's commentary upon the Vedanta, Sir W. Jones says that "it is not possible to speak with too much applause of so excellent a work; and I am confident in asserting that, until an accurate translation of it shall appear in some European language, the general history of philosophy must remain incomplete."

Sir W. Jones says of Vedanta: "The fundamental tenet of the Vedantic school consisted not in denying the existence of

[1] India: What can it teach us? p. 253.

matter, that is, of solidity, impenetrability, and extended figure (to deny which would be lunacy), but in correcting the popular notion of it, and in contending that it has no essence independent of mental perception, that existence and perceptibility are convertible terms, that external appearances and sensations are illusory and would vanish into nothing if the divine energy, which alone sustains them, were suspended but for a moment: an opinion which Epicharmus and Plato seem to have adopted, and which has been maintained in the present century with great elegance, but with little applause, partly because it has been misunderstood, and partly because it has been misapplied by the false reasoning of some popular writers, who are said to have disbelieved in the moral attributes of God, whose omnipresence, wisdom and goodness are the basis of the Indian philosophy." He adds: The system is built on the purest devotion."[1] Sir James Mackintosh, an English philospher, calls the theory (propounded by Vedanta) "refined, abstruse, ingenious and beautiful."

The Mimansa method of *Parva Paksha* (reason contra), *Uttara Paksha* (reason pro) and *Siddhant* (conclusion) of the Shastras excite Professor Max Muller's admiration, who says: "It is indeed one of the most curious kinds of literary composition that the human

[1] Sir W. Jones' Works, Vol. I, p. 165. "We might be able," says Count Bjornstjerna, "to resign ourselves with patient submission to the comfortless doctrine of Pantheism if it only concerned ourselves, but together with the hope of our own continued existence, to lose at the same time that of seeing again those whom we have most loved upon earth, to break them for ever is a reflection that bruises the heart. What! shall we first be bereaved of these beloved ones, retain nothing of them but memory's faint shadow, and then when we are called to follow them, shall even this shadow fly away from us? No; such can never be the intention of the all-bountiful Creator: He has not deposited in our hearts the tender feelings of love and of friendship in order at life's goal to rend asunder for ever the band that has been tied by them! They are of a spiritual nature, they follow the spirit beyond the boundary of life, where we shall find again those whom we have loved."—Theogony of the Hindus, p. 79. What a misunderstanding of Pantheism!

mind ever conceived. It is wonderful that the Indians should have invented and mastered this difficult form so as to have made it the vehicle of expression for every kind of learning."[1]

The six Darsanas are rarely read and understood by non-Hindus, owing partly to the extreme difficulty of the language and a peculiar and philosophic technique difficult to acquire, and partly to the want on their part of that mental equipment which is the result of high intellectual training and great *spiritual* development.

As is well known, the *Upanishads* are the fountain-head of all Hindu philosophy. They are said to be 52 in number. The Upanishads are disquisitions on philosophical subjects, and breathe an air of sublimity and spirituality which is nowhere else to be found. The profound philosophy they teach, the deep wisdom they contain, the infallible truths they establish, and the true principles they set forth are the standing marvels of Indian intellect and monuments of human genius.

In his *Philosophy of the Upanishads*, recently translated by Rev. A. S. Geden, M.A., Prof. Deussen claims for its fundamental thought "an inestimable value for the whole race of mankind." It is in "marvellous agreement with the philosophy founded by Kant, and adopted and perfected by his great successor, Schopenhauer," differing from it, where it does differ, only to excel. For, whereas the philosophy of Schopenhauer only "represents Christianity in its present form," we must have recourse to the Upanishads "if we are willing to put the finishing touch to the Christian consciousness, and to make it on all sides consistent and complete. "Professor Deussen, it is true, is kind enough to Christianity to bracket the New Testament and the Upanishads

[1] "In this method," says Prof. Max Muller, "the concatenation of *pros* and *cons* is often so complicated and the reason on both sides defended by the same author with such seriousness that we sometimes remain doubtful to which side the author leans, till we arrive at the end of the whole chapter."

as 'the two noblest products of the religious consciousness of mankind,' but leaves his readers in no doubt as to which he considers the nobler of the two"

The great German philosopher, Schopenhauer, says: "Oh! how thoroughly is the mind here washed clean of all early engrafted Jewish superstitions and of all philosophy that cringes before those superstitions. In the whole world there is no study, except that of the originals, so beneficial and so elevating as that of the Upanishads. *It has been the solace of my life, it will be the solace of my death.*"

Mr. Elphinstone, in comparing the ancient Greeks with the ancient Hindus, says:[1] "Their (Hindus) general learning was more considerable; and in the knowledge of the being and nature of God, they were already in possession of a light which was but faintly perceived even by the loftiest intellects in the best days of Athens."

[1] Elphinstone's History of India, p. 49. Bhagwat Gita has for centuries moulded the thoughts and the conduct of a large section of the Hindu nation. Bhagwat Gita is essentially a work on the Vedanta philosophy, and appears to have been composed to correct a misconception of that noble system. Owing to a misunderstanding of the teachings of this sublime philosophy, men began to neglect their duties and responsibilities, since there was only one Brahma and all else was illusion. This alarmed all good and thoughtful men, and as an antidote this excellent book, *Bhagwat Gita* was written. It is skilfully introduced as an episode in the Mahabharata. Whatever may be the *raison d'etre* of the book, it has not only fascinated the minds of Hindus but has charmed Europeans, who speak in rapturous terms of this celebrated poem.

The teaching of the Bhagwat Gita is that the zealous performance of his duty is a man's most important task, wherever he be, and in whatever position he may find himself.

Mrs. Manning says: "Bhagwat Gita is one of the most remarkable compositions in the Sanskrit language."

Professor Heeren says: "The poem certainly abounds in sublime passages which remind one of the Orphic hymn to Jupiter quoted by Stobœus."—Histocal Researches, Vol. II, p. 198.

Mr. Elphinstone says: "Bhagwat Gita deserves high praise for the skill with which it is adapted to the general Epic, and the tenderness and elegance of the narrative by means of which it is introduced."—History of Indi, p. 155.

SCIENCE.

I.—MEDICINE.

A wise physician, skill'd our wounds to heal
Is more than armies to the public weal.

—POPE.

THE science of medicine, like other sciences, was carried to a very high degree of perfection by the ancient Hindus. Their great powers of observation, generalization and analysis, combined with patient labour in a country of boundless resources, whose fertility for herbs and plants is most remarkable, placed them in an exceptionally favourable position to prosecute their study of this great science. Owing, however, to the destruction of a great part of Sanskrit literature, it is impossible to form an accurate estimate of the high proficiency attained by the Hindus in this important science. Unlike philosophy and grammar, on which subjects ancient works still extant furnish sufficient material to enable one to form a correct judgment of their pre-eminence in those branches of learning, medicine is a practical science which has long been neglected, owing to a variety of causes.

Lord Ampthill recently (February 1905) said at Madras: "Now we are beginning to find out that the Hindu Shastras also contain a Sanitary Code no less correct in principle, and that the great law-giver, Manu, was one of the greatest sanitary reformers the world has ever seen."

Professor Wilson says: "The Ancient Hindus attained as thorough a proficiency in medicine and surgery as any people whose acquisitions are recorded. This might be expected, because their patient attention and natural shrewdness would render them excellent observers, whilst the extent and fertility of their native country would furnish them with many valuable drugs and medicaments. Their diagnosis is said, in consequence, to define and distinguish symptoms with great accuracy, and their Materia Medica is most voluminous."[1]

Sir William Hunter has the following on the scope of Indian medicine: "Indian medicine dealt with the whole area of the science. It described the structure of the body, its organs, ligaments, muscles, vessels and tissues. The Materia Medica of the Hindus embraces a vast collection of drugs belonging to the mineral, vegetable and animal kingdoms, *many of which have now been adopted by European physicians*. Their pharmacy contained ingenious processes of preparation, with elaborate directions for the administration and classification of medicines. Much attention was devoted to hygiene, regimen of the body, and diet."[2]

Mr. Weber says: "The number of medical works and authors is extraordinarily large."[3]

The Ayur Veda is the oldest system of medicine in the world. The great Hindu physician, Dhanwantri,[4] imparted to his pupil Susruta the knowledge, embodied in the work that goes by his name. Charaka states that "originally the contents of his own works were communicated by Atreya Muni to Agnivesa, and by him to Charaka, who condensed where it was too prolix and expanded where it was too brief." *Susruta* and *Charaka*

[1] Wilson's Works, Vol. III, p. 269. "Materia Medica," says Weber, "generally appears to have been handled with great predilection."—*Indian Literature*, p. 270.

[2] Imperial Indian Gazetteer, "India," p. 120.

[3] Weber's Indian Literature, p. 269.

[4] The name of this great man, Dhanwantari, has become a synonym of an "adept" His name is generally pronounced before taking medicine in Rajputana, in consequence of the popular belief that his prescriptions are infallible.

are now the two most important and well known works extant on Hindu medicine.

The chief *distinction* of the modern European science of medicine is surgery. But even in surgery, as will be clear from the following quotations, the ancient Hindus attained the highest proficiency.

Mr. Weber says: "In surgery, too, the Indians seem to have attained a special proficiency, and in this department, European surgeons might, perhaps, *even at the present day* still learn something from them, as indeed they have already borrowed from them the operation of rhinoplasty."[1]

Prof. Macdonell says: "In modern days European surgery has borrowed the operation of rhinoplasty, or the formation of artificial noses, from India, where Englishmen became acquainted with the art in the last century."[2]

"Their surgery," says Elphinstone, "is as remarkable as their medicine."[3] Mrs Manning says: "The surgical instruments of the Hindus were sufficiently sharp, indeed, as to be capable of dividing a hair longitudinally."[4]

Dr. Sir W. W. Hunter says: "The surgery of the ancient Indian physicians was bold and skilful. They conducted amputations, arresting the bleeding by pressure, a cup-shaped bandage and boiling oil; practised lithotomy; performed operations in the abdomen and uterus; cured hernia, fistula, piles; set broken bones and dislocations; and were dexterous in the extraction of foreign substances from the body. A special branch of surgery was devoted to rhinoplasty, or operation for improving deformed ears and noses and *forming new ones*, a useful operation

[1] Weber's Indian Literature, p. 270.

[2] History of Sanskrit Literature, p. 427.

[3] History of India, p. 147.

[4] Ancient and Mediæval India, Vol. II, p. 346.

which European surgeons have now borrowed. The ancient Indian surgeons also mention a cure for neuralgia, analogous to the modern cutting of the fifth nerve above the eyebrow. They devoted great care to the making of surgical instruments and to the training of students by means of operations performed on wax spread on a board or on the tissues and cells of the vegetable kingdom, and upon dead animals. They were expert in midwifery, not shrinking from the most critical operations, and in the diseases of women and children. Their practice of physic embraced the classifications, causes, symptoms and treatment of diseases, diagnosis and prognosis. Considerable advances were also made in veterinary science, and monographs exist on the diseases of horses, elephants, etc."[1]

The author of the History of Hindu Chemistry says: "According to Susruta, the dissection of dead bodies is a *sine qua non* to the student of surgery, and this high authority lays particular stress on knowledge gained from experiment and observation."[2]

Dr. Seal says: "The Hindus practised dissection on dead bodies for purposes of demonstration............Post mortem operations as well as major operations in obstetric surgery (the extraction of the fœtus, etc.) were availed of for embryological observations."

A word with regard to the Veterinary Science. Mr. H. M. Elliot says: "There is in the Royal library at Lucknow a work on veterinary art, which was translated from the Sanskrit by order of Ghayas-ud-din Muhammad Shah Khilji.

This rare book, called *Kurrat-ul-mulk*, was translated as early as A.H. 783 (1381 A.D.), from an original styled Salotar, which

[1] Indian Gazetteer, "India," p. 220. See also Weber's Indian Literature, p. 270.

[2] History of Hindu Chemistry, Vol I, p. 105.

is the name of an Indian who is said to have been a Brahman, and the tutor of Susruta. The Preface says that the translation was made "from the barbarous Hindi into the refined Persian, in order that there may be no more need of a reference to infidels." The book is divided into eleven chapters and thirty sections.

Chapter	I.	On the breeds and names of horses ...	4	sections.
"	II.	On their odour, on riding, and breeding ...	4	"
"	III.	On stable management, and on wasps building nests in a stable	2	"
"	IV.	On colour and its varieties	3	"
"	V.	On their blemishes	3	"
"	VI.	On their limbs	2	"
"	VII.	On sickness and its remedies	4	"
"	VIII.	On bleeding	4	"
"	IX.	On food and diet	2	"
"	X.	On feeding for the purpose of fattening ...	3	"
"	XI.	On ascertaining the age by the teeth ...	1	"

The precise age of this work is doubtful, because, although it is plainly stated to have been translated in A. H. 783, yet the reigning prince is called Sultan Ghaias-ud-din Mohammad Shah, son of Mahmud Shah, but there is no king so named whose reign corresponds with that date. If Sultan Ghaias-ud-din Tughlak be meant, it should date sixty years earlier, and if the king of Malwa, who bore that name, be meant, it should be dated one hundred years later; either way, it very much precedes the reign of Akbar.[1]

The translator makes no mention in it of the work on the

[1] "It is curious, that without any allusion to this work, another on the veterinary art, styled Salotari, and said to comprise in the Sanskrit original 16,000 slokas, was translated in the reign of Shahjahan, 'when there were many learned men who knew Sanskrit" by Sayyad Abdullah Khan Bahadur Firoz Jung, who had found it among some other Sanskrit books, which during his expedition against Mewar, in the reign of Jehangir, had been plundered from Amar Singh, Rana of Chitor. It is divided into twelve chapters, and is more than double the size of the other."

same subject, which had been previously translated from the Sanskrit into Arabic at Baghdad, under the name of Kitab-ul-Baitarat.[1]

Professor Weber says: "In the Vedic period, animal anatomy was evidently understood, as each part had its own distinctive name." He also says: "The chapter of Amarkosha on the human body and its diseases certainly presupposes an advanced cultivation of medical science."[2]

Professor Wilson says: "There is a very large body of medical literature in Sanskrit, and some of the principal works are named by Arabic writers as having been known and translated at Baghdad in the ninth century. These works comprise all the branches of medical science, surgery included, and contain numerous instances of accurate observation and judicious treatment."

The Hindus have, through this branch of knowledge, as through many others, been the benefactors of humanity; for, Hindu medicine is the foundation upon which the building of the European medical science has been constructed. His Excellency Lord Ampthill, the late Governor of Madras, while declaring open the Madras King Institute of Preventive medicine, said: "The people of India should be grateful to him (Col. King) for having pointed out to them that they can lay claim to have been acquainted with the main principles of curative and preventive medicine at a time when Europe was still immersed in ignorant savagery. I am not sure whether it is generally known that the *science of medicine originated in India*, but this is the case, and *the science was first exported from India to Arabia and thence to Europe*. Down to the close of the seventeenth century, European physicians learnt the science from the works of Arabic doctors; while the Arabic doctors many

[1] Elliot's Historians of India, part I, pp. 263, 464.
[2] Weber's Indian Literature, p. 267.

centuries before had obtained their knowledge from the works of great Indian physicians such as Dhanwantri, Charaka, and Susruta. It is a strange circumstance in the world's progress that the centre of enlightenment and knowledge should have travelled from East to West leaving but little permanent trace of its former existence in the East."

Sir W. Hunter says: "The Hindu medicine is an independent development." Arab medicine was founded on the translations from the Sanskrit[1] treatises made by command of the Khalif of Baghdad (950-960 A.D.). European medicine down to the 17th century was based upon the Arabic, and the name of the Indian physician Charaka, repeatedly occurs in Latin translations of Avicenna (Abu Sina), Rhazes (Abu Rasi), and Serapion (Abu Sirabi).

Prof. Macdonell says: "The effect of Hindu medical science upon the Arabs after about 700 A.D. was considerable, for the Khalif of Baghdad caused several books on the subject to be translated."[2]

Mrs. Manning says: "The medical works of India had already attained world-wide celebrity when the Khalif of Baghdad collected the greatest works and summoned the most learned scientific men of their era to give brilliancy to Baghdad as a seat of learning." She adds: "It is impossible to exhibit India's ancient science to Europeans unacquainted with Sanskrit or not having access to the native medical libraries, in which we understand many medical works are withheld from Europeans."[3]

In support of the fact that Hindu medical works were largely translated by the Arabs, and that these translations formed the

[1] Csoma de Koros was the first to announce that the Thibetan *Tanjur* contains among others translations of Charaka, Susruta and Vagabhata.

[2] Sanskrit Literature, p. 427.

[3] Ancient and Mediæval India, Vol. I, pp. 353, 354.

nucleus of their science, and that after being translated into European languages they formed the backbone of the European science of medicine, the following facts may be cited:—

Barzouhyeh, a contemporary of the celebrated Sassanian king, Nosherevan (A.D. 531-572), visited India to acquire proficiency in Indian sciences.[1]

According to Professor Sachau, the learned translator of Alberuni, "some of the books that had been translated under the first Abbaside Caliphs were extant in the library of Alberune, when he wrote his 'India,' the Brahma Siddhanta or Sindhind, ... the Charaka in the edition of Ali Ibn Zain and the Panchatantra, or Kalila Damna."[2]

Almansur or Almanzar, who removed his seat from Damascus to Baghdad between 753 and 774 A.D., caused translations to be made from the Sanskrit of medical scientific works, among which we find particularised a tract upon poisons by Shank (meaning Charaka) and a treatise on medicine by Shashrud[3] (meaning Sasruta).

Mrs. Manning says: "Later Greeks at Baghdad are found to have been acquainted with the medical works of the Hindus, and to have availed themselves of their medicaments."[4] We learn with interest that Serapion, one of the earliest of the Arab writers, mentions the Indian Charaka, *praising him as an autho-*

[1] History of Hindu Chemistry, Introduction, p. 76.

[2] Alberuni's India, by Professor Sachau.

[3] Colebrooke's Algebra of the Hindus, Vol. II, p. 512. That Charaka should be changed by Arabic writers into Sarak, Susruta into Susrud, Nidana into Badan, Astanga into Asankar, and so forth, need not at all surprise us. Such transformations can well be explained on phonetic principles. Moreover, one must remember that the Indian works translated into Arabic were sometimes derived from pre-existing Pehlvi versions, and in the migrations through successive languages the names often got frightfully disfigured.

[4] Ancient and Mediæval India, Vol. I, p. 351.

rity in medicine, and referring to the *myrabalans* as forming part of Charaka's prescriptions."[1]

Rhazes was a greater physician than Serapion. He lived at Baghdad with Al Mansur. He wrote twelve books on chemistry. On two occasions, Rhazes refers to the "Indian Charaka" as an authority for statements on plants or drugs.[2]

Another celebrated medical man is Avicinna (Abu Ali Sina), called Sheikh Rais, or the prince of physicians, who succeeded Rhazes. He was the most famous physician of his time. He translated the works of Aristotle, and died in 1036 A.D. In treating of leeches, Avicinna begins by a reference to what "the Indians say," and then gives nearly the very words of Susruta, describing the six poisonous leeches, amongst which are "those called krishna or black, the hairy leech, that which is variegated like a rainbow, etc."[3]

Sultan Firoz Shah, after capturing Nagarkot, had the Sanskrit medical works found there translated into Arabic by Ayazuddin Khalid.[4]

In the reign of Harun-ul-Rashid, the Hindu medicine was not only valued by the Arabs, but Hindu physicians were actually invited to Baghdad, and they went and resided in his court. For this information we are indebted to *Abu Osaiba* whose biographies are quoted by Prof. Dietz in his *Analecta Medica*,[5] Wustenfeld, Rev. W. Cureton,[6] Flu Muller.

Abu Osaiba states that *Manka* was a Hindu, eminent in the art of medicine and learned in Sanskrit literature. He made a journey from India to Iraq, cured the Khalif Harun-ul-Rashid of an illness,

[1] Royle's Ancient Hindu Medicine, p. 36.
[2] See Royle, p. 38.
[3] Royle's Ancient Hindu Medicine, p. 38
[4] Max Muller's Science of Language, p. 167.
[5] Leipsic Edition of 1833, p. 124.
[6] Journal of the R. A. Society, Vol. VI, pp. 105-115.

and translated a work on poison by Charaka from Sanskrit into Persian. Another Hindu doctor named Saleh has also been eulogised by *Abu Osaiba*. He was, it is said, one of the most learned amongst the Hindus, and greatly skilled in curing diseases according to the Indian mode. He lived in *Iraq* during Harun's reign. He travelled to Egypt and Palestine, and was buried when he died in Egypt.

Gabriel Bactishna, a Syrian, became one on the translators of works on medicine from Sanskrit into Arabic.[1]

Professor Sachau says: "What India has contributed reached Baghdad by two different roads. Part has come directly in translations from the Sanskrit, part has travelled through Iran, having originally been translated from Sanskrit (Pali? Prakrit?) into Persian, and farther from Persian into Arabic. In this way, *e.g.*, the fables of *Kalila and Dimna* have been communicated to the Arabs, and a book on medicine, probably the famous Charaka—*of Fihrist*, p. 303.

"In this communication between India and Baghdad we must not only distinguish between two different roads, but also between two different periods."

"As Sindh was under the actual rule of the Khalif Mansur (A.D. 753-774), there came embassies from that part of India to Baghdad, and among them scholars, who brought along with

[1] See Dietz's Analecta Medica. Dr. Furnell, Dy. Surgeon-General and Sanitary Commissioner, Madras, in his lecture delivered on the 1st April, 1882, most vigorously supported the claims of Hindu medicine as one of the most ancient and the most advanced sciences ever cultivated in the world. Speaking of the importance of drinking unpolluted water, he said that "as the ancient Hindus were superior to all others in other respects, so also were they superior to the others in recognising the importance and value of *water*, as well as in insisting upon preserving the water from filth of any kind whatever." He added that in his address to the Convocation in 1879 he had said that the Hindu physicians were unrivalled in all branches of medicine at the time when the Britons were savages and used to go about quite naked. He then described the instructions contained in the Hindu medical works with regard to the use of water, which he said were most remarkable.

them two books, the *Brahma-Sidhanta* of Brahmagupta (Sindhind), and his *Khandakhadyaka* (Arkand). With the help of these pandits, Alfazari, perhaps also Yakub Ibn Tarik, translated them. Both works have been largely used, and have exercised a great influence. It was on this occasion that the Arabs *first* became acquainted with a scientific system of astronomy. They learned from Brahmagupta earlier than from Ptolemy."

"Another influx of Hindu learning took place under Harun, A.D. 786-808. The ministerial family Barmak, then at the zenith of their power, had come with the ruling dynasty from Balkh, where an ancestor of theirs had been an official in the Buddhistic temple, Naubehar, *i.e.*, *navavihara*, the new temple (or monastry). The name Barmak is said to be of Indian descent, meaning *paramaka*, *i.e.*, the superior (abbot of the *vihara*)?. Of course the Barmak family had been converted, but their contemporaries never thought much of their profession of Islam, nor regarded it as genuine. Induced probably by family traditions, they sent scholars to India, there to study medicine and pharmacology. Besides, they engaged Hindu scholars to come to Baghdad, made them the chief physicians of their hospitals and ordered them to translate from Sanskrit into Arabic, books on medicine, pharmacology, toxicology, philosophy, astrology and other subjects. Still in later centuries, Muslim scholars sometimes travelled for the same purposes as the emissaries of the Barmak, *e.g.*, Almuwaffak, not long before Alberuni's time."[1]

Mrs. Manning says: "Greek physicians have done much to preserve and diffuse the medical science of India. We find, for instance, that the Greek physician Actuarius celebrates the Hindu medicine called *triphala*. He mentions the peculiar products of India, of which it is composed, by their Sanskrit name

[1] Sachau's translation of Alberuni's India.

Myrobalans.' Ætius, who was a native of Amida in Mesopotamia, and studied at Alexandria in the fifth century, not only speaks of the *Myrobalans*, but mentions them as the proper cure for the disease called elephantiasis."

The Hindus were the first nation to establish hospitals, and for centuries they were the only people in the world who maintained them. The Chinese traveller Fahein speaking of a hospital he visited in Patliputra says: "Hither come all poor and helpless patients suffering from all kinds of infirmities. They are well taken care of, and a doctor attends them: food and medicine being supplied according to their wants. Thus they are made quite comfortable, and when they are well, they may go away."[2]

"The earliest hospital in Europe." says Mr. Vincent Smith,[3] "is said to have been opened in the tenth century."

Among the ancient Hindu physicians of note may be mentioned (1) Atreya, Agnivesa, Charaka, Dhanwantari, Susruta, Bharadvaja, Kapishthala, Bheda, Latukarna, Parasara, Harita, Kashraparu, Baijvapi, Krisa Samkrityayana, Babhravya, Krishnatreya, Auddalakie Svetaketu, Panchala, Gonardiya, Gonikaputra, Sabandhu, Samkara and Kankayana.

Nearchas relates that the Greek physicians did not know how to cure snakebite. But the Hindu physicians cured it, and notified their ability to cure all who were afflicted with it, if they came to the court of Alexander the Great.[4]

As regards their knowledge of the Science of Chemistry, Mr. Elphinstone says: "Their (Indian) chemical skill is a fact more striking and more unexpected."[5]

[1] Ancient and Mediæval India, Vol. I, p. 451.
[2] Giles' Version.
[3] Early History of India, p. 259.
[4] Wise's History of Medicine, p. 9.
[5] A famous expounder of this art (alchemy) was Nagarjuna, a native of Daihak, near Somnath. He excelled in it, and composed a book which contains

Sir P. C. Ray in his History of Hindu Chemistry says; "While *Rasaratnakara* and *Rasarnava* are Tantras pure and simple in which alchemy is incidentally dwelt upon, *Rasaratana-samuchchaya* (a modern work based on old Hindu medical works), is a systematic and comprehensive treatise on materia medica, pharmacy and medicine. Its methodical and scientific arrangement of the subject-matter would do credit to any modern work, and altogether it should be pronounced a production unique of its kind in Sanskrit literature."[1]

Dr. Ray says: "We have only to refer our readers to the chapter on the preparation of caustic alkali, in the Susruta, with the direction that the strong lye is to be 'preserved in an iron vessel' as a proof of the high degree of perfection in scientific pharmacy achieved by the Hindus at an early age. It is absolutely free from any trace of quackery or charlatanism, and is a decided improvement upon the process prescribed by a Greek writer of the eleventh century, as unearthed by M. Berthelot."[2] As regards dispensaries and hospitals, everyone knows that Buddhist India was studded with them.

In European histories of chemistry, the credit of being the first to press chemical knowledge into the service of medicine

the substance of the whole literature on this subject, and is very rare."—*History of Hindu Chemistry*, Vol. I, p. 54.

The *Englishman* (a Calcutta daily), in a leader in 1880, said: "No one can read the rules contained in great Sanskrit medical works without coming to the conclusion that in point of knowledge, the ancient Hindus were in this respect very far in advance not only of the Greeks and Romans but of Mediæval Europe."

"Nagarjuna Bodhisatva was well practised in the art of compounding medicines; by taking a preparation (pill or cake) he nourished the years of life for many hundreds of years, so that neither the mind nor appearance decayed. Satvaha-Raja had partaken of this mysterious medicine."—Beal's Buddhist Records of the Western World, Vol II, p. 212.

[1] History of Hindu Chemistry, Vol. I, p. 1.

[2] History of Hindu Chemistry, Vol. I, Introduction, p viii. In Vol. II of the same work Dr. Ray (p. 43) adds that M. Berthelot was so struck with the originality of this process that he suggested that this portion was evidently modern!!

and introduce the use of the internal administration of mercurial preparations, is given to Paracelsus (1493-1541). But, says the author of the History of Hindu Chemistry, "we have, indeed, reason to suspect that Paracelsus got his ideas from the East."[1]

Dr. Ray says: "From the evidences we have adduced all along there can now be scarcely any question as regards the priority of the Hindus in making mercurial remedies a speciality; and they are entitled to claim orginality in respect of the internal administration of metal generally, seeing that the Charaka and the Susruta, not to speak of the later Tantras, are eloquent over their virtues."[2]

In Europe, however, the medicinal virtues of mercury do not appear to have been at all ascertained even in the days of Pliny the elder; that writer termed quicksilver the *bane* and poison of all things, and what would with more propriety be called *death*-silver.[3]

Mr. Elphinstone says: "They knew how to prepare sulphuric acid, nitric acid and muratic acide; the oxide of copper, iron, lead (of which they had both the red oxide and litharge), tin and zinc; the sulphuret of iron, copper, mercury, antimony, and arsenic; the sulphate of copper, zinc and iron; and carbonates of lead and iron. Their modes of preparing these substances were sometimes peculiar."[4]

"Their use of these medicines seems to have been very bold. They were the first nation who employed minerals internally, and they not only gave mercury in that manner but arsenic and arsenious acid, which were remedies in intermittents. They have

[1] History of Hindu Chemistry, Vol. I, p. 60.

[2] History of Hindu Chemistry, Vol. I, Introduction, p. lxii.

[3] Natural History *Lile*, 33.

[4] For further information, see Dr. Royle (p. 44 and on), who particularly refers to the processes for making calomel and corrosive sublimate.

long used cinnabar for fumigations, by which they produced a speedy and safe salivation. They have long practiced inoculation.

"They cut for the stone, couched for the cataract and extracted the fœtus from the womb, and in their early works enumerate not less than 127 sorts of surgical instruments."[1]

In the course of a lecture to the natives of Bengal on National Universities in India, delivered at Calcutta, in January 1906, Mrs. Besant said: "In physics and chemistry you have advanced far more. In medicine you are still more advanced. In the West it is by no means a science but largely guess work. *Indian medicine, both of the Hindus and the Mohamedans, is superior to the medicine of the West.*"

In order to give an idea of the advanced state of Hindu science of medicine and hygiene, as well as of what we may yet expect from the continued researches of the learned in ancient Indian literature in the way of valuable additions to the modern European medical science, I cannot do better than quote the words of His Excellency Lord Ampthill, Governor of Madras, at the opening of the King Institute of Preventive Medicine in February 1905: "The Mohamedan conquests brought back to India much of the medical knowledge which had been lost for centuries, and we have proofs that the Mughal rulers were great sanitary reformers in the magnificent water works which still exist and perform their functions at various places in the north of India. Now, the British rulers of India have been bringing back yet more of the knowledge which *emanated from this country centuries ago*; and when we undertake municipal water supply

[1] Elphinstone's History of India, p 145. The author also says: "Their acquaintance with medicines seems to have been very extensive We are not surprised at their knowledge of simples in which they gave early lessons to Europe and more recently taught us the benefit of smoking *dhatura* in asthma and the use of cowitch against worms."

schemes, with filter beds and hydraulic pressure, when we build hospitals and establish medical schools, when we promulgate regulations to check the spread of plague, or when we impose on local bodies the duty of watching over the health of the people, we are not introducing any modern innovations or European fads; but merely doing that which was done conturies ago, and again centuries before that, but which has long since been forgotten by all except the historian and the archæologist. The study of these questions brings out the truth of the old saying that there is nothing new in the world. Now, this saying is even true as regards preventive medicine, which we are all apt to regard as one of the most recent discoveries of modern science. Colonel King gives clear proof that the ancient caste injunctions of the Hindus were based on a belief in the existence of transmissible agents of disease, and that both Hindus and Mohamedans used inoculation by small-pox virus as a protection against small-pox; and certain it is that long before Jenner's great discovery, or to be more correct, *re-discovery of vaccination*, this art of inoculation was used for a while in Europe, where it had been imported from Constantinople; and knowledge of medicine which flourished in the Near East at the commencement of the Christian era *emanated, as I have already shown you, from India*."

His Excellency then added: "It is also very probable, so Colonel King assures me, that the ancient Hindus used animal vaccination secured by transmission of the small-pox virus through the cow, and he bases this interesting thoery on a quotation from a writing by Dhanvantri, the greatest of the ancient Hindu physicians, which is so striking and so appropriate to the present occasion that I must take the liberty of reading it to you. It is as follows: "Take the fluid of the pock on the udder of the cow or on the arm between the shoulder and elbow of a human subject on the point of a lancet, and lance with it the arms between the shoulders and elbows until the blood appears: then mixing the fluid with the blood the fever of the small-pox will be produced. *This is vaccination pure and simple. It would seem from it that Jenner's great discovery was actually forestalled by the ancient Hindus.*"

His Excellency further said: "I cannot refrain from mentioning yet another of Colonel King's interesting discoveries, which is that the modern plague policy of evacuation and disinfection is not a bit different from that enjoined in ancient Hindu Shastras."

II.—MATHEMATICS.

In Mathematics he was greater
Than Tycho Brahe, or Erra Pater.

—BUTLER: *Hudibras.*

In mental abstraction and concentration of thought the Hindus are proverbially happy. Apart from direct testimony on the point, the literature of the Hindus furnishes unmistakable evidence to prove that the ancient Hindus possessed astonishing powers of memory and concentration of thought. Hence all such sciences and branches of study as demand concentration of thought and a highly-developed power of abstraction of the mind were highly cultivated by the Hindus. The science of mathematics, the most abstract of all sciences, must have had an irresistible fascination for the minds of the Hindus. Nor are there proofs wanting to support this statement. The most extensive cultivation which astronomy received at the hands of the Hindus is in itself a proof of their high proficieny in mathematics. The high antiquity of Hindu astronomy is an argument in support of a still greater antiquity of their mathematics. That the Hindus were selected by nature to excel all other nations in mathematics, is proved by her revealing to them the foundation of all mathematics. It has been admitted by all competent authorities that the Hindus were the inventors of the numerals. The great German critic, Schlegel, says that the Hindus invented "the decimal cyphers, the honour of which, next to letters the most important of human discoveries, has, with the common consent of historical authorities, been ascribed to the Hindus."[1]

Prof. Macdonell says: In science, too, the debt of Europe to India has been considerable. There is, in the first place, the great fact that the Indians invented the numerical figures used all over the world. The influence which the decimal system of reckoning dependent on those figures has had not only on mathematics but on the progress of civilization in general, can hardly be over-estimated. During the eighth and ninth centuries the Indians became the teachers in arithmetic and algebra of the Arabs, and through them of the nations of the West. Thus, though we call the latter science by an Arabic name, it is a gift we owe to India."[2]

After translating Vyasa Bhasya Sutra 13, Pada III, Dr. Ray says: "This conclusively proves that the decimal notation was familiar to the Hindus when the Vyasa Bhasya was written *i.e.*, centuries before the first appearance of the notation in the writings of the Arabs or the Greco Syrian intermediaries."[3]

Sir M. Monier Williams says: From them (Hindus) the Arabs received not only their first conceptions of algebraic analysis, but also those numerical symbols and decimal notations now current everywhere in Europe, and which have rendered untold service to

[1] Schlegel's History of Literature, p. 123.

[2] History of Sanskrit Literature, p. 424.

[3] History of Hindu Chemistry, Vol. II, p. 117.

the progress of arithmetical science."[1] Says Manning: "To whatever cyclopædia, journal or essay we refer, we uniformly find our numerals traced to India and the Arabs recognised as the medium through which they were introduced into Europe."[2] Sir W. W. Hunter also says: "To them (the Hindus) we owe the invention of the numerical symbols on the decimal scale. The Indian figures 1 to 9 being abbreviated forms of initial letters of the numerals themselves, and the zero, or 0, representing the first letter of the Sanskrit word for empty (*sunya*). The Arabs borrowed them from the Hindus, and transmitted them to Europe."[3]

Professor Weber says: "It is to them (the Hindus) also that we owe the ingenious invention of the numerical symbols, which in like manner passed from them to the Arabs, and from these again to European scholars. By these latter, who were the disciples of the Arabs, frequent allusion is made to the Indians and uniformly in terms of high esteem; and one Sanskrit word even (*uchcha*) has passed into the Latin translations of Arabian astronomers."[4]

Professor Wilson says: Even Delambre concedes their claim to the invention of numerical cyphers."

Arithmetic.

Mrs. Manning says: "Compared with other ancient nations, the Hindus were peculiarly strong in all the branches of arithmetic."[5] Professor Weber, after declaring that the Arabs were disciples of the Hindus, says: "The same thing (*i.e.*, the Arabs borrowed from the Hindus) took place also in regard to

[1] Indian Wisdom, p. 124.
[2] Ancient and Mediæval India, Vol I, p. 376.
[3] Imperial Gazetteer, p. 219. "India."
[4] Weber's Indian Literature, p. 256.
[5] Ancient and Mediæval India, Vol. I, p. 374.

algebra and arithmetic in particular, in both of which it appears the Hindus attained, quite independently, to a high degree of proficiency." Sir W. W. Hunter also says that "the Hindus attained a very high proficiency in arithmetic and algebra independently of any foreign influence."[1]

The English mathematician Prof. Wallace, says: "The *Lilavati* treats of arithmetic, and contains not only the common rules of that science, but the application of these to various questions of interest, barter, mixtures, combinations, permutation, sums of progression, indeterminate problems, and mensuration of surfaces and solids. The rules are found to be exact and nearly as simple as in the *present state* of analytical investigation. The numerical results are readily deduced, and if they be compared with the earliest specimens of Greek calculation, the advantages of the decimal notation are placed in a striking light."[2] It may, however, be mentioned that *Lilavati*, of which Professor Wallace speaks, is a comparatively modern manual of arithmetic; and to judge of the merits of Hindu arithmetic from this book is to judge of the merits of English arithmetic from Chamber's manual of arithmetic.

It may be added that the enormous extent to which numerical calculation goes in India, and the possession by the Hindus of by far the largest table of calculation, are in themselves proofs of the superior cultivation of the science of arithmetic by the Hindus.

GEOMETRY.

The ancient Hindus have always been celebrated for the remarkable progress they made in geometry. Professor Wallace

[1] Imperial Gazetteer, "India," p. 219.

[2] Edinburgh Review, Vol. 29, p. 147.

says: "However ancient a book may be in which a system of trigonometry occurs, we may be assured it was not written in the infancy of the science. Geometry must have been known in India *long before* the writing of the Surya Siddhanta,"[1] which is supposed by the Europeans to have been written before 2,000 B.C.[2]

Professor Wallace says: "Surya Siddhanta contains a rational system of trigonometry, which differs entirely from that first known in Greece or Arabia. In fact it is founded on a geometrical theorem, which was not known to the geometricians of Europe before the time of Vieta, about two hundred years ago. And it employs the sines of arcs, a thing unknown to the Greeks, who used the chords of double arcs. The invention of sines has been attributed to the Arabs, but it is possible that they may have received this improvement in trigonometry as well as the numerical characters from India."[3]

Mr. Elphinstone says: "In the *Surya Siddhanta* is contained a system of trigonometry which not only goes far beyond anything known to the Greeks, but involves theorems which were not discovered in Europe till two centuries ago."[4]

Professor Wallace says: "In expressing the radius of a circle in parts of the circumference, the Hindus are quite singular. Ptolemy and the Greek mathematicians in their division of the radius preserved no reference to the circumference. The use of sines, as it was unknown to the Greeks, forms a difference between theirs and the Indian trigonometry. Their rule for the computation of the lines is a considerable refinement in science first practiced by the mathematician Briggs."[5]

[1] Mill's India, Vol. II, p. 150.
[2] See Mill's India, Vol. II, p. 3, footnote.
[3] Edinburgh Encyclopædia, "Geometry," p. 191.
[4] History of India, p. 129.
[5] Mill's India, Vol. II, p. 150.

Count Bjornstjerna says: "We find in *Ayeen Akbari*, a journal of the Emperor Akbar, that the Hindus of former times assumed the diameter of a circle to be to its periphery as 1,250 to 3,927. The ratio of 1,250 to 3,927 is a very close approximation to the quadrature of a circle, and differs very little from that given by Metius of 113 to 355. In order to obtain the result thus found by the Brahmans, even in the most elementary and simplest way, it is necessary to inscribe in a circle a polygon of 768 sides, an operation, which cannot be performed arithmetically without the knowledge of some peculiar properties of this curved line, and at least an extraction of the square root of the ninth power, each to ten places of decimals. The Greeks and Arabs have not given anything so approximate."[1]

It is thus clearly seen that the Greeks and the Arabs apart, even the Europeans have but very recently advanced far enough to come into line with the Hindus in their knowledge of this branch of mathematics.

Professor Wallace says: "The researches of the learned have brought to light astronomical tables in India which must have been constructed by the principles of geometry, but the period at which they have been framed has by no means been completely ascertained. Some are of opinion that they have been framed from observation made at a very remote period, not less than 3,000 years before the Christian era (this has been conclusively proved by Mons. Bailly); and if this opinion be well founded, the science of geometry must have been cultivated in India to a considerable extent long before the period assigned to its origin in the West; so that many elementary propositions, may have been brought from India to Greece."[2] He adds: "In

[1] Theogony of the Hindus, p. 37.

[2] Edinburgh Encyclopædia, "Geometry," p. 191.

geometry there is much deserving of attention. We have here the celebrated proposition that the square on the hypotenuse of a right-angled triangle is equal to the square on the sides containing the right angle and other propositions, which form part of the system of modern geometry. There is one remarkable proposition, namely, that which discovers the area of a triangle when its three sides are known. *This do s not seem to have been known to the ancient Greek geometers.*"

The Sulva Sutras, however, date from about the eighth century B.C., and Dr. Thibaut has shown that the geometrical theorem of the 47th proposition, Book I, which tradition ascribes to Pythagoras, was solved by the Hindus at least two centuries earlier,[1] thus confirming the conclusion of V. Schrœder that the Greek philosopher owed his inspiration to India.[2]

Mr. Elphinstone says: "Their geometrical skill is shown among other forms by their demonstrations of various properties of triangles, especially one which expresses the area in the terms of the three sides, and was unknown in Europe till published by Clavius, and by their knowledge of the proportions of the radius to the circumference of a circle, which they express in a mode peculiar to themselves, by applying one measure and one unit to the radius and cirumference. This proportion, which is confirmed by the most approved labours of Europeans, was not known out of India until modern times."[3]

ALGEBRA.

The Hindus have been especially successful in the cultivation of algebra. Professor Wallace says: "In algebra the Hindus

[1] Journal of the Asiatic Society of Bengal, 1875, p. 227.
[2] See History of Hindu Chemistry, Vol. I, p. xxiv, Intro.
[3] Elphinstone's History of India, p. 130.

understood well the arithmetic of surd roots, and the general resolution of equations of the second degree, which it is not clear that Diaphantus knew, that they attained a general solution of indeterminate problems of the first degree, which it is certain Diaphantus had not attained, and a method of deriving a multitude of answers to problems of the second degree, when one solution was discovered by trial, which is as near an approach to a general solution as was made until the time of La Grange." Professor Wallace concludes by adopting the opinion of Playfair on the subject, "that before an author could think of embodying a treatise on algebra in the heart of a system of astronomy, and turning the researches of the one science to the purposes of the other, both must have been in such a state of advancement as the lapse of several ages and many repeated efforts of inventors were required to produce." "This," says Professor Wilson, "is unanswerable evidence in favour of the antiquity, originality, and advance of the Hindu mathematical science."[1]

Mr. Colebrooke says: "They (the Hindus) understood well the arithmetic of surd roots; they were aware of the infinite quotient resulting from the division of finite quantities by cipher; they knew the general resolution of equations of the second degree, and had touched upon those of higher denomination, resolving them in the simplest cases, and in those in which the solution happens to be practicable by the method which serves for quadratics; they had attained a general solution of indeterminate problems of the first degree; they had arrived at a method for deriving a multitude of solutions of answers to problems of the second degree from a single answer found tentatively."[2] "And this," says Colebrooke in conclusion, "was as near an approach to a general solution of such problems as was made

[1] Mill's India, Vol. II, p. 151, Wilson's note.

[2] Colebrooke's Miscellaneous Essays, Vol. II, p. 419.

until the days of La Grange ?"[1]

"Equally decided is the evidence," says Manning, "that this excellence in algebric analysis was attained in India independent of foreign aid."

Mr. Colebrooke says: "No doubt is entertained of the source from which it was received immediately by modern Europeans. The Arabs were mediately or immediately our instructors in this study."

Mrs. Manning says: "The Arabs were not in general *inventors but recipients*. Subsequent observation has confirmed this view; for not only did algebra in an advanced state exist in India prior to the earliest disclosure of it by the Arabians to modern Europe, but the names by which the numerals have become known to us are of Sanskrit origin."[2]

Professor Monier Williams says: "*To the Hindus is due the invention of algebra and geometry and their application to astronomy.*"[3]

Comparing the Hindus and the Greeks, as regards their knowledge of algebra, Mr. Elphinstone says: "There is no question of the superiority of the Hindus over their rivals in the perfection to which they brought the science. Not only is Aryabhatta superior to Diaphantus (as is shown by his knowledge of the resolution of equations involving several unkown quantities, and in a general method of resolving all indeterminate problems of at least the first degree) *but he and his successors press hard upon the discoveries* of algebraists who

[1] Colebrooke's Miscellaneous Essays, Vol. II, pp. 416-418. For the points in which Hindu algebra is more advanced than the Greek, see Colebrooke, p. 16.

[2] Ancient and Mediæval India, Vol. II, p. 375. "Mr. Colebrooke has fully shown that algebra had attained the highest perfection it ever reached in India before it was ever known to the Arabians. Whatever the Arabs possessed in common with the Hindus, there are good grounds to believe that they derived it from the Hindus."—Elphinstone's *India*, p. 133.

[3] Indian Wisdom, p. 185.

lived almost in our own time."[1] "It is with a feeling of respectful admiration that Mr. Colebrooke alludes to ancient Sanskrit treatises on algebra, arithmetic and mensuration."[2]

In the Edinburgh Review (Vol. XXI, p. 372) is a striking history of a problem (to find x, so that $ax^2 - b$ shall be a square number). The first step towards a solution is made by Diaphantus,[3] it was extended by Fermat, and sent as a defiance to the English algebraists in the seventeenth century, but was only carried to its full extent by the celebrated mathematician Euler, who arrives exactly at the point before attained by Bhashkaracharya"[4]

Another occurs in the same Review (Volume XXIX, p. 153), where it is stated from Mr. Colebrooke that a particular solution given by Bhashkaracharya is exactly the same as that hit on by Lord Brounker in 1657; and that the general solution of the same problem was unsuccessfully attempted by Euler and only accomplished by De la Grange in 1767 A.D., although *it had been as completely given by Brahmagupta*.

"But," says Mr. Elphinstone, "the superiority of the Hindus over the Greek algebraists is scarcely so conspicuous in their discoveries as in the excellence of their method, which is altogether dissimilar to that of Diaphantus (Strachey's *Bija Ganita* quoted in the "Edinburgh Review," Vol XXI, pp. 374,

[1] Elphinstone's India, p. 131.

[2] Manning's Ancient and Mediæval India, Vol. I, p. 374.

[3] Colebrooke says: "In the whole science he (Diaphantus) is very far behind the Hindu writers."—Essays, p. 438

[4] Elphinstone's India, p. 131. Bhashkaracharya wrote the celebrated book "Siddhanta Siromani," and treatises on algebra and arithmetic. His division of a circle is remarkable for its minute analysis, which is as follows:—

60 Vikala (Seconds)	=	A Kala (Minute).
60 Kala ...	=	A Bhaga (Degree).
30 Bhaga ...	=	A Rasi (Sign).
12 Rasi ...	=	A Bhagana (Revolution).

375), and in the perfection of their algorithm (Colebrooke's Hindu Algebra quoted in the E. R., Vol. XXIX, p. 162).

One of their most favourite processes (that called cattaca) was *not* known in Europe till published by Bachet de Mezeriac, about the year 1624, and is virtually the same as that explained by Euler (Edinburgh Review, Vol. XXIX, p. 151). Their application of algebra to astronomical investigations and geometrical demonstrations is also an invention of their own; and their manner of conducting it is even now entitled to admiration (Colebrooke, quoted by Professor Wallace; and Edinburgh Review, Vol. XXIX, p. 158).

Speaking of the Hindu treatises on algebra, arithmetic, and mensuration, Mr. Colebrooke says: "It is not hoped that in the actual advanced condition of the analytical art they will add to its resources and throw new light on the mathematical science in any other respect than as concerns its history, but had an earlier version of these treatises been completed, had they been translated and given to the public when the notice of mathematicians was first drawn to the attainments of the Hindus in astronomy and in sciences connected with it, some additions would have been then made to the means and resources of algebra, for the general solution of problems, by methods which have been reinvented or have been perfected in the last age."[1]

It is thus evident from what Mr. Colebrooke shows that the Hindu literature even in its degenerate state, and when so few works are extant, contains mathematical works that show an

[1] Colebrooke's Miscellaneous Essays, Vol. II, p. 419.

It may, however, be said that in some quarters, the genuineness of the independent solution of the problems mentioned above, and the discovery of methods similar to those of the Hindus by modern Europeans have been doubted, and such doubts may well be excused, considering the extensive intercourse that has existed between India and Europe for a long time past.

advance in the science in no way behind the latest European achievements.

As an instance of the remarkable and extensive practice and cultivation of mathematics in India, may be cited the case of a problem from *Lalita Vistar*. Mons. Wœpcke,[1] indeed is of opinion that the account in the *Lalita Vistara* problem solved by Buddha on the occasion of his marriage examination, relative to the number of atoms in the length of a *Yojana*, is the basis of the "Arenarius" of the celebrated scientist Archimedes.

The credit of the discovery of the principle of differential calculus is generally claimed by the Europeans. But it was known to the Hindus centuries ago. Bhashkaracharya, one of the world's greatest mathematicians, has referred to it in various places.

Mr. Spottiswoode says: "It must be admitted that the penetration shown by Bhashkaracharya, in his analysis is in the highest degree remarkable that the formula which he establishes, and his method, bear more than a mere resemblance—they bear a strong analogy—to the corresponding process in modern mathematical astronomy; and that the majority of scientific persons will learn with surprise the existence of such method in the writings of so distant a period and so remote a region."[2]

Mr. Lethbridge says: "Bhashkaracharya is said to have discovered a mathematical process very nearly resembling the differential calculus of modern European mathematicians."[3]

Dr. Ray, however, discusses the whole question and shows that Bhaskaracharya not only knew the principle but applied it to astronomy. He says: "The astronomical *Truti* of

[1] *Mem Surla propagation des chiffres Indians*, Paris, 1863, pp. 75-91.

[2] J. R. A. S., Vol. XVII.

[3] School History of India, Appendix A, p. ii.

time measures about the thirty-four thousandth part of a second. This is of special value in determining the exact character of Bhashkar's claim to be regarded as a precursor of Newton in the discovery of the principle of the differential calculus, as well as in its application to astronomical problems and computations. This claim, as I proceed to show, is absolutely established. It is indeed far stronger than Archimedes's to the conception of a rudimentary process of integration."[1] Dr. Ray then shows that "Mr. Spottiswoode's error in thinking that Bhashkar's method is only an analogous one but is not the differential calculus itself, is due to the insufficiency of data supplied to him for his opinion."

Dr. Ray also remarks "I may add *en passant* that Bhashkara's formula for the computation of sines also implies his use of the principle of the differential calculus."[2]

III.—ASTRONOMY.

"Ye multiplying masses of increased
And still increasing light: what are ye! what
In this blue wilderness of interminable
Air where ye roll along, as I have seen
The leaves along the limpid stream of Eden!
Is your course measured for ye? or do ye
Sweep on in your unbounded revelry
Through an ærial universe of endless
Expansion, at which my soul aches to think,
Intoxicated with eternity!"

BYRON: *Cain.*

A EUROPEAN critic says: "For a man, the most sublime study is that of astronomy." And indeed, what can be more sublime

[1] History of Hindu Chemistry, Vol. II, pp. 159, 160.

[2] Ibid, p. 163.

than the study of Nature in its broadest aspects, of the movements and the functions of those wonderful and splendid bodies with which the boundless expanse of the wide, wide space is thickly studded, where fancy is puzzled and imagination itself staggered?

> "Heaven
> Is as the book of God before thee set
> Wherein to read His wondrous words."
>
> MILTON: *Paradise Lost.*

The science of astronomy flourishes only amongst a civilized people. Hence, considerable advancement in it is itself a proof of the high civilization of a nation. Hindu astronomy, or what remains of it, has received the homage of European scholars. Dr. Sir William Hunter says: "The astronomy of the Hindus has formed the subject of excessive admiration." "Proof of very extraordinary proficiency," says Mr. Elphinstone, "in their astronomical writings are found."[1]

The Hindu astronomy not only establishes the high proficiency of our ancestors in this department of knowledge and exacts admiration and applause: it does something more. It proves the great antiquity of the Sanskrit literature and the high literary culture of the Hindus. "Mons. Bailly, the celebrated author of the History of Astronomy, inferred from certain astronomical tables of the Hindus, not only advanced progress of the science but a date so ancient as to be entirely inconsistent with the chronology of the Hebrew Scriptures. His argument was laboured with the utmost diligence, and was received with unbounded applause. All concurred at the time with the wonderful learning, wonderful civilization and wonderful institutions of the Hindus."[2] It must not, however, be forgotten, as

[1] History of India, p. 120.
[2] Mill's History of India, Vol. II, pp. 97, 98.

this celebrated astronomer (Mons. Bailly) holds, that Hindu astronomy is "the remains rather than the elements of a science"[1]

Mr. Weber says: "Astronomy was practised in India as early as 2780 B.C."[2] But some of the greatest modern astronomers have decided in favour of a much greater antiquity. Cassini, Bailly, Gentil and Playfair maintain "that there are Hindu observations extant which must have been made more than three thousand years before Christ, and which evince *even then a very high degree* of astronomical science."[3]

Count Bjornstjerna proves conclusively that Hindu astronomy was very far advanced even at the beginning of the Kaliyug, or the iron age of the Hindus (about 5,000 years ago). He says: "According to the astronomical calculations of the Hindus, the present period of the world, Kaliyug, commenced 3,102 years before the birth of Christ, on the 20th February, at 2 hours 27 minutes and 30 seconds, the time being thus calculated to minutes and seconds. They say that a conjunction of the planets then took place, and their tables show this conjunction. Bailly states that Jupiter and Mercury were then in the same degree of the ecliptic, Mars at a distance of only eight, and Saturn of seven degrees; whence it follows, that at the point of time given by the Brahmins as the commencement of Kaliyug, the four planets above-mentioned must have been successively concealed by the rays of the sun (first Saturn, than Mars, afterwards Jupiter and lastly Mercury). They thus showed themselves in conjunction; and although Venus could not then

[1] See Bailly's *Histoire de l' Astronomie Ancienne (Plutot les debris que leselemens d'une Science)*.

[2] Weber's Indian Literature, p. 30. "Biot regards the 2357 B.C. as the earliest point when the course of the moon was first watched for astronomical use"—Duncker's *History of Antiquity*, p. 284.

[3] Theogony of the Hindus, p. 32.

be seen, it was natural to say *that a conjunction of the planets then took place.* The calculation of the Brahmins is so exactly confirmed by our own astronomical tables, that nothing but an *actual observation* could have given so correspondent a result." The learned Count continues: He (Bailly) further informs us that Laubere, who was sent by Louis XIV as ambassador to the King of Siam, brought home in the year 1687, astronomical tables of solar eclipses, and that other similar tables were sent to Europe by Patouillet (a missionary in the Carnatic), and by Gentil, which latter were obtained from the Brahmins in Tirvalore, and that they *all perfectly agree in their calculations although received from different persons, at different times, and from places in India remote from each other.* On these tables, Bailly makes the following observation: The motion calculated by the Brahmins during the long space of 4,383 years (the period elapsed between these calculations and Bailly's), varies not a single *minut* from the tables of Cassini and Meyer; and as the tables brought to Europe by Laubere in 1687, under Louis XIV, are older than those of Cassini and Meyer, the accordance between them must be the result of *mutual* and exact astronomical observations." Then again, "Indian tables give the same annual variation of the moon as that discovered by Tycho Brahe, a variation unknown to the school of Alexandria, and also to the Arabs, who followed the calculations of this school."

"These facts," says the erudite Count, "sufficiently show the great antiquity and distinguished station of astronomical science among the Hindus of past ages." The Count then asks "if it be true that the Hindus more than 3,000 B.C., according to Bailly's calculation, had attained so high a degree of astronomical and geometrical learning, how many centuries *earlier* must the commencement of their culture have been, since the human mind advances only step by step on the path of science!"[1]

There are however, many other arguments to establish a far higher antiquity of the Hindu astronomy than what is assigned by Bentley. The equation of the sun's centre, according to the Indian tables, is 2° 10½′; whereas the same quantity according to the modern observations is only 1° 55½′. It is one consequence of the mutual disturbances of planets that the eccentricity of the solar orbit on which the equation just mentioned depends, was greater in former ages than it is at the present time. From the quantity which the Hindus assign to this astronomical element, M. Bailly has drawn an argument in favour of the antiquity of the Indian tables, which it must be confessed is of great weight when the difference of the Indian and European determinations is considered as arising from the gradual alteration of the planetary orbits.

2. The quantities which the Indian tables assign to other astronomical elements, *viz.*, the mean motions of Jupiter and Saturn, have been found to agree almost exactly not with what is observed at the present time, but with what the theory of gravity shows would have been observed at the beginning of the Kaliyug. Laplace discovered it after the publication of the *Astronomie Indien* and inserted it in the *Journal des Savans.*

3. M. Bailly has shown that the place of the aphelion of Jupiter's orbit, determined by the Indian tables for the beginning of the Kaliyug agrees with the modern tables of Lalande when corrected by the theoretical equations of La Grange. The same thing is true of the quantity which the Hindus assign to the equation of Saturn's centre.

4. Another argument to vindicate the great antiquity of Hindu astronomy is derived from the obliquity of the ecleptic

[1] Theogony of the Hindus, p. 37.

which the Indians state at 24°. Both observation and theory concur in showing that the obliquity of the ecliptic has been diminishing slowly for many ages preceding the present.

5. The length of the Hindu tropical year as deduced from the Hindu tables is 365 days, 5 hours, 50 minutes, 35 seconds, while La Callie's observation gives 365-5-48-49. This makes the year at the time of the Hindu observation longer than at present by 1′ 46″. It is, however, an established fact that the year has been decreasing in duration from time immemorial and shall continue to decrease. In about 40 centuries the time of the year decreases about 40½″. This, then, is *an unmistakeable proof of the very high antiquity of Indian astronomy*. The observation by the Hindus must have been in the Dwapur (more than 5,000 years ago).

It should now be quite clear that in India astronomy was cultivated and wonderful progress in the science was made at a period when the rest of world, including the whole of Europe, was completely enveloped in ignorance.

Sir W. Hunter says: "In some points the Brahmans made advances beyond Greek astronomy. Their fame spread throughout the West, and found entrance into the Chronicon Paschale (commenced about 330 A. D. and revised under Heraclius 610-641)." [1]

Mr. Elphinstone says: "In addition to the points already mentioned in which the Hindus have gone beyond the other nations, Mr. Colebrooke mentions two in astronomy. One is in their notions regarding the processions of the Equinoxes, in which they were more correct than Ptolemy, and as much so as the Arabs, who did not attain to that degree of improvement till a later period; the other relates to the diurnal revolution of the earth on its axis which the Brahmans discussed in the fifth

[1] Indian Gazetteer, Vol. IV, p. 218.

century B.C."

Sir W. Hunter says: "The Sanskrit term for the apex of a planet's orbit seems to have passed into the Latin translations of the Arabic astronomers. The Sanskrit *uccha* became the *aux* (gen. *augis*) of the later translators." (Reinaud, p. 325 and Weber, p. 257).

Professor Weber says: "The fame of Hindu astronomers spread to the West, and the Andubarius (or probably, Ardubarius), whom the Chronicon Paschale places in primeval times as the earliest Indian astronomer, is doubtless none other than Aryabhatta, the rival of Pulisa, and who is likewise extolled by the Arabs under the name of Arjabahar."[2]

Professor Wilson says: "The science of astronomy at present exhibits many proofs of accurate observation and deduction, highly creditable to the science of the Hindu astronomers. The division of the ecleptic into luner mansions, the solar zodiac, the mean motions of the planets, the procession of the equinox, the earth's self-support in space, the diurnal revolution of the earth on its axis, the revolution of the moon on her axis, her distance from the earth, the dimensions of the orbits of the planet, the calculations of eclipses are parts of a system which could not have been found amongst an unenlightened people."[3]

But the originality of the Hindus is not less striking than their proficiency. It is remarkable that the Hindu methods are all original and peculiar. Professor Wilson says: "The originality of Hindu astronomy is at once established, but it is also proved by intrinsic evidence, and although there are some remarkable coincidences between the Hindu and other systems, their methods are their own."[4] Mr. Elphinstone says: "In the more advanced

[1] History of India, p. 132, footnote.
[2] Weber's Indian Literature, p. 255.
[3] Mill's History of India, Vol. II, p. 106.
[4] Mill's History of India, Vol. II, p. 107.

stages, where they are more likely to have borrowed, not only is their mode of proceedings peculiar to themselves but it is often founded on principles, with which no other ancient people were acquainted, and showed a knowledge of discoveries not made even in Europe till within the course of the last two centuries."[1]

In the sixth volume of the Journal of the American Oriental Society, Professor Whitney published an English translation of *Surya Siddhanta* by the Rev. E. Burgess, with an elaborate commentary by himself. This paper excited comments from M. Biot, the late venerable astronomer of Paris, and from Professor Weber of Berlin. Biot believed that the Hindus derived their system of *Nakshatras* or moon stations, from the Chinese, but Professor Whitney contributed two other papers to the said Journal, in which he clearly shows that the Hindu *Nakshatra* does not mean the same thing as the Chinese *sieu*. *Sieu* means a single star, whereas *Nakshatra* expresses a *group of stars*, or rather a certain portion of the starry heavens. "Again, Professor Weber shows that the Chinese *sieu* is not traceable further than two or three centuries before Christ, while *Nākshatras* are amongst the heavenly objects mentioned in the Vedic hymns."[2] The great antiquity of the science, however, is the best proof of its originality.

The Arabs were the disciples of the Hindus in this branch of knowledge also. Professor Weber says that Hindu astronomers are extolled by the Arabs. He adds: "For, during the eighth and nineth centuries the Arabs were, in astronomy, the disciples of Hindus, from whom they borrowed the lunar mansions in their new order, and whose *Siddhants*, they frequently worked up and translated in part under the supervision of Indian

[1] Elphinstone's History of India, p. 132.

[2] W. D. Whitney, "Views of Weber and Biot respecting the Relations of the Hindu and Chinese Asterisms," p. 25.

astronomers themselves, whom the Khalifs of Baghdad, etc., invited to their courts."[1]

Dr. Robertson says: "It is highly probable that the knowledge of the twelve signs of zodiacs was derived from India."[2]

Sir W. W. Hunter says: "The Arabs became their (Hindus) disciples in the eighth century, and translated Sanskrit treatises, *Siddhants*, under the name *Sindhends*."[3] Professor Wilson says: "Indian astronomers were greatly encouraged by the early Khalifs, particularly Harun-ul-Rashid and Almamun; they were invited to Baghdad, and their works were translated into Arabic. The Hindus were, fully as much as the Greeks, the teachers of the Arabians."[4]

There are nine Siddhantas extant:[5] (1) Brahma Siddhanta, (2) Surya Siddhanta, (3) Soma Siddhanta, (4) Vrihaspati Siddhanta, (5) Gargya Siddhanta, (6) Narada Siddhanta, (7) Parasar Siddhanta, (8) Pulastya Siddhanta, and (9) Vashishta Siddhanta. Of these, the work best known to Europeans is the *Surya Siddhanta*, which is the oldest of the extant Siddhantas.[6]

Mr. Davis calculates that the celebrated Hindu astronomer Parasar, judging from the observations made by him must have lived 1391 years before Christ,[7] and consequently, says Bjuornstjerna, "had read in the divine book of the heavenly firmament long before the Chaldees, the Arabs and the Greeks."[8]

[1] Weber's Indian Literature, p. 255.

[2] Disquisition Concerning India, p. 281.

[3] Indian Gazetteer, "India," p. 218.

[4] Mill's History of India, Vol. II, p. 107.

[5] The Panch Siddhantas, or the five principal astronomical works in general use are: (1) The Paulisa Siddhanta, (2) The Romaka Siddhanta, (3) The Vashishta Siddhanta, (4) The Surya Siddhanta, Brahma Siddhanta, (5) The Pailawaha Siddhanta.

[6] Indian Wisdom, pp. 184, 185.

[7] Asiatic Researches, Vol. II, p. 288.

[8] Theogony of the Hindus, pp. 33, 34.

Mr. Houghton says : "From a text of Parasar it appears that the equinox had gone back from the *tenth* degree of *Bharani* to the first of *Aswini*, or 23 degrees and 20 minutes between the days of that Indian philosopher and year of our Lord 499, when it coincided with the origin of the Hindu ecliptic, so that Parasar probably flourished near the close of the twelfth century before Christ."

After Parasar Muni came Aryabhatta, who was a great astrologer too. He was the man who, according to the Europeans, first brought to light "diurnal revolution of the earth on its axis, and to have known the true theory of the causes of the lunar and solar eclipses, and notice the motion of solstitial and equinoctial points."[1]

His principal works are: (1) Aryabatika, (2) Dasa Gitika, (3) Aryashta Sata.

The best known astronomer who flourished after Aryabhatta's time is Varahmihira, who became pre-eminent in astrology. Mrs. Manning says: "Varahmihira may be cited as a celebrated astronomer to whom astrology was irresistibly attractive;" and again, "He is called an astronomer, but it is for astrology that we find him most celebrated. He attained excellence in each branch of the Sanhita, and before writing his celebrated treatise called the Brihat-Sanhita he composed a work on pure astronomy."[2]

Varahmihir's chief works are: (1) Vrihaj Jataka, (2) Brihat Sanhita, (3) A Summary of the original Panch Siddhantas. Mrs. Manning says: "Richness of detail constitutes the chief attraction of the book (Brihat Sanhita), a merit which was appreciated by the Arab astrologer, Albiruni (البرونی), as it will be by ourselves; for although professedly astrological, its value

[1] See Chamber's Encyclopædia.

[2] Ancient and Mediæval India, Vol. I, pp. 368, 369.

for geography, architecture, sculpture, etc., is unequalled by any Sanskrit work as yet published."[1]

The last Hindu astronomer of eminence, however, was Bhaskaracharya, who is said by Europeans to have flourished so late as the twelfth century. He expounded the law of gravity with peculiar felicity, while his mathematical works place him in the forefront of the world's great mathematicians.

The roundness of the earth and its diurnal rotation, however, were known to the Hindus from the earliest times, Says a Rishi in the *Aiteriya Brahmana:* "By this great inauguration similar to Indra's, Tura, son of Kavasha, consecrated Janamjaya, and thereby did he subdue the earth completely *round.*"[2] In *Aryabhattiyam* we read:

वृत्तभपंजरमध्ये कक्षया परिवेष्टितः खमध्यगतः ।
मृज्जलशिखिवायुमयो भूगोलः सर्वतो वृत्तः ॥

"The earth, situated in the middle of the heavens and composed of five elements, is spherical in its shape." Bhashkarachrya, in *Goladhaya*, says:

समोयेतः स्यात्परिवेः शतांशः पृथिवी च पृथिवी नितरान्तनोयान ।
नरस्य तत्पृष्ठगतस्य कृष्णा समेवतस्य प्रतिभात्यतः सा ॥

"A hundredth part of the circumference of a circle appears to be a straight line. Our earth is a big sphere, and the portion visible to man being exceedingly small, the earth appears to be flat."

Dr. H. Kern, in his paper on "Some fragments of Aryabhatta," translates a passage as follows: "The terrestrial globe, a compound of earth, fire, water, air, entirely round, and compassed by a girdle, *i.e.*, equator, stands in the air," etc., etc.

As regards the annual motion of the earth, the Rig Veda says:

[1] Ancient and Mediæval India, Vol. I, p. 370. See also Dr. Kern's Bib. Ind., Introduction, p. 27.

[2] Haug's Aiteriya Brahmana, Vol. II, p. 242

या गौर्वर्त्तनिं पर्य्येति निष्कृतं पयो दुहाना व्रतनीरवारतः ।
सा प्रब्रुवाणा वरुणाय दाशुषे देवेभ्यो दाशद्धविषा विवस्वते ॥

The diurnal motion is thus described in the Yajur Veda:

आयं गौः पृश्निरक्रमीदसदन्मातरं पुरः । पितरं च प्रयन्त्स्वः ॥

The *Aiteriya Brahmana* explains that the sun neither sets nor rises, that when the earth, owing to the rotation on its axis is lighted up, it is called day, and so on.[1]

अथ यदेनं प्रातरुदेतीति मन्यन्ते रात्रेरेव तदन्तमित्वा अथात्मानं विपर्यस्यते अहरेवावस्तात् कुरुते रात्रिं पुरस्तात । स वै एष न कदाचन निम्लोचति, न ह वै कदाचन निम्लोचति ॥

As regards the stars being stationary, Aryabhatta[2] says:

भपञ्जरः स्थिरो भूरेवावृत्यावृत्य प्रातिदैवासिकौ ।
उदयास्तमयौ संपादयते ग्रहनक्षत्राणाम् ॥

"The starry vault is fixed. It is the earth which, moving round its axis, again and again causes the rising and setting of planets and stats." He starts the question: "Why do the stars seem to move?" and himself replies: "As a person in a vessel, while moving forwards sees an immovable object moving backwards, in the same manner do the stars, however immovable, seem to move daily."[3]

The Polar days and nights of six months are also described by him.

विषुवद्वृत्तं द्युसदां क्षितेः क्षितिजमितं तथा च दैत्यानां । उत्तरयाम्यौ क्रमशो मूर्द्धार्द्धगताधुरेषायतस्तेषाम् । उत्तरगोले क्षितिजादूर्द्ध्वे परितो भ्रमन्तमादित्यम् । इव्यं त्रिदशः सततं पश्यन्त्यसुराः असव्यगं याम्य ॥

It has been remarked:

लंकापुरेऽर्कस्य यदोदयः स्यात्तदा दिनार्द्धं यमकोटिपुर्याम् ॥
भवेत्तदा सिद्धपुरेऽस्तकालः स्याद्रोमके रात्रिदलं तदैव ॥

"When it is sunrise at Lanka (the Equator) it is mid-day at Java, sunset in America, and midnight at Rome."

[1] Haug's Aiteriya Brahamana, Vol. II, p. 242.
[2] Colebrooke's Miscellaneous Essays, Vol. II, p. 392.
[3] Journal of the R.A.S., Vol. XX, p. 372.

As regards the size of the earth, it is said:

प्रोक्तो योजनसंख्यया कुपरिधिः सप्ताङ्गनन्दाब्धयस्तद्व्यासः ।
कुभुजङ्गसायकभुवः सिद्धांशकेनाधिकाः ॥

"The circumference of the earth is 4,967 yojanas, and its diameter is 1,581 1/24 yojanas." A yojana is equal to five English miles, the circumference of the earth would therefore be 24,835 miles and its diameter 7,905·5/24 miles.

The Yajur Veda says that the earth is kept in space owing to the superior attraction of the sun.

आकृष्णेन रजसा वर्त्तमानो निवेशयन्नमृतं मर्त्यं च ।
हिरण्ययेन सविता रथेना देवो याति भुवनानि पश्यन् ॥

The theory of gravity is thus described in the *Sidhanta Shiromani* centuries before Newton was born:

आकृष्टिशक्तिश्च मही तया यत् ।
स्वस्थं गुरुस्वाभिमुखं स्वशक्त्या ॥
आकृष्यते तत् पततीव भाति ।
समे समन्तात् क्व पतत्विय़ं खे ॥

"The earth, owing to its force of gravity, draws all things towards itself, and so they seem to fall towards the earth," etc., etc.

That the moon and the stars are dark bodies is thus described:—

भूग्रहभानां गोलार्द्धानि स्वच्छायया विवर्णानि ।
अर्द्धानि यथासारं सूर्याभिमुखानि दीप्यन्ते ॥

"The earth, the planets and the comets all receive their light from the sun: that half towards the sun being always bright, the colour varying with the peculiarity of the substance of each."

The Atharva Veda says: "दिवि सोमो अधिश्रितः।" 'The moon is dependent on the sun for its light."

As regards the *atmosphere* it is stated:

भूमेर्बहिर्द्वादशयोजनानि भूवायुरत्राम्बुदविद्युदाद्यम् ।

"The atmosphere surrounds the earth, and its height is 12

yojanas (about 60 English miles), and the clouds, lightening, etc., are phenomena connected with it."

Mr. Colebrooke says: "Aryabhatta affirmed the diurnal revolution of the earth on its axis. He possessed the true theory of the causes of solar and lunar eclipses and disregarded the imaginary dark planets of mythologists and astrologers, affirming the moon and primary planets (and even the stars) to be essentially dark and only illuminated by the sun." [1]

As regards the solar and lunar eclipses it is stated:

छादयत्यर्कमिन्दुर्विधुं भूमिभाः ॥

"When the earth in its rotation comes between the sun and the moon, and the shadow of the earth falls on the moon, the phenomenon is called lunar eclipse, and when the moon comes between the sun and the earth the sun seems as if it was being cut off—this is solar eclipse."

The following is taken from Varamihir's observations on the moon: "One half of the moon, whose orbit lies between the sun and the earth, is always bright by the sun's rays; the other half is dark by its own shadows, like the two sides of a pot standing in the sunshine." [2]

About eclipses he says: "The true explanation of the phenomenon is this, in an eclipse of the moon, he enters into the earth's shadow; in a solar eclipse, the same thing happens to the sun. Hence the *commencement of a lunar eclipse does not take place from the west side, nor that of the solar eclipse from the east.*" [3]

Kali Dasa says in his *Raghu Vansa*:

छाया हि भूमेः शशिनो मलत्वेनारोपिता शुद्धिमतः प्रजाभिः ।

"Jai Deva sings in the *Gita Govind*: "His heart was agitated by her sight, as the waves of the deep are affected by the lunar orb." [4]

[1] Colebrooke's Essays, Appendix G, p. 467.
[2] Brihat Sanhita, Chapter V, v. 8.
[3] Brihat Sanhita, Chapter V, v 8.
[4] Tod's Rajasthan, Vol. I, p. 543.

India has from time immemorial been the land of philosophers, poets, astronomers and mathematicians, and every now and then it produces a great genius. Less than two centuries ago, Rajputana produced an astronomer, no doubt the greatest of his time. This astronomer was no other than the famous Jai Singh of Jaipur. Sir William Hunter says: "Raja Jai Singh II constructed a set of observatories at his capital Jaipur, Muttra, Benares, Delhi and Ujjain, and *was able to correct the astronomical tables of De La Hire* published in 1702 A. D. The Raja left as a monument of his skill, a list of stars collated by himself, known as the Zij Mohammed Shahi, or Tables of Mohammed Shah. His observatory at Benares survives to this day."

The celebrated European astronomer, Mr. Playfair, says: "The Brahman obtains his result with wonderful certainty and expedition in astronomy."[1] This speaks volumes in favour of the original, advanced and scientific methods of the Hindus and their marvellous cultivation of the science. Professor Sir M. Williams says: "It is their science of astronomy by which they (Hindus) heap billions upon millions, trillions upon billions of years and reckoning up ages upon ages, æons, upon æons with even more audacity than modern geologists and astronomers. In short, an astronomical Hindu ventures on arithmetical conceptions quite beyond the mental dimensions of anyone who feels himself incompetent to attempt a task of measuring infinity." A strange confession of inferiority! Well may Mrs. Manning exclaim: "The Hindus had the widest range of mind of which man is capable."[2]

In astronomy, as in other sciences, what scanty records remain not only show the astonishing proficiency of the Hindus

[1] Playfair on the Astronomy of the Hindus. Transactions of the R. A. S. of Great Britain and Ireland, Vol. II, pp. 138, 139.

[2] Ancient and Mediæval India, Vol. I, p. 114.

in the science, but contain theories not yet understood by others. Sir M. Mon. Williams says: "A very strange theory of the planetary motion is expounded at the commencement of the *Surya Siddhanta*, Chapter II," which is unknown outside India.[1]

IV.—MILITARY SCIENCE.

My voice is still for war,
Gods! can a Roman senate long debate
Which of the two to choose, slavery or death?

ADDISON: *Cato.*

WAR is a necessary evil. Peace is the natural and desirable state, but so long as human nature is what it is, so long as selfishness, envy, avarice, vanity and a desire for self-aggrandizement are not eliminated from human nature, war will remain a necessity.

War has its ideal side and peace has its blessings. At the same time peace is no blessing if it lasts too long especially if its maintenance has to be paid for with the abandonment of the national ideals. Such a peace dishonors a nation and in such a peace small-mindedness and selfishness flourish while idealism is destroyed by materialism, and simplicity of manners by luxury. In such times money becomes all-powerful and character is of little value. The more deeply we penetrate into history the more clearly we recognise that peace is the normal and desirable state but that wars are required from time to time in order to cleanse the moral atmosphere.

[1] Monier Williams' Indian Wisdom, p. 189. Mr. C. B. Clarke, F. G. S., says in his Geographical Reader: "Till of late years we did not know *with extreme exactness* the longitudes of distant places." The ancient Hindu method of finding the longitude by first finding out the *Deshanta Gathika*, with the aid of observations made at the time of the lunar eclipse, is not only scientific but infallible.

Captain Troyer says: "All the traditions of the Hindus are filled with wars, in which religion certainly had its share. I have shown sufficiently already, without being obliged to go back so far as the contests between the Suras and the Asuras."[1]

War as an art as well as a science was equally well understood in ancient India. The nation which overran nearly the whole of the habitable globe and produced Hercules, Arjuna, Sagarji, Bali could scarcely be considered inferior to any other people in their proficiency in military science.

Being the greatest commercial nation in the ancient world, and enjoying sea trade with nealry every part of the world (see "Commerce"), they were compelled to look to their navy to guard their trade and to make it sufficiently strong to ensure their position as the "mistress of the sea." Their position in the ancient world being similar to that of England in the modern world so far as maritime affairs are concerned, their navy, too, was equally eminent and powerful. Manu mentions navigation to have existed among the Hindus from time immemorial. Strabo mentions a naval department in addition to the others in the Indian army.

Being skilful sailors from time immemorial, the Hindus were adepts at naval warfare. Colonel Tod says: "The Hindus of remote ages possessed great naval power."[2]

In the time of Emperor Chandragupta of India, one of the greatest and most successful kings known to history according to Mr. Vincent Smith—the Imperial War Office consisted of six boards, one of which was the "Board of Admiralty."[3] He further says: "When we remember Asoka's relations with Ceylon and

[1] Troyer on the Ramayana in the Asiatic Journal for October 1844, p. 514.

[2] Tod's Rajasthan, Vol. II, p. 218.

[3] Vincent Smith's Early History of India, p. 124.

Also Strabo, XV, 52.

even more distant powers, we may credit him with a sea-going fleet as well as an army."[1]

Naval warfare by Hindus is mentioned in the Ramayana Ajodhya Kandam, verses 84 and 78.

नावां शतानां पञ्चानां कैवर्तानां शतं शतम् ।
सन्नद्धानां तथा यूनां तिष्ठन्त्वित्यभ्यचोदयत् ॥

Let hundreds of Kaivarta young men lie in wait in five hundred ships (to obstruct the enemy's passage).

Manusmriti while describing the various methods and means of warfare speaks of naval warfare:—

स्यन्दनाश्वैः समेयुध्येदनूपे नौद्विपैस्तथा ।
वृक्षगुल्मावृते चापैरसिचर्मायुधैः स्थले ॥

Manu, Chapter 7, V. 192.

The ship in which the Pandava brothers escaped from the destruction planned for them, and constructed by Vidura was of a large size and was provided with machinery and all kinds of weapons of war and able to defy storms.

ततःप्रवासितो............कृताम ॥

Mahabharata Adi parva.

Dhanur Veda, the standard work on Hindu military science being lost, the dissertations on the science found in the Mahabharata, the Agni Purana, and the other works are the only sources of information on the subject left to us. Dr. Sir W. Hunter says: "There was no want of a theory of regular movements, and arrangements for the march, array, encampments, and supply of troops. They are all repeatedly described in the Mahabharata."[2]

Mr. Ward says: "The Hindu did not permit even the military art to remain unexamined. It is very certain that the Hindu kings led their own armies to the combat, and that they were prepared for this important employment by a military educa-

[1] Edicts of Asoka, Introduction, p. viii.
[2] Indian Gazetteer, "India," p. 223.

tion; nor is it less certain that many of these monarchs were distinguished for the highest valour and military skill."[1]

The ancient Hindu tactics of war were as original as valuable. It is said that the Hindus divided their army in the following manner: (1) *Uras* or centre (breast), (2) *Kakshas* or the flanks, (3) *Pakshas* or wings, (4) *Pratigraha* or the reserves, (5) *Koti* or vanguards, (6) *Madhya* or centre behind the breast, (7) *Prishtha* or back—a third line between the *madhya* and the reserve.[2]

Array of forces in action is generally termed *vyuha*.

Some *vyuhas* are named from their object. Thus (1) *Madhyabhedi*, one which breaks the centre, (2) *Antarbhedi*, that which penetrates between its division. More commonly, however, they are named from their resemblance to various objects. For instance (1) *Makaravyuha*, or the army drawn up like the Makars, a mire monster. (2) *Syenavyuha*, or the army in the form of a hawk or eagle with wings spread out. (3) *Sakatavyuha*, or the army in the shape of a waggon. (4) *Aradhachanra*, or half moon. (5) *Sarvatobhadra*, or hollow square (6) *Gomutrika*, or echelon. (1) *Danda* or staff, (2) *Bhoja* or column, (3) *Mandala*, or hollow circle, (4) *Asanhata* or detached arrangements of the different parts of the forces, the elephants, cavalry, infantry severally by themselves. Each of these *vyuhas* has sub-divisions; there are seventeen varieties of the *Danda*, five of the *Bhoga* and several of both the *Mandata* and *Asanhata*.[3]

[1] See the "Theosophist" for March 1881, p. 124.

[2] The sage Brihaspati was a great teacher of military science but unfortunately not one of his works is now extant.

[3] See Agni Purana. "The most important part of Hindu battles is now a cannonade. *In this they greatly* excel, and have occasioned heavy losses to us in all our battles with them. Their mode is to charge the front and the flanks at once, and the manner in which they perform this manœuvre has sometimes called forth the admiration of European antagonists. Elphinstone's *History of India*, p. 82.

In the Mahabharata (Vol. VI., pp. 699-729), Yudhishtira suggests to Arjuna the adoption of the form of *suchimukha*, or the needle point array (similar to the phalanx of the Macedonians), while Arjuna recommends the *vajra* or thunderbolt array for the same reason. Duryodhana, in consequence, suggests *abhedya*, or the impenetrable.

In their land army, the Hindus had, besides the infantry and the cavalry, elephants and chariots also The elephants, "the living battering rams," as Macaulay calls them, were a source of great strength when properly managed and skilfully supported by other arms. Of the elephants given by Chandragupta to Seleucus, Professor Max Duncker says: "These animals a few years later decided the day of Ipsus in Phrygia against Antogonus, a victory which secured to Seleucus the territory of Syria, Asia Minor, etc." According to Ctesias, Cyrus was defeated and killed by the enemy, only because of the strong support the latter received from the Indian elephants.[1]

As regards the soldierly qualities of the Indians even of the present day, sir Charles Napier, one of the highest authorities on the subject, says: "Better soldiers or braver men I never saw, superior in sobriety, equal in courage, and only inferior in muscular strength to our countrymen. This appears to me, as

[1] "The proficiency of the Indians in this art (management of elephants) early attracted the attention of Alexander's successors; and natives of India were so long exclusively employed in this service, that the term *Indian* was applied to every elephant-driver, to whatever country he might belong." Wilson's *Theatre of the Hindus*, Vol, I, p. 15.

"In war, the King of India was preceded by 10,000 elephants and 3,000 of the strongest and the bravest followed him."—Max Duncker's *History of Antiquity*.

"Sixty years after the death of the Enlightened, the Indians assisted the Persian King, the successor of Darius in the invasion of Greece, when they trod the soil of Hellas and wintered in Thessaly. They defeated the Greeks and saw the temple of Athens in flames.—Max Duncker's *History of Antiquity*, Vol. IV, p. 384.

far as I can judge, the true character of the Indian army in the three Presidencies, and I have had men of each under my command."[1]

The chivalrous conduct of the Indian sepoys on the occasion of the defence of Arcot by Clive, and when, towards the cl se of the war with Tippu in 1782, the whole of the force under General Mathews were made prisoners, is well known. The sepoys magnanimously and spontaneously contrived with great personal rsik to send every pie of their petty savings to their imprisoned officers, saying: "We can live upon anything, but you require mutton and beef." The conduct of the Indian sepoys shown on such occasions sheds lustre on the whole profession. General Wolsley, in a paper on "courage," contributed to a journal, highly eulogised the bravery of the Indian sepoys. Duting the siege of Lucknow," he said, "the sepoys performed wonderful feats of valour."

Mr. Elphinstone says: "The Hindus display bravery not surpassed by the most warlike nations, and will throw away their lives for any considerations of religion or honour. Hindu sepoys, in our pay have in two instances advanced after troops of the king's service have been beaten off; and on one of these occasions they were opposed to French soldiers. The sequel of this history will show instances of whole bodies of troops rushing forward to certain death."[2]

Clive, Lawrence, Smith, Coote, Haliburton and many others speak of the sepoys in the highest terms.

Now as regards the weapons used by the Hindus, Professor Wilson is assured that the Hindus cultivated archery most assiduously, and were masters in the use of the bow on horseback. Their skill in archery was wonderful. "Part of

[1] The Indian Review (Calcutta) for November 1885, p. 181.

[2] Elphinstone's History of India, p. 198.

the archery practice of the Hindus consisted in shooting a number of arrows at once, from four to nine at one time." Arjuna's feats in archery at the tournament before Draupadi's marriage, and again on the death-bed of Bhishma, must excite universal admiration.

The archery of the Hindus had something mysterious about it. The arrows returned to the archer, if they missed their aim. This was considered absurd until the discovery of the bomerang" in the hands of the Australians.[1]

Warlike weapons and splendid daggers were presented at the international Exhibitions of 1851 and 1862, and a critic speaking of them, says: "Beautiful as the jewelled arms of India are, it is still for the intrinsic merit of their steel that they are most highly prized."[2]

That the ancient Hindus were celebrated for their sword-fight is evident from the Persian phrase: "To give an Indian answer," meaning "a cut with an Indian sword." The Indian swordsmen were celebrated all over the world. In an Arabic poem of great celebrity, known as *Sabaa Moalaqa* there occurs the passage: "The oppression of near relations is more severe than the wound caused by a Hindu swordsman."[3]

Ctesias mentions that the Indian swords were the best in the world.[4]

The following fivefold classification of Hindu weapons is exhaustive: (1) Missiles thrown with an instrument or engine

[1] Besides bows, other missiles as the discus, short iron clubs, and javelins, swords. maces, battle-axes, spears shields, helmets, armour and coats of mail, etc, are also mentioned. See Wilson's Essays, Vol. II, pp. 191, 192.

[2] Manning's Ancient and Mediæval India, Vol. II, p. 365.

[3] The *Tafsir Azizi* says: تیغ هندي و خنجر رومي — اکنن آنکه انتظار کند

[4] Max Duncker's History of Antiquity, Vol. IV, p. 436.

Amir Khusrau in his Tarikhi Alai speaks of "more cutting than a Hindu sword." Elliot's History, Vol. III, p. 83.

called *yantramukta*; (2) Those hurled by hand or *hastamukta*; (3) weapons which may or may not be thrown, or *muktamukta*, as javelins, tridents, etc.; (4) which are not thrown, as swords maces, etc.; (5) Natural weapons, as fists, etc. Bhindipala, Tomara, Naracha, Prasa Rishti, Pattisa, Kripana, Kshepani, Pasa, etc., are some of the arms of the ancient Hindus now extinct.

The chief distinction of the modern military science is the extensive employment of *fire-arms*. It should, however, not be supposed that fire-arms were unknown in ancient India. Though the Hindu masterpieces on the science of war are all lost, yet there is sufficient material available in the great epics and the Puranas to prove that fire-arms were not only known and used on all occasions by the Hindus, but that this branch of their armoury had received very great development. In mediæval India, of course, guns and connons were commonly used. In the twelfth century we find pieces of ordnance being taken to battle-fields in the armies of Prithviraj. In the 25th stanza of *Prithviraja Rasa* it is said that "The calivers and connons made a loud report when they were fired off, and the noise which issued from the ball was heard at a distance of ten *cos*.

न्तप पंग नयर छुटे प्जराव।
कोटह कंगूर चठि चठि सिताव॥
अंचूर तोप छुटहि झनंकि।
दश कोश आय गोला भनंकि॥
सिरदार भार वाराह रोह।
छंगी श्मभंग वर हनै कोह॥

An Indian historian, Raja Kundan Lall, who lived in the court of the king of Oudh, says that there was a big gun named *lichhma* in the possession of His Majesty the King (of Oudh) which had been originally in the artillery of Maharaja Prithviraj of Ajmer. The author speaks of a regular science of war, of the postal department, and of public or Roman roads. See *Muntakhab Tafsee-ul-Akhbar*, pp 149, 150.

"Maffei says that the Indians far excelled the Portuguese in their skill in the use of fire-arms."[1]

Another author quoted by Bohlen speaks of a certain Indian king being in the habit of placing several pieces of brass ordnance in front of his army.[2]

"Faria-e Souza speaks of a Guzerat vessel in A.D. 1500 firing several guns at the Portuguese,[3] and of the Indians at Calicut using fire vessels in 1502, and of the Zamorin's fleet carrying in the next year 380 guns."[4]

But let us turn to ancient India. Professor Wilson says: "Amongst ordinary weapons one is named *vajra*, the thunderbolt, and the specification seems to denote the employment of some explosive projectile, which could not have been in use except by the agency of something like gunpower in its properties."[5]

As regards gunpowder," the learned Professor says: "The Hindus, as we find from their medical writings, were perfectly well acquainted with the constituents of gunpowder—sulphur, charcoal, saltpetre—and had them all at hand in great abundance. It is very unlikely that they should not have discovered their inflammability, either singly or in combination. To this inference

[1] Hist. Indica, p. 25.

[2] *Das Alte Indien*, Vol. II, p. 63.

[3] Asia Portuguesa, Tom I, Part I, Chapter 5.

[4] Ibid, Chapter 7.

[5] Wilson's Essays, Vol. II, p. 302. The Indians are from time immemorial remarkable for their skill in fireworks. The display of fireworks has been from olden days a feature of the Dasehra festival. Mr. Elphinstone says: "In the Dasehra ceremony the combat ends in the destruction of Lanka amidst a blaze of fireworks which would excite admiration in any part of the world. And the procession of the native prince on this occasion presents one of the most animating and gorgeous spectacles ever seen."—Elphinstone's *History of India*, p. 178.

à priori may be added that drawn from positive proofs, that the use of fire as a weapon of combat was a familiar idea, as it is constantly described in the heroic poems."[1]

The testimony of ancient Greek writers, who, being themselves ignorant of fire-arms used by Indians, give peculiar descriptions of the mode of Hindu warfare is significant. "Themistius mentions the Brahman *fighting at a distance with lightning and thunder*."[2]

Alexander, in a letter to Aristotle, mentions "the terrific flashes of flame which he beheld showered on his army in India." See also Dante's Inferno, XIV, 31-7.

Speaking of the Hindus who opposed Alexander the Great, Mr. Elphinstone says: "Their arms, with the exception of fire-arms, were the same as at present."[3]

Philostratus thus speaks of Alexander's invasion of the Punjab: "Had Alexander passed the Hyphasis he never could have made himself master of the fortified habitations of these sages. Should an enemy make war upon them, they drive him off by means of tempests and thunders as if sent down from Heaven. The Egyptian Hercules and Bacchus made a joint attack on them, and by means of various military engines attempted to take the place. The sages remained unconcerned spectators until the assault was made, when it was repulsed by fiery whirlwinds and thunders which, being hurled from above, dealt destruction on the invaders."[4]

Commenting on the stratagem adopted by King Hal in the battle against the king of Kashmir, in making a clay elephant

[1] Essays, Vol. II, p. 303.

[2] Orat, XXVII, p. 337. See Ap. Dutens's Origin of the discoveries attributed to the Moderns, p. 196.

[3] Elphinstone's History of India, p 241.

[4] Philostrati Vit; Apollon, Lib. II, C. 33.

which exploded, Mr. Elliot says: "Here we have not only the simple act of explosion but something very much like a fuze, to enable the explosion to occur at a particular period.'[1]

Viswamitra, when giving different kinds of weapons to Rama, speaks (in the Ramayana) of one as *agneya*, another as *shikhara*.

अग्नेयमस्त्रन्दयितं शिखरन्नाम नामतः ।

"Carey and Marshman render *shikhara* as a combustible weapon."[2]

In the Mahabharata we read of "a flying ball emitting the sound of a thundercloud which Scholiast is express in referring to artillery."[3]

The *Harivansa* thus speaks of the fiery weapon:

आग्नेयमस्त्रं लब्ध्वा च भार्गवात्सगरो नृपः ।
जिगाय पृथिवीं हत्वा तालजङ्घान्सहैहयान् ॥

"King Sagara having received *fire-arms* from Bhargava conquered the world, after slaying the Taljanghas and the Haihayas." M. Langlois says that "these fire-arms appear to have belonged to the Bhargavas, the family of Bhrigu."[4] Again,

ऊर्व्वस्तु जातकर्म्मादि तस्य कृत्वा महात्मनः ।
अध्याप्य वेदानखिलांस्ततोऽस्त्रं प्रत्यपादयत् ॥
आग्नेयन्तु महाबाहुरमरैरपि दुस्सहम् ।
स तेनास्त्रबलेनाजौ बलेन च समन्वितः ॥

"Aurva having performed the usual ceremonies on the birth of the great-minded (prince), and having taught him the Vedas,

[1] Elliot's Historians of India, Vol. I, p. 265.

[2] Various kinds of weapons are mentioned, some of which are extraordinary. As it is not known how they were made, what they were like, and how they were used, people think they are only poetic phantasies. Mr. Elliot says: "Some of these weapons mentioned above were imaginary, as for instance, the *vayava* or airy." But who would not have called the gramaphone, the cinematograph and the wireless telegraphy imaginary only 50 years ago!

[3] Bohlen, Das Alte Indien, II, 66.

[4] Harivansa, p. 68.

instructed him in the use of arms; the great-armed (Aurva) presented him the fiery weapon, which even the immortals could not stand."

Brahmastra is repeatedly mentioned in Sanskrit works. Professor Wilson, in his Sanskrit Dictionary, calls Brahmastra "a fabulous weapon, originally from Brahma." For its use see Sri Bhagwat describing the fight between the son of Drona and Arjuna with the *Brahmastra*. The Rev. K. M. Bannerjea in his work, "The Encyclopædia Bengalensis, says that the Brahmastra was probably a piece of musketry not unlike the modern matchlocks."[1] Madame Blavatsky, in her *Isis Unveiled*, also shows that "fire-arms were used by the Hindus in ancient times."[2]

In the description of Ayodhia is mentioned the fact of *yantras*[3] being mounted on the walls of the fort, which shows that cannons or machines of some kind or other were used in those days to fortify and protect citadels.

The Ramayana, while describing the fortifications, says: "As a woman is richly decorated with ornaments, so are the towers with big destructive machines."[4] This shows that cannons or big instruments of war like cannons, which discharged destructive missiles at a great distance, were in use at that time.

In descriptions of fortresses and battles, *Shataghnis* are often mentioned. *Shataghni* literally means "that which kills hundreds at once." In Sanskrit dictionaries, *Shataghni* is defined as a machine which shoots out pieces of iron and other things to kill numbers of men. Its other name is *Brischi Kali* व्रश्चिकाली[5]

[1] Encyclo Bengal, Vol. III, p. 21.

[2] Isis Unveiled, Chap. XIV.

[3] *Yantra* means "that thing with which something is thrown."

[4] Ramayana, Sunder Kand, Third Chapter, 18th verse.

[5] See Raja Sir Radh Kant Dev's *Shabdkalpadruma*.

Shataghnis and similar other machines are mentioned in the following slokas of the Ramayana.

Canto	3	...	...	Slokas 12, 13, 16 and 17.
"	4	...	...	23.
"	21	...	...	last sloka.
"	39	...	...	36.
"	60	...	...	54.
"	61	...	...	32.
"	76	...	...	68.
"	86	...	...	22.

Ramayana says that the *Shataghni* was made of iron. In the *Sunder Kand* it is compared in size with big broken trees or their huge offshoots, and in appearance said to "resemble trunks of trees." "They were not only mounted on forts but were carried to the battle-fields, and they made a noise like thunder." What else could they, therefore, be but cannons?

Besides the Ramayana, the Puranas make frequent mention of *Shataghnis* being placed on forts and used in times of emergency. See Matasya Purana (मत्स्यपुराण), "Art of Government." The name used in this Purana is *Sahastraghati* (शत and सहस्र mean hundreds and thousands or innumerable)[1]; guns and connons are mentioned as existing in Lanka (Ceylon), under Ravana. They were called *Nhulat Yantras.*

Commenting on the passage in the Code of Gentoo (Hindu) Laws that "the magistrate shall not make war with any deceitful machine or with poisoned weapons, or with cannons and guns, or any kind of fire-arms," Halhed says; "The reader will probably from hence renew the suspicion which has long been deemed

[1] *Shataghni* differed widely from *Matvala* in that the Matvala were rolled down from mountains, while *Shataghni* was an instrument from which stones and iron balls were discharged. *Jamera* was another machine that did fatal injury to the enemy by means of stones. See accounts of battles with Mohammad Kasim.

absurd, that Alexander the Great did absolutely meet with some weapons of that kind in India as a passage in Quintus Curtius seems to ascertain. Gunpowder has been known in China, as well as Hindustan, far beyond all periods of investigation. The word fire-arms is literally the Sanskrit *Agniaster*, a weapon of fire; they describe the *first species* of it to have been a kind of dart or arrow tipt with fire, and discharged upon the enemy from a bamboo. Among several extraordinary properties of this weapon, one was, that after it had taken its flight, it divided into several separate streams of flame, each of which took effect, and which, when once kindled, could not be extinguished: but this kind of *Agniaster* is now lost."[1] He adds: "A cannon is called '*Shataghni*, or the weapon that kills one hundred men at once,' and, that the Purana Sastras ascribe the invention of these destructive engines to Viswacarma, the Vulcan of the Hindus."

Mr. H. H. Elliot, Foreign Secretary to the Government of India (1845), after discussing the question of the use of fire-arms in ancient India, says: "On the whole, then, we may conclude that fire-arms of some kind were used in early stages of Indian history, that the missiles were explosive, and that the time and mode of ignition was dependent on pleasure; that projectiles were used which were made to adhere to gates and buildings, and machines setting fire to them from a considerable distance; that it is probable that saltpetre, the principal ingredient of gunpowder, and the cause of its detonation, entered into the composition, because the earth of Gangetic India is richly impregnated with it in a natural state of preparation, and it may be extracted from it by lixiviation and crystallization without the aid of fire; and that sulphur may have been mixed with it, as it is abundant in the north-west of India."[2]

[1] Halhed's Code of Gentoo Laws, Introduction, p. 52. See also *Amar Kosha* and *Sabda Kalpaddrum*, Vol. I, p. 16.

[2] Bibliographical Index to the Historians of Modern India, Vol. I, p. 373.

"Rockets," says Professor Wilson, "appear to be of Indian invention, and had long been used in native armies when Europeans came first in contact with them."

Col. Tod says: "Jud Bhan (the name of a grandson of Bajra, the grandson of Krishna), 'the rocket of the Yadus,' would imply a knowledge of gun-powder at a very remote period."[1]

Rockets were unknown in Europe till recently. "We are informed by the best authorities that rockets were first used in warfare at the siege of Copenhagen in 1807."[2] Mr. Elliot says: "It is strange that they (rockets) should now be regarded in Europe as the most recent invention of artillery."[3]

There were in ancient India machines which, besides throwing balls of iron and other solid missiles, also threw peculiar kinds of destructive liquids at great distances. The ingredients of these liquids are unknown; their effects, however, are astonishing.

Ctesias,[4] Elian[5] and Philostratus[6] all speak of an oil manufactured by Hindus and used by them in warfare in destroying the walls and battlements of towns that no "battering rams or other polioretic machines can resist it," and that "it is inextinguishable and insatiable, burning both arms and fighting men."

Lassen says: "That the Hindus had something like 'Greek fire' is also rendered probable by Ctesias, who describes their employing a particular kind of inflammable oil for the purpose of setting hostile towns and forts on fire."[7]

Eusebe Salverte, in his *Occult Sciences*, says: The fire which

[1] Tod's Rajasthan, Vol. II, p. 220.

[2] Penny Encyclopædia, V, "Rocket."

[3] Bibliographical Index to the Historians of Mohammadan India, Vol. I, p. 357.

[4] Ctesie, *Indica Excerpta*, XXVII (ed. Ber), p. 356.

[5] De Natura Animal, Lib. V., cap. 3.

[6] Philostrati *Vita Apollon*, Lib. III, cap. 1.

[7] Lassen's Ind. Alt. II, p. 641.

burns and crackles on the bosom of the waves denotes that the Greek fire was anciently known in Hindustan under the name of *barrawa*."[1]

But what establishes the superiority of the ancient Hindus over the modern Europeans in the noble game of war is the *Ashtur Vidya* of the former. "The *Ashtur Vidya*, the most important and scientific part (of the art of war) is not known to the soldiers of our age. It consisted in annihilating the hostile army by envolving and suffocating it in different layers and masses of atmospheric air, charged and impregnated with different substances. The army would find itself plunged in a fiery, electric and watery element, in total thick darkness, or surrounded by a poisonous, smoky, pestilential atmosphere, full sometimes of savage and terror-striking animal forms (snakes and tigers, etc.) and frightful noises. Thus they used to destroy their enemies.[2] The party thus assailed counteracted those effects by arts and means known to them, and in their turn assaulted the enemy by means of some other secrets of the *Ashtur Vidya.* Col. Olcott also says: "Ashtur Vidya, a science of which *our modern professors have not even an inkling,*" enabled its proficient to completely destroy an invading army, by enveloping it in an atmosphere of poisonous gases, filled with awe-striking shadowy shapes and with awful sounds." This fact is proved by innumerable instances in which it was practiced. Ramayana mentions it. Jalindhar had recourse to it when he was attacked by Mahadeva, as related in the *Kartik Mahatmya.*

Another remarkable and astonishing feature of the Hindu science of war which would prove that the ancient Hindus

[1] English Translation, Vol. II, p. 223.

[2] *Theosophist*, March 1881, p 124.

[3] In Europe, poisonous gases have been invented in war for the first time in 1915 A. D.

cultivated every science to perfection, was that the Hindus could fight battles in the air. It is said that the ancient Hindus "could navigate the air, and not only navigate it but fight battles in it, like so many war-eagles combating for the dominion of the clouds. To be so perfect in æronautics, they must have known all the arts and sciences relating to the science, including the strata and currents of the atmosphere, the relative temperature, humidity and density and the specific gravity of the various gases."[1]

Viman Vidya was a science which has now completely disappeared. A few years ago, facts concerning this science found in ancient records were rejected as absurd and impossible of belief. But wireless telegraphy and the recent developments in airships have prepared people to entertain the idea of the possibility of human knowledge advancing so far as to make it practicable for men to navigate the air as they navigate the sea. And a day will come as assuredly as that the day will follow the night, when not only will the ancient Hindu greatness in this science be recognised, but the results achieved by them will again be achieved by men.

V.—MUSIC.

Music exalts each joy, allays each grief,
Expels diseases, softens every pain,
Subdues the rage of poison and the plague,
And hence the wise of ancient days adored
One power of physic, melody and song.

ARMSTRONG: *A. P. H.*

MUSIC is the natural expression of a man's feeling. It comes naturally to man, woman and child in all conditions, at all times

[1] Colonel Olcott's lecture at Allahabad in 1881. See the *Theosophist* for March 1881.

and in all countries. "The very fact of musical utterance," says Sir Hubert Parry, "implies a genuine expansion of the nature of the human being, and is in a varying degree a trustworthy revelation of the particular likings, tastes and sensibilities of the being that gives vent to it."

The Chinese emphasise its importance by calling it "the science of sciences."

"An eminently poetical people," as the ancient Hindus were, could not but have been eminently musical also. Anne C. Wilson, in what is one of the latest attempts on the part of a European to understand Hindu music, says: "The people of India are essentially a musical race.........To such an extent is music an accompaniment of existence in India, that every hour of the day and season of the year has its own melody."[1]

Mr. Coleman says: "Of the Hindu system of music the excellent writer whom I have before mentioned (Sir W. Jones), has expressed his belief that it has been formed on better principles than our own."[2]

Colonel Tod says: "An account of the state of musical science amonsgt the Hindus of early ages and a comparison between it and that of Europe is yet a desideratum in Oriental literature. From what we already know of the science, it appears to have attained a theoretical precision yet unknown to Europe, and that a period when even Greece was little removed from barbarism." The antiquity of this most delightful art is the same as the antiquity of the Sanskrit literature itself. Anne C. Wilson says: "It must, therefore, be a secret source of pride to them to know that their system of music, as a written science, is the oldest in the world. Its principal features were given long ago in Vedic

[1] Short Account of the Hindu System of Music, by Anne C. Wilson (1904), p. 5.

[2] Coleman's Hindu Mythology, Preface, p. ix.

writings......Its principles were accepted by the Mohammedan portion of the population in the days of their pre-eminence, and are still in use in their original construction at the present day."[1]

Music has been a great favourite[2] with the Hindus from the earliest times. Even the Vedas (*e.g.*, Sam Veda) treat of this science. The enormous extent[3] to which the Hindus have cultivated this science is proved by their attainments in it. But, unhappily, the master-piece on this "Science and Art combined," the *Gandharva Veda*, is lost, and references to it in Sanskrit works alone remain to point to the high principles on which the Hindu science of music was based.

Even at the present day the *Rags* and *Ragnis* of the Hindus are innumerable, and the majority of them differ so minutely from each other that even the "cultivated ear of the musical Europeans" cannot fully understand and follow them.

Sir W. W. Hunter says: "Not content with the tones and semitones, the Indian musicians employed a more minute sub-division, together with a number of sonal modifications which the Western ear neither recognises nor enjoys. Thus, they divide the octave into 22 sub-tones instead of 12 semitones of the European scale. The Indian musician declines altogether to be judged by the few simple Hindu airs which the English ear can appreciate."[4]

Anne C. Wilson says: "Every village player knows about time, and marks it by beating time on the ground, while the audience clap their hands along with him. He has the most

[1] A Short Account of the Hindu System of Music, by A. C. Wilson, p. 9.

[2] Shakespeare says: "The man that hath no music in himself
Nor is not moved with concord of sweet sounds
Is fit for treason, stratagems and spoils;
Let no such man be trusted."

[3] "The Hindu system of music is minutely explained in a great number of Sanskrit books."—Sir W. Jones.

[4] Imperial Gazetteer, "India," p. 224.

subtle ear for time, and a more delicate perception of shades of difference than the generality of *English people can acquire*, an acuteness of musical hearing which also makes it possible for him to recognise and reproduce quarter and half tones, when singing or playing."[1]

Nor are Europeans able to imitate Hindu music. Mr. Arthur Whitten says: "But I have yet to observe that while our system of notation admits of no sound of less than half a tone, the Hindus have quarter tones, thus rendering it most difficult of imitation by Europeans. The execution of their music, I hold to be impossible to all except those who commence its practice from a very early age"[2]

He also observes: "Few of the ancient Hindu airs are known to Europeans, and it has been found impossible to set them to music according to the modern system of notation, as we have neither staves nor musical characters whereby the sounds may be accurately expressed."[3]

Mrs. Besant, in her inaugural address to the School of Indian Music in the Victoria Public Hall, Madras, delivered on 15 January 1911, after saying that the Indian music was unique, that Indians had a far larger number of musical notes than they found in the West, and that the English are required to be trained to the delicate gradations of tones, to which the Western ear was not accustomed, before they could appreciate Indian music, remarked:

"What was the radical difference between Western and Indian music? There was a profound difference that turned on the parts of the subtle body which they respectively moved; for all things had a foundation in nature, and unless

[1] Anne C. Wilson's Hindu System of Music.

[2] The Music of the Ancients, p. 22.

[3] The Music of the Ancients, p. 21.

they knew the natural basis they would find it difficult to form their opinion on the subject. The subtle body was related to the different parts of their constituents, to their passions, to their emotions. Great surges of feeling which stirred the grosser parts of the subtle body threw them into violent vibration, exactly in the same way as when they felt a passion there was a violent vibration in them. So also, if they caused the vibration, the corresponding passion was awakened in them. If they heard music appealing to the higher emotions those higher emotions were aroused in them at the call of the melody. Music which appealed to the more primitive passions of man was music where sounds were lower in tone. Lower notes would be used to rouse the more primitive passions, like love, hate, anger, jealousy. These lower notes, therefore, came from the heavier string. Finer strings gave higher notes. The Western music appealed primarily to emotions in man which had something of the passionate element in them; she did not say low, or sensual, but emotions that grew out of the passionate element—it might be love of country, sacrifice for the country; it might be the heroic feeling that desired to help the oppressed—any one of the nobler emotions in man which had its root in the passionate nature purified and refined. Those were the emotions which were stirred by Western music on the whole. Indian music began in the higher emotions and lifted them up to the spiritual sphere. The best Indian music did not touch the lower nature. It began in the purer region of high emotion and passed on into the spiritual world. As they listened to some exquisite Indian melody they lost the sense that they were present in the body at all. They found their minds stilled and quieted, and the mind vanished with the body and they found themselves raised to a purer and subtler region."

Professor Wilson says: "That music was cultivated on scientific principles is evident from the accounts given by Sir W. Jones and Mr. Colebrooke, from which it appears that the Hindus had a knowledge of the gamut, of the mode of notation, of measurement, of time, and of a division of the notes of a more minute description than has been found convenient in Europe."[1] "We understand," says Mrs. Manning, "that the Hindu musicians have not only the *Chromatic* but also the *Enharmonic* genus."[2]

The *Oriental Quarterly Review* says: "We may add that the only native singers and players whom Europeans are in the way of hearing in most parts of India, are reported by their scientific brethren in much the same light as a ballad singer at the corner of the street by the *prime soprans* of the Italian opera."[3]

Sir W. W. Hunter says: "And the contempt with which the Europeans in India regard it merely proves their ignorance of the system on which Hindu music is built up."[4] Professor Wilson says: "Europeans in general know nothing of Indian music. They hear only the accompaniments to public processions, in which noise is the chief object to be attained, or the singing of the Muhamedans, *which is Persian not Indian.*"[5]

[1] Mill's India, Vol. II, p. 153.

[2] Ancient and Mdiæval India, Vol. II, p. 141.

[3] Quarterly Review for December 1825, p. 197.

[4] Imperial Gazetteer, "India," p 224. Mrs. Anne C. Wilson says: "Not many Europeans, I fancy, would boast of being even superficially acquainted with the *Dhrupada* style of song, the popular *Tappas*, the *Thumri* songs of the N.-W. P., the *Kharkhas* or war-songs of the Rajput, the *Huttari* chants, the nursery rhymes, the wedding and cremation songs of Gujrat, the *Vernams, Pallam, Kirtans* of Madras .... Who amongst us know the lyric poetry of Vidyapati, of Chandidas, Jaideva or the well-known family of Ram Bhagan Dutt, sometimes called the "nest of singing birds!"—p. 41.

[5] Mill's India, Vol. II, p. 41. Professor Wilson adds: "The practice of art among them (Hindus) has declined in consequence probably of its suppression by the Muhamadans." Sir, W. W. Hunter says: "Hindu music after a period of excessive elaboration sank under Mussalmans."—*Imperial Gazetter*, p. 223. "However, it still preserves, in a living state, some of the earlier forms, which puzzle the student of Greek music, side by side with the most complicated development."—Sir W. W. Hunter, p. 224.

There are six *rags*, and associated with them are thirty-six female *ragnees*, which partake of the peculiar measure or quality of their males but in a softer and more feminine degree. From each of these 36 *ragnees* have been born three *ragnees* reproducing the special peculiarity of their original, and these have in their turn produced offsprings without number, each bearing a distinct individuality, to the primary *rag*, or, to use the poetic Hindu expression, "they are as numerous and alike as the waves of the sea." That the Hindu cultivated music on scientific principles is proved by the fact that, as Mr. Whitten says, these *ragas* were designed to move some passion or affection of the mind, and to each was assigned some particular season of the year, time of the day and night or special locality or district, and for a performer to sing a *rag* out of its appropriate season or district would make him, in the eyes of all Hindus, an ignorant pretender and unworthy the character of a musician."

The six principal *ragas* are the following:—

(1) *Hindaul.* It is played to produce on the mind of the hearers all the sweetness and freshness of spring; sweet as the honey of the bee and fragrant as the perfume of a thousand blossoms.

(2) *Sri Rag.* The quality of this *rag* is to affect the mind with the calmness and silence of declining day, to tinge the thoughts with a roseate hue, as clouds are gilded by the setting sun before the approach of the darkness and night.

(3) *Mugh Mallar.* This is descriptive of the effects of an approaching thunder-storm and rain, having the power of influencing clouds in times of drought.

(4) *Deepuck.* This *rag* is extinct. No one could sing it and live; it has consequently fallen into disuse. Its effect is to light the lamps and to cause the body of the singer to produce flames by which he dies.

(5) *Bhairava.* The effect of this *rag* is to inspire the mind with a feeling of approaching dawn, the caroling of birds, the sweetness of the perfume and air, the sparkling freshness of dew-dropping morn.

(6) *Malkos.* The effect of this *rag* is to produce on the mind a feeling of gentle stimulation.

There is much that is common to both the Hindu and European systems. Mr. Arthur Whitten says: "Their (Hindus) scale undoubtedly resembles our diatonic mode, and consists of seven sounds, which are extended to three octaves, that being the compass of the human voice. Their voices and music, like ours, are divided into three distinct classes. The bass, called *odarah*, or lowest notes; the tenor, called *madurrah*, or middle notes; the soprano, called the *tarrah*, or upper notes. The similarity of the formation of the ancient Hindu scale to our modern system is noteworthy. We name the sounds of our scales: Doh, Ray, Me, Fah, Sol, La, Te. That common in India is: Sa, Ray, Ga, Ma, Pa, Dha, Ne."[1] The reason of this similarity is evident. Sir W. W. Hunter says: "A regular system of notation was worked out before the age of Panini, and seven notes were designated by their initial letters. The notation passed from the Brahmans through the Persians to Arabia, and was thence introduced into European music by Guido d' Arezzo at the beginning of the eleventh century."[2]

Professor Weber says: "According to Von Bohlen and Benfey, this notation passed from the Hindus to the Persian,[3]

[1] The Music of the Ancients, pp. 21, 22.

[2] Indian Gazetteer, p. 223. See Benfey's *Indien Ersch*, p. 299, and Gruber's Encyclopædia Vol. XVIII. "Some suppose that our modern word gamut comes from the Indian *gama*—a musical scale. Prakrita is *gama*, while its Sanskrit is *grama.*"

[3] Hindu musicians used to go to foreign countries to grace the courts of foreign kings. King Behram of Persia had many Hindu musicians in his court.

and from these again to the Arabs, and was introduced into European music by Guido d' Arezzo at the beginning of the eleventh century."[1]

But the principles of Hindu music were imported into Europe much earlier than this.

Strabo says: "Some of the Greeks attribute to that country (India) the invention of nearly all the science of music. We perceive them sometimes describing the *cittiara* of the Asiatics and sometimes applying to flutes the ephithet Phrygian. The names of certain instruments, such as *nabla* and others, likewise are taken from barbarous tongues." Colonel Tod says: "This *nabla* of Strabo is possibly the *tabla*, the small tabor of India. If Strabo took his orthography from the Persian or Arabic, a single point would constitute the difference between the N (*nun*) and the T (*te*)."[2] He adds: "We have every reason to believe—from the very elaborate character of their written music, which is painful and discordant to the ear, and from its minuteness of subdivision that they had also the Chromatic scale, said to have been invented by Timotheus in the time of Alexander, who might have carried it from the banks of the Indus."[3]

Colonel Tod also says: "In the mystic dance, the *Ras Mandala*, yet imitated on the festival sacred to the sun-god Hari, he is represented with a radiant crown in a dancing attitude, playing on the flute to the nymphs encircling him, each holding a musical instrument . . . . These nymphs are also called the *nava ragni*, from *raga*, a mode of song over which each presides and *nava-rasa* or nine passions excited by the powers of harmony. May we not in this trace the origin of Apollo and the sacred Nine?"

[1] Weber's Indian Literature, p. 272.
[2] Tod's Rajasthan, Vol. I, p. 569 (P. Edition).
[3] Tod's Rajasthan Vol. I, p. 570.

Bharata, Iswara, Parana and Narada were among the great Hindu musicians of ancient India.[1] In more recent times, however, Naik Gopal and Tansen have been the most celebrated ones. About Naik Gopal, Mr. Whitten says: "Of the magical effect produced by the singing of Gopal Naik and of the romantic termination to the career of this sage, it is said that he was commanded by Akbar to sing the *raga deepuck*, and he, obliged to obey, repaired to the river Jumna, in which he plunged up to his neck. As he warbled the wild and magical notes, flames burst from his body and consumed him to ashes."[2] He adds: "It is recorded of Tansen that he was also commanded by the Emperor Akbar to sing the *sri*, or night *raga*, at midday, and the power of the music was such that it instantly became night, and the darkness extended in a circle round the palace as far as his voice could be heard." India, it seems, produced Orpheuses even so late as the 16th century A.D.

As M. Bourgault Ducondray says, Hindu music will "provide Western musicians with fresh resources of expression and with colours hitherto unknown to the palate of the musician."[3]

Mr. Clements says: "Indian Music opens up a new world to the student of harmony."[4]

[1] Weber's Indian Literature, p. 272.

[2] Music of the Ancients, p. 21. Dr. Tennet says: "If we are to judge merely from the number of instruments and the frequency with which they apply them, the Hindus might be regarded as considerable proficients in music."

The instrument *singa*, or horn, is said to have been played by Mahadeva, who alone possessed the knowledge and power to make it speak. Singular stories are related of the wonders performed by this instrument.

The *Vina* (*Beena*) is the principal stringed instrument of music amongst the Hindus at the present day.

> "Although not ocean born, the tuneful Beena
> Is most assuredly a gem of Heaven—
> Like a dear friend it cheers the lonely heart
> And lends new lustre to the social meeting;
> It lulls the pains that absent lovers feel,
> And adds fresh impulse to the glow of passion."

[3] Clement's Introduction to the Study of Indian Music, Foreword, VIII."

[4] Ibid. p. 87.

OTHER SCIENCES.

What cannot Art and Industry perform,
When Science plans the progress of their toil!

BEATTIE: *Minstrel.*

THAT in addition to the astronomical, the mathematical, the medical and the military sciences, many other equally important sciences flourished in ancient India is evident from the remains of some of the most important achievements of the Hindus. Mr. Elphinstone says: "In science we find the Hindus as acute and diligent as ever."[1]

Medical science in a flourishing condition presupposes the existence in an advanced state of several other sciences, such as botany, chemistry, electricity, etc. The Astra *Vidya* (see Military Science) presupposes the existence of the science of chemistry, dynamics, meteorology, geology, physics, and other cognate sciences in a much more advanced state than what we find them in at the present day; while the *Viman Vidya* presupposes an intimate acquaintance with an equally great number of such sciences. The huge buildings of ancient India and "those gigantic temples hewn out of lofty rocks with the most incredible labour at Elephanta, Elora and at many other places," which have not only excited admiration but have been a standing puzzle to some people, could not have come into existence if the ancient Hindus had not been masters of the science of engineering. The engineering skill of the ancients was truly marvellous. With all its advanced civilization, modern Europe has yet to build the Pyramids, or to turn huge rocks into temples. Mons. de Lesseps was no doubt an admirable representative of triumphant engineering skill, and was an honour to France, but he only followed in

[1] Elphinstone's History of India, p. 133.

the footsteps of his predecessors, who were equally great, and who, too, had at one time connected the Red Sea with the Mediterranean. Mr. Swayne says: "A French Engineer repeats the feat of the old native kings and the Greek Ptolemies in marrying by a canal the Red Sea to the Mediterranean, an achievement which will make the name of Lesseps immortal, if the canal can only be kept clear of sand."[1] The sands still maintain a threatening aspect.

As regards the Pyramids, the early fathers of the Church (Christian teachers before 500 A.D.), believed them to have fallen from Heaven, while others in Europe believed them to have sprung out of earth or to have been built by Satan and his devils.

The Mahabharata shows that the ancient Hindus had achieved wonderful advancement in mechanics. In the description of the Mayasabha, (Exhibition), which was presented by Mayasur to the Pandavas, mention is made of microscopes, telescopes, clocks, etc.

An American critic says: "Such, indeed, was the mechanism of the Mayasabha, which accommodated thousands of men, that it required only ten men to turn and take it in whatever direction they liked." There was, he also says, "the steam or the fire-engine called the *agni ruth*"

That there were powerful telescopes in ancient India is doubtless, a fact. One is mentioned in the Mahabharata. It was given by Vyasajee to Sanjai at Indraprasta, in order to witness the battle going on at Kurukshetra.[2]

As regards the science of botany, Professor Wilson says: "They (the Hindus) were very careful observers both of the

[1] Swayne's Herodotus (Ancient Classics), p. 41.

[2] See Mahabharata, Bheeshma Parva, Chapter II, sloka 10.

internal and external properties of plants, and furnish copious lists of the vegetable world, with sensible notices of their uses and names significant of their peculiarities."[1] If the *Akhbar-ul-Sadeeq*[2] is to be trusted, a Sanskrit dictionary of botany in three volumes was discovered in Kashmir in 1887.

In the play *Malati and Madhava*,[3] it is stated that the damsel drew Madhava's heart "like a rod of the ironstone gem," which clearly shows that the Hindus were acquainted with artificial magnets as well as with properties of the loadstone. Professor Wilson too, supports this view. He further says: "The Hindus early adopted the doctrine that there is no vacuum in nature, but observing that air was excluded under various circumstances from space, they devised, in order to account for the separation of particles, a subtle element, or ether, by which all interstices, the most minute and inaccessible, were pervaded, a notion which *modern philosophy intimates some tendency to adopt*, as regards the planetary movements, and it was to this subtle element that they ascribed the property of conveying sound: in which they were so far right that in vacuo there can be no sound. Air again is said to be possessed of the faculty of touch, that it is the medium through which the contact of bodies is effected—ether keeps them apart—air impels them together. Fire, or rather light, has the property of figure—Mr. Colebrooke renders it of colour. In either case the theory is true; for neither colour nor form is discernible except through the medium of light. Water has the property of taste, an affirmation perfectly true; for nothing is sensible to the palate until it is dissolved by the natural fluids."[4]

[1] Mill's History of India, Vol. II, p. 97, footnote.

[2] Akhbar-ul-Sadeeq, dated 25th November 1887, p. 7.

[3] See also Manning's Ancient and Mediæval India, Vol. II, p. 209.

[4] Mill's India, Vol. II, pp. 95, 96.

The influence of the moon in causing tides seems to have been known to the Hindus from the earliest times.

Raghuvansa (V. 61) says:

तं तस्थिवांसं नगरोपकंठे ।
तदागमारूढगुरुत्वहर्षः ॥
प्रत्युज्जगाम क्रथकैशिकेन्द्रः ।
चन्द्रं प्रवृद्धोर्मिरिवोर्मिमाली ॥

That the Hindus were excellent observers and became great naturalists becomes clear from Professor Wilson's note on a verse of the drama of *Mrichchhakati*.

Charudatta says:

> "The elephants' broad front, when thick congealed
> The dried up dew, they visit me no more."

Wilson says: "At certain period a thick dew exhales from the elephant's temples. This peculiarity, though known to Strabo, seems to have escaped naturalists till lately, when it was noticed by Cuvier."[1]

Facts regarding diamonds, pearls, sapphires, etc., are mentioned with care, which shows that the ancient Hindus were thoroughly well versed in the sciences and the arts relating to fishery and to mining, and the processes of separating and extracting various substances from the earth.

That the ancient Hindus were masters of the sciences of chemistry, mechanics, meteorology is proved by one of the most wonderful of human achievements. This was the *Viman Vidya*. The airships of the Western world give us an idea of what *vimans* may have been like. Fifty years ago a *viman* was considered an impossiblity. But happily those days of Western scepticism are over, and a *viman*, for its practical advantages, is looked upon as an ideal of scientific achievement. A European critic says:

[1] The Theatre of the Hindus, Vol. I, p. 22, footnote.

"*Viman Vidya* (navigation of the air) was a complete science amongst the ancient Hindus. They were its masters and used it for all practical purposes."

This indicates their mastery of the arts and sciences on which the *Viman Vidya* is based, including a knowledge of the different strata and the currents of the atmospheric air, the temperature and density of each, and various other minor particulars. *Viman Vidya* is thus clearly mentioned in the Vedas. The Yajur-Veda (VI, 21) says:

समुद्रङ्गच्छ स्वाहा अन्तरिक्षङ्गच्छ स्वाहा देवम् सवितारङ्गच्छ स्वाहा ॥

Manu also says:

संशोध्य त्रिविधं मार्गं षड्विधं च बलं स्वकम् ।
सांपरायिककल्पेन यायादरिपुरं शनैः ॥

This science is said by some to have been a part of the more comprehensive science called "the Vayu Vidya" mentioned in the *Satpat Brahmana*, XI and XIV.

Prof. Weber says: "*Sarpa Vidya* (serpent science) is mentioned in the *Satpat Brahmana* XIII, as a separate science and *Vish Vidya* (science of poisons) in the Asvalayana Sutra."[1] "Sivedasa, in his Commentary of Chakrapani, quotes Patanjali as an authority on *Lohasastra*, or 'the Science of Iron,'."[2]

The Greeks derived their knowledge of electricity from India. Thales, one of the Greek sages, learned during his tour in India that when *amber* was rubbed with silk it acquired the property of attracting light bodies.

Not only were the sciences of electricity and magnetism extensively cultivated by the ancient Hindus, but they received high development in ancient India. The Vedantist says that lightning comes from rain. This can be easily demonstrated by the

[1] Weber's Indian Literature, p. 265.

[2] History of Hindu Chemistry, Vol. I, p. 55.

well-known experiments of Touilet and others: all these prove that Hindu sages perfectly understood all the electrical magnetic phenomena. The most significant proof of the high development of these sciences is to be found in the facts that they were made to contribute so much to the every day comfort and convenience[1] of the whole community, and that their teachings were embodied in the daily practices of the ancient Hindus, which does the highest credit to their practical wisdom and their scientific mind.

Sleep is necessary not only to enjoy sound health but to keep the body and soul together. The question now is in what way to sleep to derive the greatest benefit from this necessary operation of nature. Its solution by the ancient Hindus not only proves them to have been masters of the sciences of magnetism and electricity, but shows the spirit of Hinduism, which cannot be commended too highly for its readiness at all times and in all directions to adopt and assimilate the teachings of science. Every Hindu is instructed by his or her mother and grandmother to lie down to sleep with the head either eastward or southward.

Babu Sita Nath Roy cites slokas from the Sastras, which enjoin this practice. The *Ahnika Tuttwa*, a part of our Smiriti Sastras, says: "1. The most renowned *Garga rishi* says that man should lie down with his head placed eastward in his own house, but if he long for longevity he should lie down with his

[1] As an instance of such practical adaptations of their scientific discoveries, the following may be useful. Visitors to Simla are familiar with the sight of young native children placed in a position in which they are exposed to the constant trickling of a stream of water. This custom is generally considered a cruel one, although it has not been shown that it promotes a high rate of mortality. The object is to put the young ones to sleep, and the means are probably not more injurious than many of the patent foods and medicines which are the *civilized* substitutes. At the same time it is startling to find that Sir Joseph Fayrer, President of the Medical Society, is trying to introduce the hill custom in England. He says that the flowing of water on the vertex of the cranium never fails to induce sleep and that parents who are tormented with fretful children have only to pop them under an improvised water-spout.

head placed southward. In foreign places he may lie down with his head placed even westward, but never and nowhere should he lie down with his head placed northward."

"2. Markandeya, one of the much revered Hindu sages says that man becomes learned by lying down with his head placed eastward, acquires strength and longevity by lying down with his head placed southward, and brings upon himself disease and death by lying down with his head placed northward."

The learned writer found another sloka in the Vishnu Purana, which says: "Oh king! It is beneficial to lie down with the head placed eastward or southward. The man who always lies down with his head placed in contrary directions becomes diseased."

After stating certain facts regarding magnetism and electricity necessary to enable a man (unacquainted with the elements of these sciences) to understand his explanation, Babu Sita Nath Roy says: "According to what has been just now said, it is not very difficult to conceive that the body of the earth on which we live is being always magnetised by a current of thermal electricity produced by the sun. The earth being a round body, when its eastern part is heated by the sun its western part remains cold. In consequence a current of thermal electricity generated by the sun travels over the surface of the earth from east to west. By this current of thermal electricity the earth becomes magnetised and its geographical north pole being on the right-hand side of the direction of the current, is made the magnetic north pole, and its geographical south pole being on the left-hand side of the same current, is made the magnetic south pole. That the earth is a great magnet requires no proof more evident than that by the attractive and repulsive powers of its poles, the compass needle, in whatever position it is placed, is invariable turned so as to point out the north and the south by its two ends or poles. In the equatorial region of the earth the compass needle stands horizontally, on account of the equality of attraction exerted on its poles by those of the earth; but in the polar region the needle stands obliquely, that is, one end is depressed and the other end is elevated on account of the inequality of attraction exerted on its poles by those of the earth. Such a position of the needle in polar regions is technically termed the dip of the needle.

"It has been found by experiments that the human body is a magnetisable object, though far inferior to iron or steel. That it is a magnetisable object, is a fact that cannot be denied, for in addition to other causes there is a large percentage of iron in the blood circulating throughout all the parts of the body.

"Now, as our feet are for the most part of the day kept in close contact with the surface of that huge magnet—the earth—the whole human body therefore becames magnetised. Further, as our feet are magnetised by contact with the northern hemisphere of the earth, where exist all the properties of north polarity, south polarity is induced in our feet, and north polarity, as a necessary consequence, is induced in our head. In infancy the palms of our hands are used in walking as much as our feet, and even later on the palms generally tend more towards the earth than towards the sky. Consequently south polarity is induced in them as it is in our feet. The above arrangement of poles in the human body is natural to it, and therefore conducive to our health and happiness. The body enjoys perfect health if the magnetic polarity natural to it be preserved unaltered, and it becomes subject to disease if that polarity be in the least degree altered or its intensity diminished.

"Although the earth is the chief source whence the magnetism of the human body is derived, yet it is no less due to the action of oxygen. Oxygen gas being naturally a good magnetic substance, and being largely distributed within and without the human body, helps the earth a good deal in magnetising it.

"Though every human body is placed under the same conditions with regard to its magnetisation, yet the intensity and permanance of the magnetic polarity of one are not always equal to those of another. These two properties of the human body are generally in direct ratio to the compactness of its structure and the amount of iron particles entering into its composition.

"Now it is very easy to conceive that if you lie down with your head placed southward and feet northward, the south pole of the earth and your head,—which is the north pole of your body, and the north pole of the earth and your feet, which are the two branches of the south pole of your body,—being in juxta-position, will attract each other, and thus the polarity of the body natural to it will be preserved; while for the same reason, if you lie with your head placed northward and feet southward, the similar poles of your body and the earth being in juxta-position will repel each other, and thereby the natural polarity of your body will be destroyed or its intensity diminished. In the former position the polarity your body acquires during the day by standing, walking and sitting on the ground, is preserved intact at night during sleep; but in the latter position the polarity which your body acquires during the day by standing, walking and sitting on the ground is altered at night during sleep.

"Now as it has been found by experiment that the preservation of natural magnetic polarity is the cause of health, and any alteration of that polarity is the cause of disease, no one will perhaps deny the validity of the *slokas* which instruct us to lie down with our heads placed southward, and never and nowhere to lie down with our heads placed northward."

Now, why in those two *slokas* the eastern direction is preferred to the western for the placing the head in lying down, is explained thus: "It has been established by experiments in all works on medical electricity that if a current of electricity pass from one part of the body to another, it subdues all inflammations in that part of the body, where it enters into and produces some inflammation in the part of the body whence it goes out. This is the sum and substance of the two great principles of *Anelectrotonus* and *Catelectrotonus*, as they are technically called by the authors of medical electricities."

"Now, in lying down with the head placed eastward, the current of thermal electricity which is constantly passing over the surface of the earth from east to west, passes through our body also from the head to the feet, and therefore subdues all inflammation present in the head, where it makes its entrance. Again, in lying down with the head placed westward, the same current of electricity passes through our body from the feet to the head, and therefore produces some kind of inflammation in the head, whence it goes out. Now, because a clear and healthy head can easily acquire knowledge, and an inflamed, or, in other words, congested head is always the laboratory of vague and distressing thoughts, the venerable sage *Markandaya* was justified in saying that man becomes learned by lying down with his head placed eastward, and is troubled with distressing thoughts by lying down with his head placed westward."[1]

There are other time-honoured practices, which are founded upon a knowledge of the principles of electricity and magnetism. For instance, we find that (1) Iron or copper rods are inserted at the tops of all temples; (2) Mindulies (metallic cells) made of either gold, silver or iron, are worn on the diseased parts of the

[1] Arya Magazine for December, 1881, p. 211.

body; (3) Seats made of either silk, wool, *kusa*, grass or hairy skins of the deer and tiger are used at the time of saying prayers. Those who are acquainted with the principles of electricity will be able to account for these practices. They know that the function of the rod or the *trisula* (trifurcated iron rod) placed at the top of the Hindu temples is analogous to a lightning conductor. The mindulies perform the same functions as electrical belts and other appliances prescribed in the electrical treatments of disease. The golden temple of Vishweshwar at Benares is really a thunderproof shelter. Professor Max Muller recommends the use of a copper envelope to a gunpower magazine to exclude the possibility of being struck by lightning. The woollen and the skin *asans* (seats) protect our lives during a thunderstorm from the action of a return shock, and keeps our body insulated from the earth.

There is another practice among the Hindus which is explained by an Austrian scientist. In representation, "around the head of each of the Hindu gods is the aureole" But why they should be so represented was a mystery until now. Baron Von Reichenbach, an Austrian chemist of eminence, thus explains it. He says: "The human system in common with every animate and inanimate natural object, and with the whole starry heavens, is pervaded with a subtle aura, or, if you please, imponderable fluid, which resembles magnetism and electricity in certain respects, and yet is analogous with neither. This aura, while radiating in a faint mist from all parts of our bodies, is peculiarly bright about the head, hence the aureole. "In fact," says Col. Olcott, "we see that Reichenbach was anticipated by the Aryans (Hindus) in the knowledge of the Odic *aura*." And yet "we might never have understood what the nimbus about Krishna meant, but for this Vienna chemist, so perfect is the sway of ignorance over this once glorious people."[1]

Another practice of the Hindus which is ridiculed by non-Hindus, is that "when they sit down to eat, every man is isolated from his neighbours at the feast; he sits in the centre of a square traced upon the floor, grandsire, father and son, brother and uncle, avoiding touching each other quite as scrupulously as though they were of different castes. If I should handle a Brahman's brass platter, his *lotah* or other vessel for food and drink, neither he nor any of his caste would touch it, much less eat or drink from it until it had been passed through fire: if the utensil were of clay it must be broken. Why all these? That no affront is meant by avoidance of contact is shown in the careful isolation of members of the same family from each other. The explanation, I submit, is that every Brahman was supposed to be an individual evolution of psychic force, apart from all consideration of family relationship: if one touched the other at his particular time when the vital force was actively centred upon the process of digestion, the psychic force was liable to be drawn off, as a leaden jar charged with electricity is discharged by touching it with your hand. The Brahman of old was an initiate, and his evolved psychic power was employed in the *agnihotra* and other ceremonies. The case of the touching of the eating or drinking vessel, or the mat or clothing of a Brahman by one of another caste of inferior psychic development, or the stepping of such a person upon the ground within a certain prescribed distance from the sacrificial spot, bear upon this question. In this same plate of Baron Reichenbach's the figure F represent the aura streaming from the points of the human hand. Every human being has such an aura, and the aura is peculiar to himself or herself as to quality and volume.

[1] Col. Olcott's lecture delivered at the Town Hall, Calcutta, on 5th April, 1882.

Now, the aura of a Brahman of the ancient times was purified and intensified by a peculiar course of religious training—let us say psychic training—and if it should be mixed with the aura of a less pure, less spiritualized person, its strength would of necessity be lessened, its quality adulterated. Reichenbach tells us that the odic emanation is conductible by metals, lower than electricity, but more rapidly than heat, and that pottery and other clay vessels absorb and retain it for a great while. Heat he found to enormously increase quantitatively the flow of odyle through a metal conductor. The Brahman, then, in submitting his odylicaly-tainted metallic vessel to the fire, is but experimentally carrying out the theory of Von Reichenbach.

ARTS.

Mr. E. B. Havell, the celebrated art critic, says:—

"Art will always be caviare to the vulgar, but those who would really learn and understand it should begin with Indian art, for true Indian art is pure art, stripped of the superfluities and vulgarities which delight the uneducated eye. Yet Indian art, being more subtle and recondite than the classic art of Europe, requires a higher degree ef artistic understanding, and it rarely appeals to European *dilettanti*, who, with a smattering of perspective, anatomy, and rules of proportion, added to their classical scholarship, aspire to be art critics, amateur painters, sculptors or architects and these unfortunately have the principal voice in art administration in India." [1]

In the chapter on the "Inspiration of Indian Art" in his great work "Indian Sculpture and Painting," Mr. Havell, after describing the spiritual character of the Hindus and the meaning they understood of the winds which swept through the forest trees, the waters which poured down from the Heaven-built Himalayas, the power and beauty of the rising and the setting sun, the radiant light and heat of midday, the glories of the Eastern moonlit nights, the majestic gathering of the monsoon clouds, the fury of the cyclone, the lightning flash and thunder and the cheerful dripping of the life-giving rain, says: "From this devout communion with nature in all the marvellous diversity of her tropical moods, came the inspiration of an art possessing richness of imagery and wealth of elaboration which seem bewildering and annoying to our dull Northern ways of thinking." [2]

[1] Havell's Indian Sculpture and Painting, p. 69.

[2] Indian Sculpture and Painting, p. 68.

Comparing the European and Hindu art, Mr. E. B. Havell, says: "European art, has, as it were, its wings clipped: it knows only the beauty of earthly things. Indian art soaring into the highest empyrean, is ever trying to bring down to earth, something of the beauty of the things above."[1]

"It is curious that archæologists who are so concerned in trying to prove that nearly all Indian art was derived from the West, should seem to be only dimly aware of the immeasurably greater debt which European art and science owe to India, for they very rarely dwell upon it. From the time of the break-up of the Roman Empire, and even some centuries before, down to the days of the Renaissance, there was flowing into Europe a continuous under-current of Indian science, philosophy and art, brought by the art-workers of the East............Indian idealism during the greater part of this time was the dominant note in the art of Asia which was thus brought into Europe............The spirit of Indian idealism breathes in the Mosaics of St. Mark's at Venice, just as it shines in the mystic splendours of the Gothic Cathedrals............When a new inspiration comes into European art it will come again from the East."

As regards the position India occupies in the world of art, Mr. E. B. Havell says: "To form a just estimate of any national art we must consider not what that art has borrowed, but what it has given to the world. Viewed in this light, Indian art must be placed among the greatest of the great schools, either in Europe or in Asia. None of the great art schools are entirely indigenous and self-contained, in the archæological sense; there is none which did not borrow material from other countries, and the schools of Greece and Italy are no exception to this rule. What India borrowed from outside her own world, was repaid a

[1] Havel's Indian Sculpture and Painting, p. 24.

hundredfold by products of her own creative genius. If she took this from here, that from there, so did Greece, so did Italy: but out of what she took came higher ideals than Greece ever dreamt of, and things of beauty that Italy never realised. Let these constitute India's claim to the respect and gratitude of humanity."[1]

I.—ARCHITECTURE AND SCULPTURE.

I asked of Time for whom these temples rose
That prostrate by his hands in silence lie;
His lips disdained the mystery to disclose,
And borne on swifter wings he hurried by!
The broken columns whose? I asked of Fame
(His kindling breath gives life to works sublime);
With downcast looks of mingled grief and shame
She heaved the uncertain sign and followed *Time.*
Wrapt in amazement over the smouldering pile
I saw oblivion pass with giant strides,
And while his visage wore Pride's scornful smile,
Haply these vast domes that even in ruin shine
"*I reck not whose,*" he said "*they now are mine.*"

Byron.

There is another unmistakeable proof of the wonderful civilization of the ancient Hindus—it is their architecture. The magnificent Hindu temples, the splendid palaces, the formidable forts and the wonderful caves are truly monuments of human genius and marvels of human industry and skill. They have excited the admiration of European critics, and have elicited expressions of wonder and amazement from them. Mrs. Manning says: "That ancient architecture of India is so amazing that the first European observers could not find terms sufficiently intense to express their wonder and admiration, and although

[1] Havell's Indian Sculpture and Painting, p. 169.

the vividness of such emotions subsides on more intimate acquaintance, the most sober critics still allow that it is both wonderful and beautiful."[1]

Strength and durability, beauty and majesty are the characteristics of the Hindu style of architecture. Mahmud Ghaznavi writing to the Khalif from Mathura said that the buildings of India were surely not less strong than the Mohammedan faith. Such expressions of wonder from one of the greatest fanatics that ever lived is significant evidence of the highest development of the art of architecture in India.

Mr. Thornton says: "The ancient Indian erected buildings the solidity of which has not been overcome by the revolution of thousands of years."[2]

After speaking of Hindu sculpture, Professor Weber continues: "A far higher degree of development was attained by architecture of which some most admirable monuments still remain."[3] While describing the structure of a building, Mr. Elphinstone says: The posts and lintels of the doors, the panels and other spaces are enclosed and almost covered by deep orders of mouldings and a profusion of arabesques of plants, flowers, fruits, men, animals and imaginary beings; in short, of every embellishment that the most fertile fancy could devise. These arabesques, the running pattern of plants and creepers in particular, are often of an elegance *scarcely equalled in any other part of the world.*[4]

Mr. Havell in his remarkable book "Indian Sculpture and Painting" describes (pp. 110-131) the splendid shrine of

[1] Ancient and Mediæval India, Vol. I, p. 391.

[2] Thornton's Chapters from the British History of India.

[3] Weber's Indian Literature, p. 274.

[4] Elphinstone's History of India, p. 160. The author also says: "Perhaps the greatest of all the Hindu works are the tanks. The Hindu wells are also very remarkable."

Borobudur, built in the eighth century A.D., and says: "The great building from the basement to the seventh storey was adorned with a series of wonderful sculptures and reliefs extending in the aggregate for a length of nearly three miles (p. 114).........To compare them with the Panathenaic frieze of the Parthanon would serve no useful purpose, though as artistic achievements of the highest class the best Borobudur sculptures would not suffer by the comparison. There is as little kinship between the academic refinement of the Parthanon sculptures and this supremely devout and spontaneous art as there is between Indian and Hellenic religious thought...........A very near parallel may be found in the celebrated bronze doors of the Baptistery of Florence by Lorence Ghiberti, one of the great master-pieces of Italian art, of which Michel Angelo is reported to have said that they were "fit to be the gates of Paradise." In these gates a number of Biblical scenes are treated in a series of relief panels with similar accessories to those used by the Borobudur sculptors, *i.e.*, the figures are accompanied by representations of temples, houses, trees, clouds, water and landscape subjects. The Italian master has achieved a technical triumph which won for him the rapturous applause of the *Virtuosi* of his day, yet by the use of perspective and an excessive number of planes of relief, in the attempt to produce the illusion of pictorial effects, he has sacrificed breadth and dignity and overstepped the limitations of the plastic art. In spite of its extraordinary technical qualities the main impression given by Ghiberti's master-piece is that the artist was more concerned in exhibiting his skill to his fellow-citizens than in producing the most perfect and reverent rendering of the sacred subject. The Borobudur sculptors, with much deeper reverence and less self-consciousness, show conclusively that art is greater than artifice. The very simplicity and unaffected *naivete* of their style are much more impressive and convincing than the elaborate efforts of the Italian, who with all his wonderful technique is far behind in imagination and artistic feeling. Specially in the magnificent conventionalism of the accessories—the trees, buildings, ships, etc.—does the art of Borobudur rise above the art of Ghiberti.........The spiritual power of their (Borobudur sculptors) art has broken the chains of technical rules, risen above all thought of what critics call right or wrong, and speaks with divinely-inspired words straight to the heart of the listener. In this heaven-born quality of inspiration European art has rarely equalled and never excelled, the art of Borobudur...........These Borobudur sculptors have known how to convey the essence of truth as it is found in Nature without obtruding their own personality or relying on any of common tricks of their craft. Their art, used only in the service of truth and religion, has made their hands the obedient tools of a heaven-sent inspiration; and their unique power of realising this with a depth and sincerity unsurpassed in the art of any land or in any epoch, gives them a right to rank among the greatest of the symbolists in the whole history of art." Mr. Havell concludes: "And while there is no living artist within the boundaries of Europe who can produce anything, either in painting or in sculpture, to be placed side by side with these wonderful reliefs, and while the living traditions of this great art still linger in several parts of India, we establish schools to teach Indians painting and sculpture as they are taught in Europe, send out sculptors to decorate Indian buildings and flatter ourselves that by the annual fine art exhibitions which amuse Anglo-Indian *dilettanti* we are helping to elevate the taste of the Indian public."[1]

Of the sculptures in Prambanum, Sir Stamford Raffles, the

[1] Havell's Indian Sculpture and Painting. He adds "The story of these Sculptures of Borobudur is a liberal art education in itself."—p. 130.

British Governor of Java, says: "In the whole course of my life I have never met with such stupendous and finished specimens of human labour, and of the science and taste of age long since forgot, crowded together in so small a compass as in this little spot."[1]

The Hindu colonists from the Punjab who colonised Cambodia[2] in the fourth century A.D., carried with them the art traditions of the Cashmere School and built temples which according to Fergusson, "are large and as richly ornamented as any to be found in any part of the world."

Of the pagoda at Rameshwaram, Lord Valentia says: "The whole building presents a magnificent appearance, which we might in vain seek adequate language to describe."[3]

After giving a description of the pagoda at Chidambaram, 27 miles south of Pondicherry, Professor Heeren says: "On the other side of the large tank is the most wonderful structure of all. This is a sanctuary or chapel in the middle of an enormous hall, 360 ft. long x 260 ft. in breadth, and supported by upwards of one thousand pillars, each thirty feet high and disposed in regular order."[4] Dr. Robertson thus speaks of the Hindu architectural elegance: "Some of the ornamental parts are finished with an elegance entitled to the admiration of the most ingenious artists."[5]

The cave temples are not only peculiar to this country but show the highest artistic genius of the people. Professor

[1] History of Java, Vol. II, p. 15.

[2] History of Java, Vol. II, p. 137.

[3] Travels. Vol I, pp. 340, 341. "Several monuments in Northern India some of which were ascribed to Asoka, are recorded to have attained a height of from 200 to 400 ft., and to this day the summit of the Jetwana Lama Dagaba in Ceylon towers 251 ft. above the level of the ground." V. A. Smith's History of Fine Art in India and Ceylon.

[4] Heeren's Historical Researches, Vol. II, p. 95

[5] Dr. Robertson's Works, Vol. XII, "Disquisition Concerning India," p. 16.

Heeren[1] thus speaks of the Elora temples: "All that is great, splendid and ornamental in architecture above ground is here seen, also beneath the earth—staircases, bridges, chapels, columns and porticos, obelisks, colossal statues and reliefs sculptured on almost all the walls, representing Hindu deities." An English critic says: "All this wonderful structure, the variety, richness and skill displayed in the ornaments surpass all description."[2]

Mr. Grifiths says: "During my long and careful study of the caves I have not been able to detect a single instance where a mistake has been made by cutting away too much stone; for, if once a slip of this kind occurred it could only have been repaired by the insertion of a piece which would have been a blemish."[3]

Speaking of the Halebid temple, Mr. Vincent A. Smith says: One of the most marvellous exhibitions of human labour to be found even in the patient East. The architectural frame-work, it will be observed, is used mainly as a back-ground for the display of an infinity of superb decoration, which leaves no space uncovered and gives the eye no rest."[4] Of the Ballari temples, Mr. V. A. Smith says: "It is impossible, we are assured, to describe the requisite finish of the greenstone or hornblende pillars, or to exaggerate the marvellous intricacy and artistic finish of the decoration in even the minutest details......Both the intricate geometrical patterns of the ceilings and the foliated work covering every other part of the building exhibit the greatest possible exuberance of varied forms boldly designed and executed with consummate mastery of technical details. No chased work in

[1] See Historical Researches, Vol. II, pp. 60-70. "Magnitude," says Professor Wilson, "is not the only element of beauty in the cavern temples. The columns are carved with great elegance and fitness of design. Notice is taken of the numerous remains of temples in various parts of India in which extreme architectual beauty is to be found.—Mill's History of India, Vol. II, p 15.

[2] Asiatic Researches, Vol. III, p. 405.

[3] The Paintings in the Buddhist Cave temples of Ajanta.

[4] History of Fine Art in India, p. 42.

gold or silver could possibly be finer, and the patterns to this day are copied by goldsmiths, who take casts and moulds from them though unable to reproduce the sharpness and finish of the originals.[1]

Professor Heeren says: "It is not without an involuntary shudder that we pass the threshold of these spacious grottoes, and compare the weight of these ponderous roofs with the apparent slenderness and inadequacy of its support, an admirable and ingenious effect which must have required no ordinary share of abilities in the architect to calculate and determine!" The learned Professor concludes: "Such are the seven Pagodas or ancient monuments so-called, at Mavalipuram on the Coromandel coast, of which extraordinary buildings it will be hardly too much to assert that they will occupy a most distinguished place in the scale of human skill and ignenuity."[2]

Baron Dalberg was greatly struck with the architecture of Dwarka, which he calls "the wonderful city," and says: "The natives of that country (India) have carried the art of constructing and ornamenting excavated grottoes to a much higher degree of perfection than any other people."[3]

Comparing the Hindu with the Greek and the Egyptian architecture, Professor Heeren says: "In the richness of decoration bestowed on their pilasters, and among other things, in the execution of statues resembling caryatides they (the Hindus) far surpass both those nations (the Greeks and Egyptians)."

"The best Indian Sculpture," says Mr. E. B. Havell "touched a deeper note of feeling and finer sentiments than the best Greek."[4] Mr. Havell gives in Plate XLII a head of Buddha

[1] History of Fine Art in India, p. 44.

[2] Historical Researches, Vol. II, p. 78. Sakya Pandmrita is the name of the sculptor of the grottoes of Ellora.

[3] Geographical Ephemerides, Vol. XXXII, p. 12.

[4] Havell's Indian Sculpture and Painting, p. 142.

and says: "There is in this art a depth and spirituality which never entered into the soul of Greece."[1]

Mrs. Manning says: "The caves are remarkable also for the use of stucco and paint not merely on the walls but on the roof and pillars. And the frets and scrolls are of such beauty and elegance as to rival those at Pompeii and the Baths of Titus.' —The Kailas and the other excavations of Western India excite our awe and wonder."[2] She adds: "India is most famous for pillared architecture." The pillared colonnades or choultries connected with the Southern temples are the most extraordinary buildings.[3]

Buddhism gave a great stimulus to the development of architecture in ancient India; and with the spread of Budhism in foreign countries, the Buddhistic style of architecture was largely borrowed by foreign nations. Professor Weber hits the point when he says: "It is, indeed, not improbable that our Western steeples owe their origin to the imitation of the Buddhistic topes."[5]

Speaking of the Monolithic pillars of Emperor Asoka Mr. Vincent A. Smith in his History of Fine Art in India and Ceylon (p. 22) says: "The fabrication, conveyance and erection of monoliths of such enormous size—the heaviest weighing fifty tons—are proofs that the engineers and stone cutters of Asoka's age were not inferior in skill and resource to those of any *time* or country." "Of the Abacus of these monoliths Mr. V. A. Smith says: "Whatever the device selected, it is invariably well executed, and chiselled with that extraordinary precision and accuracy which characterise the workmanship of the Maurya

[1] Ibid, p. 144.

[2] Ancient and Mediæval India, Vol. I, p. 404. See also Fergusson's History of Architecture, Vol. II, pp. 499-501. The Karli Cave is the most perfect specimen of the cave temples.

[3] Ancient and Mediæval India, Vol. II, p. 420.

[4] Ancient and Mediæval India, Vol. I, p. 418.

[5] Indian Literature, p. 274.

age and have never been surpassed in Athens or elsewhere—p. 59." Of the capital of the Sarnath pillar, discovered in 1905 A.D., Mr. Vincent A. Smith says: "It would be difficult to find in any country an example of ancient animal sculpture superior or even equal to this beautiful art of arts, which successfully combines realistic modelling with ideal dignity, and is finished in every detail with perfect accuracy."—History of Fine Art in India, p. 60.

Speaking of the Jain columns in the South Kanara District, Mr. Walhouse says: "The whole capital and canopy are a wonder of light, elegant, highly-decorated stone-work; and nothing can surpass the stately grace of these beautiful pillars, whose proportions and adaptations to surrounding scenery are always perfect and whose richness of decoration never offends."[1]

Speaking in 1908 A.D. of the influence of Indian Art on the art of Europe and Asia, Mr. E. B. Havell says: "In the early centuries of the Christian era, and from this Indian source, came the inspiration of the great schools of Chinese painting, which from the seventh to the thirteenth centuries stood first in the whole world............The influence of India's artistic culture can be clearly traced, not only in Byzantine Art but in the Gothic cathedrals of the middle ages. Europe is very apt to dwell upon the influence of Western Art and Culture upon Asiatic civilization, but the far greater influence of Asiatic thought, religion and culture upon the Art and Civilization of Europe is rarely appraised at its proper value............From the seaports of her Western and Eastern coasts, India at this time sent streams of colonists, missionaries and craftsmen all over Southern Asia, Ceylon, Siam and far-distant Cambodia. Through China and Korea, Indian Art entered Japan about the middle of

[1] Indian Antiquary, Vol. V, p 39.

the sixth century. About A.D. 603 Indian colonists from Gujrat brought Indian Art into Java, and at Borobudur, in the 8th and 9th centuries, Indian Sculpture achieved its greatest triumphs. Some day when European Art criticism has widened its present narrow horizon, and learnt the foolishness of using the art standards of Greece and Italy as a tape wherewith to measure and appraise the communings of Asia with the Universal and the Infinite it will grant the nameless sculptors of Borobudur an honorable place among the greatest artists the world has ever known."[1]

Col. Tod says: "The Saracen arch[2] is of Hindu origin," and yet some would deny the existence of arches in the architecture of ancient India.[3] Mr. Vincent A. Smith says: "During the early centuries of the Christian era the Hindus knew the principle of true arch."[4]

Speaking of the methods which English critics of things Indian adopt, Mr. Havell says: "If Indians were to apply to European art the same methods of exegesis as archæologists

[1] Havell's Indian Sculpture and Painting.

[2] Tod's Rajasthan, Vol. I, p. 781. Colonel Tod, speaking of the *Aahai-din-ka-Jhonpra* at Ajmer, says: "I may further, with this temple and screen before us, speculate on the possibility of its having furnished some hints to the architects of Europe. It is well-known that the Saracenic arch has crept into many of those structures called Gothic, erected in the 12th and 13th centuries, when a more florid style succeeded to the severity of the Saxon or Roman: but I believe it has been doubted whence the Saracens obtained their model: certainly it was neither from Egypt nor from Persia." He then goes on to surmise that the influence of the early Caliphs of Baghdad (who were as enlightened as powerful), on European society was great, and that the victories of the Caliph's lieutenants produced no trifling results to the arts, that "this very spot, Ajmer was visited by the first hostile force which Islam sent across the Indus," and that the arches of the "temple" at Ajmer may thus be the models of the arches that were subsequently introduced amongst the Saracens.

[3] "The finest example of the triumphal arches is at Barnagar, north of Guzerat, which is the richest specimen of Hindu art."—Elphinstone's History of India, p. 163.

[4] History of Fine Art in India and Ceylon, p. 13.

ADHAI-DIN-KA-JHONPRA, AJMER.

apply to Indian, it would be easy for them to leave Europe with hardly a shred of originality."[1]

Sir Williams Hunter says: "Although Mohamedans brought their new forms of architecture, nevertheless Hindu Art powerfully asserted itself in the imperial works of the Mughals, and has left behind memorials which extort the admiration and astonishment of our age. The palace architecture of Gwalior, the mosques and mausoleums of Agra and Delhi, with several of the older temples of Southern India, stand unrivalled for grace of outline and elaborate wealth of ornament."

' When Timur, the ancestor of the Indian Mughul dynasty, withdrew his hordes from Northern India in 1398 after ravaging it with fire and sword, he took back with him as captives all the masons who had built the famous mosque at Ferozabad, in order that they might build one like it at Samarkand. Thus Indian art fulfilled once more its civilising mission, and when two and a half centuries later, Timur's descendant Shah Jahan was building the famous Taj Mahal at Agra, some of the principal masons were brought from Samarkand—probably descendants of Timur's captives."

Mr. Coleman says: "The remains of their architectural art might furnish the architects of Europe with new ideas of beauty and sublimity."[2]

"Indian art" says Havell "is always superbly decorative."[3] "English decorative art, to quote Sir W. W. Hunter once more, "in our day has borrowed largely from Indian forms and patterns. The exquisite scrolls of the rock temples at Karli and Ajanta, the delicate marble tracery and flat-wood carving of Western India, the harmonious blending of forms and colours in the fabrics of

[1] Havell's Indian Sculpture and Painting, p. 104.

[2] Hindu Mythology, Preface, p. ix.

[3] Havell's Indian Sculpture and Painting, p. 69.

Kashmir, have contributed to *the restoration of taste in England.*"[1]

Mr. Coleman says: "The ancient Hindu sculpture can boast of an almost unrivalled richness and beautiful minuteness of floral ornaments which claim and excite our warmest admiration."[2]

"No nation" says Mr. V. A. Smith,[3] has "surpassed the Indians in the variety and delicacy of the floral designs enriching their sculptures and pictures."

Speaking of a figure of Prajnaparamita, the Buddhist counterpart of Saraswati—Divine Wisdom—Mr. E. B. Havell says: "The beautiful stone figure of Prajnaparamita from Java, now in the Ethnographic Museum at Leyden, is a wonderful realization of these exalted ideals and worthy to rank as one of the most spiritual creations of art, Eastern or Western."[4]

"Hindu sculpture," says Mr. E. B. Havell, "has produced a master-piece in the great stone alto—relievo of Durga slaying the demon Mahisha, found at Singasari in Java, and now in the Ethnographic Museum, Leyden.........Judged by any standard it is a wonderful work of art, grandly composed, splendidly thorough in technique, expressing with extraordinary power and concentrated passion the wrath and might of the supreme Benificence

[1] Imperial Indian Gazetteer, Art "India," p. 225. "Indian art work, when faithful to native designs, has obtained the highest honours at the various International Exhibitions of Europe." Such is Indian art even in these degenerate days!

The reason is, art in India is not yet dead. The great art critic, Mr. E. B. Havell, says: "The secularised and denationalised art of Europe has no affinity with the living art of India, and we, aliens in race, thought and religion, have never taken any but a *dilettante*, archæological or commercial interest in it. Its deeper meanings are hidden from us, and those spiritual longings and desires, which come straight from the heart of a people, to find expression in their poetry, music, and their art, strike no chord of sympathy in ours."—Indian Sculpture and Painting, p. 3.

[2] Hindu Mythology. Preface, p. vii.

[3] History of Fine Art in India, p 79.

[4] Havell's Indian Sculpture and Painting, p. 51.

Temple of Ranpur.

roused to warfare with spirit of Evil. The student will find in this phase of Indian imaginative art an intensity of feeling—a wonderful suggestion of elemental passion transcending all the feeble emotions of humanity—a revelation of powers of the unseen which nothing in European art has ever approached, unless it be in the creations of Michel Angelo or in the music of Wagner.[1]

Of the colossal warhorse placed outside the Southern facade of the black Pagoda at Kanarak in Orissa, built about the middle of the thirteenth century by Narsigha I, Mr. Havell says: "Here Indian sculptors have shown that they can express with as much fire and passion as the greatest European art the pride of victory and the glory of triumphant warfare, for not even Homeric grandeur of the Elgin marbles surpasses the magnificent movement and modelling of this Indian Achilles, and the superbly monumental warhorse in its massive strength and vigour is not unworthy of comparison with Verocchio's famous masterpiece at Venice."[2]

"The grand temple at Barolli (Rajputana)," says the English translator of Heeren's Historical Researches, "contains unrivalled specimens of sculpture, some parts of which, especially the heads, in the language of an eye witness, would be no disgrace to *Canova* himself."

Colonel Tod, after carefully examining and exploring the temple, exclaims: "To describe its stupendous and diversified architecture is impossible; it is the office of the pen alone, but the labour would be endless. *Art seems to have exhausted itself*, and we are perhaps now for the first time fully impressed with the beauty of Hindu sculpture. The columns, the ceilings, the external roofing where each stone presents a miniature temple, one rising over another until the crown, by the urn-like *kalas*,

[1] Havell's Indian Sculpture and Painting, p. 62.
[2] Ibid p. 147.

distract our attention. The carving on the capital of each column would require pages of explanation, and the whole, in spite of its high antiquity, is in wonderful preservation.

"The doorway, which is destroyed, must have been curious, and the remains that choke up the interior are highly interesting. One of these specimens was entire and unrivalled in taste and beauty."[1]

Even of the Indian art of the present day, Mr. Havell says: "Europe of the present day has in art far more to learn from India than to teach."[2]

II.—PAINTING.

WRITING on the technique of the Ajanta paintings, Mr. Griffiths, who superintended the copying of them by his students in the Bombay School of Art, says:—

"The artists who painted them were giants in execution. Even on the vertical sides of the walls some of the lines, which were drawn with one sweep of the brush, struck me as being very wonderful; but when I saw long, delicate curves drawn without faltering, with equal precision, upon the horizontal surface of a ceiling, where the difficulty of execution is increased a thousandfold it appeared to me nothing less than miraculous."[3]

"The Chinese Schools owed their inspiration originally to the art of India In the early centuries of the Christian era the traditions of Indian religious art had been taken into Turkistan and China by Indian Buddhist missionaries and

[1] Tod's Rajasthan, Vol. II, p. 704. Col Tod says: "In short, it would require the labour of several artists for six months to do anything like justice to the wonders of Barolli."

[2] Havell's Indian Sculpture and Painting, p. 130.

[3] Indian Antiquary, Vol. III, p. 24.

craftsmen, and by Chinese students taught in Indian Universities."[1]

Abul Fazal, the Mohammedan historian, says of Hindu painters: "Their pictures surpass our conception of things. Few indeed in the whole world are found equal to them."[2] Even Mr Mill says: "The Hindus copy with great exactness, even from nature..............They draw portraits both of individuals and of groups with a minute likeness."

Mr. Havell says: "Among Rembrandt's pen and ink studies collected in the British Museum, the Louvre and elsewhere, a number have been identified as copies or adaptations of Indian miniatures, and it has been shown that from them chiefly, Rembrandt derived the Oriental atmosphere for his Biblical subjects."

Mr. Vincent A. Smith in his History of Fine Art in India and Ceylon (p. 6) says: "The remarkable success attained by Hindu Art, both plastic and pictorial in the treatment of plant motives and the representation of indigenous animals is unsurpassed."

III.—WEAVING.

> The whole world without art and dress
> Would be but one great wilderness.
>
> —BUTLER.

INDIANS, even of the present day, are remarkable for their delicacy of sense, especially their nicety of touch. Not only is their observation very accurate and minute, which has given a peculiar charm to their poetry and their fine arts, but their delicate and tactile sensibility, with their general delicacy of

[1] Havell's Indian Sculpture and Painting, p. 186.
[2] Blochman's Ain-i-Akbari, Vol. 1, p. 108.

sense, has enabled them to achieve a peculiar excellence in many of the industrial arts and manufactures. Mr. James Mill says: "The delicate frame of the Hindu is accompanied with an acuteness of external sense, particularly of touch, which is altogether unrivalled, and the flexibility of his fingers is equally remarkable."[1]

Mr. Orme says: "The hand of the Indian cookwench shall be more delicate than that of an European beauty. The skin and features of a porter shall be softer than those of a professed *petit maitres*. The women wind off the raw silk from the pod of the worm. A single pod of the raw silk divided into 20 different degrees of fineness, and so exquisite is the feeling of these women that whilst the thread is running through their fingers so swiftly that their eye can be of no assistance, they will break it off exactly as the assortments change at once from the first to the twentieth, from the nineteenth to the second."[2]

It appears that nature herself has bestowed the gift of excellence in arts and manufactures on the patient, skilful Hindu. The other nations appear to be constitutionally unfit to rival the Hindus in the finer operations of the looms, as well as in other arts that depend upon the delicacy of sense.

Nature gave India another advantage, Mr. Mill says: "His (Hindu) climate and soil conspired to furnish him with the most exquisite material for his art, *the finest cotton which the earth produces*."[3] Alas! that cotton has now disappeared.

[1] Mill's India, Vol. II, p. 17.

[2] People and Government of Hindustan, pp. 409 and 413.

[3] Mill's History of India, Vol. II, p. 17. This shows that India is capable of producing and in ancient times did produce the finest cotton used in weaving. In those days India had not to look to Egypt and America for cotton of a superior quality to enable her to manufacture finer muslins to clothe her sons and daughters. It would be interesting to many to learn that cotton is thought to have "reached Europe in the time of the Crusade, through the medium of the Arabs, the Arab word *kuta* becoming our cotton." Mrs. Manning's Ancient and Medieval India, Vol. II, p 356.

Mr. Elphinstône, speaking of Indian cotton cloth, says, "the beauty and delicacy of which was so long admired, and which, in fineness of texture, has never yet been approached in any country."[1] Mr. Murray says: "Its fabrics, the most beautiful that human art has anywhere produced, were sought by merchants at the expense of the greatest toils and dangers."[2]

Mr. Thornton says that the Indian muslins are "fabrics of unrivalled delicacy and beauty."[3]

Mr. Bott, in his work, "Cotton Manufactures of Dacca," says that Aurangzeb once reproved his daughter for showing her skin through her clothes. The daughter justified herself by asserting that she had on seven suits, or *jamas*.[4] After comparing the finest fabrics of India and of England, Dr. Watson decides in favour of the Indian fabrics. He finds the yarn *finer than any yet produced in Europe*, while the twisting given to it by the Hindu hands makes it more durable than any machine-made fabric.

"Shawls made in Kashmir," says Mrs. Manning, are still

[1] Elphinstone's History of India, pp. 163, 164.

[2] Murray's History of India, p. 27.

[3] Thornton's Chapters of the British History of India. Buddha forbids the use of fine muslin by religious women, because he once saw Gang-Dgah-mo (a woman having upon her a very fine linen which was sent to Gsal-rgyal by the king of Kalighana) naked while she was wearing a full muslin dress. See also Journal of the Asiatic Society of Bengal, VI, 1837 "Cosma's Analysis of the Dulva." To give an idea of the value of such fine muslins, Dr. Watts says that in 1776 A.D., the finest muslin reached the price of £56 per piece (Textile Manufactures, p. 79).

[4] Mr. Elphinstone says: "Gold and silver brocades were also favourites, and were, perhaps, original manufactures in India." See Colebroke, Asiatic Researches, Vol. V, p. 61. *Rudra Yamla Tantra*, in an enumeration of Hindu castes, mentions Pundracas or Pattasutracaras, or feeders of silk-worms and silk twisters: this authority, therefore, in conjunction with the frequent allusion to silk in most ancient Sanskrit books, may be considered as decisive of the question, provided the antiquity of the Tantra be allowed, of which Mr. Colebrooke seems to have no doubt. Silk is, moreover, mentioned throughout the Archipelago by its Sanskrit name, *Sutra*, which proves its Indian origin.

unrivalled."[1] Even James Mill says: "Of the exquisite degree of perfection to which the Hindus have carried the productions of the loom it would be idle to offer any description; as there are few objects with which the inhabitants of Europe are better acquainted, whatever may have been the attainment in this art of other nations of antiquity (the Egyptians, for example, whose fine linen was so eminently prized), the manufacture of no modern nation can, in delicacy and fineness, vie with the texture of Hindustan."[2]

Mrs. Manning says: "Some centuries before our era they produced muslins of that exquisite texture which even our nineteenth century machinery cannot surpass."[3] The Encyclopædia Britannica says that the exquisitely-fine fabrics of cotton have attained to such perfection that the modern art of Europe, with all the aid of its wonderful machinery; has *never yet rivalled in beauty* the product of the Indian loom."[4]

A critic says: "Carpets are made at Masulipatam with unrivalled Hindu taste," to which Mrs. Manning adds: "Carpets have also been made in later days in Government prisons, under British superintendeuce; the result proves that *we must not attempt to teach art to India.*"[5]

Dr. Forbes Watson, in his work on the Textile Manufactures of India gives an interesting account of a series of experiments made on both the European and the Indian muslins, to determine their cliams to superiority. The result was altogether in favour

[1] The presentation of Kashmir shawls to Sita supplies an additional proof in favour of the high antiquity of these celebrated fabrics."

[2] Mill's History of India, Vol. II, p. 16.

[3] Ancient and Mediæval India, Vol. I, p. 359.

[4] Encyclopædia Britannica, p. 446 (Weaving).

[5] Ancient and Medieval India, Vol. II, p. 363. Professor Heeren says: "The variety of cotton fabrics mentioned even by the author of Periplus as articles of commerce is so great that we can hardly suppose the number to have increased afterwards."

of the Indian fabrics. He concludes: "However viewed, therefore, our manufacturers have something still to do. With all our machinery and wondrous appliances we have hitherto been unable to produce a fabric which, for fineness or utility, can equal the woven air of Dacca, the product of arrangements, which appear rude and primitive, but which in reality are admirably adapted for the purpope."

IV.—STEEL AND IRON MANUFACTURES.

As regards iron manufactures, Professor Wilson says "Casting iron is an art that is practised in this manufacturing country (England) only within a few years. The Hindus have the art of smelting iron, of welding it, and of making steel, and have had these arts from times immemorial."[1]

Dr. Ray says: "Coming to comparatively later times, we find that the Indians were noted for their skill in the tempering of steel. The blades of Damascus were held in high esteem, but it was from India that the Persians, and, through them, the Arabs learnt the secret of the operation. The wrought-iron pillar close to the Kutub, near Delhi, which weighs ten tons and is some 1,500 years old, the huge iron girders at Puri, the ornamental gates of Somnath, and the 24-feet wrought-iron gun at Nurvar, are monuments of a bye-gone art, and bear silent but eloquent testimony to the marvellous metallurgical skill attained by the Hindus."

Manufacturing steel, however, is a very ancient art, and what is remarkable is that steel made in ancient India was as good as the best steel *now* manufactured in Europe or America. In 1913-14 Mr. Bhandarkar, Supdt. of Archaeology, Western

[1] Mill's History of India, Vol. II, p 47.

Circle discovered two pieces of steel under an old column near Bhilsa (Gwalior State) and sent them for examination to Sir Robert Hadfield an expert on iron matters. On analysing it he found the piece to be of such unusual value and interest that in his presidential address at the meeting of the Faraday Society in November last, he could not help making a prominent mention of it. "One of the special points," he says, "is that notwithstanding the large number of specimens of ancient iron and supposed steel I have examined during the last few years, none of them have sufficient carbon to be termed steel in our modern time meaning. This specimen is probably the first to be exhibited in modern times of an ancient piece of high carbon steel which has been hardened by quenching." Mr. Bhandarkar adds: "It is impossible to overrate the importance of this discovery......... It would have been considered the height of archæological blasphemy if they had been told that the Hindus could manufacture steel and that even so early as B. C. 140, to which date the column has to be assigned."[1]

Regarding the Kutub pillar, Fergusson says: "It has not, however, been yet correctly ascertained what its age really is. There is an inscription upon it, but without a date. From the form of its alphabet, Prinsep ascribed it to the third or fourth century. Mr. Fergusson continues: "Taking A. D. 400 as a mean date—and it certainly is not far from the truth—it opens our eye to an unsuspected state of affairs, to find the Hindus at that age capable of forging a bar of iron larger than any that have been forged even in Europe up to a very late date, and not frequently even now. As we find them, however, a few centuries afterwards using bars as long as this *lat* in roofing the porch of the temple at Kanaruc, we must now believe that they were much

[1] Progress Report of the Archæological Survey of India, Western Circle, for the year ending March 1915, pp. 59, 60.

more familiar with the use of this metal than they afterwards became. It is almost equally startling to find that after an exposure to wind and rain for fourteen centuries it is unrusted, and the capital and inscription are as clear and as sharp now as when put up fourteen centuries ago. There is no mistake about the pillar being of pure iron. General Cunningham had a bit of it analysed in India by Dr. Murray, and another portion was analysed in the school of mines here by Dr. Percy. Both found it pure malleable iron without any alloy."[1]

Mrs. Manning says: "The superior quality of Hindu steel has long been known, and it is worthy of record that the celebrated Damascus blades, have been traced to the workshops of Western India." She adds: "Steel manufactured in Cutch enjoys at the present day a reputation not inferior to that of the steel made at Glasgow and Sheffield."[2] Mrs. Manning also says: "It seems probable that ancient India possessed iron more than sufficient for her wants, and that the Phœnicians fetched iron with other merchandise from India."[3]

V.—OTHER ARTS.

Professor Weber says: "The skill of the Indians in the production of delicate woven fabrics, in the mixing of colours, the working of metals and precious stones, the preparation of essences and in all manner of technical arts, has from early times enjoyed a worldwide celebrity."[4]

Professor Wilson says: "They had acquired remarkable

[1] History of Indian and Eastern Architecture, p. 508; Ed. 1899.

[2] Ancient and Mediæval India, Vol. II, p. 365.

[3] Ancient and Mediæval India, Vol. II, p. 364. See also "Commerce."

[4] Weber's Indian Literature, p. 275.

proficiency in many of the ornamental and useful arts of life."[1]

As regards dyeing, Mr. Elphinstone says: The brilliancy and permanence of many of the dyes, have not yet been equalled in Europe."[2] He adds: "The brilliancy of their dyes is remarked on as well as their skill in manufactures and imitations of foreign objects.[3]

Dr. Tennent and even Mr. James Mill admit that the Indian colours are the most brilliant on earth. The Hindus were the earliest nation who discovered the art of extracting colours from plants. The names by which several plants are known in foreign countries bear testimony to this fact. Indigo is so called after *India*. Pliny used to write *indico*.[4]

After mentioning that Varahmamihra gives recipes for artificial imitations of natural flower scents, etc., Dr. Ray says: "To these classes of professional experts were due three of the great Indian discoveries in the chemical arts and manufactures which enabled India to command for more than a thousand years the markets of the East as well as the West, and secured to her an easy and universally recognised pre-eminence among the nations of the world in manufactures and exports."[5]

Bancroft gives much praise to the "natives of India for having so many thousand years ago discovered means by which the colourable matter of the plants might be extracted exygenated and precipitated from all other matters combined with it." Even Mill is constrained to say: "Among the arts of the Hindus, that of printing and dyeing their cloths has been celebrated; and the beauty and brilliancy, as well as durability of the colours they

[1] Mill's History of India, Vol. II, p. 233.

[2] History of India, p. 164.

[3] History of India, p. 243. See Strabo, lib. xv, p. 493.

[4] He says: "Cast the right indico upon the live coals, it yieldeth a flame of most excellent purple."—Manning's Ancient and Mediæval India, Vol. II, p. 355.

[5] History of Hindu Chemistry, Vol. II, p. 133.

produce, are worthy of particular praise."[1]

Mr. Elphinstone says: "The taste for minute ornaments fitted them to excel in goldsmiths' work."[2]

Professor Heeren says: "The art of working in ivory must have attained a high degree of perfection."

What is most remarkable, however, is the simplicity of their processes and the exceedingly small number of the instruments with which they work. Stavorinus writes: "Their artificers work with so little apparatus and so few instruments, that an European would be astonished at their neatness and expedition."[3]

Dr. Mann, Principal, Agricultural College, Poona, found the mortar used in an ancient column near Bhilsa "to be lime mortar of the best kind." "This analysis," he says, "gives the idea of a well-made mortar, prepared with a full recognition of the purpose served by sand and clayey matter in making the material as well as lime. In this respect it appears to be far an advance of many Phœnician and Greek mortars, which contain far too little sand for the best results." Mr. Bhandarkar further says: This was another startling discovery, as all archæologists were convinced that the old Hindus did not know the use of lime mortar. This was believed to have been first introduced into India by the Muhammadans, and to hold therefore that it was known to them at such an early period as B.C. 250, to which time the brick wall has to be ascribed, was considered to be a mere figment of the imagination. Dr. Mann's analysis, however,

[1] Mill's India, Vol. II, p. 31. "In some of the delicate manufactures, however," says Mill, "particularly in weaving, spinning, and dyeing, the Hindus rival all nations as in the fabrication of trinkets too." Professor Heeren says: "The dress of the Hindus seemed extraordinary white to the Greeks."—Historical Researches, Vol. II, p. 272.

[2] Elphinstone's History of India, p. 164. "The Hindus cut the precious stones, polish them to a high degree of brilliancy and set them neatly in gold and silver."—Mill's History of India, Vol. II, p. 30.

[3] Stavorinus' Voyage, p. 412. Foster was astonished to see their instruments and their simple processes.—Asiatic Researches, Vol. II, p. 272.

destroys another cherished belief.'"[1]

Dr. Royle is of opinion that the system of rotation of crops has been derived from India. The Hindu farmer understands extremely well how to maintain the productive power of his land.[2]

Professor Wilson says: "The use of glass for windows is a proof of civilization that neither Greek nor Roman refinement presents."[3]

Pliny says that the best glass ever made was India glass.[4]

Dr. Forbes Watson says: The study of Indian art might in numberless ways improve the character of the everyday articles around us (Englishmen)."[5]

Chamber's Encyclopædia says: "In manufacture, the Hindus attained to a marvellous perfection at a very early period, and the Courts of Imperial Rome glittered with gold and silver brocades of Delhi. The muslins of Dacca were famous ages ago throughout the civilized world. In the International Exhibition of 1862, splendid specimens of gorgeous manufactures and the patient industry of the Hindus were displayed. Textile fabrics of inimitable fineness, tapestry glittering with gems, rich embroideries and brocades, carpets wonderful for the exquisite harmony of colour, enamel of the most brillant hue, inlaid wares that require high magnifying power to reveal their minuteness, furniture most elaborately carved, sword of curious forms and excellent temper are amongst the objects that prove the *perfection of art* in India."[6]

[1] Progress Report of the Archæological Survey of India, Western Circle, for the year ending March 1915, p. 60.

[2] Dr Roxburgh fully approves of the Hindu system of agriculture. Sir T. Munro calls it "a good system."

[3] Mill's India, Vol. II, p. 46.

[4] Ray's History of Hindu Chemistry, Vol. II, p. 223. "Lenses and mirrors of various kinds are mentioned, the spherical, oval being well known."——p. 223.

[5] Lord Dufferin once said: "The West has still much to learn from the East in matters of dress." Of the much-dispised *dhoti*, Mrs. Manning says: "Any dress more perfectly convenient to walk, to sit, to lie in, it would be impossible to invent."—Ancient and Mediæval India, Vol. II, p. 358.

[6] Chamber's Encyclopædia, p. 543.

COMMERCE AND WEALTH.

I.—COMMERCE.

> But chief by numbers of industrious hands
> A nation's wealth is counted; numbers raise
> Warm emulation; where that virtue dwells
> There will be traffic's seat; there will she build
> Her rich emporium.
>
> —DYER: *Fleece.*

THOUGH Indians have practically no hand now in the commerce of the world, yet there was a time when they were the masters of the seaborne trade of Europe, Asia and Africa. They built ships, navigated the sea, and held in their hands all the threads of international commerce, whether carried on overland or by sea.

As their immense wealth was in part the result of their extensive trade with other countries, so were the matchless fertility of the Indian soil and numberless products of Hindu arts and industries the cause of the enormous development of the commerce of ancient India. As Cowper says:

> "And if a boundless plenty be the robe,
> Trade is a golden girdle of the globe."

India, which, according to Chamber's Encyclopædia, "has been celebrated during many ages for its valuable natural productions, its beautiful manufactures and costly merchandise,"[1] was, says the Encyclopædia Britannica, "once the seat of commerce."[2]

Mrs. Manning says: "The indirect evidence afforded by

[1] Chamber's Encyclopædia, Vol. V, p. 536.

[2] Encyclopædia Britannica, Vol. XI, p. 446.

the presence of Indian products in other countries coincides with the direct testimony of Sanskrit literature to establish the fact that the ancient Hindus were a commercial people."[1] She concludes: "Enough has now been said to show that the Hindus have ever been a commercial people."[2]

Dr. Caldwell says: "It appears certain from notices contained in the Vedas that Aryans of the age of Solomon practiced foreign trade in ocean-going vessels."[3]

Professor Heeren says: "The Hindus in their most ancient works of poetry are represented as a commercial people."[4]

In the Rig Veda, a passage (I. 25·7) represents Varuna having a full knowledge of the sea routes, and another (I. 56·2) speaks of merchants going everywhere and frequenting every part of the sea for gain.

The Ramayana refers to the Yavan Dvipa and Suvarna Dvipa (Java and Simatra) and to the *Lohta Sayara* or the Red Sea.

यत्नवन्तो यवद्वीपं सप्तराज्योपशोभितम् ।
सुवर्णरूप्यकद्वीपं सुवर्णाकरमण्डितम् ॥
. . . .
ततो रक्तजलं भीमं लोहितं नामसागरम् ।

The late Professor Buhler says: "References to sea voyages are also found in two of the most ancient *Dharma Sutras*."

The dramas Sakuntala, Ratnavali of king Harsha, Sisupalvadha of Magha, relates stories of sea voyages of merchants and others, and the fabulous literature of India is replete with stories of sea voyages by Hindus.

The author of *Indian Shipping* recently published, says:[5] "For full thirty centuries India stood out as the very heart of the old world and maintained her position as one of the foremost

[1] Ancient and Mediæval India, Vol. II, p. 353.
[2] Ancient and Mediæval India, Vol. II, p. 354.
[3] Grammer of the Dravidian Languages, p. 122.
[4] Heeren's Historical Researches, Vol. II, p. 266.
[5] Indian Shipping, by R. Mukerjee, p. 4, Introduction.

maritime countries. She had colonies in Pegu, in Cambodia, in Java, in Sumatra, in Borneo and even in the countries of the Farther East as far as Japan. She had trading settlements in Southern China, in the Malayan Peninsula, in Arabia and in all the chief cities of Persia and all over the East Coast of Africa. She cultivated trade relations not only with the countries of Asia, but with the whole of the then known world, including the countries under the dominion of the Roman Empire, and both the East and West became the theatre of Indian commercial activity and gave scope to her naval energy and throbbing international life." According to R. Sewell, "there was trade both by sea and overland with Western Asia, Greece, Rome and Egypt as well as China and the East."[1]

Mr. Rhys Davids says: "Communication both inland and foreign was of course effected by caravans and water. The caravans are described as consisting of 500 carts drawn by oxen. They go both east and west from Benares and Patna as centres. The objective was probably the parts on the West Coast, those on the sea board of Sobira (the Sophir 'Ophir' of the Septuagint) in the Gulf of Cutch or Bharukaccha. From here there was interchange by sea with Baveru (Babylon) and probably Arabia, Phœnicia and Egypt. Westward merchants are often mentioned as taking ships from Benares or lower down at Champa, dropping down the great river, and either coasting to Ceylon or adventuring many days without sight of land, Suvarnabhumi (Chryse Chersonesus, or possibly inclusive of all the coast of Farther India)."[2]

In Sanskrit books we constantly read of merchants, traders, and men engrossed in commercial pursuits. Manu Smriti, the oldest lawbook in the world, lays down laws to govern

[1] Imperial Gazetteer, New Edition, Vol. II, p. 325.
[2] The Journal of the Royal Asiatic Society for 1901.

commercial disputes having reference to seaborne traffic as well as the inland and overland commerce. In *Sakuntala* we learn of the importance attached to commerce, where it is stated "that a merchant named Dhanvriddhi, who had extensive commerce had been lost at sea and had left a fortune of many millions." In *Nala and Damyanti*, too, we meet with similar incidents.

Sir W. Jones is of opinion that the Hindus "must have been navigators in the age of Manu, because bottomry is mentioned in it."[1] In the *Ramayana*, the practice of bottomry is distinctly noticed.[2] Mr. Elphinstone says: "The Hindus navigated the ocean as early as the age of Manu's Code, because we read in it of men well acquainted with sea voyages."[3]

According to Professor Max Duncker, ship-building was known in ancient India about 2000 B.C. It is thus clear that the Hindus navigated the ocean from the earliest times, and that they carried on trade on an extensive scale with all the important nations of the whole world.

Mr. A. M. T. Jackson, I.C.S., says: "The Buddhist Jatakas and some of the Sanskrit law books tell us that ships from Bhroach and Supara traded with Babylon (Baveru) from the 8th to the 6th century B.C."[4]

Rev. J. Foulkes says: "The fact is now scarcely to be doubted that the rich Oriental merchandise of the days of King Hiram and King Solomon had its starting place in the seaports of Dakhan (Deccan), and that with a very high degree of probability some of the most esteemed of the spices which were carried into Egypt by the Midianitish merchants of Genesis xxxvii. 25-28,

[1] Asiatic Researches, Vol. II, p. 284. Manu speaks of "merchants who traffic beyond the sea and bring presents to the king."—India in Greece.

[2] See Ramayana, III, 237.

[3] Elphinstone's History of India, p. 166. "The word used in the original for sea is not applicable to inland waters."

[4] Bombay City Gazetteer, Vol. II, chap IV, p. 3.

and by the sons of the Patriarch Jacob (Gen. xliii. 11) had been cultivated in the spice gardens of the Dakhan.[1]

The age that produced such enterprising Brahman missionaries who led the Barbarian conquerors captive and spread the light of Brahmanism beyond the eastern mountains and seas, also produced many mighty seamen. Pliny the elder (A.D. 23-79) writes: "The same Nepos, when speaking of the northern circumnavigation, relates that to Q. Metellus Celer, the colleague of Africanus in the consulship, but then a proconsul in Gaul, a present was given by the King of Suevi, consisting of some Indians who, sailing from India for the purpose of commerce, had been driven by storms into Germany.

The *Yuktiulpataru* classifies ships according to their sizes and shapes. The *Rajavalliya* says that the ship in which King Sinhaba of Bengal sent Prince Vijaya, accommodated full 700 passengers, and the ship in which Vijaya's Pandyan bride was brought over to Ceylon carried 800 passengers on board.[2] The ship in which Buddha in the Supparaka Bodhisat incarnation made his voyages from Bharukachha (Broach) to the "sea of the seven gems,"[3] carried 700 merchants besides himself. The *Samudda Vanija Jataka* mentions a ship which accommodated one thousand carpenters.

With Phœnicia and Babylon, the Indians enjoyed trade from the earliest times. Dr. Sayce, the famous Assyrialogist, says that the Indians traded by sea with Babylon as early as B.C. 3000, when Ur Bagas, the first King of United Babylonia, ruled in Ur of the Chaldees.[4] Mr. Kennedy[5] says: "The evidence warrants us in the belief that maritime commerce between India and Babylon

[1] The Indian Antiquary, Vol. VIII.
[2] Turnour's *Mahavanso*, p. 46.
[3] Hardy's Manual of Buddhism, p. 13.
[4] Hibbert Lectures for 1887 A.D.
[5] Journal of the Royal Asiatic Society for 1898 A.D.

flourished in the 7th and 6th but more especially in the 6th century B.C. It was chiefly in the hands of Dravidians, although Aryans had a share in it, and as Indian traders settled afterwards in Arabia and on the east coast of Africa, and as we find them settling at this very time on the coast of China, we cannot doubt that they had their settlements in Babylon also."

In the tenth century B.C., Solomon of Israel and Hiram of Tyre sent ships[1] to India, whence they carried away ivory, sandalwood, apse, peacocks, gold, silver, precious stones, etc., which they purchased from the tribe of *Ophir*.[2] Now Ptolemy says there was a country called Abhiria at the mouth of the river Indus. This shows that some people called Abhir must have been living there in those days. We find a tribe called "Abhir" still living in Kathyawar, which must, therefore, be the *Ophir* tribe mentioned above. Professor Lassen thinks "Ophir" was a seaport on the south-west coast of India. Mrs. Manning says it was situated on the western coast of India.

As, however, the authors of Smith's Dictionary of the Bible think that *Ophir* was situated somewhere in Africa, let us go a little more closely into the question of the tribe. Let us first see if the articles imported by the Navy of Tarshish were procurable in India, and if they were, whether they were also procurable in Africa or any other country.

Among the things sent by the Hindus to Solomon and Hiram were peacocks. Now, these birds were nowhere to be found in those days except India, where they have existed from the earliest times. "We frequently meet in old Sanskrit poetry with sentences like these: 'Peacocks unfolding in glittering glory all their green and gold;' 'peacocks dancing in wild glee at the approach

[1] Called the "Navy of Tarshish." See also the book of Chronicles.
[2] Max Duncker's History of Antiquity, Vol. IV; and Manning's Ancient and Mediæval India, Vol. II, p. 349.

of rain;' 'peacocks around palaces glittering on the garden walls.' Ancient sculpture, too, shows the same delight in peacocks, as may be seen, for instance, in graceful bas-reliefs on the gates of *Sanchi* or in the panels of an ancient palace in Central India, figured in Tod's *Rajasthan* (p. 405)."

At the same time it is quite certain that the peacock was not generally known in Greece, Rome, or Egypt before the time of Alexander of Macedon, whose followers were astonished to see such a beautiful bird in India. It was after Alexander's time that peacocks came to be imported direct from India or through Persia into Greece. It was the Romans, however, who most delighted in the bird, admired it, and spent immense sums of money on it. It was the height of luxury for the high Roman dames and the old Roman epicures to have tongues of peacocks served to them at their tables.

There is, however, conclusive evidence to prove that Solomon and Hiram got their peacocks from India. This evidence is the name which the bird received in the Holy Land. "The word for peacock in Hebrew is universally admitted to be foreign; and Gesenius, Sir Emerson Tennent, and Professor Max Muller appear to agree with Professor Lassen in holding that this word as written in Kings and Chronicles is derived from the Sanskrit language."[1]

In the Hebrew text the word for peacock is *tuki*, while the ancient, poetical, purely Tamil-Malayalam name of the peacock is *tokei*, the bird with (splendid tail).[2]

Now, with regard to *ivory*. It was largely used in India, Assyria, Egypt, Greece and Rome. Elephants are indigenous in India and Africa, and the ivory trade must be either of Indian origin or African. But the elephants were scarely known to the

[1] Ancient and Mediæval India, Vol. II, p. 350.

[2] Caldwell's Grammar of the Dravidian Languages, p. 91.

ancient Egyptians,[1] and Professor Lassen decides that elephants were neither used nor tamed in ancient Egypt.

In ancient India, however, as is well known, they were largely used and tamed. No description of a king's procession or of a battle is to be met with but elephants are mentioned in it. No chieftain was without his elephants. The elephant is an emblem of royalty and a sign of rank and power. The god Indra, too, has his "Airawat." Then, the Sanskrit name for a domestic elephant is *ibha*, and in the bazars of India *ibha* was the name by which the elephant's tusks were sold. In ancient Egypt, ivory was known by the name *ebu*. Professor Lassen thinks "that the Sanskrit name *ibha* might easily have reached Egypt through Tyre, and become the Egyptian *ebu*. It is thus very probable that India first made Egypt acquainted with ivory. Strabo (XV. 37) says: "Ivory grows there (India)." Mrs. Manning says: "It is believed that by this name, or by words derived from it, ivory must have been introduced into Egypt and Greece. Although by what process *ibha* was changed into the Greek *elephas*, is not satisfactorily explained."[2]

Though ivory was known in Greece before the time of Homer, who speaks of it as largely used, the elephant itself was unknown to the Greeks until the day of Arabella, where they saw Darius aided by war elephants with their drivers from India. It was here that the Greeks for the first time saw these animals armed with tusks, which were familiar to them in trade. They gave the name of *elephas* to the animal itself, whose tusks were known to them by the name. By this name also, Aristotle made the animal famous in Eurpe. We thus see that from India were first imported ivory and peacocks into Egypt, Greece, Palestine and Persia and that the "Ophir" is no other than the *Ahir* tribe of India.

[1] Ancient and Mediæval India, Vol. II, p. 351.
[2] Alterthumskunde, Vol I., p. 351.

Direct evidence is, however, available now on the subject. The late Professor Buhler says: "The now well-known Baveru Jataka to which Professor Minayef first drew attention, narrates that Hindu merchants exported peacocks to Baveru. The identification of Baveru with Babiru or Babylon is not doubtful," and considering the "age of the materials of the Jatakas, the story indicates that the *Vanias* of Western India undertook trading voyages to the shores of the Persian Gulf and of its rivers in the 5th, perhaps even in the 6th century B.C. Just as in our days, this trade very probably existed already in much earlier times, for the Jatakas contain several other stories describing voyages to distant lands and perilous adventures by sea, in which the names of the very ancient Western ports of Surparaka-Supara and Bharukaccha-Broach are occasionally mentioned."[1]

It would be interesting to many to learn that "it was in India that the Greeks first became acquainted with sugar."[2] Sugar bears a name derived from the Sanskrit. With the article the name travelled into Arabia and Persia, and thence became established in the languages of Europe.[3]

Mr. Maunder says: "In the reign of Seleucidæ, too, there was an active trade between India and Syria."[4] Indian iron[5] and coloured cloths and rich apparels[6] were imported into Babylon and Tyre in ships from India. There were also commercial routes to Phœnicia, through Persia, which will be mentioned later on.

We have already seen that India exported her merchandise to Egypt. Mr. Elphinstone says: "The extent of the Indian

[1] Jataka iii No. 339. Cowell's Cambridge Edition.
[2] Ancient and Mediæval India, Vol. II, p. 353.
[3] See Lassen, p. 318.
[4] Maunder's Treasury of History, p. 775.
[5] "Phœnicians fetched iron with other merchandise from India"—Ancient and Mediæval India, Vol. II, p. 364.
[6] See Heeren's Historical Researches, Vol. II, p. 272.

trade under the first Ptolemies is a well-known fact in history."[1]

In the Book of Genesis we read that Joseph was sold by his brethren to the "Ishmaelites come from Gilead, with their camels bearing spicery, balm and myrrh going to carry it down to Egypt."[2] Here, Dr. Vincent observes, we find "a caravan of camels loaded with the spices of India and balm and myrrh of Hadramaut." Some suppose that myrrh used to be imported into Egypt by the Abyssinians, in whose country it largely grows. But the most conclusive proof of its importation from India is the name which it took in Egypt. Dr. Royle[3] observes that myrrh is called *bal* by the Egyptians, while its Sanskrit name is *bola*, bearing a resemblance which leaves no doubt as to its Indian manufacture. Silk, pearls, diamonds, calicoes, and other commodities of India were also imported into Alexandria in Egypt, which remained for ages the chief emporium of the Eastern commerce.

This trade was carried on from Myos Hormos, the chief port on the Red Sea, where the Indian fleets arrived. It is said that the articles were carried from here to Coptos, and thence to Alexandria on the Nile.[4] In the middle ages also trade on an extensive scale was carried on between India and Egypt, whence frankincense, an article of perfumery, is said to have been imported from Egypt into India.[5] Periplus clearly says that there was much direct intercourse between ancient India and Egypt.[6] Mr. Davies says: "But apart from this occasional intercourse, a constant trade was carried on between Alexandria and Western India. There was also an overland route through Palmyra."[7]

[1] Elphinstone's History of India, Vol. I, p. 141.
[2] Genesis, Chapter xxvii, v. 25.
[3] Royle's Ancient Hindu Medicine, "Myrrh," p. 119.
[4] Encyclopædia Britannica, Vol. XI, p. 450.
[5] Ibid, p. 446.
[6] See Heeren's Historical Researches, Vol. II, p. 300.
[7] Davie's Bhagwat Gita, p. 195.

"It was by sea and after Claudius, by the open sea, that the bulk of merchandise from Indian south coast ports was carried to the Arabian marts and Alexandria." [1]

There was also an active trade between India and Greece. The mention of ivory by Homer and of several other Indian articles assign the trade a very ancient date. In addition to ivory, India also supplied indigo (as mentioned in Periplus) to Greece. The writer in Chamber's Encyclopædia (Vol. V, p. 557) says that indigo was imported into Greece and Rome from India, whence also the inhabitants of the former countries derived their knowledge of its use. In India it is called *nil*, whence is derived the *anil* of the Portuguese and the *neel* of the Arabs. Homer knew *tin* by its Sanskrit name. Professor Max Duncker says that the Greeks used to wear silken garments which were imported from India, and which were called "Sindones," or "Tyrian robes."

Rome appears to be one of the important cities in Europe with which ancient India had considerable trade. The chief articles exported from India, in addition to those already mentioned, are, according to Periplus,[2] cotton cloth, muslin, chintz of various kinds, cinnamon [3] and other spicery, diamonds, pearls, onyx stone, emeralds, and many other inferior stones.[4] Ctesias [5] adds steel, drugs, aromatics, calicoes [6] and lac.[7] Spicery appears to have been exported from India from the earliest times. Professor Heeren says: "India is the mother-country of spices, and from the most ancient times she supplied the whole Western world with that

[1] Journal of the R. A. S. for 1904, "Roman Coins."
[2] Periplus, p. 28.
[3] To Ctesias (400 B.C.) Cinnamon was known only by its Indian name *Karpion* (Tamil *Karupa*).
[4] Pliny's Natural History, xxxvii. c. i.
[5] Indica, Chapter iv.
[6] Encyclopædia Britannica, Vol. XI, p. 459.
[7] Ctesias, Indica, Chapter xxi.

article.[1] Pepper was very largely exported from India in the time of Theophrastos,[2] who distinguishes several varieties of it. With pepper, its name also migrated through Persia to the West.[3] Mrs. Manning says: "Nard or spikenard, cassia, calamus and what appears to be the bdellium of Scripture may be traced to India, where scents were early valued and carefully prepared."[4]

Roman coins in large quantities are found in places in Southern India, whence beryl, pepper, pearls and minerals were exported to Rome. Some of these are described by Mr. Sewell. "These hoards," he says, "are the product of 55 separate discoveries, mostly in the Coimbatore and Madura districts."[5]

Mr. Momensen in his Provinces of the Roman Empire (Vol. II, p. 301), says: "Somewhat further to the south at Kananor numerous Roman gold coins of the Julio Claudian epoch have been found, formerly exchanged against the spices destined for the Roman kitchens."

Trade with Rome assumed such proportions that later on large numbers of Romans came and settled in South India. Mr. Vincent Smith[6] says: "There is good reason to believe that considerable colonies of Roman subjects engaged in trade were settled in Southern India during the first two centuries of our era.."

Of the products of loom, silk was more largely imported from India into ancient Rome than either in Egypt or in Greece. "It so allured the Roman ladies," says a writer, 'that it sold for its weight in gold."[7] "The most valuable of the exports of India was silk, which under the Persian Empire is said to have been

[1] Heeren's Historical Researches, Vol. II, p. 274.
[2] Theophrastos: Historical Plant, IX, 22.
[3] Sanskrit *pippali*, whence the Latin *piper* and pipper.
[4] Ancient and Mediæval India, Vol. II, p. 353.
[5] Journal of the R. A. S. for 1904, "Roman Coins."
[6] Early History of India, pp. 400, 401.
[7] Encyclopædia Britannica, Vol. XI, p. 459.

exchanged by weight in gold."[1] It is evident that "there was a very large consumption of India manufactures in Rome. This is confirmed by the elder Pliny, who complained that there was "no year in which India did not drain the Roman Empire of a hundred million sesterces (£1,000,000)......so dearly dó we pay for our luxury and our women."[2] The annual drainage of gold from Rome and its provinces to India was estimated by him at 500 steria, equal to about Rs. 4,000,000.[3] "We are assured on undisputed authority that the Romans remitted annually to India a sum equivalent to £4,000,000 to pay for their investments, and that in the reign of Ptolemies, 125 sails of Indian shipping were at one time lying in the ports whence Egypt, Syria, and Rome itself were supplied with the products of India."[4]

Arabia being the nearest of the countries situated to the west of India, was the first to which the Indian commercial enterprises by sea were directed. The long-continued trade with Arabia dates from a very remote antiquity. "The labours of Von Bohlen (*Das Alte Indien*, Vol I, p. 42), confirming those of Heeren and in their turn confirmed by those of Lassen (*Ind Alt.* Vol. II, p. 580), have established the existence of a maritime commerce between India and Arabia from the very earliest period of humanity."[5] Lassen also says that the Egyptians wrapped their mummies in Indian Muslin.

Agarthchides,[6] President of the Alexandrian Library, who is mentioned with respect by Strabo, Pliny and Diodorus, and who lived upwards of 300 years before the time of Periplus, noticed the active commercial intercourse kept up between Yemen and

[1] Indian Shipping, p 83.
[2] Pliny: Natural History.
[3] Encyclopædia Britannica, Vol XI, p 460.
[4] Life in Western India (Guthrie), from Tod's Western India, p. 221. Strabo (ii, v, 12) saw about 120 ships sail from Myos Hormos to India.
[5] Hist. Anc. del orient, Eng. edition, II, pp. 299-301.
[6] Geogr. Min. I, p. 66.

Pattala—a seaport in Western India, which Mr. Pottinger indentifies with the modern Hyderabad, Sindh. Pattala in Sanskrit means a "commercial town," "which circumstance. if it is true," says Professor Heeren, "would prove the extreme antiquity of the navigation carried on by the Indus."[1] Agatharchides saw large ships coming from the Indus and Pattala.

Periplus, written by a great sailor who navigated the Red Sea, the Persian Gulf, the Malabar and Coromandel coasts and resided for many years at Broach, mentions "large Hindu ships off East African, Arabian and Persian ports and Hindu settlements on the north coast of Socotra." It also says that the inhabitants of the Coromandel coast traded in vessels of their own with those of Malabar.

The importance of trade was highly appreciated by the people of Kalinga—a Kingdom on the Eastern seaboard of India. Inscriptions "speak of navigation and ship commerce as forming part of the education of the princes of Kalinga."[2] Professor Max Duncker says: "Trade existed between the Indians and Sabæans on the coast of South Arabia before the tenth century B.C."[3]—the time when, according to the Europeans, Manu lived. In the days of Alexander, when the Macedonian general, Nearchus, was entering the Persian Gulf, Muscat was pointed out to him as the principal mart for Indian products, which were transmitted thence to Assyria.

That this trade was chiefly in the hands of the Indians up to the beginning of the last century is proved by what Mr Cloupet, a not very ancient writer, says: "The commerce of Arabia Felix," he says, "is entirely in the hands of the banias of Gujrat, who from father to son have established themselves in the country

[1] Historical Researches, Vol. II, p. 299.
[2] Hunter's Orissa, Vol I, p. 197.
[3] Duncker's History of Antiquity, Vol. IV, p. 156.

and are protected by the Government in consideration of a certain import levied upon their estimated property."[1]

Egypt was not the only part of Africa with which the Hindus traded in olden days. The eastern coast of Africa called Zanzibar and the provinces situated on the Red Sea carried on an extensive trade with ancient India. Myos Hormos, as has been stated before, was the chief emporium of Indian commerce on the Red Sea. Of the trade with Zanzibar, Periplus gives us pretty full information. After enumerating the commercial stations on the coast as far as the promontory of Rhapta, now called Delgado, which was the most southerly point of his geographical knowledge, and after describing their mercantile relations with Egypt, he continues: "Moreover, indigenous products such as corn, rice, butter, oil of seasamum, coarse and fine cotton goods, and cane-honey (sugar) are regularly exported from the interior of Ariaka (Conkan), and from Barygaza (Baroucha) to the opposite coast."[2]

This trade is also noticed by Arrian, who adds that "this navigation was regularly managed." Professor Heeren thinks that the trade with the gold countries of Africa will serve to explain the great abundance of this metal in India.

The African trade, too, was in the hands of the Hindus. Periplus[3] calls our attention to the fact that the banians of India as well as merchants of Greece and Arabia, established themselves at Socotra,[4] near the Gulf of Aden, beside the Cape of Guardafui. Professor Heeren[5] says it is a well-known fact that the banians or Hindu merchants were in the habit of traversing the ocean and settling in foreign countries. The fact that thousands of Hindus

[1] From the accounts of Mr. Cloupet in Allgem, Geogr. Ephem, for November 1810, p. 235.
[2] Periplus, p. 8.
[3] Periplus, p. 17.
[4] It was formerly called the Island of Dioscorids.
[5] Historical Researches, Vol. II.

from Gujarat and its neighbouring provinces are even now found settled in the eastern districts of Africa, proves that in ancient times Indians in large numbers had settled in Africa for purposes of commerce.

The Eastern countries with which ancient India traded were chiefly China, Transgangetic Peninsula and Australia. Professor Heeren says that "the second direction which the trade of India took was towards the East, that is, to the Ultra-Gangetic Peninsula, comprising Ava,[1] Mallaca,[2] etc., etc. The traffic with these countries would, of course, be carried on by sea only, though the transmissi n of goods across the Bay of Bengal could not be attended with much difficulty."[3]

J. Takakusu says: "That there was a communication or trade between India and China from about 400 A.D. down to 800 A.D. is a proven fact. Not to speak of any doubtful records we read in the Chinese and Japanese books, Buddhist or otherwise, of *Indian merchant ships* appearing in the China Sea; we know definitely that Fahien (399-415 A.D.) returned to China *via* Java by an Indian boat.........and further in the Tang dynasty an eyewitness tells us that there were in 750 A.D. many Brahman ships in the Canton River."[4]

This commerce was actively carried on in the days of Periplus, as it actually mentions a place situated on the Coromandel coast, from which the passage was usually made to Chrysa, which appellation, according to Ptolemy,[5] denoted Malacca, but according to the author of Periplus, the whole of the Trans-gangetic Peninsula.[6]

[1] Its Sanskrit name is *Auga*, which is noticed in the Ramayana.

[2] Col. Wilford interprets the Sanskrit *Yamala* by Mallaca. See Asiatic Researches, Vol. VIII, p. 302.

[3] Historical Researches, Vol. II, p. 296.

[4] Journal of the R. A. S., Great Britain and Ireland, Octr. 1905, p. 872.

[5] See Mannert, Vol. V, p. 242.

[6] Periplus, p. 34.

Mr. Vincent Smith says: "Ancient Tamil literature and the Greek and Roman authors prove that in the first two centuries of the Christian era the ports on the Coromandel or Chola coast enjoyed the benefits of active commerce with both East and West. The Chola fleets . . . crossed the Indian ocean to the islands of the Malaya Archipelago."[1]

Professor Heeren says: "The Hindus themselves were in the habit of constructing the vessels in which they navigated the coast of Coromandel, and also made voyages to the Ganges and the peninsula beyond it. These vessels bore different names according to their size."[2] Nothing, indeed, could furnish better proof that this commerce did not originate from an intercourse with the Greeks, but was the sole product of ancient native industry, a fact which receives additional confirmation from the existence of commercial towns and ports on the Coromandel coast from time immemorial. Masulipatam, with its cloth manufactures, as well as the mercantile towns situated on the mouth of the Ganges, have already been noticed as existing in the time of Periplus; and if we allow these places to have been even then very ancient, of which there is scarcely any doubt, have we not equal reason for believing their commerce and navigation to be so also?"[3]

Even so late as the 17th century A.D. this port retained its importance as a commercial mart. Tavernier in 1666 A.D. said: "Masulipatam is the only place in the Bay of Bengal from which vessels sailed eastwards for Bengal, Arrakan, Pegu, Siam, Sumatra, Cochin China and the Manillas and West to Hormuz, Makha and Madagascar."[4]

[1] Early History of India, p. 415.
[2] Some were called *Sangara*, *others Colandiaphonta*, and so on.
[3] Historical Researches, Vol. II, p. 296.
[4] Ball's Translation, I, 174.

Ceylon.

A few words regarding the commercial importance of Ceylon will not be out of place. According to Cosmos, Ceylon was at one time the centre of Hindu commerce, for which purpose, indeed, its natural situation and commodious havens afforded singular opportunities.[1]

Ceylon has been known by variety of names in the East as well as in Europe. It was called Taprobane, a name first used by "Onesicritus"[2] and ingeniously derived from *Top*, an island, and Rahan or Ravan, an ancient king conquered by Maharaja Ram Chandra.[3] Ptolemy remarks that it was formerly called *Palæsimundi* (which Pliny confirms), but that in his own time it was called Salice, and the natives Saloe (whence Selan and Ceylon). It was called *Sinhala Dvipa* by the Hindus. The name Sinhala was given to the Island by Prince Vijaya of Bengal, who according to *Mahawansa* conquered and colonised the island about 550 B.C.

In Ptolemy's accounts of Ceylon we find its coast well furnished with commercial ports.[4] Talacori, Modutti, Amurogramum, Moagramum (Mahagram, a great city) are among the principal commercial cities described by him. Professor Heeren says: "It (Ceylon) was noted for commercial navigation before 500 B.C."[5]

From Arrian we known that the northern part of Ceylon was in a very highly-civilized state, and that it was a seat of extensive commerce with the countries from the farthest China

[1] Professor Heeren says: "Commercial History of India is dependent on that of Ceylon."—Historical Researches, Vol. II, p. 440.
[2] Historical Researches, Vol. II, p. 417.
[3] Asiatic Researches, Vol. V, p. 39.
[4] Ptolemy Chapter XII.
[5] Historical Researches, Vol. II, p. 437.

in the East to Italy in the West.[1]

Pliny says: "Taprobane was for a long time considered to be a second world and went by the appellation of Antichthones," which proves its reputation as a seat of commerce and civilization.

Some idea of the extent of the ancient commerce of Ceylon can be gathered from the accounts which Cosmos gives of it, though at a comparatively later date. After describing the situation of the island and the name by which the Hindus called it, he says: From *all* India, Persia, Ethiopia, between which countries it is situated in the middle, an infinite number of vessels arrive at, as well as go from, Ceylon. From the interior of the continent, as for instance from China and other commercial countries, it receives silk, aloes, cloves, and other productions, which it exports to Malabar, where the pepper grows, and to Calliene (near Bombay), whence is brought steel and cloth, for this latter is also a great commercial port. It likewise makes consignments to Sindh on the borders of India, whence come musk and castoreum; and also to Persia, Yemen, and Adule. From all these countries it receives articles of produce, which again it transmits into the interior, together with its own productions. Selandiv (*Sinhal Dwipa*) is consequently a great emporium, and being situated in the middle of the Indian Ocean, it receives merchandise from, as well as sends it to, all parts of the world."[2]

Professor Heeren adds: "From Pliny, who quotes the testimony of ancient historians, namely, those of Alexander's age, who first discovered Taprobane to be an island, we learn that Ceylon enjoyed this commercial reputation in the time of the Ptolemies, and even in that of Alexander. If we extend this period but a century and a half further back, which no one

[1] Historical Researches, Vol. II, p. 432.
[2] Historical Researches, Vol. II, p 298.

surely will consider unreasonable, we come at once to the interesting *historical fact* that during a space of a thousand years, that is from 500 B.C. to 500 A.D., the island of Ceylon, so conveniently situated for such a purpose, continued to be the great emporium of the Hindu-carrying trade, from Adule on the coast of Africa, Yemen and Malabar and the Ultra Gangetic Peninsula, even to China." He also says: "Ceylon was the common mart of Australian commerce."[1]

That a considerable portion of ancient India was closely connected with that of Ceylon is clear, not only from the remains of Hindu civilization still everywhere visible in the island, but also from the express testimony of the writers on the subject. The island of Ceylon has been celebrated in the historical and fabulous writings of India as being very prosperous and wealthy. "Golden Lanka" is a trite phrase in India. The island was politically, socially, in religion, and, till very recently, even physically—after Ram Chandra's celebrated stone bridge—a part of India. It was inhabited by Hindus, who, so far as nationality, language, religion and civilization are concerned, belonged to the same stock as their brethren of India. It enjoyed, therefore, an equally considerable refinement and civilization. When the British first went to Ceylon, "they beheld with astonishment the stupendous remains of ancient civilization, not merely temples and other edifices, but what is still more extraordinary, tanks of such amazing extent as to deserve the name of lakes." Her ancient prosperity, her material strength, her moral and social achievements have all been testified to by many European writers. Arrian, Cosmos[2] and a host of other great writers, travellers and annalists of the first

[1] Historical Researches, Vol. II, p. 426.

[2] A merchant who travelled about 560 A.D., in the reign of Emperor Justinian II as far as Adula, at that time a celebrated port belonging to the King of Axume, in Ethiopia, near Arkeeko.

centuries of the Christian era unanimously declare that Ceylon occupied the foremost position in the commercial transactions of the ancient world.

It has already been remarked that the Alexandrian historians were the first to discover that Ceylon was an island. Professor Heeren says: "It is, however, quite evident from the testimony of Arrian that much of what is advanced respecting the trade of Ceylon may, with equal justice, be applied to the opposite coast of Malabar."

The sea-coast of India was naturally well-furnished with harbours and havens to cope with commerce on a gigantic scale. Professor Heeren says: "Commercial towns and ports existed on the Coromandel coast from time immemorial. The coast of Coromandel, and specially the southern part, is represented by Ptolemy to have been thickly-studded with a series of commercial towns."[1]

Extensive commerce bespeaks advanced civilization. Mr. Elphinstone says: "The numerous commercial cities and ports for foreign trade which are mentioned in Periplus, attest the progress of the Indians in a department which, more than any other, shows an an advance condition of the nation."[2]

LAND TRADE.

The land trade of India extended to China, Turkistan, Persia, Babylon, and sometimes also to Egypt, Greece and Rome. Mr. Vincent says: "The country in the north with which India traded

[1] Historical Researches, Vol. II, p. 297. The chief ports mentioned in Periplus, p. 30, are: (1) Bryguza (Bharouch); (2) Miziris (Mangalore); (3) Nelkynda (Neliceram); (4) Patala (Hyderabad in Sindh); (5) Calliene (Gallian, situated over against Bombay), and the islands of Elephanta and Salsette. In addition to these, Cosmos names Sindus (Sindh); Orrbota (Surat); Calliene; Sibor; Parti; Mangarath; Salopatana; Nelopatana; Pudapatana.

[2] History of India p. 241.

was China."[1] The author of Periplus, after describing the geographical position of China, says: "Silk was imported from that country, but the persons engaged in this trade were the Indians themselves." It may, however, be added, in the words of an English critic:[2] "It is not improbable that silk was also indigenous in India even at a remote epoch."[3]

As regards the trade with central and northern Asia, we are told that "the Indians make expeditions for commercial purposes into the golden desert *Ideste*, desert of Cobi, in armed companies of a thousand or two thousand men. But, according to report, hey do not return home for three or four years." The *Takhti, Suleman*, or the stone tower mentioned by Ptolemy and Ctesias was the starting point for Hindu merchants who went to China.

Professor Heeren says: "By means of this building it is easy to determine the particular route as well as the length of time employed by the Hindu merchants in their journey to China. If we assume Cabul, or rather Bactria, as their place of departure, the expedition would take a north-easterly direction as far as the forty-first degree of north latitude. It would then have to ascend the mountains, and so arrive at the stone tower through the defile of Hoshan, or Owsh. From thence the route led by Cashgar, beyound the mountains, to the borders of the great desert of Cobi, which it traversed probably through Khoten and Asku (the Casia and Auxazia of Ptolemy). From these ancient towns the road lay through Koshotei to Sechow on the frontiers of China, and thence to Pekin, a place of great antiquity, if we are to understand it as the metropolis of Serica, which, indeed, the accounts of Ptolemy would hardly leave any

[1] Vincent, Vol. II, pp. 574, 575. The author says: "The name China is of Hindu origin and comes to us from India."

[2] Asiatic Researches, Vol. II, p. 286. See also Schlegel, *Berlin Calendar* p. 9 (Edition 1829).

[3] See also "Art of Weaving."

room to doubt. The whole distance amounts to upwards of two thousand five hundred miles."[1]

As regards Western Asia, Professsor Heeren says that the Palmyrians, in addition to their commerce by land, exercised also a sea-trade with India."[2]

"After the decline of Rome," says the Encyclopædia Britannica, "Bassora became the chief commercial mart, and to Ormus merchandise from India was brought."[3]

India traded with Europe by sea as well as by land. The writer quoted above says: "The produce of India was also brought to Europe by other routes, namely (1) by the way of Palmyra, then a flourishing city, and thence to Rome and other Western cities, through the ports of Syria; (2) across the Himalaya mountains to the Oxus, thence to the Caspian Sea, and finally to its ultimate markets of Europe."[4]

Foreign trade of a nation presupposes development of its internal trade. Specially is this true of a large country like India, with its varied products, vast population and high civilization. Professor Lassen of Paris considers it "remarkable that the Hindus themselves discovered the rich, luxurious character of India's products; many of them are produced in other countries, but remained unnoticed until sought for by foreigners, whereas the most ancient Hindus had a keen enjoyment in articles of state and luxury. Rajas and other rich people delighted in sagacious elephants, swift horses, splendid peacocks, golden decorations, exquisite perfumes, pungent peppers, ivory, pearls, gems, etc., and consequently caravans were in continued requisition to carry down these and innumerable other matters between the north and the south and the west and the east of their vast and varied country.

[1] Historical Researches, Vol. II, p. 290.
[2] Historical Researches, Vol. II, p. 490 (Appendix IX).
[3] Encyclopædia Britannica, Vol. XI, p. 460.
[4] Encyclopædia Britannica, Vol. XI, p. 459.

These caravans, it is conjectured, were met at border stations and about ports by western caravans or ships bound to or from Tyre and Egypt, or to or from the Persian Gulf and Red Sea."[1]

Professor Heeren remarks: "The internal trade of India could not have been inconsiderable, as it was in a certain degree prescribed by nature herself."[2] Royal roads were constructed all over the country from east to west and from north to south, in addition to the numberless rivers, along the banks of which considerable commerce was carried on.

Strabo, Plutarch, and Apollodorus agree in their statements that India had considerable trade roads in all directions, with *mile stones*, and was provided with inns for travellers. (See Strabo, Chap. XV, pp. 474 and 487). And these "roads," says Heeren, "were planted with trees and flowers."[3]

The Great Asoka, who according to Mr. Vincent Smith "rightfully claims a place in the front rank of the great monarchs, not only of India, but of the world,"[4] says in his Pillar Edict VII, "On the roads I have had banyan trees planted to give shade to man and beast: I have had groves of mango trees planted; and at every half *kos* I have had wells dug; resthouses have been erected; and numerous watering places have been prepared here and there for the enjoyment of man and beast."[5] This is more than has ever been attempted in India since.

Active internal commerce was carried on in northern India along the course of the Ganges. Here was the royal highway extending from Taxila on the Indus through Lahore to Palibhotra (in Behar, and which was 10,000 stadia in length).[6]

[1] See Ancient and Mediæval India, Vol. II, p. 348.
[2] Historical Researches, Vol. II, p. 267.
[3] Historical Researches, Vol II, p. 279.
[4] Early History of India, p. 131.
[5] Early History of India, by V. Smith, p. 162.
[6] Strabo, p. 1,010. Pliny also speakes of it in his Natural History, Vol. VI, p. 21.

Ramayana, too, mentions another road leading from Ayodhya (Oudh) by Hastinapur on the Jamna, through Lahore, to the city of *Giniberaja* in the Punjab.

Periplus, too, after saying that "the Ganges and its tributary streams were the grand commercial routes of northern India," adds that the "rivers of Southern Peninsula also were navigated."[1]

Dr. Vincent says that the Ayeen Akbari mentions 40,000 vessels as employed in the commerce of the Indus and that it was this commerce that furnished Alexander with the means of seizing, building, hiring or purchasing the fleet with which he fell down the stream."[2]

Dr. Robertson says: "If we could give credit to the account of the invasion of India by Semiramis no fewer than 4,000 vessels were assembled in the Indus to oppose her fleet (Diod. Sical. lib. ii, cap. 74). It is remarkable that when Mahmud of Ghazni invaded India a fleet was collected on the Indus to oppose his, consisting of the same number of vessels."[3]

According to Arrian, the commercial intercourse between the eastern and western coasts was carried on in country-built ships.

Periplus again says that "in Dachhanabades *Dakshina Patha* of Sanskrit, or the Deccan) there are two very distinguished and celebrated marts, named Tagara and Pluthama,[4] whence merchandise was brought down to Barygaza (Baraunch or Broach).

Ozene[5] (Ujjan) was one of the chief marts for internal traffic, and supplied the neighbouring country with all kinds of merchandise. It also became the emporium of foreign commerce.

[1] Periplus, p. 29.

[2] Commerce of the Ancients, Vol. I, p. 12.

[3] Disquisition Concerning Ancient India, p. 196.

[4] For the identification of these two places, see Elphinstone's "India," p. 223, footnote. "Tagara remained for 2,000 years the great emporium of the Mediterranean commerce."—Heeren.

[5] Historical Researches, Vol. II, p. 280.

It transported Indian products to Barygaza, and was a celebrated depot of the produce of more distant and northern couutries.

Fairs were an important vehicle of trade, and were introduced in every part of the country. A large concourse of people assemble at these fairs in different seasons for the purpose of exchanging merchandise as well as discussing religious and national topics. Even now lakhs of people assemble at Hardwar, Benares, Allahabad, on the banks of Nerbudda and other places.[1]

Regarding these Hindu fairs, Mr. Elphinstone says: "Indian fairs have strong resemblance to those of England. But no assemblage in England can give a notion of the lively effect produced by the prodigious concourse of people in white dresses and bright-coloured scarfs and turbans, so unlike the black head-dresses and dusky habits of the North."[2]

Mrs. Manning says that the Hindus traded even in the Vedic period, "and the activity in trade thus early noted has continued to be the characteristic of the county."[3]

The Encyclopædia Britannica says: "It (India) exported its most valuable produce, its diamonds, its aromatics, its silks, and its costly manufactures. The country, which abounded in those expensive luxuries, was naturally reputed to be the seat of immense riches, and every romantic tale of its felicity and glory was readily believed. In the Middle Ages, an extensive commerce with India was still maintained through the ports of Egypt and the Red Sea; and its precious produce imported

[1] "The almost innumerable crowds that yearly flock to Benares, Jagan Nath and elsewhere, amounting to many hundred thousand of souls, would obviously give rise to a species of commerce."—*Historical Researches*, Vol. II, p. 279. [For an account of fairs at Hardwar, see Hardwicke's accounts of it in the Asiatic Researches, Vol. II, p. 312, where he says that two-and-a-half lakhs of souls assemble every year, while on the occasion of *Kumbh* the number is many times larger].

[2] Elphinstone's History of India, p. 179. He also remarks that "many such places are also amongst the celebrated marts for the transfer of merchandise."

[3] Ancient and Mediæval India, Vol. II, p. 347.

into Europe by the merchants of Venice, confirmed the popular opinion of its high refinement and its vast wealth."[1]

II.—WEALTH.

Rich in the gems of India's gaudy zone.

CAMPBELL: *Pleasures of Hope.*

IF HISTORY proves anything, it proves that in ancient times India was the richest country in the world. The fact that she has always been the cynosure of all eyes, Asiatic or European, that people of less-favoured climes have always cast longing looks on her glittering treasures, and that the ambition of all conquerors has been to possess India, prove that she has been reputed to be the richest country in the world.

Her sunny climate, unrivalled fertility, matchless mineral resources and world-wide exports in ancient times helped to accumulate in her bosom the wealth which made her the happy hunting ground of adventurers and conquerors. Professor Heeren says: "India has been celebrated even in the earliest times for its riches."[2] Dr. Wise says that the wealth, splendour and prosperity of India had made a strong impression on the mind of Alexander the Great, and that when he left Persia for India, he told his army that they were starting for that "Golden India" where there was endless wealth, and that what they had seen in Persia was as nothing compared to the riches of India. Chamber's Encyclopædia says: "India has been celebrated during many ages for its wealth."[3] The writer of the article "Hindustan"

[1] Encyclopædia Britannica, Vol. XI, p. 446. Foreign commerce on such a gigantic scale as described above was one of the principal causes of the immense riches of ancient India.

[2] Heeren's Historical Researches, Vol. II, p. 268.

[3] Chambers's Encyclopædia, Vol. V, Art. "India," p. 536.

in the Encyclopædia Britannica remarks that India "was naturally reputed to be the seat of immense riches."[1] Milton voiced the popular belief when he sang of the wealth of India:

> "High on a throne of royal state which far
> Outshone the wealth of Ormuz and of Ind,
> Or where the gorgeous East with richest hand
> Showers on her kings barbaric, pearls and gold."

An idea of the immense wealth of India could be gathered from the fact that when Sultan Mahmud Ghaznavi destroyed the far-famed temple of Somnath he found such immense riches and astonishing diamonds cooped up in the single "Idol of Siva" that it was found quite impossible to calculate the value of that booty.[2] After a stay at Mathura for 26 days, in which he collected large idols of gold and silver in thousands, many set with priceless jewels, Mahmud went to Kanauj, which so astonished the tyrant and his followers, though long familiar with wealthy cities like Mathura, that they declared that Kanauj was only rivalled in splendour and magnificence by the high heavens.

Gold, the emblem of wealth, was first found in India. Herodotus speaks of India as being "rich in gold."[3] It is a well known fact that the Indian province of the Empire of Darius (Gandhara-Kabul) alone paid its revenue or tribute in gold, every other part of his Empire paying in silver. The amount of gold paid by Indians was £1,290,000 a year. India was the home of diamonds and other precious stones in ancient times. Periplus says that "the Greeks used to purchase pieces of gold from the Indians." Nelkynda or Neliceram, a port near Calicut on the Malabar Coast, is said to have been the only market for pearls in the world in ancient times.

[1] Encyclopædia Britannica, Vol. XI, p. 446.
[2] See Lethbridge's "History of India."
[3] Herodotus, iii. 106 and McCrindle's Ancient India as described in Classical literature.

Chamber's Encyclopædia says that the minerals of India are rich and varied. Diamonds, emeralds, plumbago, beryl, topazes are among its products. Gold has been found in India from time immemorial. The Deccan and the Malabar Coast are believed to be the gold-bearing districts,[1] and at Dharwar, quartz reefs of the richest description have been found.

Pliny calls India "the sole mother of precious stones" and the "great producer of the most costly gems."

India has been famous for diamonds, pearls, topazes, sapphires, rubies, emeralds, lazuli, corals and other jewels.[2] The most famous pearls and stones are all of Indian origin. The pearl presented by Julius Cæsar to Servilia, the mother of Brutus, as well as the famous pearl ear-ring of Cleopatra, were obtained from India. The most famous diamonds[3] in the world are natives of India. Though the Pitt (or the Regent as it is now called) weighs 136⅞ carats and is large in size, yet the *Koh-i-noor*, weighing only 106½ carats,[4] hallowed by ages of romantic history, is the most famous diamond in the world. Both were taken from India to England. The Pitt, however, after being reduced in cutting from 410 to 136⅞ carats was sold in 1717 to the Regent of France, the Duke of Orleans. It may still be seen at the Louvre, Paris. It is valued at £480,000, the *Koh-i-noor* at only £140,000. But the mythological and historical value of the *Koh-i-noor* is untold.

[1] Periplus (p. 36) speaks of gold mines situated in the Lower Gangetic Plain. Pliny speaks of gold and silver mines in the mountains of Capitalia, which are represented by him as the highest of the Ghat Range.—Heeren's Historical Researches, Vol. II.

[2] "India can claim for its own all the finely coloured stones of blue, green and red not however yellow diamonds."—Baner and Spencier.

[3] Dr. Ray says: "It is sometimes asserted that the phosphorescence of diamond was first observed in 1663 A.D. by the celebrated Robert Boyle. Bhoja (11th century), however, mentions this property."—History of Hindu Chemistry, Vol. II, p. 40.

[4] When the *Koh-i-noor* first reached England it weighed 186⅛ carats.

It was the wealth of India that impelled the rude Arabs to invade this country, and led the half-civilized Tartars to overrun it. It was the wealth of India that attracted Nadir Shah to India, from whence he returned laden with immense booty, and caused the Abdali chief to renew his attacks on it.

May be, as Sophocles sings[1] that,

> "Gold is the worst of ills
> That ever plagued mankind: this wastes our cities,
> Drives forth their natives to a foreign soil,
> Taints the pure heart, and turns the virtuous mind
> To basest deed."

Yet gold has its virtues. It was gold which not only enabled England to save herself and Europe in the last century but decided the fate of Napolean Bonaparte.[2]

---

[1] Antigone, Act I.

[2] The great French statesman and historian, LaMartine in his history of the Restoration, Vol. I, p. 72, says: "By this treaty (of Chaumont) England took into pay 500,000 soldiers of the sovereigns of the North." See also p. 33. The representatives of the Allied Powers at Vienna, declared him an outlaw but declined to oppose him for want of funds. On this, England granted them large subsidies. Thus began the war that ended in the crowning mercy of Waterloo. LaMartine in his remarkable History of the Restoration, Vol. II, p. 213, says England paid a war subsidy of 125,000,000 francs to the coalition. This was in addition to the subsidy granted to Louis XVI for 80 thousand troops. See Ibid, p. 289.

RELIGION.

True Religion
Is always mild, propitious and humble,
Plays not the tyrant, plants no faith in blood,
Nor bears destruction on her chariot wheels,
But stops to polish, succour and redress,
And builds her grandeur on the public good.

J. MILLER.

RELIGION, the balm for afflicted minds, is, as Bacon observes, "the chief bond of human society." It is the most powerful factor in the regulation of human affairs. As a man's company gives us a key to the general principles which guide his conduct, so does a nation's religion give us a clue to those general principles and natural forces which are at work in it for good or for evil, and which will lead it either towards civilization and enlightenment or towards degeneration and darkness. As the habitual actions and trifling acts of a man are clearly stamped with the characteristics of his personality, so is the religion of a nation an index to mark its position in the scale of civilization.

Thus religion is one of the tests of civilization. And true religion, which is only another name for *Gyana* or true knowledge, is a result of pre-eminence in morals, philosophy, literature, science and general culture.

"The Indians," says Prof. Macdonell, "are the only division of the Indo-European family which has created a great national religion—Brahmanism—and a great world religion, Buddhism; while the rest far from displaying originality in this sphere, have long since adopted a foreign faith."[1]

[1] Macdonell's Sanskrit Literature, p. 7.

The present religion of the masses in India should not be literally taken to be the religion of their ancestors, and the nature of their religion should not be judged from the religious system of the modern Hindus. The once highly-spiritual religion of the Hindus has, so far as the masses are concerned, now become thoroughly materialised to mark their degradation, and things earthly are now installed in the place which was once occupied by the eternal principle of all things.

The Vedic religion is the knowledge, the recognition of the eternal principles of being, of God, of spirit and matter, and their relation to one another as revealed to men in the Vedas.

Unbounded sympathy with humanity and infinite love for all God's creatures, which are the results of the noblest influences of true religion, found their supreme expression in India. No nobler sacrifice can be imagined than that involved in the resolution of the Indian who said: "Never will I seek nor receive private individual salvation—never enter into final peace alone; but for ever and everywhere will I live and strive for the universal redemption of every creature throughout the world. Until all are delivered, never will I leave the world of sin, sorrow, and struggle, but will remain where I am."[1]

The Hindu religion is the knowledge and the comprehension of those eternal principles which govern nature and man, those immutable laws which from one view point are called "science," and from another "true philosophy." It concerns itself not with things true under certain conditions or at certain times: its precepts are ever true, true in the past, true in the present, true in the future.

True knowledge being one, it takes, without any distinction, into its fold, Indians, Arabs, Europeans, Americans, Africans,

[1] Buddhist Catena.

Chinese, and others. Its principles circumscribe the globe and govern all humanity.

The Hindu or the Vedic religion is not, like other religions, a confession of weakness, an humble admission of the helplessness of humanity, and an absolute reliance on an external power—on a particular person—for the salvation of mankind. The Hindu religion is a confident assertion of supreme manhood—an assertion full of dignity and independence. It towers high above other faiths, inasmuch as its teachings are elevating and energising as of no other great faith.

In an article on the "Vital Value in the Hindu God Idea, in the *Hibbert Journal*, Mr. W. Tully Seegar frankly admits that the Hindu idea is much more highly developed than that of modern Christianity, and concludes: "Enough has been said to suggest the probability that the Hindu conceptions regarding 'the Self,' are just what the Occident needs and must appropriate, if it is to see through life's falsities and lay hold of its spiritual realities. If the term Christian must be retained, let it be preserved in a form that will serve the purpose of doing away with its puerile ecclesiasticism—namely Neo-Christian. The latter-day influx of Orientalism among us is preparing the way for a fusion of its purer elements with Western individualism, and the outcome that may be looked for is the *Religion of the divine self*, the most hopeful and national of all methods of overcoming the sways of the senses of the spirit."

Schlegel says: "It cannot be denied that the early Indians possessed a knowledge of the true God. All their writings are replete with sentiments and expressions, noble, clear, severely grand, as deeply conceived as in any human language in which men have spoken of their God."[1]

The Rev. J. Bryce admits that "there is every reason to

[1] Wisdom of the Ancient Indians.

believe that there existed a period in the Hindu history when the Brahma was the sole object of religious adoration."[1] Rev. Mr. Ward says: "It is true, indeed, that the Hindus believe in the unity of God. 'One Brahma without a second,' is a phrase very commonly used by them when conversing on subjects which relate to the nature of God. They believe also that God is Almighty, All-wise, Omnipotent, Omniscient."

Mr. Charles Coleman says: "The Almighty, Infinite, Eternal, Incomprehensible, Self-existent Being; He who sees everything though never seen; He who is not to be compassed by description and who is beyond the limits of human conception is Brahma, the one unknown true Being, the Creator, the Preserver and Destroyer of the universe. Under such and innumerable other definitions is the Deity acknowledged in the Vedas, or the sacred writings of the Hindus."[2]

Col. Kennedy says: "Every Hindu who is in the least acquainted with the principles of his religion must in reality acknowledge and worship God in unity."

Count Bjornstjerna, after giving a quotation from the Vedas, says: "These truly sublime ideas cannot fail to convince us that the Vedas recognise only one God, who is Almighty, Infinite, Eternal, Self-existent, the Light and the Lord of the Universe."[3]

Maurice is assured "that the Brahman is seeking after one Divine unseen object, nay, that his aim in his whole life and discipline is to purify himself from outward, sensible things, that he may approach nearer to this one source of Illumination."[4] Mr. Colebrooke says that "the ancient Hindu religion, as founded on the Hindu Scriptures, recognised but one God."[5]

[1] Sketch of the State of British India.
[2] Mythology of the Hindus.
[3] Theogony of the Hindus, p. 53.
[4] Religions of the World, p. 44.
[5] Asiatic Researches, Vol. VIII, p. 385. See also Paterson's "Origin of Hindu religion" in the Asiatic Researches.

"It is very doubtful," says Prof. Monier Williams, "whether idolatry existed in the time of Manu's compilation of the Smriti."[1]

Of the much-abused institution of Shraddhas, Prof. Max Muller says: "The worship of the ancestors and the offering of Shraddhas have maintained much of their old sacred character. They have sometimes been compared to the communion in the Christian Church, and it is certainly true that many natives speak of their funeral and ancestral ceremonies with a hushed voice and with real reverence. They alone seem still to impart to their life on earth a deeper significance and higher prospect. I could go even a step further and express my belief that the absence of such services for the dead and of ancestral commemorations is a real loss in our own religion. Almost every religion recognises them as tokens of a loving memory offered to a father, to a mother, or even to a child, and though in many countries they may have proved a source of superstition, there runs through them all a deep well of living human faith that ought never to be allowed to perish."[2]

The distinguishing feature of Hinduism, however, is that it is a thoroughly scientific religion. Religion and science went hand-in-hand in ancient India. The religious tenets of other nations have been proved, and are admitted by men of culture and thought to be in conflict with the teaching of modern science. In India, however, theology is founded upon philosophy and science. The Vedic religion is, therefore, thoroughly scientific. Major Cunningham says: "In the East, however, philosophy has always been more closely allied to theology than in civilized Greece or modern Europe."[3]

An eminent Frenchman says that the Hindu Revelation

[1] Indian Wisdom, p. 226.
[2] India: What can it teach us? p 242.
[3] Cunningham's History of the Sikhs, p. 25.

is "of all Revelations the only one whose ideas are in complete harmony with modern science."

No religion in the world claims to be in complete harmony with the spirit of modern science except the Vedic religion. Buddhism, being only a modified from of Hinduism, does not differ materially from the Vedic religion in its scientific aspects.

The Vedic religion was not like the so-called Hindu religion of the present day, exclusive and confined to Indians. It was universal, and non-Indians like the Greeks, Scythians, Huns and others, were included in its fold. Inscriptions recently discovered show that Greeks and others embraced Hinduism and were freely admitted in Hinduism.

The Hunas, under their leader Toramana, founded a great empire early in the sixth century. These new-comers were converted to Brahmanism and greatly helped the Brahmans to re-establish their supremacy. Mihirakula, the successor of Toramana, was a worshipper of Siva and a very cruel persecutor of the Buddhists. According to Hiuen Tsang, Mihirakula destroyed Buddhist Stupas and Sangharamas, and slaughtered countless followers of Buddha. Kalhana, in his Rajatarangini (I. vv. 312-316), preserves a Kashmir tradition of his age (12th century) which says that Mihirakula "re-established pious observances in this land which, overrun by impure Daradas, Bhauttas, and Mlechchhas, had fallen off from the sacred law."

Mrs. Besant, said at Calcutta: "India is the mother of religion. In her are combined science and religion in perfect harmony, and that is the Hindu religion, and it is India that shall be again the spiritual mother of the world."[1]

[1] Mrs. Besant's lecture at the Grand Theatre, Calcutta on 15th January 1906. In the course of the lecture, Mrs. Besant said: "In the nineteenth century one of the postulates of science was that life, thought, and consciousness were all results of certain molecular arrangements of matter. Brain, the speaker added, secreted thought as the liver secreted bile. The whole materialistic science tended

The Vedas do not teach such unscientific absurdities as that out of nothing came something, or that the sun was created after the creation of the earth. Miss F. P. Cobbe very justly observes: "For ages back, and markedly since the days of Spinoza, facts have been known to learned men utterly at variance with the received doctrines of the infallibility of Scripture, or even of its historical accuracy."[1]

Mr. Froude says: The truth of the Gospel history is now more widely doubted in Europe than at any time since the conversion of Constantine."[2]

Bishop Colenso says: "I assert without fear of contradiction that there are multitudes now of the more intelligent clergy who do *not* believe in the reality of the Noachian deluge as described in the Book of Genesis."[3]

Mr. J. A. Langland says: "The philosophy and the religion

to show that life was the result of an arrangement of matter. Where the mechanical arrangement of matter failed, there thought failed. Intelligence and consciousness were simply the result of matter. That was the idea repeated in Tyndal's famous treatise—'we must see in matter a permanent potency of every form of life.' But Hinduism proclaimed exactly the opposite. It taught that life was primary and matter secondary. Matter was simply a tool, instrument, vehicle. This was clearly explained in the Upanishads, in the problem of *atma*. It was shown how the unembodied *atma* was in the body. The body was the dwelling-house of the embodied *atma*. It is written that the *atma* desired to see and the eye was there. The *atma* desired to hear and the ear was there, the *atma* desired to think and the mind was there. Consciousness was primary, *atma* was primary, while the senses, organs, the body were secondary. This was the Hindu teaching. The later discoveries of science also taught that consciousness is the creator and the matter is the form." The speaker then stated, by way of illustration, that "man had legs, as was plain to her audience, and they were able to walk; and such was the case with other senses. But modern science taught exactly the opposite. It declared that creatures with legs desired to walk and legs were gradually formed by slow degrees after repeated efforts. The desire was an aspect of consciousness and not an arrangement of matter. The creatures wanted to move, so the organs of locomotion were gradually and duly built. The function of sight did not come from the eye; it was the result of perception in consciousness."

[1] Broken Lights.

[2] Short Studies on Great Subjects, Vol. I, p. 278.

[3] Pentateuch and Book of Joshua, Part II, Preface.

of to day (Christianity) are opposed. The teachings of our divines and the teachings of our thinkers are antagonistic."[1]

The Vedic *dharma*, however, never feared scientific advancement, nor was it ever guilty of the terrors of the Inquisition. It never shed the blood of a Galilio, a Copernicus or a Bruno.[2]

The Countess of Jersey says in the *Nineteenth Century*: "But to the higher caste Hindu (provided he knew anything about Hinduism) Christianity offers no solution to his doubts and to his fears. The doctrines of the Upanishads (the philosophical speculations of the Vedas) *satisfy the utmost longing of the mind.* The acute logic of the ancient Rishis has raised a bulwork of argument to support the huge fabric of Hindu thought. The doctrine of *Karma* offers the simplest and most reasonable answer to the obvious inequalities and striking contrasts in this visible world of happiness and suffering. The ferment and unrest of the soul in the search of knowledge is soothed and laid at rest when the object of contemplation is reduced to a figure-head and finally a point in space. The contemplation of point in space results in a self-absorbing delight which knows no end, and which places the soul high above all carnal wants and aspirations. This is the goal of Hindu philosophy. *Christianity has nothing to offer to those who are dissatisfied with Hinduism.*"[3]

[1] Religious Scepticism and Infidelity.

[2] "Although steadfast in his faith, the Hindu is not fanatical, he never seeks to make proselytes. If the Creator of the world, he says, had given the preference to a certain religion, this alone would have prevailed upon the earth; but as there are many religions, this proves the approbation of them by the Most High . . . . They (the Hindus) regard God as present in the mosques with those who kneel before the cross, and in the temple where Brahma is worshipped. And is not this faith more in accordance with the true doctrine of Christ than that which lighted the *Auto da fe* for the infallibility of the Popes, for the divinity of Mary, and for the miracles of the saints!"—*Theogony of the Hindus*, pp. 67, 68

[3] *Times of India* (Weekly Edition) for 25th May 1889. Chaplain Della Valle, author of "A Voyage to East India," thus concludes the chapter "On the Moralities of the Hindu: "O! what a sad thing it is for Christians to

It has been shown that almost every part of the world was, at some remote period, conquered and colonised by the ancient Hindus. Similarly, it will be found that the different nations of the ancient world derived their religion from ancient Aryavarta.

Even at the present moment more than half of the human race are the express followers of the religions that emanated from India. If the population of the world be taken in round numbers, at 1,000,000,000 we shall find from authentic records, that 530,000,000 men profess Hinduism and Buddhism (the religions that originated in India), while only 470,000,000 men follow religions which are of non-Indian origin. Rev. Mr. Ward says: "Their (Hindus) philosophy and religion still prevail over the greater portion of the globe, and that it is Hinduism which regulates the forms of worship and modes of thinking and feeling and acting throughout Japan, China, Tartary, Hindustan, the Burman Empire, Siam, Ceylon, etc."[1]

It is equally clear that the religions that did not originate in India have been strongly influenced by Hindu religious thought. Bjornstjerna says: "Buddhism has also extended its doctrines among most of the other religious systems." The Mosaic cosmogony, still believed in by the Jews and others, is derived from the Hindu system of cosmogony.

come short of Indians even in moralities, come short of those, who themselves believe to come short of Heaven?' The Chaplain thus closes his interesting work on the subject of conversion, which is as remote from accomplishment at this day as it was at that distant period: "Well known it is that the Jesuit there, who, like the Pharisees 'that would compass sea and land to make one proselyte' (Matt. 23-25), have sent into Christendom many large reports of their great conversions of infidels in East India. But all these boastings are but reports: the truth is, that they have there spilt the precious water of baptism upon some few faces, working upon the necessity of some poor men, who for want of means, which they give them, are contented to wear crucifixes, but for want of knowledge in the doctrine of Christianity are only in name Christians."—*A Voyage to East India*, pp. 402, 417, 418 and 480.

[1] Mythology of the Hindus, Preface, p. xviii.

The origin of the Greek Church of Christianity is thus explained by Mr. Princep: "The Buddhists of the West, accepting Christianity on its first announcement, at once introduced the rites and observances which for centuries had already existed in India. From that country Christianity derived its monarchical institutions, its forms of ritual and church service, its councils or convocations to settle schisms on points of faith, its worship of relics and working of miracles through them, and much of the discipline and of the dress of the clergy, even to the shaven heads of the monks and friars."[1]

Some of the most important of the Christian ethical teachings may be found word for word in the writings of the Hindu philosophers, who flourished centuries before the birth of the Saviour. The corner-stone of Christian ethics, "Do unto others as thou wouldst they should do unto thee," is nothing more than the teaching of Yajnvalkya, who says: "It is not our hermitage, still less the colour of skin that produces virtue, virtue must be practiced. Therefore, *let no one do to others what he would not have done to himself.*"[2]

Mons. Delbos says that "the religious aspirations of that (Hindu) civilization are found grandly expressed in the Rig Veda. That civilization pervades in every corner of the civilized world, and is around and about us every day of our lives."[3]

It is an observation of Hume that one generation does not go off the stage at once and other succeed, as is the case with silk-worms and butterflies. There is a varying margin, says Mr. Payne, into which the men of one age and those of the succeeding are blended.

[1] Princep's Mongolia and Tartary.

[2] See Max Muller's India: What can it teach us? p. 74.

[3] Mons. Delbos' paper on the Vedas read before the International Literary Association at Paris on 14th July 1884.

In the same way, one religion never completely dies out to be succeeded by another altogether new and independently developed. As a rule, new religions are evolved out of the old ones, and the old ones are in a way the parents of the new religions. Christianity is evolved out of the Mosaic Scripture, which again is derived from the religion of the ancient Egyptians, which was derived from India. Muhamadanism, some writers hold, is a mixture of the Mosaic Scriptures, Christianity and the Parsee religion (which was derived from Hindustan), strongly tinged with the native spirit and singlemindedness of the Arabs and the democratic principles of their social system.

Buddhism, as is well known, was only a revolt against Brahmanical tyranny. It is essentially Hinduism. Mr. Vincent Smith says: "Both Buddhism and Jainism, which as systems known to us date from 500 B.C. in round numbers, may be regarded as *offshoots* or sects of Hinduism."[1]

Prof. Rhys Davids says: "Buddhism is essentially an Indian system. The Buddha himself was, throughout his carer, characteristic Indian......he was the greatest and wisest and best of Hindus"[2]

Professor Weber[3] says: "Buddhism, in fact, may be regarded as a reformed phase of Hindu religion and ethical activity." Again, about the teaching of Buddha, he says: "This teaching contains in itself absolutely nothing new. On the contrary it is essentially identical with the corresponding Brahmanical doctrine; only the fashion in which Buddha proclaimed and disseminated it was something altogether novel and unwonted." Buddhism was founded by Sakya Sinh or Sakya Muni,[4] the son of Shudho-

[1] History of Fine Arts in India and Ceylon, p. 9.

[2] American Lectures on the History of Religions, p. 117.

[3] Weber's Sanskrit Literature, pp. 285 and 289.

[4] Buddha as a child, was also called Siddharatha.

dhana, king of Kapilavastu, situated to the north of Behar. According to Buddhistic writers, however, he was the third Buddha, not the first, there being twenty-two Buddhas in all. There have been several Buddhas[1] who differ among themselves as they differ from the Hindus. But they all agree in the following points: (1) They acknowledge the Vedic *dharma* as the foundation of their own. (2) They admit, in conjuction with this doctrine, a divine *triad*, which combines the principle of the Trinity with that of the unity, although frequently under other names than those of the Trimurtee of the Brahmans. (3) In acknowledging the doctrine of the transmigration of the soul. (4) Regarding the soul as an emanation of the Divine Being, which after having accomplished its transmigration, returns to its high origin.[2] Buddhism differs from *popular Hinduism* in the following particulars: (1) It does not acknowledge the Vedas as a revelation from God, but only regards them as a highly deserving human composition, cantaining great but not revealed truths. (2) It does not recognise the division of castes, as Hinduism does. (3) It considers the inferior gods and demi-gods of the Brahman religion merely as holy men sent by the Almighty for the benefit of the human race. "These Buddhas, therefore, were like Luther, Calvin and Huss, reformers of religion." (4) Their idea of God is different from the Hindu idea.

Sir E. Arnold says: "Buddhism has in it the eternity of a universal hope, the immortality of a boundless love, an indestructible element of faith in final good and the proudest assertion ever made of human freedom."[3]

[1] Theogony of the Hindus, p. 89.

[2] This shows the origin of Buddhism to have taken place after the Mahabharata, when the Vedanta came to be received as an *Advaita* system. Its rejection of the caste system also points to the same period, as it was after the Mahabharata that the system began to be abused.

[3] Light of Asia, Preface, p. xiii.

As regards the propagation of Buddhist doctrines, it is probable that at one time they spread over the whole world. In Burma, Siam, in most of the islands of the Indian Archipelago and Ceylon, in Thibet, Mongolia, Japan, Nepal, Bhutan and the Lesser Thibet it is still the prevailing religion; but that at one time it spread to Turkistan, Persia, Egypt, and Rome, and even to Scandinavia and the British Islands, is most probable.[1]

Count Bjornstjerna says: "It is called *Godama's* (Gautama's), doctrine in Assam, Pegu, Ava and Ceylon; *Sumana's* doctrine in Siam; *Amidha Buddha's* in Japan, *Fo's* or *Fahi's* in China and Cochin-China; *Sakya Singh's* in Eastern Bengal and Nepal, *Dharma Ray's* in Bootan; *Adi Buddha's* in Great Thibet; *Mahamuni's* in Lesser Thibet and *Sakya Muni's* in Mongolia and Mants-Chouri."[2]

"The Buddhist Monks, Bharana and Matanga, who first carried Buddhism to China, during the reign of the Han Emperor Mingti in A.D. 65, were natives of Gandhara (Punjab), of which the capital was Takshila. Some authors conjecture the Gœti of the Chinese to be the same as the Greek Scythi, who were no other than the parent stock of the Hindu Sakya race."[3]

[1] "That the true seat of Buddhism," says Bjornstjerna, "in ancient times was Hindustan is attested by the temples of Ellora, Elephanta and Ajanta, of which the greater part were dedicated to Buddha, and also by the most authentic Hindu records. In a conversation with Bogle (the British envoy at Thibet) the Dalai Lama stated that Brahma, Vishnu and Shiva were worshipped by the inhabitants of Thibet, but the lesser gods of India were not otherwise regarded by them than holy men (Buddhism); that the people of Thibet, from 700 to 800 years back possessed many temples in India, but that the Brahmans had destroyed them, and that India was the real native seat of their gods and doctrines; he therefore begged the English envoy to obtain permission from the Governor-General that they might again erect temples on the shores of the Ganges."—Theogony of the Hindus, p. 98.

[2] Theogony of the Hindus, p. 86. A. H. Bitchourin, a Russian translator of Chinese religious books, says that Buddhism universally prevails in the highland of Central Asia.

[3] See Sarat Chander Das. "Universities in India," in the *Hindustan Review* for March 1906.

"The foot-prints of Buddha were worshipped by his followers and were called *Phrabat*. They were engraved on rocks and hills, where people flocked from all parts of the country to worship them. They have now been found to be existing in most countries. These foot-prints are regarded by the Buddhists in the same light as the rainbow in the religions founded on the Mosaic records, namely, as an assurance that the deluge shall not return. Six such Phrabats are found in the East, one of them singularly enough in Mecca, whither the Buddhists made pilgrimages long before the rise of Islamism."[1] This proves the prevalence of Buddhism in Arabia in ancient times.

Bjornstjerna continues: "But Buddhism has also penetrated to the banks of the Nile, of which we have many proofs. The so-called Hermes Scriptures (the name of the sacred writings of the Egyptians) contain a metaphysical treatise in the form of a dialogue between Hermes and Thodh, Bodh, Buddh, which throughout exhibits the doctrines of Buddhism; they speak of the *pre-existence* of the soul, of its transmigrations upon earth (Metempsychosis), of its *emanation* from the Divine Being, and of its *final return* to its high original."[2] There is another early Egyptian writing, Pimander's Hermes Trismegistus, in a dialogue form between Pimander and Thodh, which develops the Buddhist doctrine of Trinity.

Count Bjornstjerna again says: "The Chaldeans, the Babylonians and the inhabitants of Colchis derived their religion and culture from India."[3] "That a system of Hinduism," says

[1] Theogony of the Hindus, pp. 92, 93. After discoursing on Socrates, Epicurus, Zoroaster and Confucius, Schlegel says: "But they were not so generally revered as benefactors of their country: whilst for numerical influence, Gautama Buddha swayed the destinies of more millions of human beings than the four together."—History of Literature, p. 124.

[2] Theogony of the Hindus, p. 100.

[3] Theogony of the Hindus, p. 38.

Colonel Tod, "pervaded the whole Babylonian and Assyrian empires, Scripture furnishes abundant proofs in the medium of the various types of the Sungod, Bal Nath, whose pillar adorned every mount and every grove."[1]

"The Samaritans in Aram were Buddhists, as also the Essenes in Palestine, at least as to their private doctrine, for outwardly they followed the Mosaic law." The Gnostics were divided into two classes: (1) The Egyptians and (2) The Asiatics; and "the adherents of the latter," says Bjornstjerna "were in fact Buddhists who in a great measure adopted the external forms of Christianity, because they regarded Jesus as a Buddha who had appeared on earth in accordance with their own tenets."[2]

Count Bjornstjerna continues: "Even the Druids in ancient Britian were Buddhists; they adopted the metempsychosis, the pre-existence of the soul and its return to the realms of universal space. They had a divine *Triad* consisting of a creator, preserver and destroyer as with the Buddhists (and Hindus). The Druids constituted a sacerdotal order which reserved to itself alone the interpretation of the mysteries of religion."[3]

The Druids propagated their doctrines in Gaul during the time of Cæsar, whence they penetrated in the West to the Celtic tribes in Spain, and in the East to Germany and Cimbrian peninsula.

"The spread of Buddhism to the above-mentioned parts of the world was for the most part anterior to Christianity; simultaneously with the establishment of this creed, Buddhism penetrated as far as the Altai mountains in Asia and the Scandinavian peninsula in Europe. Into the last-named peninsula

[1] Tod's Rajasthan, Vol. I, p. 605.
[2] Theogony of the Hindus, p. 101.
[3] Theogony of the Hindus, p. 104.

it was introduced by *Sigge-Fridulfson*, surnamed *Odin* (in the ancient Scandinavian dialect *Whodin*; *in* is the article which added to Whod, Bhodd, Buddh, makes Whodin—Odin), chief of an Asiatic tribe called Asar."[1]

Buddhism being only a particular form of Hinduism, not only is Hinduism the groundwork of Buddhism, but the mythology and the traditions of both are necessarily one and the same. Hence, wherever Buddhism has spread through the exertions of the Indians or wherever the Buddhist Hindus migrated, there is found between the religion, mythology, and scientific and philosophical writings of India and of those countries, an affinity too close to be only accidental. In the case of Scandinavia, however, the resemblance is so close that without assuming the migration of the Hindus into the country, it cannot otherwise be explained satisfactorily. "All the Indo-Scythian invaders of India," says Colonel Tod, "held the religion of Buddha, and hence the conformity of manners and mythology between the Scandinavians or German tribes and the Rajputs."[2]

(1) After giving a few questions with their answers from the Edda of the Scandinavians and a few similar ones from the Vedas, the Swedish Count Bjornstjerna concludes: "All these questions are so exceedingly similar to those which the angels make to Brahma and the answers similar to those of Brahma in the Vedas, that *we can scarcely question the derivation of the Edda from the Veda*."[3]

(2) "A common symbol of the Creator among the Hindus (from whom it passed into Egypt) was the scarabæus or beetle.

[1] Theogony of the Hindus, p. 105. The author says: "It seems to be the same tribe which came by sea to *Etruria*."

[2] Tod's Rajasthan, Vol. I, p. 65.

[3] Theogony of the Hindus, pp. 107 and 108.

In Scandinavia, likewise, this insignificant insect was sacred, and bore the name of the god Thor."

(3) "The resemblance between the *serpent* of *Midgard* in the Edda and the serpent of Vishnu in the Veda is also worthy of remark, both being described as having encircled the world."

(4) "But what is most deserving of observation is the accordance between the gates of *Walhall* and the Indian ages of the world, or yugs. According to the Edda, Walhall has 540 gates; if this number be multiplied by 800, the number of Einheriers who can march[1] out abreast from each gate, the product will be 432,000, which forms the very elementary number for the so-frequently-named ages of the world or *yugs*, adopted both in the doctrine of Brahma and Buddha, of which the one now in course will extend to 432,000 years, the the three preceding ones corresponding to this number multiplied by 2, 3, and 4."

Between the nomenclatures of the Scandinavian and Hindu mythologies there is a remarkable resemblance. Love is in Swedish, *karlek*: Bengali, *karlekeya*; while Swerga is the Swedish name of Sweden and is situated near the North pole. *Skand*, the God of war, reigns there (Scandinavia), and seven steps (zones) lead thither, of which the most northern is named *Thule*, the ancient name of Sweden."[2]

It appears that the Hindu settlers migrated to Scandinavia before the Mahabharata, taking their philosophy and religion with them, but were soon absorbed by the natives owing to their inferiority in numbers.

Count Bjornstjerna says: "We have seen how Buddhism has

[1] "Five hundred and forty doors, I believe to be in Walhall. Eight hundred Einheriers can go out abreast when they are to fight against the Ulfven (the wolf). Here is meant the fatal encounter with *Fenris Ulfven* at the end of the world, when Odin, at the head of 432,000 armed Einheriers takes the field against them.—(See the Edda).

[2] Theogony of the Hindus, p. 109.

spread first over the two peninsulas of India and afterwards proceeded to Ethiopia, Egypt, China, Corea, Thibet; it penetrated to Chaldea, Phœnicia, Palestine, Colchis, Greece, Rome, Gaul, and Britain."[1] It is thus clear that Buddhism, or rather Reformed Hinduism, at one time spread over almost every country of the ancient world. We have already seen (see Colonization) that Egypt and Greece were colonized by the Hindus in ancient times: those settlers must have taken with them their religion from ancient India. Direct and conclusive proofs, however, are available to prove that the religion of the ancient Egyptians and ancient Greeks was derived from India. On Comparing the religious systems of the Egyptians and the Hindus we are struck by their resemblance to each other. "Both proceed from monotheistic principles and degenerate into a polytheistic heathenism though rather of a symbolic than of a positive character. The principle of Trinity with that of the Unity, the pre-existence of the soul, its transmigration, the division of castes into priests, warriors, traders and agriculturists are the cardinal points of both systems. Even the symbols are the same on the shores of the Ganges and the Nile. Thus we find the *Lingam* of the Siva temples of India in the *Phallus* of the Ammon temples of Egypt—a symbol also met with on the head-dress of the Egyptian gods. We find the *lotus flower* as the symbol of the sun both in India and in Egypt, and we find symbols of the immortality of the soul in both countries. The power of rendering barren women fruitful ascribed to the temples of *Siva* in India, was also ascribed to the temples of *Ammon* in Egypt; a belief retained to our days, for the Bedouin women may still be seen wandering around the temple of *Ammon* for the purpose of obtaining this blessing."[2]

[1] Theogony of the Hindus, p. 101.
[2] Theogony of the Hindus, pp. 40 and 41.

Several names of Hindu mythology are recognised in Egypt: "Thus, *Ammon*, the supreme god of Egyptians corresponds to *Aum* of the Hindus; and the Brahminical *Siva* is found in the temple to which Alexander the Great made his pilgrimage from Egypt, and which yet bears this name." These resemblances between the two systems of religion prove that the one is derived from the other. The following arguments advanced by Count Bjornstjerna prove conclusively that the Hindu religion is the source of the Egyptian religion:—

(1) "It is testified to by Herodotus, Plato, Solon, Pythagoras and Philostratus that the religion of Egypt proceeded from India.

(2) "It is testified by Niebuhr, Valentia, Champollian, and Waddington, that the temples of Upper Egypt are of greater antiquity than those of Lower Egypt; that the temples in Meroe are more ancient than those of Elephantine and Thebes; these more ancient than the temples of Tentyra and Abydos; and these again more ancient than those of Memphis, Heliopolis and Sais; that consequently the religion of Egypt, according to the testimony of those monuments, proceeded *from the South*, which cannot be from any other land than from Ethiopia and Meroe, to which country it came from India, as testified by the above-named Greek authorities.

(3) "The chronicles found in the temples of Abydos and Sais, and which have been transmitted to us by Josephus, Julius Africanus and Eusebius all testify that the religious system of the Egyptians proceeded from India.

(4) "We have Hindu chronologies (besides those of Puranas concerning the *Yugs*, which are nothing but astronomical allegories) which go still further back in time than the tables of the Egyptian kings, according to Manetho.

(5) "There is a tradition among the Abyssinians which they say they have possessed from time immemorial, and which

is still equally received among the Jews and the Christians of that country, that the first inhabitants (they say *Cush*, grandson of Noah, with his family) came over the chain of mountains, which separates the highlands of Abyssinia from the Red Sea and the Straits of Babel Mandeb from a remote Southern country. The tradition further says that they built the city of *Axum* early in the days of Abraham, and that from thence they spread themselves, following the River Nile downwards until they became (as Josephus says) the Meroetes; namely, the inhabitants of that part of *Nubia*, which being sitnated between the *Nile* and its conflux the *Atbara*, forms what is commonly called the island of Meroe, from which they spread further down the river to Egypt." Count Bjornstjerna thus concludes: "It appears from the abovementioned grounds that the Hindus have a greater claim to the primogeniture of religion, and consequently to the primogeniture of civilization than the people of ancient Egypt."[1]

The cosmogony of the whole world has been derived from India. That the Greeks derived theirs from the Hindus may be seen in the accounts which *Damascius has given of the doctrine of Orpheus*. It is as follows: "In the beginning was *Kronos*, who out of *chaos* created *æther* (day) and *erebos* (night); therein he laid an egg (Hindu) from which came *Phanes*, furnished with three heads (the Brahmin Trimurti). *Phanes* created the man and the woman from whom the human race is derived. The cosmogony of the Egyptians also adopts the Hindu egg which, divided into two, formed heaven and earth (*vide* Diodorus and Plutarch)."[2]

The Mosaic system of cosmogony was derived from India. Count Bjornstjerna says: "If we reflect upon all these testimonies respecting Mose s, and consider the place (Aeliopolis) where

[1] Theogony of the Hindus, pp. 43-46.
[2] Theogony of the Hindus, pp. 130 and 131.

he studied, and if we also recollect that the religion of the Egyptians was derived from India, we find a clue from whence Moses must partly have obtained his *cosmogony*, and also his religious system, which like the Vedas, was constructed upon monotheistic principles."[1]

The present cosmogony prevalent in the Christian and Mohamedan countries is also of Indian origin. The Buddhistic cosmogony is as follows: "In the beginning the earth was uninhabited, at which time the inhabitants of Heaven or of Bhurana (angels) used to visit the earth. These glorious beings consisting of men and women, through the purity of their spirit, had never yet cherished any ***sensual desires***, when Adi Buddha (the supreme God) infused into them the desire to taste the fruit of a tree resembling the almond, which excited the sensual appetite in them, and they afterwards disdained to return to Bhurana, and thus became the parents of the human race."[2] That this is the source from which the Bible and the Quran derived their common system of cosmogony there can scarcely be any doubt. It is thus perfectly clear that every system of cosmogony, whether ancient or modern, owes its origin to the Hindus.

The mythology of the Greeks, the Egyptians and the Assyrians is wholly founded on the Hindus mythology. Professor Max Muller says: "The poetry of Homer is founded on the mythology of the Vedas,"[3] and without the Veda, he says a little further, "the science of mythology would have remained a mere guess-work and without a safe basis."[4]

[1] Theogony of the Hindus, p. 144.
[2] Theogony of the Hindus, p. 131.
[3] Chips from a German Workshop, Vol. III, p. 79.
[4] Chips from a German Workshop, Vol. III, p. 96.

The gods and goddesses of Greece are but copies of their Hindu originals.

Jupiter	...	stands for	Indra.
Juno	...	"	Durga or Parwati (Indrani).
Apollo	...	"	Krishna.
Venus	...	"	Rati.
Ceres	...	"	Sri.
Cybele	...	"	Prithvi.
Neptune and Uranus		"	Varuna.
Minerva	...	"	Saravsati.
Mars	...	stands for	Skand.
Pluto	...	"	Yama.
Plutus	...	"	Kuvera.
Vulcan	...	"	Vishvakarma.
Cupid	...	"	Kama.
Mercury	...	"	Narada.
Aurora	...	"	Ushas.
AEolus	...	"	Vayu.
Janus	...	"	Ganesa.
Dioscuri (Castor and Pollux)			Aswini Kumara.
Styx	...	"	Vaitarni.
Ida	...	"	Kailas.
Olympus	...	"	Meru.

The Ramayana and the Mahabbarata are the sources of the Homeric poems, and the mythology of the Greeks is, to a great extent, only an adaptation of the Hindu mythology to local life and traditions of Greece.

The Christian mythology, too, is derived from that of the Hindus. Both Mr. Maurice[1] and Sir W. Jones[2] believe Rama to be Raamah of Scripture, son of Cush (Genesis, Chapter x. verse 7). It is thus clear to a student of comparative mythology that the Hindu deities are the objects of worship in some form or other throughout the world.

[1] Maurice's History, Vol. III, p. 104.
[2] Sir W. Jones in the Asiatic Researches, Vol. II, p. 40

Mr. W. D. Brown says: "By careful examination the unprejudiced mind cannot but admit that Hindu is the parent of the literature and theology of the world. The researches and investigations made in Sanskrit language, which was once spoken in that country, by scholars like Max Muller, Jaccolliot, Sir William Jones and others, have found in the ancient records of India the strongest proofs that thence were drawn many or nearly all the favourite dogmas which later theologians have adopted; and the strongest proofs show to the thoughtful student that the ancient Hindus were neither the practisers of idolatry nor the unlearned. uncivilized, barbaric race they have usually been thought, but a people enjoying a measure of inspiration that might be envied by more pretentious nations. And I have not the least doubt that these translations of ancient Hindu literature will confound the so-called modern civilizations, that they will look upon India as a century flower once more coming into full bloom, wafting forth its delicious fragrance, and will beg for a slip from its branches."

BIBLIOGRAPHICAL INDEX.

WORKS BY

HAR BILAS SARDA, F.R.S.L.

HINDU SUPERIORITY.

(*P.P. 428*+xxxii.)

Full cloth, royal octavo, gilt lettered, and illustrated ... *Rs. 6*

1. **The Liberty Review** (LONDON):—"The facts which he brings forward to establish the pre-eminence of India in every department and sphere of human activity are of a character which it would be difficult to dispute, and the style in which they are set forth is both clear and picturesque."

2. **The Indian Mirror** (CALCUTTA):—"M. Har Bilas Sarda, B.A., F.R.S.L., has done an inestimable service to his country by publishing a remarkable book entitled 'Hindu Superiority.'......The book under review is a scholarly attempt to determine that position of unrivalled greatness. Let every patriotic Hindu come and cast a glance at the inspiriting picture of his country's post greatness painted in the pages of Hindu Superiority. It is needless to dwell at length upon the vast erudition and antiquarian research of the author. The book is a priceless treasure. His method of treatment is scientific. We would earnestly exhort our countrymen professing the Hindu faith to peruse the book with care and attention."

3. **The Indian World** (CALCUTTA):—"Mr. Sarda's book is the most interesting account of the ancient civilization of India that we have ever had the pleasure of reading. Mr. Sarda's style is easy, clear and sometimes rises even to eloquence; his manner of presenting an argument or advancing a theory is always happy and attractive; his study is encyclopædic. He demolishes for good the theory of the Hellenic origin of Indian civilization. To the future historian of India this book will prove a mine of information, *to the student of the civilization of the world it will be indispensable.*"

4. **The Morning Post** (DELHI):—"As a contribution to the history of his country, it is intensely interesting from beginning to end. As a brief synopsis of a vast subject, the work is a most valuable contribution to our knowledge."

5. **The Amrita Bazar Patrika**:—"The researches of the author prove his tireless energy, his uncommon industry and his vast knowledge."

Ajmer:

Historical and Descriptive.

With 29 full page illustrations, full cloth, gilt lettered ... ... Rs. 5

The Morning Post (DELHI):—"For the book under review we have nothing but praise. It is the work of a scholar in love with his subject, and his research in all the by-ways of Indian history does him great credit. The book is well bound, neatly printed and profusely illustrated, and will prove of immense use to visitors and residents of Ajmer."

The Indian Antiquary (BOMBAY):—"The author has spared no pains to make his book as accurate, full and reliable as it was possible to do. The reader is sure to be amazed at the mass of information so critically collected and so interestingly set forth."

The Hindustan Review (ALLAHABAD):—"We can unreservedly commend it to all lovers of the picturesque in India and to all students of its history. The book is beautifully got-up and embellished with 29 most excellent illustrations.

Dr. A.F.R. Hoernle, C.I.E., LL.D., (ENGLAND):—"I write to congratulate you on the production of your book 'Ajmer: Historical and Descriptive.' It is replete with useful and interesting information, and the illustrative plates give a good idea of the fine sights of Ajmer."

The Celebrated Poetess, Mrs. Sarojini Naidu of Hyderabad:—"I think your book is most interesting, not merely useful as a guide to visitors to Ajmer, but of great interest to every reader who has the 'pride of country' in his veins. It is really a patriotic kind of work to write so comprehensive, instructive and attractive a history of a city famous and dear to every Indian, whether he bathe spiritually in Brahma's Lotus Lake or bow his head at the Chishti shrine."

The Prithviraja Vijaya.

Price: As. 8.

The Modern Review (CACUTTA):—"This essay contains a highly valuable and critical account of a Sanskrit poem on Prithviraj.........Mr. Sarda learnedly compares six chronological tables of Prithviraj's dynasty from six different sources, and gives interesting descriptions of Ajmer city and the king's personal appearance."

Maharana Sāngā.

Price Rs. 2-8-0.

The Modern Review:—Mr. Sarda's book is the most up-to-date. His facts are based on contemporary records, inscription and official chronicles. Being a gentleman of the Rajput country and fully familiar with the living traditions of history still current in that country and with Indo-Mohammedan histories he occupies an unrivalled position as a Rajput historian. His writings have the further advantage of being products of a pen used to judicial weighing of facts. *It is really an epic booklet.* Personalities vie with each other in nobleness, valour and sense of honour *The mind becomes awestricken by stories which are more romantic, than the greatest romances. Their virtues thrill the heart and electrify the soul.*

Dr. A. Vincent Smith, Litt D. (Oxford).—This book on Maharana Sanga is well turned out and carefully printed. The author has used Sanskrit Hindi and Persian materials as well as the ordinary books in English, and the *book thus possesses independent value as a work of original research.*

The New India:—"The present reviewer can recommend the present volume as one which will hold the undivided attention of any one who comes to it for the story of the great Rajput who is its hero. The reign of the last of the Indian Sovereigns under whom all the Rajput tribes combined is full of incident, and the character of the Maharana is one which lends itself to enthusiastic treatment. He was a true Rajput and our author responds to the chivalrous outlook on life which is summed up in that name."

The Bengalee:—*The Democratic Ideal Among Hindoos.* His (Har Bilas Sarda's) life of Maharana Sanga, the greatest of the rulers of Mewar, save and except Rana Pratap is an illuminating record of Rajput daring and achievement coupled with Rajput chivalry and generosity. Nor is this the sole merit of the work. It throws an interesting side-light on ancient Hindu ideals and institutions, of especial value in these days."

The Hindustan Review:—Mr. Har Bilas Sarda is indefatigable in popularizing his researches in the history of Rajputana. After having dealt with the career of Maharana Kumbha which we noticed at the time of its appearance in terms of appreciation he has now placed before the reading public Maharana Sanga, which is a very well-written sketch of the famous Maharana Sangram Singh, one of the greatest and most forceful rulers of Mewar, The book deals with heroic times and is a meritorious contribution to Indian historical literature. It should form a capital prize-book in schools and colleges.

Maharana Kumbha.

SOVEREIGN, SOLDIER AND SCHOLAR.

Full cloth, gilt lettered and illustrated ... ... Rs. 2.

Mahamahopadhyaya P. Har Prasada Sastri, C.I.E., Vice-President, Asiatic Society of Bengal:—"Many thanks for your most valuable present. Your Maharana Kumbha will be appreciated throughout Bengal. It gives a very full account of the man and his times. Your book reads like a novel. Your book will be a very desirable addition to my library."

Mr. K. P. Jayaswal, M.A. (Oxon), Bar-at-law, late Lecturer in History in Calcutta University:—"I think highly of the book. I hope you would contribute more to a critical study of Rajputana history as you have done in this case."

New India (MADRAS):—"The author is an able writer and the theme suits his pen. Besides, when three Rajputs like Chonda, Kumbha and Jodha are shown playing their parts simultaneously in a book like this, the story cannot but be of absorbing interest."

The Hindustan Review (ALLAHABAD):—"Mr. Har Bilas Sarda is a specialist in the history and traditions of Rajputana, and his knowledge of the subject has been well utilized by him in his historico-biographical sketch called "Maharana Kumbha." Mr. Sarda has produced an exceedingly interesting account of his life and heroic career. The book embodies the results of the latest researches in the history of Rajputana and forms a notable addition to the ranks of Indian biographies in English."

The Mahratta (POONA): "The author has made full use of all the inscriptions, manuscripts and other resources to bring his information up to date.........We can heartily commend the book to the public. Books of this sort unveiling our real past—full of many a glorious deed—serve to strengthen our faith in our future."

The Hindu (MADRAS):—The long reign of Kumbha............has been well dealt with by the author in a charming way.........The book embodies some of the results of the researches in the history of Rajputana and is writen in an attractive and interesting style. We hope it will meet with such encouragement from the public as it rightly deserves."

Mr. C. W. Waddington, M.A., C.I.E., C.V.O., Principal, Mayo College (AJMER):—"Such trustworthy accounts based on latest information drawn from inscriptions and monuments, not only fill an immediate want in our knowledge, but will form an invaluable nucleus for a completely authentic history which we may hope will be some day published."

Mr. A. T. Holme, I. C. S., Resident of Mewar:—"It is very nicely got up and most interesting."